The Rite of Vajrayogini Self-Initiation

Khenpo Lama Migmar Tseten

Mangalamkosha Publications
PO Box 391042
Cambridge, Ma 02139 USA
www.lamamigmar.net

ISBN 979-8509203329

Preface

This book provides an extensive collection of Vajrayogini's self initiation practices compiled with Tibetan, phonetics, and English translation by Khenpo Lama Migmar from traditional sources. These practices for accumulating merit and wisdom will guide us to reach Vajrayogini's stage, the union of wisdom and compassion. It is our hope that the following pages offer a window into the awakened state and inspire you in your own practice. May all sentient beings everywhere experience peace.

Important requirement: It is very important to receive the empowerment, transmission, and instruction from a Master who holds the Vajrayogini Naropa lineage to do these practices.

Mangalamkosha Publications

Cambridge, MA

May 2021

Acknowledgments

Mangalamkosha wishes to thank the following people who have helped to bring this text to completion: Lama Karma Dhondup, Malcolm Smith, Osa Manell, Dr. Allie Aitken, Dr. Raga Markely, Meg Hutchinson, Dr. Rory Lindsay, and Dr. J.Y. Chen.

Contents

Appendix

༄༅། །རྗེ་བཙུན་རྡོ་རྗེ་རྣལ་འབྱོར་མ་ནཱ་རོ་མཁའ་སྤྱོད་ཀྱི་སིནྡྷུ་རའི་དཀྱིལ་འཁོར་སྒྲུབ་མཆོད་བདག་འཇུག་གི་ཆོ་ག་མཁའ་སྤྱོད་སྒྲུབ་པའི་ཉེ་ལམ་གྱི་ལྷན་ཐབས་དཀྱུས་སུ་བཙུག་པ་ནག་འགྲོས་བཀླག་ཆོག་གསལ་བའི་མེ་ལོང་ཞེས་བྱ་བ་བཞུགས་སོ།།

The Clear Mirror

A Liturgical Arrangement
Containing the Supplements for the "Quick Path of Khecarī: the Puja Sādhana of the Sindhura Maṇḍala of Noropa Khecarī Jetsun Vajrayoginī and Rite of Self-Initiation"

༄༅། །ཨོཾ་བདེ་ལེགས་སུ་གྱུར་ཅིག

Oṁ, May it be auspicious!

རྗེ་བཙུན་རྡོ་རྗེ་རྣལ་འབྱོར་མ་ནཱ་རོ་མཁའ་སྤྱོད་ཀྱི་སིནྡྷུ་རའི་དཀྱིལ་འཁོར་བསྒྲུབ་ཅིང་མཆོད་པ་དང་། བདག་ཉིད་འཇུག་ཅིང་དབང་བླང་བའི་ཆོ་ག་མཁའ་སྤྱོད་སྒྲུབ་པའི་ཉེ་ལམ་ཞེས་བྱ་བ་ཚར་ཆེན་རྡོ་རྗེ་འཆང་ཆེན་པོའི་གསུང་ཇི་ལྟ་བ་བཞིན་ལ་མཆོད་ཕྲེང་རྒྱས་པ་དང་ཚོགས་མཆོད་སོགས་ཁ་སྐོང་བསྣན་པའི་ནག་པོ་འགྲོ་ཞེས་བཀླག་ཆོག་གསལ་བའི་མེ་ལོང་བཀོད་པ་ལ། བླ་མ་དང་རྗེ་བཙུན་རྡོ་རྗེ་རྣལ་འབྱོར་མ་དབྱེར་མེད་པའི་ཞབས་ལ་གུས་པ་ཆེན་པོས་ཕྱག་འཚལ་ལོ། དེ་ལ་འདིར་འཁོར་ལོ་བདེ་མཆོག་རྣལ་འབྱོར་གསང་མཐའི་དཀྱིལ་འཁོར་དུ་དབང་བསྐུར་བ་ལེགས་པར་ཐོབ་ཅིང་། དམ་ཚིག་དང་སྡོམ་པར་ལྡན་པས། རྗེ་བཙུན་མ་འདི་ཉིད་ཀྱི་སིནྡྷུ་རའི་དཀྱིལ་འཁོར་དུ་བྱིན་རླབས་ལེགས་པར་ཐོབ་པའི་རྣལ་འབྱོར་པ་དག་གིས་ཆོས་བཅུ་རྣམ་པ་གཉིས་ལ་སོགས་པ་དུས་ཁྱད་པར་ཅན་གྱི་ཚེ། རྗེ་བཙུན་མ་འདི་ཉིད་ཀྱི་སིནྡྷུ་རའི་དཀྱིལ་འཁོར་བསྒྲུབ་ཅིང་མཆོད་པ་དང་། བདག་ཉིད་འཇུག་ཅིང་དབང་བླང་བར་འདོད་པས། རང་ཉིད་ཀྱི་སྒྲུབ་ཁང་ལ་སོགས་པ་དབེན་ཞིང་ཡིད་དང་མཐུན་པའི་གནས་སུ་ཆག་ཆག་དང་ཕྱི་དོར་ལ་སོགས་པ་ལེགས་པར་བྱས། བླ་མ་དང་རྗེ་བཙུན་མའི་བྲིས་སྐུ་དང་། འབུར་སྐུ་ལ་སོགས་པའི་རྟེན་ཡོད་ན་ཚུལ་བཞིན་བཤམས་པའི་དྲུང་དུ། འཐས་ཤིང་དོས་སྙོམས་པའི་ས་གཞིའམ། སྟེགས་བུ་ལ་སོགས་པ་བ་བྱུང་ལྔ་དང་དྲི་བཟང་གི་ཆུས་བྱུགས། ཁྲུ་གང་ལ་སོགས་པའི་ཚད་ཀྱིས་ཟླུམ་བསྐོར་བྱ།

དེའི་ཕྱིར་རོལ་དུ་སོར་ཕྱེད་ཙམ་བསྐྱེད་པའི་ཀླུམ་སྐོར་གཉིས་པ་བྱ། ནང་གི་ཀླུམ་སྐོར་དང་མཐུན་པར་ཆོས་འབྱུང་ཉིས་བརྩེགས་ཀྱི་ཐིག་གདབ། དེ་ལ་ཚོན་དབྱེ་བ་ནི། ཆོས་འབྱུང་གཉིས་དམར་པོ་ཐིག་གི་གཙོད་མཚམས་རེ་ཁྲ་དཀར་པོ། ནང་གི་ཀླུམ་སྐོར་དང་ཆོས་འབྱུང་གི་བར་གྱི་ཁྲམས་ལྗང་གུ། མུ་ཁྱུད་སྔོན་པོ། མུ་ཁྱུད་ཀྱི་ཕྱི་ནང་གཉིས་ཀའི་རེ་ཁྲ་དཀར་པོ། ཆོས་འབྱུང་གཉིས་ཀྱི་དབུས་སུ་ཟླ་གདན་གྱི་སྟེང་དུ་ཚོམ་བུ་དམར་པོ་བཀོད་པ་ནི་སྐུ་ཚོམ་བུའི་དཀྱིལ་འཁོར་ཞེས་བྱ་བ་ཡིན་ལ། འདི་ཉིད་འཇུག་པ་བདེ་བར་འདོད་ན། རས་སམ་དར་དམར་པོ་ལ་བྲིས་ཀྱང་རུང་ཞེས་ཀྱང་གསུངས། དེའི་སྟེང་དུ་མཧཱི་ལ་སོགས་པའི་ཐོད་པ་མཚན་ཉིད་དང་ལྡན་པའི་ནང་དུ། ཆང་ལ་སྦྲང་དམ་བུ་རམ་ལ་སོགས་པ་སྦྱར་བདུད་རྩི་རིལ་བུའི་ཕྱེ་མ་བཏབ་པ་དཔྲལ་བ་རང་ཉིད་ལ་ཕྱོགས་པར་བཞག དེ་ནི་གསུང་བདུད་རྩིའི་དཀྱིལ་འཁོར་ཞེས་བྱ་བ་ཡིན། དེའི་ཁར་ཞིང་བུ་ཕྲ་མོས་རྒྱ་གྲམ་བྱས་ལ་དར་དམར་གྱིས་བཀབ། དེའི་སྟེང་དུ་མེ་ལོང་དམ་མ་འབྱོར་ན་ཤིང་ལེབ་ལ་སོགས་པའི་ཁར་སིནྡྷུ་ར་ཚགས་ལ་བཙགས་པ་ཁོད་སྙོམས་པར་བཀྲམ། གསེར་གྱི་ཐུར་མའམ། མེད་ན་དོ་རྗེའི་རྩེ་མོས་ཆོས་འབྱུང་གྲུ་གསུམ་ཉིས་བརྩེགས་ཀྱི་དབུས་སུ་རྒྱ་ཡིག་གམ་བོད་ཡིག་གང་ཡང་རུང་བའི་བཾ་ཡིག་བྲིས་པའི་མཐར་མདུན་ནས་གཡོན་སྐོར་གྱིས་ཨོཾ་གསུམ་མའི་སྔགས་ཕྲེང་མགོ་ཕྱིར་བསྟན་འཁོར་ཡུག་ཏུ་བྲིས། དེ་ཡང་ཨོཾ་གསུམ་དང་། དེའི་རྗེས་སུ། སརྦ་དང་། བུདྡྷ་དང་། ཌཱ་ཀི་དང་། ནཱི་ཡེ་དང་། བཛྲ་དང་། ཝརྞི་དང་། ནཱི་ཡེ་དང་། བཛྲ་དང་། བཻ་རོ་དང་། ཙ་ནཱི་ཡེ་དང་། ཧཱུཾ་གསུམ་དང་། ཕཊ་གསུམ་དང་། སྭཱ་ཧཱ་རྣམས་རིམ་བཞིན་བྲི་བ་མ་གཏོགས་འབྲུ་རེ་རེ་ནས་བཟློག་པ་ནི་མི་མཛད། དེའང་ཤར་དྲང་པོར་ཨོཾ་དང་། བྱང་དུ་ཌཱ་དང་། ནུབ་ཏུ་རྦ་དང་། ལྷོར་ནི་བྲིས་ན་ཆ་སྙོམས་པར་འབྱུང་ངོ། མདུན་རྒྱབ་གཉིས་སྤྱངས་པའི་གྲྭ་བཞིར་དགའ་བ་འཁྱིལ་པ་རེ་བྲིའོ། དེ་ནི་ཐུགས་སིནྡྷུ་རའི་དཀྱིལ་འཁོར་ཞེས་བྱ་བ་ཡིན་ནོ། དེ་རྣམས་ཀྱི་སྟེང་དུ་དར་དམར་རམ། ལིང་དམར་རམ། རས་དམར་གང་ཡང་རུང་བའི་གུར་ཁང་ལེགས་པ་ཕུབ། ཟན་གཙང་མའི་རིལ་བུ་ཆུང་དུ་ལ་རས་དཀར་གྱི་སྟོད་བུ་བཙུགས་པ་འབྲི་མོག་གི་མར་ཁུའི་ཁ་དོག་བསྒྱུར་བ་སིནྡྷུ་རའི་མཎྜལ་གྱི་སྟེང་དམ་མདུན་ཕྱོགས་གང་རུང་དུ་བཞག སྒྲུབ་མཆོད་རྐྱང་པའི་དུས་མ་བཞམས་ཀྱང་རུང་། དེའི་མཐའ་བསྐོར་དུ་ཆུ་གཉིས་སྔོན་དུ་འགྲོ་བའི་ཉེར་སྤྱོད་ལྔ་ཕྱོགས་མཚམས་རེ་རེར་བཀོད་པ་གཡོན་སྐོར་དུ་བཞམ། དཀུ་བག་ཅན་གྱི་གཏོར་མ་ལྔ་ཚར་རམ། བསྟུན་གསུམ་དུ་བྱས་པ་མཎྜལ་གྱི་མདུན་ནམ། རྒྱབ་ཕྱོགས་གང་བདེ་བར་བཞམ། སློབ་དཔོན་གྱི་མདུན་དུ་བུམ་པ་བཅུད་དང་ལྡན་པ་མགུལ་ཆིངས་དམར་པོ་ཁ་རྒྱན་དུང་ཆོས་རྡོར་གཟུངས་རྣམས་ཚང་བ། དོ་རྗེ་དྲིལ་བུ་ནང་མཆོད་མེ་ཏོག་དང་བཅས་པ། ཚོགས་ཀྱི་འཁོར་ལོའི་ཡོ་བྱད་རྣམས་ཀྱང་མ་ཚང་བ་མེད་པ་བཞམ། དེ་དག་ནི་ཚོ་གར་མ་གཏོགས་པའི་སྦྱོར་བའོ།

In the Liturgy of the Clear Mirror, the liturgical arrangement for ease of use according to "The Shortcut to Khecarī" the puja Sādhana of the sindhura maṇḍala of Jetsun Vajrayoginī and the rite of the self-initiation composed by Tsarchen Vajradhara, supplemented with the extensive garland of offerings, the Ganapūjā, and so on, I [Nesar Je Kunga Legpe Jungne] pay homage with devotion to the feet of the guru and the Jetsun Vajrayoginī inseparable.

Here, those yogis and yoginīs who have obtained empowerment into the ultimate secret maṇḍala of Chakrasamvara, have kept their samayas and vows, and have perfectly obtained the blessing into the sindhura maṇḍala of Jetsunma herself, who wish to accomplish the sindhura maṇḍala of the Jetsunma herself on two tenths (Ḍākinī days of the lunar calendar) and other occasions, make offerings and take the self-initiation must sprinkle water, clean, and so on in their practice room which is in a isolated location and conducive to the mind.

If one has representations, such as base images of paintings and statues and so on, set them up properly. In front of these, smear ground that has a leveled edges and surface or a raised platform with the five substances of the cow and scented water, make a circle that is a cubit in diameter. Make a second circle outside that one that is half a finger width larger in diameter. Lay out two stacked dharmakaras equal with the inner circle. The colors of the two dharmakaras are red outlined in white. The space between the dharmakaras and the inner circle is green; the outer border is blue; it's inner and outer edges are outlined in white. Placing a red pile on top of a moon seat in the center of the two dharmakaras is called the "pile maṇḍala of the body." It is said that those wish for an easy start may draw this on red cloth or silk.

On the top of this, there is a tripod and so on. Inside of a skull with the proper characteristics mix alcohol with honey or jaggery, etc. Place a pill or powder of amrita, and place the forehead of the skull towards oneself. That is called the amrita maṇḍala of speech.

On top of the skull make a cross with small sticks and cover it with red cloth. On top of that, place a mirror or if one cannot use one, place a flat piece of wood, on which sift and spread sindhura evenly. Draw two stacked dharmakaras with a golden stick, or if one does not have that, use the tip of a vajra.

*In the center of that, draw a Vaṁ in either Sanskrit (वं) or Tibetan (བཾ) letter. Starting from the front, on the periphery, write the triple Oṁ mantra circling to the left with the head of the syllables facing out. Apart from writing them in reverse order, the syllables them selves are not reversed. Three Oṁs, sarva, buddha, ḍāki, nīye, vajra, varṇṇa, nīye, vajra, vairo, canīye, three Hūms, three Phaṭs svāhā (*ཨོཾ་ཨོཾ་ཨོཾ་སརྦ་བུདྡྷ་ཌཱ་ཀི་ཎཱི་ཡེ་བཛྲ་ཝརྞྞཱི་ཡེ་བཛྲ་བཻ་རོ་ཙ་ནཱི་ཡེ་ཧཱུྃ་ཧཱུྃ་ཧཱུྃ་ཕཊ་ཕཊ་ཕཊ་སྭཱ་ཧཱ*). Further, if one draws Oṁ (*ཨོཾ*) in the front, which is the east, Ḍā (*ཌཱ*) in the north, Ṇṇa (*ཎྞ*) in the west, and Ṇī (*ཎཱི*) in the south, it will be even. That is called the sindhura maṇḍala of mind.*

Above this, cover it well with a tent of either red silk, red canvas, or red cloth. Place cotton wicks in small pills of pure dough and color them with a dye made from Drimog (Onosma hookeri), placing them above or in front of the sindhura maṇḍala. However, when doing only the accomplishment offering, it is fine if they are not prepared.

Surrounding this, set up the offering bowls of sense objects, beginning with two waters in each direction, arranging them circling to the left. Arrange five kubagchan tormas, or to abbreviate, three, either front or in back of the maṇḍala whichever is easiest.

In front of the master, there is vase with the essential substances, tied at the neck with a red cloth with a lid ornament, a conch vessel, a vajra and dharani thread all complete, along with a vajra, bell, the inner offering and flowers.

Arrange the articles of the ganacakra without leaving anything out.

Those are the preparations that are not included in the ritual.

Prayer to the Gurus of the Lineage

ཚོ་གར་གཏོགས་པའི་སྦྱོར་བ་ལ་ཐོག་མར་བརྒྱུད་པའི་གསོལ་འདེབས་ནི།

The preparations included in the ritual begins with offering a supplication to the lineage.

རྒྱལ་བ་རྒྱ་མཚོའི་རིགས་བདག་རྡོ་རྗེ་ཆོས།།
རྒྱལ་བའི་ཡུམ་མཆོག་རྡོ་རྗེ་རྣལ་འབྱོར་མ།།
རྒྱལ་སྲས་ཐུ་བོ་ན་རོ་ཏ་པའི་ཞབས།།
གསོལ་བ་འདེབས་སོ་ལྷན་སྐྱེས་ཡེ་ཤེས་སྩོལ།།

Gyal-Wa Gya-Tsoy Rig Dag Dor-Je Chö
Gyal-Way Yum Chog Dor-Je Nal-Jor-Ma
Gyal-Se Thu-Wo Na-Ro Ta-Pay Shab
Söl-Wa Deb-So Lhen-Kye Ye-She Tsöl

To the feet of Vajradharma, the master of the family
of oceans of victors,
to Vajrayoginī the supreme mother of the victors
and to powerful Nāropa, the son of the victors:
I offer a supplication, please grant me the connate wisdom.

གསང་ཆེན་སློབ་བཤད་འཛིན་པའི་ཕམ་ཐིང་པ།།
གསང་མཛོད་ཀུན་གྱི་གཉེར་གྱུར་ཤེས་རབ་བརྩེགས།།
གསང་སྔགས་རྒྱ་མཚོའི་མངའ་བདག་མལ་ལོའི་ཞབས།།
གསོལ་བ་འདེབས་སོ་ལྷན་སྐྱེས་ཡེ་ཤེས་སྩོལ།།

Sang Chen Lob-She Zin-Pay Pham-Ting-Pa
Sang Zö Kün Gyi Ter Gyur She-Rab Tseg
Sang Ngag Gya-Tsoy Nga Dag Mal Loy Shab
Söl-Wa Deb-So Lhen-Kye Ye-She Tsöl

To the feet of the Pamthingpas, holder of the disciple's explanation of the great secret,
to She-Rab Tsek, the treasurer of all treasuries of secrets,
and to Mal Lotsawa, master of the ocean of secret mantra:
I offer a supplication, please grant me the connate wisdom.

རྡོ་རྗེ་འཆང་དབང་བླ་ཆེན་ས་སྐྱ་པ།།
རྡོ་རྗེའི་སྲས་མཆོག་རྗེ་བཙུན་བསོད་ནམས་རྩེ།།
རྡོ་རྗེ་འཛིན་པའི་གཙུག་རྒྱན་གྲགས་པའི་ཞབས།།
གསོལ་བ་འདེབས་སོ་ལྷན་སྐྱེས་ཡེ་ཤེས་སྩོལ།།

Dor-Je Chang Wang La-Chen Sa-Kya-Pa
Dor-Jey Se Chog Je-Tsün Sö-Nam Tse
Dor-Je Zin-Pay Tsug Gyen Drag-Pay Shab
Söl-Wa Deb-So Lhen-Kye Ye-She Tsöl

To the feet of Great guru Sakyapa, powerful Vajradhara,
Jetsun Sonam Tsemo, the supreme vajra son
and Drakpa Gyaltsen, crown ornament of vajra holders:
I offer a supplication, please grant me the connate wisdom.

ས་སྐྱ་པཎ་ཆེན་གངས་ཅན་མཁས་པའི་རྗེ།།
ས་གསུམ་སྐྱེ་དགུའི་གཙུག་རྒྱན་འཕགས་པའི་མཆོག།

ས་སྐྱའི་བསྟན་འཛིན་ཞང་སྟོན་ཆོས་རྗེའི་ཞབས།།
གསོལ་བ་འདེབས་སོ་ལྷན་སྐྱེས་ཡེ་ཤེས་སྩོལ།།

Sa-Kya Pan-Chen Gang-Chen Khay-Pay Je
Sa Sum Kye Gui Tsug Gyen Phag-Pay Chog
Sa-Kyey Ten-Zin Shang-Ton Chö-Jey Shab
Söl-Wa Deb-So Lhen-Kye Ye-She Tsöl

To the feet of the great paṇḍita of the Sakyapas, lord of Himālayan scholars,
to supreme Phagpa, the crown ornament of all beings in heaven, earth and below
and Shangton Choeje, holder of the Sakya doctrine:
I offer a supplication, please grant me the connate wisdom.

གྲུབ་པའི་དབང་པོ་ན་བཟའ་བྲག་ཕུག་པ།།
གྲུབ་མཆོག་མཁས་པའི་དེད་དཔོན་ཆོས་ཀྱི་རྗེ།།
གྲུབ་རིགས་སྙན་བརྒྱུད་མངའ་བདག་ཡར་ཀླུང་པར།།
གསོལ་བ་འདེབས་སོ་ལྷན་སྐྱེས་ཡེ་ཤེས་སྩོལ།།

Drub-Pay Wang-Po Na-Za Drag-Phug-Pa
Drub-Chog Khe-Pay De-Pon Chö-Kyi-Je
Drub Rig Nyen-Gyü Nga-Dag Yar-Lung-Par
Söl-Wa Deb-So Lhen-Kye Ye-She Tsöl

To the feet of Naza Dragpugpa, the lord of siddhas,
to Lama Dampa, the Lord of Dharma, the captain of scholarly supreme siddhas

and to Yarlungpa, master of the aural lineage
of the family of siddhas:
I offer a supplication, please grant me the connate wisdom.

བདག་གཞན་འགྲོ་བའི་སྐྱབས་མགོན་རྒྱལ་བ་མཆོག།
བདག་ཉིད་ཆེན་པོ་འཇམ་དབྱངས་ནམ་མཁའི་མཚན།།
བདག་ཆེན་ཆོས་རྗེ་བློ་གྲོས་རྒྱལ་མཚན་ཞབས།།
གསོལ་བ་འདེབས་སོ་ལྷན་སྐྱེས་ཡེ་ཤེས་སྩོལ།།

Dag-Shen Dro-Way Kyab-Gon Gyal-Wa Chog
Dag-Nyi Chen-Po Jam-Yang Nam-Khay Tsen
Dag Chen Chö-Je Lo-Dö Gyal-Tsen Shab
Söl-Wa Deb-So Lhen-Kye Ye-She Tsöl

To the feet of Gyalwa Chog, protector of myself and others,
to one named Jamyang Namkha, the great being
and to the great lord, the lord of Dharma, Lodro Gyaltsen.
I offer a supplication, grant me the connate wisdom.

བཀའ་དྲིན་མཉམ་མེད་རྗེ་བཙུན་རྡོ་རིང་པ།།
བཀའ་བཞིན་སྒྲུབ་པའི་བསྟན་འཛིན་བློ་གསལ་དབང་།།
བཀའ་བརྒྱུད་གསང་ཆེན་སྨྲ་བ་མཁྱེན་བརྩེའི་ཞབས།།
གསོལ་བ་འདེབས་སོ་ལྷན་སྐྱེས་ཡེ་ཤེས་སྩོལ།།

Ka-Drin Nyam Me Je-Tsün Do-Ring-Pa
Ka-Shin Drup-Pay Ten-Zin Lo-Sel Wang
Ka-Gyü Sang Chen Ma-Wa Khyen-Tsey Shab
Söl-Wa Deb-So Lhen-Kye Ye-She Tsöl

To the feet of Jetsun Doringpa, with unparalleled kindness,
to powerful Losal, the holder of the teachings who
accomplished what has been ordered,
and to Khyentse Wangchuk, the teacher of the great secret
lineage of instruction:
I offer a supplication, please grant me the connate wisdom.

རིག་སྔགས་འཆང་བ་བླབ་གསུམ་རྒྱལ་མཚན་དང་།།
རིགས་བརྒྱའི་ཁྱབ་བདག་དབང་ཕྱུག་རབ་བརྟན་དཔལ།།
རིག་གྲོལ་མཐར་ཕྱིན་རྗེ་བཙུན་བཀའ་འགྱུར་བ།།
གསོལ་བ་འདེབས་སོ་ལྷན་སྐྱེས་ཡེ་ཤེས་སྩོལ།།

Rig Ngag Chang-Wa Lab-Sum Gyal-Tsen Dang
Rig Gyay Khyab-Dag Wang-Chug Rab-Ten Pal
Rig Dröl Thar Chin Je-Tsün Kan-Gyur-Wa
Söl-Wa Deb-So Lhen-Kye Ye-She Tsöl

To the feet of Labsum Gyaltsen, the vidyāmantradhara;
to Wangchuk Rabten, sovereign of a hundred families,
and to Jetsun Kangyurwa, who reached ultimate knowledge
and liberation:
I offer a supplication, please grant me the connate wisdom.

དཀྱིལ་འཁོར་རྒྱ་མཚོའི་ཁྱབ་བདག་ཞྭ་ལུ་བ།།
དཀྱིལ་འཁོར་ཀུན་གྱི་གཙོ་བོ་མཁྱེན་རབ་རྗེ།།
དཀྱིལ་འཁོར་འཁོར་ལོའི་བདག་པོ་རྣམ་གཉིས་ལ།།
གསོལ་བ་འདེབས་སོ་ལྷན་སྐྱེས་ཡེ་ཤེས་སྩོལ།།

Kyil-Khor Gya-Tsoy Khyab-Dag Sha-Lu-Wa
Kyil-Khor Kün Gyi Tso-Wo Khyen-Rab Je
Kyil-Khor Khor-Loy Dag-Po Nam Nyi La
Söl-Wa Deb-So Lhen-Kye Ye-She Tsöl

To the feet of Shaluwa, sovereign of an oceans of maṇḍalas,
to Lord Khyenrab, chief of all maṇḍalas
and to the two lords of the wheel of maṇḍalas:
I offer a supplication, please grant me the connate wisdom.

སྙན་བརྒྱུད་གདམས་པའི་གཏེར་མཛོད་སྨོར་ཆེན་རྗེ།།
སྙན་བརྒྱུད་མངའ་བདག་ཀུན་དགའ་ལེགས་འབྱུང་ཞབས།།
སྙན་བརྒྱུད་སྤེལ་མཁས་ཀུན་དགའ་བློ་གྲོས་ལ།།
གསོལ་བ་འདེབས་སོ་ལྷན་སྐྱེས་ཡེ་ཤེས་སྩོལ།།

Nyen-Gyü Dam-Pay Ter Zö Mor-Chen Je
Nyen-Gyü Nga-Dag Kün-Ga Leg Jung Shab
Nyen-Gyü-Pal Khe Kün-Ga Lo-Drö La
Söl-Wa Deb-So Lhen-Kye Ye-She Tsöl

To the feet of Lord Morchen, the treasury of the instructions of the aural lineage,
to Kunga Lekjung, the master of the aural lineage, and
to Kunga Lodro, the scholar who spread the aural lineage:
I offer a supplication, please grant me the connate wisdom.

ས་གསུམ་སྐྱེ་རྒྱུའི་གཉེན་གཅིག་ཐར་རྩེ་རྗེ།།
ས་བསྟན་ཉིན་མོར་བྱེད་པའི་ནམ་མཁའ་ལེགས།།

ས་བཅུའི་དབང་ཕྱུག་བསྟན་པའི་ཉི་མ་ལ།།
གསོལ་བ་འདེབས་སོ་ལྷན་སྐྱེས་ཡེ་ཤེས་སྩོལ།།

Sa Sum Kye-Gui Nyen Chig Thar-Tse Je
Sa Ten Nyin-Mor Je-Pay Nam-Kha Leg
Sa Chui Wang-Chuk Ten-Pay Nyi-Ma La
Söl-Wa Deb-So Lhen-Kye Ye-She Tsöl

To the feet of Lord Thartse, sole friend of all beings in heaven, earth and below,
to Namka Lek, the one who illuminates the teachings of the Sakya,
and to Tenpei Nyima, lord of the tenth stage:
I offer a supplication, please grant me the connate wisdom.

སྒྲུབ་པའི་སར་བཞུགས་ངག་དབང་རིན་ཆེན་དང་།།
སྒྲུབ་པ་མཆོག་བརྙེས་ཀུན་དགའ་བསྟན་འཛིན་ཞབས།།
སྒྲུབ་གཉིས་དཔལ་སྟེར་འཇམ་དཔལ་བཟང་པོ་ལ།།
གསོལ་བ་འདེབས་སོ་ལྷན་སྐྱེས་ཡེ་ཤེས་སྩོལ།།

Drup-Pay Sar Shug Nga-Wang Rin-Chen Dang
Drup-Pa Chog Nye Kün-Ga Ten-Zin Shab
Drup Nyi Pal-Ter Jam-Pal Zang-Po La
Söl-Wa Deb-So Lhen-Kye Ye-She Tsöl

To the feet of Nga-Wang Rinchen, who resides on the stage of accomplishment,
to Kunga Tenzin, the one who attained supreme siddhi,

and to Jampal Zangpo, the glorious treasure of the
two kinds of siddhi:
I offer a supplication, please grant me the connate wisdom.

འཇམ་དཔལ་དབྱངས་དངོས་མཁྱེན་བརྩེའི་དབང་པོ་དང་།།
འཇམ་དཔལ་སྒྲུབ་པ་བློ་གཏེར་དབང་པོའི་ཞབས།།
འཇམ་དབྱངས་རྣམ་འཕྲུལ་ཆོས་ཀྱི་ཉི་མ་ལ།།
གསོལ་བ་འདེབས་སོ་ལྷན་སྐྱེས་ཡེ་ཤེས་སྩོལ།།

Jam-Pal Yang Ngö Khyen-Tsey Wang-Po Dang
Jam-Pal Drup-Pa Lo Ter Wang-Poy Shab
Jam-Yang Nam-Trul Chö-Kkyi Nyi-Ma La
Söl-Wa Deb-So Lhen-Kye Ye-She Tsöl

To the feet of Khyentse Wangpo, Manjushri in person,
to Loter Wangpo, the one who accomplished Manjushri,
and to Choekyi Nyima, the emanation of Manjushri;
I offer a supplication, please grant me the connate wisdom.

རྣམ་དག་རྒྱུད་སྡེའི་མན་ངག་ལ་དབང་ཞིང་།།
རྣམ་མང་གདུལ་བྱའི་བློ་གྲོས་རྒྱས་མཛད་པ།།
རྣམ་འདྲེན་མཆོག་གྱུར་གཞན་ཕན་སྙིང་པོ་ལ།།
གསོལ་བ་འདེབས་སོ་ལྷན་སྐྱེས་ཡེ་ཤེས་སྩོལ།།

Nam-Dag Gyü-Dey Men Ngag La Wang Shing
Nam Mang Dul-Jay Lo-Drö Gye-Zé-Pa
Nam-Dren Chog-Gyur Shen-Phen Nying-Po La
Söl-Wa Deb-So Lhen-Kye Ye-She Tsöl

To Shenphen Nyingpo, the one with authority over the
intimate instructions of the pure tantras,
the one who increases the intelligence of disciples in many
ways,
the one who is the supreme leader of all,
I offer a supplication, please grant me the connate wisdom.

རིགས་དང་དཀྱིལ་འཁོར་རྒྱ་མཚོའི་ཁྱབ་བདག་མཆོག།
དྲན་པས་སྲིད་ཞིའི་གདུང་བ་སེལ་མཛད་པ།།
བཀའ་དྲིན་མཉམ་མེད་རྩ་བའི་བླ་མ་ལ།།
གསོལ་བ་འདེབས་སོ་ལྷན་སྐྱེས་ཡེ་ཤེས་སྩོལ།།

Rig Dang Kyil-Khor Gya-Tsoy Khyab-Dag Chog
Dren-Pé Si Shiy Dung-Wa Sel Zé-Pa
Ka-Drin Nyam-Mey Tsa-Way La-Ma La
Söl-Wa Deb-So Lhen-Kye Ye-She Tsöl

To the root guru of unparalleled kindness
sovereign of oceans of families and maṇḍalas,
who removes the torment of existence and peace
through being recalled:
I offer a supplication, please grant me the connate wisdom.

དཔལ་འབྱོར་གྲུ་ཆེན་མི་རྟག་དྲན་པ་ཡི།།
བ་དན་དཀར་པོས་བསྐྱོད་པའི་ལས་འབྲས་ཀྱི།།
བླང་དོར་མཐུན་པའི་རླུང་གིས་རབ་བསྐུལ་ནས།།
འཇིགས་རུང་འཁོར་བའི་མཚོ་ལས་སྒྲོལ་བར་ཤོག།

Thal-Jor Dru Chen Mi-Tag Dren-Pa Yi
Ba-Den Kar-Pö Kyö-Pay Lé De Kyi
Lang-Dor Thün-Pay Lung Gi Rab-Kul Ne
Jig-Rung Khor-Way Tso Lé Dröl-War Shog

May I be freed from the terrifying ocean of saṃsāra
in the great ship of freedom and endowments,
moved by the white sail of recalling impermanence,
driven by the favorable wind of adopting and abandoning karma and its results.

བསླུ་མེད་སྐྱབས་གནས་གཙུག་གི་ནོར་བུར་བསྟེན།།
མ་གྱུར་འགྲོ་བའི་དོན་ཆེན་སྙིང་ལ་ཞུགས།།
རྡོར་སེམས་བདུད་རྩིས་ཉེས་པའི་དྲི་མ་བཀྲུས།།
རྗེ་བཙུན་བླ་མའི་ཐུགས་རྗེས་སྐྱོང་བར་ཤོག།

Lu-Me Kyab-Ne Tsug Gi Nor-Bur Ten
Ma-Gyur Dro-Way Don Chen Nying La Shug
Dor-Sem Dü-Tsi Nye-Pay Dri-Ma Tru
Je-Tsün La-May Thug-Je Kyong-War Shog

Relying upon the crown jewel of the non-deceptive places of refuge,
the great benefit of migrating mother beings present in my heart,
the taint of faults washed by the amrita of Vajrasattva,
may I be nurtured by the compassion of the Jetsun guru.

ཡིད་འོང་རྒྱལ་ཡུམ་ཕྱི་ཡི་རྣལ་འབྱོར་མ།།
བཾ་ཡིག་ནང་གི་རྡོ་རྗེ་བཙུན་མོ་མཆོག།
སེམས་ཉིད་སྟོང་གསལ་གསང་བའི་མཁའ་སྤྱོད་ཡུམ།།
རང་ཞལ་མཐོང་བའི་རྩེ་དགས་རོལ་པར་ཤོག།

Yi Ong Gyal-Yum Chi Yi Nal-Jor-Ma
Vaṁ Yig Nang Gi Dor-Je Tsun-Mo Chog
Sem-Nyi Tong Sal Sang-Way Kha-Chö Yum
Rang Shal Thong-Way Tse Ge Röl-Par Shog

The beautiful mother of the victors is the outer Yoginī,
the syllable Vaṁ is the inner supreme Vajra Queen,
clear and emptiness mind essence is the secret Khecarī,
may I enjoy the delightful revelry of seeing my own face.

སྣོད་ཀྱི་འཇིག་རྟེན་ཨེ་ཡིག་གཞལ་མེད་ཁང་།།
བཅུད་ཀྱི་སེམས་ཅན་བཾ་ཡིག་རྣལ་འབྱོར་མ།།
ཟུང་འཇུག་བདེ་བ་ཆེན་པོའི་ཏིང་འཛིན་གྱིས།།
ཅིར་སྣང་དག་པའི་སྣང་བར་འཆར་བར་ཤོག།

Nö Kyi Jig-Ten E Yig Shal-Me Khang
Chü-Kyi Sem-Chen Vaṁ Yig Nal-Jor-Ma
Zung-Jug De-Wa Chen-Poy Ting-Zin Gyi
Chir Nang Dag-Pay Nang-War Char-War Shog

The universe is the syllable *E*, the celestial mansion,
sentient beings are *Vaṁ*, Yoginī.

May whatever appears arising as pure vision
with the samādhi of the great bliss of union.

དེ་ལྟར་ཕྱོགས་དང་ཟླ་བའི་རྣལ་འབྱོར་གྱིས།།
ནམ་ཞིག་དུས་ན་དགའ་མ་བྱི་རུའི་མདོག།
ལི་ཁྲིའི་སྐྲ་གྲོལ་དམར་སེར་མིག་གཡོ་མས།།
མངོན་སུམ་རིག་འཛིན་གྲོང་དུ་འཁྲིད་པར་ཤོག།

De-Tar Chog Dang Da-Way Nal-Jor Gyi
Nam-Shig Dü Na Ga-Ma Chi-Rüi Dog
Li-Tiy Ta-Dröl Mar-Ser Mig Yo-Mé
Ngön-Sum Rig-Zin Drong-Du Ti-Par Shog

As such, through the eleven yogas
when the time has come, may a coral colored maiden
with vermilion hair and flirtatious orange eyes
lead one in person to the city of vidyādharas.

སིནྡྷུར་ལངྐ་ལི་ཡི་སྡོང་བུར་བཅས།།
རོ་ལྡན་གནས་སུ་བསྒྲུབས་ཤིང་ཡུལ་ཀུན་ཏུ།།
ཉུལ་བས་གང་གི་མཛོད་སྤུར་འཁྱིལ་རིས་ཅན།།
འཕོས་པའི་མཛེས་མས་མཁའ་སྤྱོད་འཁྲིད་པར་ཤོག།

Sin-Dhur Lang-Ka Li-Yi Dong-Bur Ché
Ro-Den Ne-Su Drub Shing Yül Kün-Tu
Nyul-Way Gang Gi Zö Pur Khyil Ri-Chen
Pho-Pay Ze-Mé Kha-Chö Ti-Par Shog

May whoever practices the rite of sindhura and the langkali
tree
in a charnel ground, roaming through all lands,
meet a beauty to whom the swirl
on their forehead transfers and be lead to Khecharī.

ནང་གི་ཕག་མོ་གཟུང་འཛིན་འཁྲི་ཤིང་བཅོམ།།
མཆོག་གི་དྷཱུ་ཏིར་ཞུགས་པའི་གར་མཁན་མ།།
ཚངས་པའི་སྒོ་ནས་སྤྲིན་ལམ་དབྱིངས་སུ་འཕོན།།
ཁྲག་འཐུང་དཔའ་བོར་འཁྱུད་ཅིང་རོལ་པར་ཤོག།

Nang Gi Phag-Mo Zung Zin Ti Shing Chom
Chog Gi Dhu-Tir Shug-Pay Gar-Khen-Ma
Tsang-Pay Go Ne Trin Lam Ying Su Thon
Trag Thung Pa-Wor Khyü Ching Röl Par Shog

The inner Vārāhī who destroys the creeper of subject and
object,
is the dancer who enters the supreme avadhūti;
ejected from the aperture of crown into the expanse of the
sky,
may she play in the embrace of heroic Heruka.

ལྟེ་བའི་པདྨོར་རླུང་ལྷའི་ཏི་ལ་ཀ།
རྩེ་གཅིག་བསྒོམས་པའི་ཁ་སྦྱོར་རྣལ་འབྱོར་གྱིས།།
ལུས་སེམས་རྩ་ལ་དྲི་བཞོན་ཞུགས་པ་ཡི།།
བདེ་བ་མཆོག་གིས་བདག་རྒྱུད་ཚིམས་པར་ཤོག།

Te-Way Pe-Mor Lung Ngay Ti-La-Ka
Tse Chig Gom-Pay Kha-Jor Nal-Jor Gyi
Lü Sem Tsa La Di Shon Shug-Pa Yi
De-Wa Chog Gi Dag Gyü Tsim-Par Shog

In the lotus of the navel is a tilaka of five vāyus,
through practicing one-pointedly on the yoga of uniting the vāyus,
the vāyu is gathered into the channels of the body and mind:
may my mind be satisfied with supreme bliss.

ཐ་མལ་འོད་ཀྱི་གཏུམ་མོ་མཛེས་ལྡན་མ།།
དྷཱུ་ཏཱིར་འཛུམ་དཀར་བཞད་པའི་རོལ་རྩེད་ཀྱིས།།
ཧཾ་ཡིག་གཞོན་ནུ་ཡོངས་སུ་མཉེས་བྱས་ནས།།
ཟུང་འཇུག་བདེ་བ་ཆེན་པོའི་ས་ཐོབ་ཤོག།

Tha-Mal Ö Kyi Tum-Mo Ze-Den-Ma
Dhu-Tir Zum Kar Zhe-Pay Röl-Tse Kyi
Ham Yig Shon-Nu Yong-Su Nye-Je Ne
Zung-Jug De-Wa Chen-Poy Sa Thob Shog

The beautiful ordinary and light caṇḍālī girl with a playful smiling face, in the avadhūti,
having pleased the youth, the syllable *Haṁ*,
may I attain the stage of the great bliss of union.

སྐྱེ་འགག་གནས་གསུམ་བྲལ་བ་གདོད་མའི་གཞིས།།
སྟོང་གསལ་བརྗོད་དུ་མེད་པ་གཉུག་མའི་ངང་།།

ཟུང་འཇུག་བློ་འདས་རང་སེམས་རྣལ་འབྱོར་མར།།
རང་ངོ་ཤེས་ནས་རྟག་ཏུ་སྐྱོང་བར་ཤོག།

Kye Gag Ne Sum Drel-Wa Dö-May Shi
Tong Sal Jo Du Me-Pa Nyug-May Ngang
Zung-Jug Lo-Dé Rang-Sem Nal-Jor-Mar
Rang Ngo-She Ne Tag-Tu Kyong-War Shog

The original nature is free from arising, ceasing and abiding,
the innate state is inexpressible emptiness and clarity,
Yoginī, my mind, is union beyond thought:
having recognized my own face may it always be sustained.

རྩ་རླུང་ཐིག་ལེ་ཨེ་ཝཾ་དབྱིངས་སུ་ཐིམ།།
སེམས་ཉིད་བདེ་ཆེན་ཆོས་སྐུའི་དཔལ་ཐོབ་ནས།།
བགྲང་ཡས་གཟུགས་སྐུའི་རྣམ་རོལ་དཔག་མེད་ཀྱིས།།
ནམ་མཁའི་མཐའ་ཀླས་འགྲོ་འདི་སྐྱོང་བར་ཤོག།

Tsa Lung Thig-Le E Wam Ying Su Thim
Sem Nyi De-Chen Chö-Kyui Pal Thob Ne
Drang Ye Zug-Kui Nam-Röl Pag-Me Kyi
Nam-Khay Tha-Le Dro Di Kyong-War Shog

After the channels, vāyu, bindu, and *E Vaṁ* dissolve into the dhātu,
the glory of the dharmakāya of great bliss, the mind essence, is obtained,
may these migrating beings in limitless space be nurtured
with infinite transformations of countless rūpakāyas.

Preliminaries

སྔོན་འགྲོ་གཏོར་མ་ཆུ་ཆང་གིས་སྦྱངས་ལ།

ཨོཾ་སུམྦྷ་ནི་སུམྦྷ་ཧཱུྃ་ཧཱུྃ་ཕཊ།

ཨོཾ་གྲྀཧྞ་གྲྀཧྞ་ཧཱུྃ་ཧཱུྃ་ཕཊ།

ཨོཾ་གྲྀཧྞ་པ་ཡ་གྲྀཧྞ་པ་ཡ་ཧཱུྃ་ཧཱུྃ་ཕཊ།

ཨོཾ་ཨཱ་ན་ཡ་ཧོཿ བྷ་ག་ཝཱན་བིདྱ་རཱ་ཛ་ཧཱུྃ་ཧཱུྃ་ཕཊ། ཀྱིས་བསང་།

The preliminaries, purify the torma with water and alcohol, cleansing them with:

Oṁ sumbha nisumbha huṁ hūṁ phaṭ

Oṁ grihaṇa grihaṇa huṁ hūṁ phaṭ

Oṁ grihaṇapaya grihaṇapaya huṁ hūṁ phaṭ

Oṁ ānayaho bhagavān vidyārāja huṁ hūṁ phaṭ

ཨོཾ་སྭ་བྷཱ་ཝ་ཤུདྡྷཿ སརྦ་དྷརྨཱཿ སྭ་བྷཱ་ཝ་ཤུདྡྷོ྅ཧཾ། གིས་སྦྱངས།

Purify with:

Oṁ svabhāva shuddhaḥ sarva dharmāḥ svabhāva shuddho' haṁ

ཨོཾ་ཨཱཿ ཧཱུྃ་ཧ་ཧོཿ ཧྲཱིཿ དང་ལག་པ་གཡས་གཡོན་དབུས་གསུམ་བསྟན་པ་དང་བྱ་ཁྱུང་གི་ཕྱག་རྒྱས་བྱིན་གྱིས་བརླབས།

Show the right hand, then the left, place them in the center and bless with garuda mudra:

Oṁ āḥ hūṁ ha hoḥ hrīḥ

སླར་ཡང་། ཨོཾ་ཨཱཿ ཧཱུྃ་ལན་གསུམ།

Further, recite three times:

Oṁ āḥ hūṁ

Torma for the Ḍākinīs

དེ་ནས་མཁའ་འགྲོ་སྤྱི་གཏོར་ནི།

ཕཻཾ་ཞེས་དང་། ཨོཾ་བཛྲ་ཨཱ་རལླི་ཧོཿ ཛཿ ཧཱུྃ་བཾ་ཧོཿ བཛྲ་ཌཱ་ཀི་ནཱི་ས་མ་ཡ་སྟྭཾ། དྲྀ་ཤྱ་ཧོཿ ཞེས་བརྗོད།

Recite:

Phaiṁ, oṁ vajra āralli hoḥ, jaḥ hūṁ vaṁ hoḥ, vajraḍākinī samaya stvaṁ drishya hoḥ

རང་གི་སྙིང་གའི་ས་བོན་གྱི་འོད་ཟེར་གྱིས་འཛམ་བུའི་གླིང་ན་གདོད་ནས་གྲུབ་པའི་དུར་ཁྲོད་བརྒྱད་མདུན་གྱི་ནམ་མཁར་བྱོན་པར་བསམས་ལ། དེ་རྣམས་ལ་གཏོར་མ་ཕུལ་བར་བསམས་ཏེ། ཐལ་མོ་ཁ་གྱེན་དུ་བྱེ་ལ།

Rang Gi Nying-Gay Sa-Bon Gyi Ö-Zer Gyi Zam-Bui-Ling Na Dö-Ne Drup-Pay Dur-Trö Gye Dün-Gyi Nam-Khar Jon-Par Sam La, De-Nam La Tor-Ma Phul-War Sam Te Tal-Mo Kha Gyen-Du Che La

Imagine that light rays from the seed syllable in one's heart bring the eight charnel grounds that formed at the beginning in Jambudvipa into the space in front of oneself. Imagine that one is offering the torma to them and cup one's palms.

ཨོཾ་ཁ་ཁ་ཁཱ་ཧི་ཁཱ་ཧི། སརྦ་ཡཀྵ་རཀྵ་ས། བྷཱུ་ཏ་པྲེ་ཏ་པི་ཤཱ་ཙ། ཨུནྨཱ་ད། ཨ་པསྨཱ་ར། ཌཱ་ཀ་ཌཱ་ཀི་ནྱ་ད་ཡ། ཨི་མཾ་བ་ལིཾ་གྲྀཧྞ་ནྟུ། ས་མ་ཡ་རཀྵནྟུ། མ་མ་སརྦ་སིདྡྷིཾ། མེ་པྲ་ཡཙྪནྟུ། ཡ་ཐཻ་བཾ། ཡ་ཐེཥྚཾ། བྷུཉྫ་ཐ། ཛི་གྷྲ་ཐ། པི་བ་ཐ། མཱ་ཏི་ཀྲ་མ་ཐ། མ་མ་སརྦ་ཀཱརྻ་སཏྭ་ཁཾ། བི་ཤུདྡྷི་ཡ། ས་ཧ་ཡི་ཀཱ་བྷ་ཝནྟུ། ཧཱུྃ་ཧཱུྃ་ཕཊ་ཕཊ་སྭཱ་ཧཱ། ཞེས་ལན་གསུམ་གྱིས་ཕུལ།

Repeating the offering three times:

Oṁ Kha kha khāhi khāhi, sarva yaksha rākshasa bhuta preta pishāci, unmāda, apasmāra, ḍāka ḍākinyā daya imaṁ baliṁ ghrihaṇantu, samaya rakshantu mama sarva siddhim me prayacchantu, yathaivaṁ, yathaishtaṁ, bhujñatha, jighatha, pipatha, mātikramatha, mama sarva karya, satsukhaṁ vishuddhaya, sahayika bhavantu huṁ hūṁ phaṭ phaṭ svāhā

ཨོཾ་བཛྲ་ཨརྒྷཾ་ཨཱཿ ཧཱུྃ། ཨོཾ་བཛྲ་པཱདྱཾ་ཨཱཿ ཧཱུྃ། ཨོཾ་བཛྲ་པུཥྤེ་ཨཱཿ ཧཱུྃ། ཨོཾ་བཛྲ་དྷཱུཔེ་ཨཱཿ ཧཱུྃ། ཨོཾ་བཛྲ་ཨཱ་ལོ་ཀེ་ཨཱཿ ཧཱུྃ། ཨོཾ་བཛྲ་གནྡྷེ་ཨཱཿ ཧཱུྃ། ཨོཾ་བཛྲ་ནཻ་ཝི་དྱེ་ཨཱཿ ཧཱུྃ། ཨོཾ་བཛྲ་ཤབྡ་ཨཱཿ ཧཱུྃ། བར་ཕྱིས་མཆོད།

Make offerings with:

Oṁ vajra arghaṁ āḥ hūṁ
Oṁ vajra pādyaṁ āḥ hūṁ[1]
Oṁ vajra puṣpe āḥ hūṁ
Oṁ vajra dhūpe āḥ hūṁ
Oṁ vajra āloke āḥ hūṁ
Oṁ vajra ghande āḥ hūṁ
Oṁ vajra naividye āḥ hūṁ
Oṁ vajra shabda āḥ hūṁ

ནང་མཆོད་ཕུལ་ཏེ། ཨོཾ་ཨཱཿ ཧཱུྃ། སངས་རྒྱས་མཁའ་འགྲོ། རྡོ་རྗེ་མཁའ་འགྲོ། རིན་ཆེན་མཁའ་འགྲོ། པདྨ་མཁའ་འགྲོ། སྣ་ཚོགས་མཁའ་འགྲོ་ལ་སོགས་པ་གནས་གསུམ་གྱི་དཔའ་བོ་དང་མཁའ་འགྲོ་མ་རྣམས་ཀྱི་ཞལ་དུ་མཆོད་པ་དམ་པ་འབུལ་ལོ། ཞེས་བརྗོད།

---

[1] Some manuscripts have ཨོཾ་བཛྲ་ཨརྒྷཾ་སྭཱ་ཧཱ། ཨོཾ་བཛྲ་པཱདྱཾ་སྭཱ་ཧཱ། *(Oṁ vajra arghaṁ svāhā, Oṁ vajra pādyaṁ svāhā).*

Oṁ āḥ hūṁ, Sang-Gyé Khan-Dro, Dor-Je Khan-Dro, Rin-Chen Khan-Dro, Pad-Ma Khan-Dro, Na-Tsog Khan-Dro La Sog Pa Ne Sum Pa-Wo Dang Khan-Dro-Ma Nam Kyi Shal Du Chö-Pa Dam-Pa Bül Lo

Make the inner offering by reciting:

Oṁ āḥ hūṁ, this sublime offering is made to the mouths of the Buddha ḍākinī, Vajra ḍākinī, Ratna ḍākinī, Padma ḍākinī, Viśva ḍākinī, and so on, all the heroes and ḍākinīs of the three places.

དྲིལ་བུ་ཆིག་བརྡུང་བྱ་ཞིང་།
ལྷ་ཡི་ཚོགས་རྣམས་མ་ལུས་དང་།།
ཀླུ་ཡི་ཚོགས་རྣམས་མ་ལུས་དང་།།
གནོད་སྦྱིན་ཚོགས་རྣམས་མ་ལུས་དང་།།
སྲིན་པོའི་ཚོགས་རྣམས་མ་ལུས་དང་།།
འབྱུང་པོའི་ཚོགས་རྣམས་མ་ལུས་དང་།།
ཡི་དྭགས་ཚོགས་རྣམས་མ་ལུས་དང་།།
ཤ་ཟའི་ཚོགས་རྣམས་མ་ལུས་དང་།།
སྨྱོ་བྱེད་ཚོགས་རྣམས་མ་ལུས་དང་།།
རྗེད་བྱེད་ཚོགས་རྣམས་མ་ལུས་དང་།།
མཁའ་འགྲོའི་ཚོགས་རྣམས་མ་ལུས་དང་།།
མ་མོའི་ཚོགས་རྣམས་མ་ལུས་དང་།།
དེ་ལ་སོགས་ཏེ་འབྱུང་པོའི་ཚོགས།།
མ་ལུས་པར་ནི་ཐམས་ཅད་དག།
འདིར་གཤེགས་བདག་ལ་དགོངས་སུ་གསོལ།།

Lha Yi Tsog-Nam Ma-Lü Dang
Lu Yi Tsog-Nam Ma-Lü Dang
Nö-Jin Tsog-Nam Ma-Lü Dang
Sin-Poy Tsog-Nam Ma-Lü Dang
Jung-Poy Tsog-Nam Ma-Lü Dang
Yi-Dak Tsog-Nam Ma-Lü Dang
Sha-Zay Tsog-Nam Ma-Lü Dang
Nyo-Je Tsog-Nam Ma-Lü Dang
Ji-Je Tsog-Nam Ma-Lü Dang
Khan-Droy Tsog-Nam Ma-Lü Dang
Ma-Moy Tsog-Nam Ma-Lü Dang
De-La-Sok Te Jung-Pay Tsog
Ma-Lü-Par Nï Tham-Ché Dak
Dir Shek Dak La Gong-Su-Söl

Ring the bell one time for each line:

The whole assembly of devas,
the whole assembly of nāgas,
the whole assembly of yakṣas,
the whole assembly of rākṣasas,
the whole assembly of bhūtas,
the whole assembly of pretas,
the whole assembly of piśācīs,
the whole assembly of unmādas,
the whole assembly of apasmāras,
the whole assembly of ḍākinīs,
the whole assembly of mātrikās,
likewise all assemblies of the bhūtas without missing,
please come here and take heed of me!

བསྟན་པ་བསྲུང་དང་འགྲོ་བའི་དོན་མཛད་ཕྱིར།།
ཐུགས་དམ་བཅས་ཤིང་ཞལ་གྱིས་བཞེས་པ་རྣམས།།
དཔལ་ཆེན་བཀའ་སྡོད་ཡིད་ལྟར་མགྱོགས་པ་ཡི།།
འཇིགས་པའི་གཟུགས་ཅན་དྲག་གཏུམ་མི་བཟད་པ།།
གདུག་པ་འདུལ་མཛད་ནག་པོའི་ཚོགས་རྣམས་འཇོམས།།
རྣལ་འབྱོར་ལས་ལ་འབྲས་བུ་སྟེར་མཛད་ཅིང་།།
མཐུ་སྟོབས་བྱིན་རླབས་བསམ་གྱིས་མི་ཁྱབ་པའི།།
གནོད་སྦྱིན་ཚོགས་སོགས་བརྒྱད་ལ་ཕྱག་འཚལ་ལོ།།
སྡེ་བརྒྱད་བཙུན་མོ་སྲས་དང་གཡོག་བཅས་ཀྱིས།།
དངོས་གྲུབ་ཀུན་གྱི་བཀའ་དྲིན་བདག་ལ་སྩོལ།།

Ten-Pa Sung Dang Dro-Way Dön Zé Chir
Tuk-Dam Ché Shing Zhel-Gyi Zhe-Pa Nam
Pal-Chen Ka-Dö Yi-Tar-Gyok-Pa Yi
Jik-Pay-Zuk Chen Drak-Tum Mi-Zé-Pa
Duk-Pa Dül-Zé Nak-Poy Tsog-Nam Jom
Nal-Jor Lé La Dre-Bu Ter Zé Ching
Thu-Top Jin-Lap Sam-Gyi-Mi-Khyap-Pay
Nö-Jin Tsog Sok Gye La Chak-Tsal-Lo
De-Gye Tsün-Mo Se Dang Yok Ché Kyi
Ngö-Drup Kün Gyi Ka-Drin Dak La Tsöl

In order to guard the teachings and benefit migrating beings,
those with commitments and promises,
who abiding by the command of the great glorious one, as fast as thought,
with terrifying forms, wrathful and fearsome,

tame the wicked and conquer those of the dark side.
Make the activities of the yogin bear fruit.
Homage to the eight assemblies of the yakṣas, and so on,
who have inconceivable power, strength, and blessing.
Eight classes, with your queens, sons and servants,
kindly grant me all siddhis.

རྣལ་འབྱོར་བདག་ཅག་འཁོར་བཅས་ལ།།
ནད་མེད་ཚེ་དང་དབང་ཕྱུག་དང་།།
དཔལ་དང་གྲགས་དང་སྐལ་པ་བཟང་།།
ལོངས་སྤྱོད་རྒྱ་ཆེན་ཀུན་ཐོབ་ཅིང་།།

Nal-Jor Dak-Chak Khor-Ché La
Ne-Mi Tse Dang Wang-Chuk Dang
Pal Dang Drak Dang Kal-Pa-Zang
Long-Chö Gya-Chen Kün-Thop Ching

May we yogins along with our retinue
attain health, longevity, power,
prestige, fame, good fortune,
and vast enjoyments.

ཞི་དང་རྒྱས་ལ་སོགས་པ་ཡི།།
ལས་ཀྱི་དངོས་གྲུབ་བདག་ལ་སྩོལ།།
དམ་ཚིག་ཅན་གྱིས་བདག་ལ་སྲུངས།།
དངོས་གྲུབ་ཀུན་གྱི་སྟོང་གྲོགས་མཛོད།།

Zhi Dang Gye La Sok-Pa Yi
Lé Kyi Ngö-Drup Dak La Tsöl
Dam-Tsik-Chen Gyi Dak La Sung
Ngö-Drup Kün Gyi Tong-Drok-Zö

Grant us the siddhis of
the activities of pacifying, increasing, and so on.
Samaya holders, protect me!
Assist me in all siddhis.

དུས་མིན་འཆི་དང་ནད་རྣམས་དང་།།
གདོན་དང་བགེགས་རྣམས་མེད་པར་མཛོད།།
རྨི་ལམ་ངན་དང་མཚན་མ་ངན།།
བྱ་བྱེད་ངན་པ་མེད་པར་མཛོད།།

Dü-Min-Chi Dang Ne Nam Dang
Dön Dang Gek Nam Me-Par Zö
Mi-Lam Ngen Dang Tsen-Ma Ngen
Ja-Je-Ngen-Pa Me-Par Zö

Prevent untimely death, illnesses,
attacks, and obstructors!
Prevent bad dreams, bad omens,
and negative activities.

འཇིག་རྟེན་བདེ་ཞིང་ལོ་ལེགས་དང་།།
འབྲུ་རྣམས་འཕེལ་ཞིང་ཆོས་འཕེལ་དང་།།
དགེ་ལེགས་ཐམས་ཅད་འབྱུང་བ་ཡི།།
ཡིད་ལ་འདོད་པ་ཀུན་སྒྲུབ་ཤོག།

Jik-Ten-De Zhing Lo-Lek Dang
Dru Nam Pel Zhing-Chö Pel Dang
Ge-Lek Tham-Ché Jung-Wa Yi
Yi-La Dö-Pa Kün-Drup Shok

May there be happiness in the world,
good harvests, increased grains yields, and increased Dharma.
All positive things arise,
and all the wishes in the mind be accomplished.

དཔལ་ལྡན་བླ་མ་དམ་པ་རྣམས་ཀྱི་ཐུགས་དགོངས་རྫོགས་པ་དང་། ནམ་མཁའ་དང་མཉམ་པའི་སེམས་ཅན་ཐམས་ཅད་ཀྱི་དོན་དུ། ཕྱག་རྒྱ་ཆེན་པོ་མཆོག་གི་དངོས་གྲུབ་རྗེ་བཙུན་རྡོ་རྗེ་རྣལ་འབྱོར་མའི་གོ་འཕང་ཐོབ་པར་བྱ་བའི་ཕྱིར་དུ། རྗེ་བཙུན་རྡོ་རྗེ་རྣལ་འབྱོར་མའི་སིནྡྷུ་རའི་དཀྱིལ་འཁོར་བསྒྲུབ་ཅིང་མཆོད་པ་དང་། བདག་ཉིད་འཇུག་ཅིང་དབང་བླང་བར་འཚལ་ན་དཀར་ཕྱོགས་ལ་མངོན་པར་དགའ་བའི་སྲུང་མ་ཁྱད་པར་ཅན་ཁྱེད་རྣམས་ཀྱིས་མཆོད་སྦྱིན་གྱི་གཏོར་མ་རྒྱ་ཆེན་པོ་འདི་བཞེས་ལ། དཀྱིལ་འཁོར་ཆེན་པོའི་བྱ་བ་མཐར་མ་ཕྱིན་གྱི་བར་དུ་བར་ཆད་ཐམས་ཅད་བསྲུང་བ་དང་། དེ་ནས་ཀྱང་བདག་ཅག་རྣལ་འབྱོར་འཁོར་དང་བཅས་པ་བྱང་ཆུབ་མ་ཐོབ་ཀྱི་བར་གྱི་བར་ཆད་ཐམས་ཅད་བསྲུང་བ་དང་། བྱང་ཆུབ་སྒྲུབ་པའི་སྟོངས་གྲོགས་མཛད་དུ་གསོལ། གང་དག་ནག་པོའི་ཕྱོགས་སུ་ཞུགས་པ་གསང་སྤྱོད་བལྟ་བར་མི་དབང་བའི་བགེགས་དང་ལོག་པར་འདྲེན་པ་ཐམས་ཅད་སའི་ཕྱོགས་འདིར་མ་གནས་པར་གཞན་དུ་སོང་ཞིག

Pal-Den La-Ma Dam-Pa Nam Kyi Thug Gong Dzog-Pa Dang, Nam-Kha Dang Nyam-Pay Sem-Chen Tham-Ché Kyi Don Du, Chag-Gya Chen-Po Chog Gi Ngö-Drup Je-Tsün Dor-Je Nal-Jor-May Go-Phang

Thop-Bar Ja-Way Chir Du, Je-Tsün Dor-Je Nal-Jor-May Sin-Dhu-Ray Kyil-Khor Drub Ching Chö-Pa Dang, Dag-Nyi Jug Ching Wang Lang-War Tsel Na Kar-Chog La Ngön-Par Ga-Way Sung-Ma Khye-Par Chen Khye-Nam Kyi Chö Jin Gyi Tor-Ma Gya-Chen-Po Di She La, Kyil-Khor Chen-Poy Ja-Wa Thar-Ma Chin Gyi Bar Du Bar-Ché Tham-Ché Sung-Wa Dang, De Ne Kyang Dag-Chag Nal-Jor Khor Dang Ché Pa Jang-Chub Ma Thob Kyi Bar Gyi Bar Ché Tham-Ché Sung-Wa Dang, Jang-Chub Drub-Pay Tong Drog Zé Du Söl, Gang Dag Nag-Poy Chog Su Gyur-Pa Sang Chö Ta-War Mi Wang-Way Geg Dang Log-Pa Dren-Pa Tham-Ché Say Chog Dir Ma Ne-Par Shen-Du Song Shig

In order to accomplish the intention of glorious sublime gurus, to benefit sentient beings equal with space, and for the sake of obtaining the supreme siddhi of mahamudra, the stage of the Jetsun Vajrayoginī, while performing the Sādhana with the offering to the sindhura maṇḍala and self-initiation of Jetsun Vajrayoginī, special protectors who delight in the positive side, may you accept this vast torma offering. Until we complete the activities of the great maṇḍala, guard us against all obstacles. Please assist us to accomplish awakening and protect us, yogins and our retinue, from all obstacles until we attain awakening.

Whoever has turned to the dark side, all obstructors and misleading spirits who have no ability to observe secret conduct, you must not stay here, go somewhere else!

ཨོཾ་སུམྦྷ་ནི་སུམྦྷ་ཧཱུྃ་ཧཱུྃ་ཕཊ།

ཨོཾ་གྲྀཧྞ་གྲྀཧྞ་ཧཱུྃ་ཧཱུྃ་ཕཊ།

ཨོཾ་གྲྀཧྞ་པ་ཡ་གྲྀཧྞ་པ་ཡ་ཧཱུྃ་ཧཱུྃ་ཕཊ།

ཨོཾ་ཨཱ་ན་ཡ་ཧོཿ བྷ་ག་ཝཱན་བིདྱཱ་རཱ་ཛ་ཧཱུྃ་ཧཱུྃ་ཕཊ།

ལན་གསུམ་བརྗོད་ཅིང་རྡོ་རྗེ་དྲིལ་བུ་གསོར་དཀྲོལ་དྲག་ཏུ་བྱ། གཏོར་མ་ཕྱིར་ས་གཙང་སར་དོར་རོ།

Recite three times, rotate the vajra and ring the bell loudly, throw the torma outside on a clean ground:

Oṁ sumbha nisumbha huṁ hūṁ phaṭ

Oṁ grihaṇa grihaṇa huṁ hūṁ phaṭ

Oṁ grihaṇapaya grihaṇapaya huṁ hūṁ phaṭ

Oṁ ānayaho bhagavān vidyārāja huṁ hūṁ phaṭ

Blessing of the Place and Offerings

གནས་དང་མཆོད་པའི་ཡོ་བྱད་བྱིན་གྱིས་བརླབས་པ་ནི།

ༀ་སུམྦྷ་ནི་སུམྦྷ་ཧུྃ་ཧཱུྃ་ཕཊ།
ༀ་གྲྀཧྞ་གྲྀཧྞ་ཧུྃ་ཧཱུྃ་ཕཊ།
ༀ་གྲྀཧྞ་པ་ཡ་གྲྀཧྞ་པ་ཡ་ཧུྃ་ཧཱུྃ་ཕཊ།
ༀ་ཨཱ་ན་ཡ་ཧོཿ བྷ་ག་ཝཱན་བིདྱཱ་རཱ་ཛ་ཧུྃ་ཧཱུྃ་ཕཊ། གྱིས་བསང་།

Then bless the place and offerings. Cleanse with:
Oṁ sumbha nisumbha huṁ hūṁ phaṭ
Oṁ grihaṇa grihaṇa huṁ hūṁ phaṭ
Oṁ grihaṇapaya grihaṇapaya huṁ hūṁ phaṭ
Oṁ ānayaho bhagavān vidyārāja huṁ hūṁ phaṭ

ༀ་སྭ་བྷཱ་ཝ་ཤུདྡྷཿ སརྦ་དྷརྨཱཿ སྭ་བྷཱ་ཝ་ཤུདྡྷོ྅ཧཾ། གིས་སྦྱངས།

Purify with:
Oṁ svabhāva shuddhaḥ sarva dharmāḥ svabhāva shuddho' haṁ

སྟོང་པའི་ངང་ལས་གནས་ཁང་བྷྲཱུྃ་ལས་རིན་པོ་ཆེ་སྣ་ཚོགས་ལས་གྲུབ་པའི་གཞལ་ཡས་ཁང་གྲུ་བཞི་སྒོ་བཞི་པ། རྟ་བབས་བཞིས་མཛེས་པ། རྒྱན་ཐམས་ཅད་ཀྱིས་བརྒྱན་པ། མཚན་ཉིད་ཐམས་ཅད་ཡོངས་སུ་རྫོགས་པའི་ནང་དུ་ཨ་ལས་ཡེ་ཤེས་ཀྱི་ཀ་པཱ་ལ་ཡངས་ཤིང་རྒྱ་ཆེ་བ་རྣམས་ཀྱི་ནང་དུ་ཧཱུྃ་ཞུ་བ་ལས་བྱུང་བའི་ལྷ་རྫས་ལས་གྲུབ་པའི་མཆོད་ཡོན། ཞབས་བསིལ། མེ་ཏོག བདུག་སྤོས། མར་མེ། དྲི་ཆབ། ཞལ་ཟས། རོལ་མོ་རྣམས་བཟང་ཞིང་རྒྱ་ཆེ་བ། དངས་ཤིང་ཐོགས་པ་མེད་པ། ས་དང་ནམ་མཁའ་བར་སྣང་ཐམས་ཅད

གང་བ། འཕགས་པ་ཀུན་ཏུ་བཟང་པོའི་རྣམ་པར་ཐར་པ་ལས་བྱུང་བའི་མཆོད་པའི་སྤྲིན་གྱི་ཕུང་པོ་ལྟ་བུ། བསམ་གྱིས་མི་ཁྱབ་པ། བླ་མ་དང་། རྗེ་བཙུན་རྡོ་རྗེ་རྣལ་འབྱོར་མའི་ལྷ་ཚོགས་སངས་རྒྱས་དང་བྱང་ཆུབ་སེམས་དཔའ་ཐམས་ཅད་ཀྱི་སྤྱན་ལམ་དུ་འབྱུང་ཞིང་རྒྱས་པར་གྱུར་ཅིག

Tong-Pay Ngang Lé Ne Khang Bhrum Lé Rin-Po-Che Na-Tsog Lé Drub-Pay Shel-Ye-Khang Dru Shi Go Shi-Pa, Ta Bab Shi Ze-Pa, Gyen Tham-Ché Kyi Gyen-Pa, Tsen-Nyi Tham-Ché Yong-Su Zog-Pay Nang Du Ah Lé Ye-She Kyi Ka-Pa-La Yang Shing Gya-Che-Wa Nam Kyi Nang Du Hūṁ Shu-Wa Lé Jung-Way Lha Zé Lé Drub-Pay Chö-Yon, Shab-Sil, Me-Tog, Dug-Po, Mar-Me, Dri-Chab, Shal-Ze, Röl-Mo Nam Zang Shing Gya-Che-Wa, Dang Shing Thog-Pa Me-Pa, Sa Dang Nam-Kha Bar-Nang Tham-Ché Gang-Wa, Phag-Pa Kün-Tu Zang-Poy Nam-Par Thar-Pa Lé Jung-Way Chö-Pay Trin Gyi Phum-Po Ta-Bu, Sam Gyi Mi Khyab-Pa, La-Ma Dang, Je-Tsün Dor-Je Nal-Jor-May Lha Tsog Sang-Gyé Dang Jang-Chub Sem-Pa Tham-Ché Kyi Chen Lam Du Jung Shing Gye-Par Gyur Chig

From the state of emptiness, one's residence from *Bhrūm* (བྷྲཱུྃ) arises as a celestial mansion made of jewels with four doors and four pediments, which is adorned with all ornaments and completed with all characteristics. Inside of this, from *Ah* (ཨ) arises wisdom kapalas, wide and vast, in which the divine substances of offerings arising from the melting of *Hūṁ* (ཧཱུྃ), drinking water, washing water, flowers, incense, lamps, scented water, food and music. They are of excellent quality, vast, pure, and without impediment, filling the earth, space and sky, an inconceivable cloud of offerings coming from the liberation of Ārya Samantabhadra appeared and increased in front of the Guru, Jetsun Vajrayogini's assemblage with buddhas and bodhisattvas.

ཨོཾ་བཛྲ་ཨརྒྷཾ་ཨཱཿ ཧཱུྃ། ཨོཾ་བཛྲ་པཱདྱཾ་ཨཱཿ ཧཱུྃ། ཨོཾ་བཛྲ་པུཥྤེ་ཨཱཿ ཧཱུྃ། ཨོཾ་བཛྲ་དྷཱུཔེ་ཨཱཿ ཧཱུྃ།
ཨོཾ་བཛྲ་ཨཱ་ལོ་ཀེ་ཨཱཿ ཧཱུྃ། ཨོཾ་བཛྲ་གནྡྷེ་ཨཱཿ ཧཱུྃ། ཨོཾ་བཛྲ་ནཻ་ཝི་དྱེ་ཨཱཿ ཧཱུྃ། ཨོཾ་བཛྲ་ཤབྡ་
ཨཱཿ ཧཱུྃ། རྣམས་ཕྱག་རྒྱ་དང་བཅས་པས་བྱིན་གྱིས་བརླབས།

Bless with the mudras:

Oṁ vajra arghaṁ āḥ hūṁ

Oṁ vajra pādyaṁ āḥ hūṁ

Oṁ vajra puṣpe āḥ hūṁ

Oṁ vajra dhūpe āḥ hūṁ

Oṁ vajra āloke āḥ hūṁ

Oṁ vajra ghande āḥ hūṁ

Oṁ vajra naiwidye āḥ hūṁ

Oṁ vajra shabda āḥ hūṁ

རྣམ་མཁའ་མཛོད་ཀྱི་ཕྱག་རྒྱ་དཔྲལ་བར་བཅས་ལ།
ཨོཾ་བཛྲ་སྥ་ར་ཎ་ཁཾ་ཞེས་པས་མང་པོར་སྤེལ།

With the treasury of space mudra at one's forehead, multiply with:

Oṁ vajra spharaṇa khaṁ

ཨོཾ་བཛྲ་གྷཎྚེ་ར་ཎི་ཏ། པྲ་ར་ཎི་ཏ། སཾ་པྲ་ར་ཎི་ཏ། སརྦ་བུདྡྷ་ཀྵེ་ཏྲ་པྲ་ཙ་ལི་ཏེ། པྲཛྙཱ་པཱ་ར་མི་ཏ་ན་ད་སཾ་བྷ་ཝེ་ཏ། བཛྲ་དྷརྨ་ཧྲི་ད་ཡ་སནྟོ་ཥ་ཎི་ཧཱུྃ་ཧཱུྃ་ཧཱུྃ་ཧོ་ཧོ་ཧོ་ཨ་ཁཾ་སྭཱ་ཧཱ།

ཞེས་ལན་གསུམ་བརྗོད་པས། དང་པོས་མཆོད་ཡུལ་རྣམས་མདུན་གྱི་ནམ་མཁར་སྤྱན་དྲངས། གཉིས་པས་དེ་དག་གི་གནས་ཁང་བྱིན་གྱིས་བརླབ། གསུམ་པས་མཆོད་པ་བྱིན་གྱིས་བརླབ་པར་བསམ་ལ་རོལ་ཆེན་བྱ། དེ་ནས་མཎྜལ་ཞུ་འབུལ་སྤྱི་ལྟར་བྱས་ལ།

Oṁ vajraghaṇḍe raṇita praraṇita saṁpraraṇita sarvabuddha kṣetra pracalite prajñāpāramitā nāda saṁbhaveta vajradharma hridaya santoṣaṇi hūṁ hūṁ hūṁ ho ho ho akhaṁ svāhā

Recite this three times. During the first recitation, the receivers of the offerings are invited into the space in front of oneself. The second recitation blesses their dwelling place. During the third recitation, imagine that the offerings are blessed and play the music. Next, make the requesting maṇḍala offering according to the general method.[2]

[To practice uncommon Vajrayoginī Sādhana, go to page 293 then continue with "Front Generation" on page 57.]

---

[2] Some manuscripts have ཕྱག་བཅོ་བརྒྱད་མ་བདེ་ཀྱེ་ལྟར་བྱས་ལ། instead of སྤྱི་ལྟར་བྱས་ལ།

Refuge and Enlightenment Thought

སྐྱབས་འགྲོ་སེམས་བསྐྱེད་ཧེ་རུ་ཀའི་བསྒོམ་བཟླས་བདེ་མཆོག་ལྟར་བྱས་པས་རྒྱུད་སྦྱངས། བདག་བསྐྱེད་རྫོགས་པ་བཟླས་པ་ལ་ཐུག་གི་བར་དུ་སྒྲུབ་ཐབས་ཀྱི་ངག་འདོན་ལྟར་ཉམས་སུ་བླངས། ཞེས་གསུངས་པས་སྐྱབས་ཡུལ་གསལ་བཏབ་ལ།

Purify one's continuum with refuge, the generation of bodhicitta and the meditation and recitation of the Heruka Vajrasattva according to Chakrasamvara. Then, perform the complete self generation up to the [mantra] recitation according to the sādhana practice. Visulize the objects of refuge according to the instruction.

བདག་དང་འགྲོ་བ་ནམ་མཁའ་དང་མཉམ་པའི་སེམས་ཅན་ཐམས་ཅད་དུས་འདི་ནས་བཟུང་སྟེ། ཇི་སྲིད་བྱང་ཆུབ་སྙིང་པོ་ལ་མཆིས་ཀྱི་བར་དུ་དཔལ་ལྡན་བླ་མ་དམ་པ་རྣམས་ལ་སྐྱབས་སུ་མཆིའོ། རྫོགས་པའི་སངས་རྒྱས་བཅོམ་ལྡན་འདས་རྣམས་ལ་སྐྱབས་སུ་མཆིའོ། དམ་པའི་ཆོས་རྣམས་ལ་སྐྱབས་སུ་མཆིའོ། འཕགས་པའི་དགེ་འདུན་རྣམས་ལ་སྐྱབས་སུ་མཆིའོ། ཞེས་ལན་གསུམ་བདུན་སོགས་བརྗོད།

Dag Dang Dro-Wa Nam-Kha Dang Nyam-Pay Sem-Chen Tham-Ché Dü Di Ne Zung Te, Ji Si Jang-Chub Nying-Po La Chi Kyi Bar Du Pal-Den La-Ma Dam-Pa Nam La Kyab Su Chi'o, Zog-Pay Sang-Gyé Chom-Den-Dé Nam La Kyab Su Chi'o, Dam-Pay Chö Nam La Kyab Su Chi'o, Phag-Pay Gen-Dun Nam La Kyab Su Chi'o

Thus recite three or seven times:

From this time forth until the seat of awakening is reached, I and all sentient beings equal with space go for refuge to the glorious sublime gurus; go for refuge to the perfect Bhagavān Buddhas; go for refuge to the sublime Dharma; and go for refuge to the Noble Sangha.

བླ་མ་དང་དཀོན་མཆོག་རིན་པོ་ཆེ་རྣམ་པ་གསུམ་ལ་བདག་ཕྱག་འཚལ་ཞིང་སྐྱབས་སུ་མཆིའོ། ཁྱེད་རྣམས་ཀྱིས་བདག་གི་རྒྱུད་བྱིན་གྱིས་བརླབ་ཏུ་གསོལ། ཞེས་ཚར་གཅིག་བརྗོད།

La-Ma Dang Kon-Chog Rin-Po-Che Nam-Pa Sum La Dag Chag Tsel Shing Kyab Su Chi'o, Khye-Nam Kyi Dag Gi Gyü Jin Gyi Lab-Tu Söl

Thus recite once:

I pay homage and go for refuge to the guru and the Precious Three Jewels. May you please bless my continuum.

བདག་གིས་རྫོགས་པའི་སངས་རྒྱས་ཀྱི་གོ་འཕང་ཐོབ་པར་བྱ་ལ། སེམས་ཅན་ཐམས་ཅད་སྲིད་པའི་སྡུག་བསྔལ་གྱི་རྒྱ་མཚོ་ཆེན་པོ་ལས་བསྒྲལ་བར་བྱ། དེའི་ཆེད་དུ་རྡོ་རྗེ་རྣལ་འབྱོར་མའི་ལམ་གྱི་རིམ་པ་ཟབ་མོ་ཉམས་སུ་བླང་བར་བྱའོ། ཞེས་ལན་གསུམ་བརྗོད།

Dag Gi Zog Pay Sang-Gyé Kyi Go Phang Thop-Par Ja La, Sem-Chen Tham-Ché Si-Pay Dug Ngel Gyi Gya-Tso Chen-Po Lé Dral-War Ja, Dey Ché-Du Dor-Je Nal-Jor-May Lam Gyi Rim-Pa Zab-Mo Nyam Su Lang-War Ja'o

Thus recite three times:

I should achieve the stage of complete enlightenment to liberate all sentient beings from the great ocean of suffering. For that purpose, I shall practice this profound stages of Vajrayoginī's path.

Recitation and Meditation of Vajrasattva

རང་གི་སྤྱི་བོར་པདྨ་དང་ཟླ་བའི་གདན་ལ་སྐད་ཅིག་གི་བཅོམ་ལྡན་འདས་རྡོ་རྗེ་སེམས་དཔའ་དཔལ་ཧེ་རུ་ཀ་སྐུ་མདོག་དཀར་པོ་ཞལ་གཅིག་ཕྱག་གཉིས་ཀྱིས་རྡོ་རྗེ་དང་དྲིལ་བུ་འཛིན་པས་ཡུམ་ལ་འཁྱུད་པ། རུས་པའི་རྒྱན་དྲུག་གིས་བརྒྱན་ཅིང་ཞབས་རྡོ་རྗེའི་སྐྱིལ་མོ་ཀྲུང་གིས་བཞུགས་པ། རང་འདྲའི་རིགས་བདག་གི་དབུ་རྒྱན་ཅན། དེའི་པང་ན་ཡུམ་རྡོ་རྗེ་སྙེམས་མ་སྐུ་མདོག་དཀར་མོ་གྲི་གུག་དང་ཐོད་པ་འཛིན་པ། ཕྱག་རྒྱ་ལྔས་བརྒྱན་པ་དང་མཉམ་པར་སྦྱོར་བའི་ཡབ་ཀྱི་ཐུགས་ཀར་ཟླ་བའི་སྟེང་དུ་ཧཱུྃ་དཀར་པོ། དེ་ལས་འོད་ཟེར་འཕྲོས། ཕྱོགས་བཅུའི་དེ་བཞིན་གཤེགས་པ་ཐམས་ཅད་ཀྱི་ཐུགས་ཀྱི་སྙིང་པོ་ཡེ་ཤེས་ཀྱི་བདུད་རྩི་སྤྲིན་དྲངས་ནས་ཧཱུྃ་ལ་ཐིམ།

Rang Gi Chi-Wor Pad-Ma Dang Da-Way Den La Ke-Chig Gi Chom-Den-Dé Dor-Je Sem-Pa Pal He-Ru-Ka Ku Dog Kar-Po Shal Chig Chag Nyi Gyi Dor-Je Dang Dril-Bu Zin-Pé Yum La Khyü-Pa, Rü-Pay Gyen Drug Gi Gyen Ching Shab Dor-Jey Kyil-Mo Tung Gi Shug Pa, Rang Dray Rig Dag Gi Wu Gyen Chen, Dey Pang Na Yum Dor-Je Nyem-Ma Ku Dog Kar-Mo Ti Gug Dang Thö-Pa Zin-Pa, Chag-Gya Nge Gyen-Pa Dang Nyam-Par Jor-Way Yab Kyi Thug Kar Da-Way Teng Du Hūṁ Kar-Po, De Lé Ö-Zer Trö, Chog Chui De-Shin Sheg-Pa Tham-Ché Kyi Thug Kyi Nying-Po Ye-She Kyi Dü-Tsi Chen Drang Ne Hūṁ La Tim

Bhagavan Vajrasattva Shri Heruka instantly appears on a lotus[3] and moon disc on one's crown. His body is white in color. He has one face and two hands which hold a vajra and

[3] The stem of the lotus is inserted into the aperture of Brahma.

bell. He embraces the mother. Adorned with six ornaments of bone, he sits with his feet crossed in vajra posture. The master of his family adorns his head. In his lap is Mother Vajragarvi, whose body is white in color. Holding a curved knife and skullcup, she is adorned by the five mudras and she is in union with the father.

In the father's heart there is a moon disc, upon which is a *Hūṁ* (ཧཱུྃ). Rays of light shine from this syllable inviting the essence of the mind of all tathāgatas of the ten directions in the form of wisdom amrita to dissolve into the *Hūṁ* (ཧཱུྃ).

བཅོམ་ལྡན་འདས་བདག་དང་སེམས་ཅན་ཐམས་ཅད་ཀྱི་ཚེ་འཁོར་བ་ཐོག་མ་མེད་པ་
ནས་བསགས་པའི་སྡིག་སྒྲིབ་ཉེས་ལྟུང་དྲི་མའི་ཚོགས་ཐམས་ཅད་རྩ་བ་ནས་བྱང་ཞིང་
དག་པར་བྱིན་གྱིས་བརླབ་ཏུ་གསོལ། ཞེས་གསོལ་བ་བཏབ་པས་ཧཱུྃ་ལས་བདུད་རྩི་
བབས། ཡབ་ཀྱི་སྐུ་གང་། རྡོ་རྗེའི་ལམ་བརྒྱུད། ཡུམ་གྱི་པདྨ་ར་བབས། ཡུམ་གྱི་སྐུ་གང་།
ཡབ་ཡུམ་གཉིས་ཀའི་སྐུ་ཐམས་ཅད་ལས་བདུད་རྩིའི་རྒྱུན་བབས། བདག་གི་སྤྱི་གཙུག་
ནས་ཞུགས་པས་ལས་ངན་སྡིག་སྒྲིབ་ཐམས་ཅད་དུད་ཁུ་དང་ནག་ཁྲག་གི་རྣམ་པས་
བཤང་གཅི་གཉིས་དང་། རྐང་མཐིལ་གཉིས་ནས་འཐོན། ལུས་ཐམས་ཅད་བདུད་རྩི་
དཀར་པོས་ཁེངས་པར་གྱུར་པར་བསམས་ལ།

Chom-Den-Dé Dag Dang Sem-Chen Tham-Ché Kyi Tse Khor-Wa Thog-Ma Me-Pa Ne Sag-Pay Dig Dib Nye-Tung Dri-May Tsog Tham-Ché Tsa-Wa Ne Jang Shing Dag-Par Jin Gyi Lab-Tu Söl, She Söl-Wa Tab-Pé Hūṁ Lé Dü-Tsi Bab, Yab Kyi Ku Gang, Dor-Jey Lam

Gyü, Yum Gyi Pad-Mar Bab, Yum Gyi Ku Gang, Yab-Yum Nyi-Kay Ku Tham-Ché Lé Dü-Tsiy Gyün Bab, Dag Gi Chi Tsug Ne Shug-Pé Lé Ngen Dig Drib Tham-Ché Dü-Khu Dang Nag Trag Gi Nam-Pé Shang Chi Nyi Dang, Kang Thil Nyi Ne Thon, Shul Tham-Ché Dü-Tsi Kar-Po Kheng-Par Gyur

"Bhagavan, bless us to cleanse and purify all the taints of the misdeeds, obscurations, faults, and downfalls that I and all sentient beings have accumulated from time without beginning in the samsara."

Having offered the supplication, amrita flows from the *Hūṁ* (ཧཱུྃ), filling the body of the father, passing through his vajra, and filling the body of the mother. A stream of amrita descends from the father and mother's union. Since it enters through one's crown, all of the illnesses, evil spirits, misdeeds, and obscurations leave through the rectum, urethra, and the soles of the feet in the form of soot, pus, blood, and creatures. All of the empty places are filled with white amrita.

Thus imagine.

ཨོཾ་ཤྲཱི་བཛྲ་ཧེ་རུ་ཀ་ས་མ་ཡ་མ་ནུ་པཱ་ལ་ཡ། ཧེ་རུ་ཀ་ཏྭེ་ནོ་པ་ཏིཥྛ། དྲྀ་ཌྷོ་མེ་བྷ་ཝ། སུ་ཏོ་ཥྱོ་མེ་བྷ་ཝ། ཨ་ནུ་རཀྟོ་མེ་བྷ་ཝ། སུ་པོ་ཥྱོ་མེ་བྷ་ཝ། སརྦ་སིདྡྷི་མྨེ་པྲ་ཡཙྪ། སརྦ་ཀརྨ་སུ་ཙ་མེ་ཙིཏྟཾ་ཤྲི་ཡཾ་ཀུ་རུ་ཧཱུྃ། ཧ་ཧ་ཧ་ཧ་ཧོཿ བྷ་ག་ཝཱན། བཛྲ་ཧེ་རུ་ཀ་མཱ་མེ་མུཉྩ། ཧེ་རུ་ཀོ་བྷ་ཝ། མ་ཧཱ་ས་མ་ཡ་ས་ཏྭ་ཨཱཿ ཧཱུྃ་ཕཊ། ཉི་ཤུ་རྩ་གཅིག་བཟླ།

Recite the mantra twenty-one times:

Oṁ shṛī vajraheruka samayamanupālaya heruka twenopatiṣṭha dṛiḍho me bhava sutosyo me bhava anurakto me bhava suposyo me bhava sarva sidhhim me prayaccha sarva karmasu ca me cittaṁ shriyaṁ kuru hūṁ ha ha ha ha hoḥ bhagavān vajraheruka mā me muñca heruko' bhava mahāsamayasattva āḥ hūṁ phaṭ

བདག་ནི་མི་ཤེས་རྨོངས་པ་སྟེ། །
དམ་ཚིག་ལས་ནི་འགལ་ཞིང་ཉམས། །
བླ་མ་མགོན་པོས་སྐྱབས་མཛོད་ཅིག །
གཙོ་བོ་རྡོ་རྗེ་འཛིན་པ་སྟེ། །
ཐུགས་རྗེ་ཆེན་པོའི་བདག་ཉིད་ཅན། །
འགྲོ་བའི་གཙོ་ལ་བདག་སྐྱབས་མཆི། །

Dag Ni Mi She Mong Pa Te
Dam-Tsig Lé Ni Gal Shing Nyam
La-Ma Gon-Po Kyab Zö Chig
Tso-Wo Dor-Je Zin-Pa Te
Thug-Je Chen-Poy Dag-Nyi Chen
Dro-Way Tso La Dag Kyab Chi

I am ignorant and confused,
I have transgressed and damaged my samaya.
Guru and protector, please shelter me!
To the chief holder of the vajra
endowed with a compassionate nature,
the chief of all migrating beings, I go for refuge.

སྐུ་གསུང་ཐུགས་རྩ་བ་དང་ཡན་ལག་གི་དམ་ཚིག་ཉམས་པ་ཐམས་ཅད་མཐོལ་ལོ་བཤགས་སོ། །སྡིག་སྒྲིབ་ཉེས་ལྟུང་དྲི་མའི་ཚོགས་ཐམས་ཅད་རྩ་བ་ནས་བྱང་ཞིང་དག་པར་བྱིན་གྱིས་བརླབ་ཏུ་གསོལ། ཞེས་གསོལ་བ་བཏབ་པས་རྡོ་རྗེ་སེམས་དཔའ་ཡབ་ཡུམ་འོད་དུ་ཞུ་སྟེ་སྤྱི་བོ་ནས་རང་ལ་ཐིམ་པས་རང་གི་ལུས་ཤེལ་སྒོང་གཡའ་དག་པ་ལྟ་བུར་གྱུར།

Ku Sung Thug Tsa-Wa Dang Yen-Lag Gi Dam-Tsig Nyam-Pa Tham-Ché Thol Lo Shag So, Dig Drib Nye-Tung Dri-May Tsog Tham-Ché Tsa-Wa Ne Jang Shing Dag-Par Jin Gyi Lab-Tu Söl, She Söl-Wa Tab-Pé Dor-Je Sem-Pa Yab-Yum Ö Du Shu Te Chi-Wo Ne Rang La Thim-Pé Rang Gi Lü Shel Gong Ya Dag-Pa Ta-Bur Gyur

I reveal and confess all my damaged root and branch samayas of body, speech, and mind. Please bless me to cleanse and purify all accumulations of misdeeds, obscurations, faults, and downfalls.

Having offered the supplication, Vajrasattva father and mother melt into light and dissolve into oneself through one's crown. Imagine that one's body becomes like a flawless crystal ball.

Guru Yoga

བླ་མའི་རྣལ་འབྱོར་ནི།

མདུན་གྱི་ནམ་མཁར་སེང་གེས་བཏེགས་པའི་རིན་པོ་ཆེའི་ཁྲི་སྣ་ཚོགས་པདྨ་དང་ཟླ་བའི་གདན་གྱི་སྟེང་དུ། རྩ་བའི་བླ་མ་རྗེ་བཙུན་རྡོ་རྗེ་ཆོས་ཀྱི་རྣམ་པ་ཅན། སྐུ་མདོག་དམར་པོ་ཞལ་གཅིག་ཕྱག་གཉིས་ཀྱི། གཡས་པས་བདེ་སྟོང་གི་སྒྲ་སྒྲོགས་པའི་ཌཱ་མ་རུ་འཁྲོལ་བ། གཡོན་པས་ཐོད་པ་བདུད་རྩིས་གང་བ་ཐུགས་ཀར་འཛིན་པ། གྲུ་མོ་གཡོན་ན་ཁ་ཊྭཾ་ག་བསྣམས་པ། ཞབས་རྡོ་རྗེའི་སྐྱིལ་མོ་ཀྲུང་གིས་བཞུགས་པ། རུས་པའི་རྒྱན་དྲུག་གིས་བརྒྱན་ཅིང་། གཞོན་ནུ་ལང་ཚོ་དར་ལ་བབས་པ། སྐྱབས་གནས་ཀུན་འདུས་ཀྱི་ངོ་བོར་གྱུར།

Dün Gyi Nam-Khar Sen-Ge Teg-Pay Rin-Po-Chey Ti Na Tsog Pad-Ma Dang Da-Way Den Gyi Teng Du, Tsa-Way La-Ma Je-Tsün Dor-Je Chö Kyi Nam-Pa Chen, Ku Dog Mar-Po Shal Chig Chag Nyi Kyi, Yé-Pé De Tong Gyi Dra Drog-Pay Da-Ma-Ru Tröl-Wa, Yön-Pé Thö-Pa Dü-Tsi Gang-Wa Thug Kar Zin-Pa, Tru-Mo Yön Na Kha-Tam-Ga Nam-Pa, Shab Dor-Jey Kyil Mo Trung Gi Shug Pa, Rü-Pay Gyen Drug Gi Gyen Ching, Shon-Nu Lang Tso Dar La Bab Pa, Kyab-Ne Kün Dü Kyi Ngo-Wor Gyur

In the space in front, on top of a multicolored throne of jewels supported by lions, on a lotus and moon seat is one's root guru in the form of Jetsun Vajradharma. He is red in color, with one face, two hands. His right hand plays a damaru with the sound of bliss and emptiness. His left hand holds a skull full of amrita to his heart. He holds a khaṭvāṅga staff in the crook of his left elbow. He sits with his feet in vajra posture. He is youthful, adorned with the six bone ornaments. He is the essence of all places of refuge.

དུས་གསུམ་སངས་རྒྱས་ཐམས་ཅད་ཀྱི་ངོ་བོ་བླ་མ་རིན་པོ་ཆེ་ལ་ཕྱག་འཚལ་ཞིང་སྐྱབས་སུ་མཆིའོ། །བདག་གི་རྒྱུད་བྱིན་གྱིས་བརླབ་ཏུ་གསོལ། ཞེས་ལན་གསུམ་སོགས་གསོལ་བ་བཏབ་པས།

Dü Sum Sang-Gyé Tham-Ché Kyi Ngo-Wo La-Ma Rin-Po-Che La Chag Tsal Shing Kyab Su Chi'o, Dag Gi Gyü Jin Gyi Lab-Tu Söl

Repeat this three times and offer the supplication:
I pay homage and go for refuge to the precious guru, the essence of the buddhas of the three times. Please bless my continuum.

བླ་མ་འོད་དུ་ཞུ་ནས་སྤྱི་བོ་ནས་རང་ལ་ཐིམ་པས།

La-Ma Ö Du Shu Ne Chi-Wo Ne Rang La Thim-Pe

The guru melts into light and dissolves into one's crown.

Self Generation

རང་གི་སྙིང་གར་ཨེ་ཨེ་ལས་ཆོས་འབྱུང་དམར་པོ་གྲུ་གསུམ་ཉིས་བརྩེགས་ཀྱི་ནང་དུ་ཨ་ལས་ཟླ་བའི་དཀྱིལ་འཁོར་གྱི་དབུས་སུ་བཾ་ཡིག་དམར་པོའི་མཐར་གཡོན་བསྐོར་དུ། ཨོཾ་ཨོཾ་ཨོཾ་སརྦ་བུདྡྷ་ཌཱ་ཀི་ནཱི་ཡེ་བཛྲ་ཝརྞ་ནཱི་ཡེ། བཛྲ་བཻ་རོ་ཙ་ནཱི་ཡེ། ཧཱུྃ་ཧཱུྃ་ཧཱུྃ། ཕཊ་ཕཊ་ཕཊ་སྭཱ་ཧཱ། ཞེས་པའི་སྔགས་ཕྲེང་ཁ་དོག་དམར་པོས་བསྐོར་བ་ལས་འོད་ཟེར་འཕྲོས་ལུས་ཐམས་ཅད་གང་། ལུས་ངག་ཡིད་གསུམ་གྱི་སྡིག་སྒྲིབ་དག ལུས་འོད་ཀྱི་གོང་བུར་གྱུར། དེ་ཡོངས་སུ་གྱུར་པ་ལས། རང་ཉིད་རྡོ་རྗེ་རྣལ་འབྱོར་མའི་སྐུར་གྱུར་པ་ནི། སྣ་ཚོགས་པདྨ་དང་ཉི་མའི་གདན་ལ་ཞབས་གཡས་བརྐྱང་བས་དུས་མཚན་མ་དམར་མོའི་ནུ་མའི་སྙིང་ནས་མནན་པ། གཡོན་བསྐུམ་པས་འཇིགས་བྱེད་ནག་པོའི་མགོ་བོ་རྒྱབ་ཏུ་བལྟབ་ནས་མནན་པ། སྐུ་མདོག་དམར་མོ་བསྐལ་པའི་མེ་ལྟ་བུའི་གཟི་བརྗིད་ཅན། ཞལ་གཅིག་ཕྱག་གཉིས་སྤྱན་གསུམ་དག་པ་མཁའ་སྤྱོད་དུ་གཟིགས་པ། ཕྱག་གཡས་རྡོ་རྗེས་མཚན་པའི་གྲི་གུག་ཐུར་དུ་བརྐྱངས་ནས་འཛིན་པ། གཡོན་པས་ཐོད་པ་ཁྲག་གིས་གང་བ་སྟེང་ཕྱོགས་སུ་བཟུང་ནས་ཞལ་གྱེན་དུ་ཕྱོགས་པས་གསོལ་བ། ཕྲག་པ་གཡོན་པར་རྡོ་རྗེས་མཚན་པའི་ཁ་ཊྭཱཾ་ག་ལ་ཌཱ་མ་རུ་དང་དྲིལ་བུ་དང་། འཕན་རྩེ་གསུམ་པ་འཕྱང་བཞིན་པ་བསྣམས་པ། དབུ་སྐྲ་ནག་པོ་སིལ་བུར་གྱུར་པས་སྐུ་སྨད་ཡན་ཆད་ཁེབས་པ། ལང་ཚོ་དར་ལ་བབ་ཅིང་འདོད་པའི་ནུ་འབུར་རྒྱས་པ་བདེ་བ་བསྐྱེད་པའི་ཉམས་ཅན། མི་མགོ་སྐམ་པོ་ལྔའི་དབུ་རྒྱན་དང་སྐམ་པོ་ལྔ་བཅུའི་དོ་ཤལ་ཅན། གཅེར་བུ་ཕྱག་རྒྱ་ལྔས་བརྒྱན་པ། རྣམ་སྣང་གི་ཅོད་པན་ཅན་ཡེ་ཤེས་ཀྱི་མེ་འབར་བའི་དབུས་ན་བཞུགས་པའོ།།

Rang Gi Nying Gar E E Lé Chö-Jung Mar-Po Dru Sum Nyi Tseg Kyi Nang Du Ah Lé Da-Way Kyil-Khor Gyi Wü-Su Vaṁ Yig Mar-Poy Thar Yön Khor Du, Oṁ oṁ oṁ sarvabuddhaḍākinīye vajra varnanīye, vajra vairocanīye, hūṁ hūṁ hūṁ, phaṭ phaṭ phaṭ svāhā, Zhe-Pay Ngag

Treng Kha-Dog Mar-Po Kor-Wa Lé Ö-Zer Trö Lü Tham-Ché Gang, Lü Ngag Yi Sum Gyi Dig Drib Dag, Lü Ö Kyi Gong Bur Gyur, De Yong Su Gyur Pa Le, Rang Nyi Dor-Je Nal-Jor-May Kur Gyur Pa Ni, Na Tsog Pad-Ma Dang Nyi-May Den La Shab Yé Kyang-We Dü-Tsen-Ma Mar-Moy Nu-May Teng Ne Nen-Pa, Yön Kum-Pé Jig-Je Nag-Poy Go-Wo Gyab Tu Tab Ne Nen-Pa, Ku Dog Mar-Mo Kal-Pay Me Ta-Bui Zi Ji Chen, Shal Chig Chag Nyi Chen Sum Dag-Pa Kha-Chö Dü Zig-Pa, Chag Yé Dor-Jé Tsen-Pay Tri Gug Thur Du Kyang Ne Zin-Pa, Yön-Pé Thö-Pa Trag Gi Gang-Wa Teng Chog Su Zung Ne Shal Gyen Du Chog-Pé Söl-Wa, Trag-Pa Yön-Par Dor-Jé Tsen-Pay Kha-Tam-Ga La Da-Ma-Ru Dang Dril-Bu Dang, Phen-Tse Sum-Pa Chang Shin-Pa Nam-Pa, Wu-Tra Nag-Po Sil Bur Gyur-Pé Ku Ke Yen-Ché Kheb Pa, Lang Tso Dar La Bab Ching Dö-Pay Nu-Bur Gye-Pa De-Wa Kye-Pay Nyam Chen, Mi Go Kam-Po Ngay Wu Gyen Dang Kam-Po Nga Chui Do Shal Chen, Cher-Bu Chag-Gya Nge Gyen-Pa, Nam-Nang Gi Chö-Pen Chen Ye-She Kyi Me Bar-Way Wu-Na Shug-Pa'o

In one's heart arises a double dharmakāra from *E E* (ཨེ་ཨེ་). Inside that, a moon maṇḍala arises from *Ah* (ཨ). In the center of which, there is a red *Vaṁ* (བྃ) surrounded by the red mantra garland circling to the left:

Oṁ oṁ oṁ sarvabuddhaḍākinīye vajra varnanīye vajra vairocanīye hūṁ hūṁ hūṁ phaṭ phaṭ phaṭ svāhā.

Rays of light shine from the *Vaṁ* (བྃ) encircled by the mantra garland filling the entire body. The misdeeds and obscurations of body, voice, and mind are purified. The body is transformed into a ball of light.

From the complete transformation of that, one is in the form of Vajrayoginī standing on a multicolored lotus and a sun seat. Her extended right leg presses down on red Kālaratri's breasts; her contracted left leg presses down on black Bhairava's head which is bent backwards. She is red in color, brilliant as the fire at the end of the eon. She has one face, two hands, and three eyes which gaze into the Khecari realm. Her right hand extends downwards holding a curved knife marked with a vajra. Her left hand holds aloft a skull filled with blood from which she drinks with her upturned face. On her left shoulder is a khaṭvāṅga staff marked with a vajra, from which hang a damaru, a bell, and three banners. Her black hair is loose and falls to her waist. She has reached the fullness of youth, her breasts swelling with passion. She has an expression that generates bliss. She has a diadem of five dried human heads and a necklace of fifty dried ones. She is naked, adorned with five bone ornaments. She has a crown of Vairocana. She stands in the center of the blazing fire of wisdom.

དེའི་གནས་རྣམས་སུ་ཟླ་བའི་དཀྱིལ་འཁོར་གྱི་སྟེང་དུ་ལྟེ་བར་ཨོཾ་བཾ་དམར་པོ་རྡོ་རྗེ་ཕག་མོ། སྙིང་གར་ཧཾ་ཡོཾ་སྔོན་མོ་གཤིན་རྗེ་མ། ཁར་ཧྲིཾ་མོཾ་དཀར་མོ་རྨོངས་བྱེད་མ། དཔྲལ་བར་ཧྲིཾ་ཧྲིཾ་སེར་མོ་སྐྱོད་བྱེད་མ། སྤྱི་གཙུག་ཏུ་ཧཱུཾ་ཧཱུཾ་ལྗང་ཁུ་སྐྲག་བྱེད་མ། ཡན་ལག་ཐམས་ཅད་ལ་ཕཊ་ཕཊ་དུད་ཁ་ཙཎྜི་ཀའི་ངོ་བོ་གྱུར།

Dey Ne Nam Su Da-Way Kyil-Khor Gyi Teng Du Te-War Oṁ Vaṁ Mar-Po Dor-Je Phag-Mo, Nying Gar Haṁ Yoṁ Ngon-Mo Shin-Je-

Ma, Khar Hriṁ Moṁ Kar-Mo Mong-Je-Ma, Tel-War Hriṁ Hriṁ Ser-Mo Kyo-Je-Ma, Chi Tsug Tu Hūṁ Hūṁ Jang Khu Tag-Je-Ma, Yen-Lag Tham-Ché La Phaṭ Phaṭ Dü-Kha Chan-Di-Kay Ngo-Wo Gyur

On top of moon discs at these locations on one's body are:

red *Oṁ Vaṁ* (ཨོཾ་བཾ) on the navel,

the essence of Vārāhī;

blue *Haṁ Yoṁ* (ཧཾ་ཡོཾ) on the heart,

the essence of Yāminī;

white *Hriṁ Moṁ* (ཧྲཱིཾ་མོཾ) on the mouth,

the essence of Mohinī;

yellow *Hriṁ Hriṁ* (ཧྲཱིཾ་ཧྲཱིཾ) on the forehead,

the essence of Saṁcālinī;

green *Hūṁ Hūṁ* (ཧཱུཾ་ཧཱུཾ) on the crown,

the essence of Saṁtrāsinī;

smoky *Phaṭ Phaṭ* (ཕཊ་ཕཊ) on all the limbs,

the essence of Caṇḍikā.

སྙིང་གའི་ཐུགས་ཕྲེང་ལས་འོད་ཟེར་འཕྲོས་ཏེ། བ་སྤུའི་བུ་ག་ནས་ཕར་སོང་། རིགས་དྲུག་གི་སེམས་ཅན་ཐམས་ཅད་ལ་ཕོག་པས། སྡིག་སྒྲིབ་བག་ཆགས་དང་བཅས་པ་སྦྱངས། དེ་ཐམས་ཅད་རྡོ་རྗེ་རྣལ་འབྱོར་མའི་སྐུར་གྱུར།

Nying Gay Ngag Treng Lé Ö-Zer Trö Te, Ba-Pui Bu-Ga Ne Phar Song, Rig Drug Gi Sem-Chen Tham-Ché La Phog-Pe, Dig Drib Bag-Chag Dang Ché-Pa Jang, De Tham-Ché Dor-Je Nal-Jor-May Kur Gyur

Light rays shine from the mantra garland of the heart and leave through the pores. The light rays touch all the sentient beings of the six realms, purifying all their misdeeds, obscurations, and traces. They all transform into Vajrayoginī.

འབར་བའི་ཕྱག་རྒྱ་དཔྲལ་བའི་དབུས་སུ་གཡོན་བསྐོར་དུ་ལན་གསུམ་བསྐོར་ཞིང༌། ངག་ཏུ།
ཕཻཾ།

Rotate the blazing mudra in the center of the forehead three times and recite:
Phaiṁ

རང་གི་སྙིང་གའི་བྃ་ཡིག་ལས་འོད་ཟེར་འཕྲོས། འོག་མིན་ནས་རྗེ་བཙུན་རྡོ་རྗེ་རྣལ་འབྱོར་མ་ལ་ཕྱོགས་བཅུའི་དཔའ་བོ་དང་རྣལ་འབྱོར་མ་ཐམས་ཅད་ཀྱིས་བསྐོར་བ་དང་འགྲོ་བ་རྣལ་འབྱོར་མར་གྱུར་པ་ཐམས་ཅད་ཀྱང་བདག་ཉིད་ལ་ཐིམ་པར་གྱུར།

Rang Gi Nying Gay Vaṁ Yig Lé Ö-Zer Trö, Og-Min Ne Je-Tsün Dor-Je Nal-Jor-Ma La Chog Chui Pa-Wo Dang Nal-Jor-Ma Tham-Ché Kyi Kor-Wa Dang Dro-Wa Nal-Jor-Mar Gyur-Pa Tham-Ché Kyang Dag Nyi La Thim-Par Gyur

Rays of light shine from the *Vaṁ* (བྃ) syllable in one's heart. Jetsun Vajrayoginī surrounded by heroes and yoginīs in the ten directions comes from Akaniṣṭha along with sentient beings transformed into Vajrayoginīs, all dissolve into oneself.

ཛཿ ཧཱུྃ་བཾ་ཧོཿ ཞེས་པ་དང་། པད་ཀོར་གྱི་མཐར་འཁྱུད་པའི་རྒྱ་བྱས་ལ།
ཨོཾ་ཡོ་ག་ཤུདྡྷཿ སརྦ་དྷརྨཱཿ ཡོ་ག་ཤུདྡྷོ྅ ཧཾ། ཞེས་བརྗོད།

Recite:
Jaḥ hūṃ vaṃ hoḥ

Do the lotus round and perform the mudra of embracing at the end, and:
Oṁ yogaśuddhaḥ sarva dharmāḥ yogaśuddho'haṁ

རང་གི་སྙིང་གར་ཆོས་འབྱུང་གྲུ་གསུམ་དམར་པོ་ཉིས་བརྩེགས་ཀྱི་ནང་དུ་ཟླ་བའི་དཀྱིལ་འཁོར་གྱི་དབུས་སུ་བཾ་ཡིག་ལ་སྔགས་ཕྲེང་ཁ་དོག་དམར་པོས་གཡོན་དུ་བསྐོར་བ་ལས་འོད་ཟེར་དམར་པོ་དཔག་ཏུ་མེད་པ་འཕྲོས། སེམས་ཅན་ཐམས་ཅད་ཀྱི་སྡིག་སྒྲིབ་སྦྱངས། སངས་རྒྱས་ཐམས་ཅད་མཆོད། དེ་རྣམས་ཀྱི་བྱིན་རླབས་ནུས་མཐུ་འོད་ཟེར་དམར་པོའི་རྣམ་པར་སྤྱན་དྲངས། སྔགས་ཕྲེང་ལ་ཐིམ་པས་རྒྱུད་བྱིན་གྱིས་བརླབ་པར་གྱུར།

Rang Gi Nying Gar Chö-Jung Dru Sum Mar-Po Nyi Tseg Kyi Nang Du Da-Way Kyil-Khor Gyi Wü-Su Vaṁ Yig La Ngag Treng Kha-Dog Mar-Po Yön Du Kor-Wa Lé Ö-Zer Mar-Po Pag Tu Me-Pa Trö, Sem-Chen Tham-Ché Kyi Dig Drib Jang, Sang-Gyé Tham-Ché Chö, De-Nam Kyi Jin-Lab Nu Thu Ö-Zer Mar-Poy Nam-Par Chen Drang, Ngag Teng La Thim-Pé Gyü Jin Gyi Lab-Par Gyur

In one's heart, there is a red double dharmakāra. Inside of which, on the center of a moon disc is a *Vaṁ* (བཾ) syllable surrounded by a red mantra garland circling to the left. Immeasurable red light rays shine from that purifying the misdeeds and obscurations of all sentient beings, and making offerings to all the buddhas. All of their blessings, power, and force are invited in the form of red light rays, which dissolve into the mantra garland, thus one's continuum is blessed.

ཨོཾ་ཨོཾ་ཨོཾ་སརྦ་བུདྡྷ་ཌཱ་ཀི་ནཱི་ཡེ། བཛྲ་ཝརྞ་ནཱི་ཡེ།བཛྲ་བཻ་རོ་ཙ་ནཱི་ཡེ། ཧཱུྃ་ཧཱུྃ་ཧཱུྃ། ཕཊ་ཕཊ་ཕཊ་སྭཱ་ཧཱ། ཞེས་བརྒྱ་རྩ་ལ་སོགས་པ་བཟླས།

Recite hundred times, and so on:

Oṁ oṁ oṁ sarvabuddhaḍākinīye vajra varnanīye vajra vairocanīye hūṁ hūṁ hūṁ phaṭ phaṭ phaṭ svāhā

སྙིང་གའི་ཆོས་འབྱུང་ཟླ་བ་ཡིག་འབྲུ་དང་བཅས། བདེ་བ་བསྐྱེད་པར་འདོད་ན་གསང་གནས་དང་། མི་རྟོག་པ་བསྐྱེད་པར་འདོད་ན་ལྟེ་བར་ཕབས་ཏེ། མདུན་རྒྱབ་སྤངས་པའི་གྲྭ་བཞིར་དགའ་བ་འཁྱིལ་པ་གཡོན་སྐོར་དུ་འཁོར་བ་དང་། སྔགས་ཕྲེང་ལན་གསུམ་མམ་བདུན་ལ་སོགས་པ་གློག་པའི་ཚུལ་དུ་སེམས་གཏད་ནས། རླུང་ཁ་སྦྱོར་ཅི་ཐུབ་འཛིན། རང་གི་སྨིན་མཚམས་དང་། གསང་གནས་སུ་དགའ་འཁྱིལ་གཡོན་བསྐོར་དུ་ཤུགས་དྲག་ཏུ་འཁོར་བ་ལ་སེམས་གཏད་ནས་རླུང་ཁ་སྦྱོར་བཟུང་། དགའ་འཁྱིལ་གཉིས་མཐར་སྙིང་གའི་བཾ་ཡིག་ལ་ཐིམ་པར་བསམ་མོ།

The dharmakara at the heart, along with the moon and syllables, drops to the secret place if one wishes to generate bliss or to the navel if one wishes to generate nonconceptuality. Apart from the front and back tips, the four bliss swirls spin to the left. Focus the mind on the syllables of the mantra and read three or seven times. After this, unify the vāyus (vase retention) and hold as long as possible. Focus the mind on the bliss swirls spinning intensively at the one's brow and the secret place, unify the vāyus (vase retention) and hold. Finally, imagine the two bliss swirls dissolve into the Vaṁ (བཾ) at the heart.

Front Generation

དེ་ནས་མདུན་གྱི་ནང་མཆོད་དང་མཊྷིའི་སྟེང་གི་གསུང་བདུད་རྩིའི་དཀྱིལ་འཁོར་ལ་དམིགས་ཏེ།

ཨོཾ་སུམྦྷ་ནི་སུམྦྷ་ཧཱུྃ་ཧཱུྃ་ཕཊ།

ཨོཾ་གྲྀཧྞ་གྲྀཧྞ་ཧཱུྃ་ཧཱུྃ་ཕཊ།

ཨོཾ་གྲྀཧྞ་པ་ཡ་གྲྀཧྞ་པ་ཡ་ཧཱུྃ་ཧཱུྃ་ཕཊ།

ཨོཾ་ཨཱ་ན་ཡ་ཧོཿ་བྷ་ག་ཝཱན་བི་དྱཱ་རཱ་ཛ་ཧཱུྃ་ཧཱུྃ་ཕཊ། ཀྱིས་བསང་།

Visualize the inner offering in front of oneself and the speech maṇḍala of amrita above the tripod; cleanse with:

Oṁ sumbha nisumbha huṁ hūṁ phaṭ

Oṁ grihaṇa grihaṇa huṁ hūṁ phaṭ

Oṁ grihaṇapaya grihaṇapaya huṁ hūṁ phaṭ

Oṁ ānayaho bhagavān vidyārāja huṁ hūṁ phaṭ

ཨོཾ་སྭ་བྷཱ་ཝ་ཤུདྡྷཿ་སརྦ་དྷརྨཱཿ་སྭ་བྷཱ་ཝ་ཤུདྡྷོ྅ཧཾ། གིས་སྦྱངས།

Purify with:

Oṁ svabhāva shuddhaḥ sarva dharmāḥ svabhāva shuddho' haṁ

སྟོང་པའི་ངང་ལས་ཨ་ལས་བྱུང་བའི་ཐོད་པ་ཡངས་ཤིང་རྒྱ་ཆེ་བའི་ནང་དུ་ཤ་ལྔ་བདུད་རྩི་ལྔ་ཡེ་ཤེས་ལྔ་རྣམས་ཞུ་བ་ལས་བྱུང་བའི་ཡེ་ཤེས་ཀྱི་བདུད་རྩིའི་རྒྱ་མཚོ་ཆེན་པོར་གྱུར་པར་བསམས་ལ།

Tong-Pay Ngang Lé Ah Lé Jung-Way Thö-Pa Yang Shing Gya Che Way Nang Du Sha Nga Dü-Tsi Nga Ye-She Nga Nam Shu-Wa Lé Jung-Way Ye-She Kyi Dü-Tsiy Gya-Tso Chen-Por Gyur Par Sam La

Imagine that an *Ah* (ཨ) arises out of the state of emptiness. That *Ah* (ཨ) turns into a vast and wide skull, in which is a great ocean of wisdom amrita that comes from the melting of the five meats, five amritas, and five wisdoms.

ཨོཾ་ཨཱཿ ཧཱུྃ་ཧ་ཧོཿ ཧྲཱིཿ ཞེས་ཕྱག་རྒྱ་བཅས་པ་ལན་གསུམ་བརྗོད།

Recite the following three times with the mudra:
Oṁ āḥ hūṁ ha hoḥ hrīḥ

དེ་ནས་དཀྱིལ་འཁོར་གསུམ་ཆར་ལ་དམིགས་ཏེ།
ཨོཾ་སུམྦྷ་ནི་སུམྦྷ་ཧཱུྃ་ཧཱུྃ་ཕཊ།
ཨོཾ་གྲྀཧྞ་གྲྀཧྞ་ཧཱུྃ་ཧཱུྃ་ཕཊ།
ཨོཾ་གྲྀཧྞ་པ་ཡ་གྲྀཧྞ་པ་ཡ་ཧཱུྃ་ཧཱུྃ་ཕཊ།
ཨོཾ་ཨཱ་ན་ཡ་ཧོཿ བྷ་ག་ཝཱན་བིདྱཱ་རཱ་ཛ་ཧཱུྃ་ཧཱུྃ་ཕཊ། ཀྱིས་བསང་།

After that is the visualization of three maṇḍalas; cleanse wth:
Oṁ sumbha nisumbha huṁ hūṁ phaṭ
Oṁ grihaṇa grihaṇa huṁ hūṁ phaṭ
Oṁ grihaṇapaya grihaṇapaya huṁ hūṁ phaṭ
Oṁ ānayaho bhagavān vidyārāja huṁ hūṁ phaṭ

ཨོཾ་སྭ་བྷཱ་ཝ་ཤུདྡྷཿ སརྦ་དྷརྨཱཿ སྭ་བྷཱ་ཝ་ཤུདྡྷོ྅ ཧཾ། གིས་སྦྱངས།

Purify with:
Oṁ svabhāva shuddhaḥ sarva dharmāḥ svabhāva shuddho' haṁ

སྟོང་པའི་ངང་ལས་ཡཾ་ལས་རླུང་གི་དཀྱིལ་འཁོར། རཾ་ལས་མེའི་དཀྱིལ་འཁོར། ཝཾ་ལས་ཆུའི་དཀྱིལ་འཁོར། ལཾ་ལས་སའི་དཀྱིལ་འཁོར། སུཾ་ལས་རི་རབ་ཀྱི་སྟེང་དུ། ཨ་ལས་ཡེ་ཤེས་ཀྱི་ཀ་པཱ་ལ་ཡངས་ཤིང་རྒྱ་ཆེ་བ་བདུད་རྩི་ལྔས་ཡོངས་སུ་གང་བའི་སྟེང་དུ། ཧཱུྃ་ལས་སྣ་ཚོགས་རྡོ་རྗེའི་ལྟེ་བ་ལ་ཧཱུྃ་གིས་མཚན་པ། དེ་ལས་འོད་ཟེར་ཕྱོགས་བཅུར་འཕྲོས་པས། འོག་རྡོ་རྗེའི་ས་གཞི། ཁོར་ཡུག་རྡོ་རྗེའི་ར་བ་དང་དྲ་བ། སྟེང་རྡོ་རྗེའི་གུར་དང་བླ་བྲེ། ཕྱི་རོལ་ཐམས་ཅད་མདའི་དྲ་བ་དང་ཡེ་ཤེས་ཀྱི་མེ་རི་རབ་ཏུ་འབར་བ་དང་བཅས་པའི་ནང་དུ། དུར་ཁྲོད་ཆེན་པོ་བརྒྱད་ཀྱིས་ཡོངས་སུ་བསྐོར་བའི་དབུས་སུ་ཨེ་ཨེ་ལས་ཆོས་འབྱུང་དམར་པོ་གྲུ་གསུམ་ཉིས་བརྩེགས་ཀྱི་ནང་དུ་ཟླ་བའི་དཀྱིལ་འཁོར་གྱི་དབུས་སུ་བཾ་ཡིག་དམར་པོའི་མཐར་གཡོན་སྐོར་དུ། ཨོཾ་ཨོཾ་ཨོཾ་སརྦ་བུདྡྷ་ཌཱ་ཀི་ནཱི་ཡེ། བཛྲ་ཝརྞ་ནཱི་ཡེ།བཛྲ་བཻ་རོ་ཙ་ནཱི་ཡེ། ཧཱུྃ་ཧཱུྃ་ཧཱུྃ། ཕཊ་ཕཊ་ཕཊ་སྭཱ་ཧཱ། ཞེས་པའི་སྔགས་ཕྲེང་ཁ་དོག་དམར་པོས་བསྐོར་བ་ལས་འོད་ཟེར་འཕྲོས། འཕགས་པ་མཆོད་སེམས་ཅན་གྱི་དོན་བྱས། ཚུར་འདུས་ཡིག་འབྲུ་རྣམས་ལ་ཐིམ་པ་ཡོངས་སུ་གྱུར་པ་ལས། རྗེ་བཙུན་རྡོ་རྗེ་རྣལ་འབྱོར་མའི་སྐུར་གྱུར་པ་ནི།

Tong-Pay Ngang Lé Yaṁ Lé Lung Gi Kyil-Khor, Raṁ Lé Mey Kyil-Khor, Vaṁ Lé Chui Kyil-Khor, Laṁ Lé Say Kyil-Khor, Suṁ Lé Ri-Rab Kyi Teng Du, Ah Lé Ye-She Kyi Ka-Pa-La Yang Shing Gya Che-Wa Dü-Tsi Nge Yong Su Gang Way Teng Du, Hūṁ Lé Na Tsog Dor-Jey Te-Wa La Hūṁ Gi Tsen-Pa, De Lé Ö-Zer Chog Chur Trö-Pe, Og Dor-Jey Sa-Shi, Khor Yug Dor-Jey Ra-Wa Dang Dra-Wa, Teng Dor-Jey Gur Dang La-Dre, Chi Röl Tham-Ché Day Dra-Wa Dang Ye-She Kyi Me-Ri Rab-Tu Bar-Wa Dang Ché-Pay Nang Du, Dur Trö Chen-Po Gye Kyi Yong Su Kor-Way Wü-Su E E Lé Chö-Jung Mar-Po Dru Sum Nyi Tseg Kyi Nang Du Da-Way Kyil-Khor Gyi Wu-Su Vaṁ Yig Mar-Poy Tha Yön Kor Du, Oṁ oṁ oṁ sarvabuddhaḍākinīye vajra varnanīye vajra vairocanīye hūṁ hūṁ hūṁ phaṭ phaṭ phaṭ svāhā, She Pay Ngag

Teng Kha-Dog Mar-Po Kor-Wa Lé Ö-Zer Trö, Phag-Pa Chö, Sem-Chen Gyi Don Je, Tsur Dü Yig Dru Nam La Thim-Pa Yong Su Gyur-Pa Lé, Je-Tsün Dor-Je Nal-Jor-May Kur Gyur-Pa Ni

From the state of emptiness arises *Yaṁ* (ཡྃ); from which arises an air maṇḍala; from *Raṁ* (རྃ) arises a fire maṇḍala; from *Vaṁ* (ཝྃ) arises a water maṇḍala; from *Laṁ* (ལྃ) arises a earth maṇḍala; from *Suṁ* (སུྃ) arises Mt. Sumeru. On top of this, from *Ah* (ཨཿ) arises a wisdom kapala that is vast and wide, totally filled with the five amritas. Upon this, from *Hūṁ* (ཧཱུྃ) arises a visvavajra, marked with a *Hūṁ* at the center. Since light rays shine from it into the ten directions, there is a vajra ground below, surrounding with a fence of the vajra net; above is a vajra canopy tent; on the periphery, there is a net of arrows along with the wisdom fire blazing like mountains.

Inside of this, totally surrounded by the eight charnel grounds, in the center, from *E E* (ཨེ་ཨེ) arises a doubled dharmakāra. Inside that, a moon maṇḍala arises from *Ah* (ཨཿ). In the center of which, there is a red *Vaṁ* (བྃ) surrounded by the red mantra garland circling to the left:

Oṁ oṁ oṁ sarvabuddha ḍākinīye vajra varṇanīye
vajra vairocanīye hūṁ hūṁ hūṁ phaṭ phaṭ phaṭ svāhā,

Light shines from the mantra rosary, making offerings to the nobles, benefiting all sentient beings, and then returning and absorbing into the syllables. From the complete transformation of that, the syllables turn into Vajrayoginī.

སྣ་ཚོགས་པདྨ་དང་ཉི་མའི་གདན་ལ་ཞབས་གཡས་བརྐྱང་པས་དུས་མཚན་མ་དམར་མོའི་ནུ་མའི་སྟེང་ནས་མནན་པ། གཡོན་བསྐུམ་པས་འཇིགས་བྱེད་ནག་པོའི་མགོ་བོ་རྒྱབ་ཏུ་བསྣུན་ནས་མནན་པ། སྐུ་མདོག་དམར་མོ་བསྐལ་པའི་མེ་ལྟ་བུའི་གཟི་བརྗིད་ཅན། ཞལ་གཅིག་ཕྱག་གཉིས་སྤྱན་གསུམ་དག་པ་མཁའ་སྤྱོད་དུ་གཟིགས་པ། ཕྱག་གཡས་པས་རྡོ་རྗེས་མཚན་པའི་གྲི་གུག་ཐུར་དུ་བརྐྱང་ནས་འཛིན་པ། གཡོན་པས་ཐོད་པ་ཁྲག་གིས་གང་བ་སྟེང་ཕྱོགས་སུ་བཟུང་ནས་ཞལ་གྱེན་དུ་ཕྱོགས་པས་གསོལ་བ། ཕྲག་པ་གཡོན་པར་རྡོ་རྗེས་མཚན་པའི་ཁ་ཊྭཾ་ག་ལ་ཌཱ་མ་རུ་དང་དྲིལ་བུ་དང་འཕན་རྩེ་གསུམ་པ་འཕྱང་བཞིན་པ་བསྣམས་པ། དབུ་སྐྲ་ནག་པོ་སིལ་བུར་གྱུར་པས་སྐུ་སྐེད་ཡན་ཆད་ཁེབས་པ། ལང་ཚོ་དར་ལ་བབས་ཅིང་འདོད་པའི་ནུ་འབུར་རྒྱས་པ། བདེ་བ་བསྐྱེད་པའི་ཉམས་ཅན། མི་མགོ་སྐམ་པོ་ལྔའི་དབུ་རྒྱན་དང་། སྐམ་པོ་ལྔ་བཅུའི་དོ་ཤལ་ཅན། གཅེར་བུ་ཕྱག་རྒྱ་ལྔས་བརྒྱན་པ། ཡེ་ཤེས་ཀྱི་མེ་འབར་བའི་དབུས་ན་བཞུགས་པའོ།

Na Tsog Pad-Ma Dang Nyi-May Den La Shab Yé Kyang Pé Dü-Tsen-Ma Mar-Poy Nu-May Teng Ne Nen-Pa, Yön Kum-Pé Jig-Je Nag-Poy Go-Wo Gyab Tu Tab Ne Nen-Pa, Ku Dog Mar-Po Kel-Pay Me Ta-Bui Zi Ji Chen, Shal Chig Chag Nyi Chen Sum Dag-Pa Kha-Chö Du Zig-Pa, Chag Yé-Pé Dor-Je Tsen-Pay Tri Gug Thur Du Kyang Ne Zin-Pa, Yön-Pé Thö-Pa Trag Gi Gang-Wa Teng Chog Su Zung Ne Shal Gyen Du Chog-Pe Söl-Wa, Trag-Pa Yön-Par Dor-Je Tsen-Pay Kha-Tam-Ga La Da-Ma-Ru Dang Dril-Bu Dang Phen-Tse Sum-Pa Chang Shin-Pa Nam-Pa, Wu-Tra Nag-Po Sil Bur Gyur-Pé Ku Ke Yen-Ché Kheb Pa, Lang Tso Dar La Bab Ching Dö-Pay Nu-Bur Gye-Pa, De-Wa Kye-Pay Nyam Chen, Mi Go Kam-Po Ngay Wu-Gyen Dang, Kam-Po Nga Chui Do Shal Chen, Cher-Bu Chag-Gya Nge Gyen-Pa, Ye-She Kyi Me Bar-Way Wü-Na Shug-Pa'o

She stands on a multicolored lotus and sun seat. Her extended right leg presses down on red Kālarātri's breasts; her contracted left leg presses down on black Bhairava's head which is bent backwards. She is red in color, brilliant as the fire at the end of the eon. She has one face, two hands, and three eyes which gaze into the Khecarī realm. Her right hand extends downwards holding a curved knife marked with a vajra. Her left hand holds aloft a skull filled with blood from which she drinks with her upturned face. On her left shoulder is a khaṭvāṅga staff marked with a vajra, from which hang a damaru, a bell, and three banners. Her black hair is loose and falls to her waist. She has reached the fullness of youth, her breasts swelling with passion. She has an expression that generates bliss. She has a diadem of five dried human heads and a necklace of fifty dried ones. She is naked, adorned with five bone ornaments. She stands in the center of the blazing fire of wisdom.

དེ་ནས་འབར་བའི་ཕྱག་རྒྱ་སྨིན་མཚམས་སུ་གཡོན་སྐོར་དུ་ལན་གསུམ་བསྐོར་ཞིང་། དག་ཏུ།
ཕཻཾ།

Rotate the blazing mudra in the center of the forehead three times and recite:

Phaiṁ

རང་གི་ཐུགས་ཀའི་ཕྃ་ཡིག་ལས་འོད་ཟེར་འཕྲོས་པས། འོག་མིན་ནས་རྗེ་བཙུན་རྡོ་རྗེ་རྣལ་འབྱོར་མ་ལ་སངས་རྒྱས་དང་བྱང་ཆུབ་སེམས་དཔའ་དཔའ་བོ་དང་རྣལ་འབྱོར་མའི་ཚོགས་དཔག་ཏུ་མེད་པས་བསྐོར་བ་ཨོཾ་བཛྲ་ས་མ་ཛཿ ཞེས་སྤྱན་དྲངས།

Rang Gi Tuk Kay Vaṁ Yig Lé Ö-Zer Trö Pe, Og-Min Ne Je-Tsün Dor-Je Nal-Jor-Ma La Sang-Gyé Jang-Chup Sem-Pa Pa-Wo Dang Nal-Jor-May Tsog Pak Tu Me Pé Kor-Wa, Oṁ vajra samājaḥ She Chen Drang

Light rays shining from the *Vaṁ* (བཾ) syllable within one's heart summon Jetsun Vajrayoginī from the realm of Akanishta, surrounded by an assembly of immeasurable buddhas, bodhisattvas, heroes, and yoginīs, *Oṁ vajra samājaḥ.*

ཛཿ ཧཱུྃ་བཾ་ཧོཿ གཉིས་སུ་མེད་པར་ཐིམ། པད་ཀོར་གྱི་མཐར་འཁྱུད་པའི་ཕྱག་རྒྱ་བཅས་ལ།
ཨོཾ་ཡོ་ག་ཤུདྡྷཿ སརྦ་དྷརྨཱཿ ཡོ་ག་ཤུདྡྷོ྅ཧཾ།

With *Jaḥ hūṁ vaṁ hoḥ*, they are absorbed nondually.

At the end of lotus rolls, make the mudra of embrace with:
Oṁ yogaśuddhaḥ sarva dharmāḥ yogaśuddho'haṁ

དེའི་གནས་རྣམས་སུ་ཟླ་བའི་དཀྱིལ་འཁོར་གྱི་སྟེང་དུ། ལྟེ་བར་ཨོཾ་བཾ་དམར་མོ་རྡོ་རྗེ་ཕག་མོ། སྙིང་གར་ཧཾ་ཡོཾ་སྔོན་མོ་གཤིན་རྗེ་མ། ཁར་ཧྲིཾ་མོཾ་དཀར་མོ་རྨོངས་བྱེད་མ། དཔྲལ་བར་ཧྲིཾ་ཧྲིཾ་སེར་མོ་སྐྱོད་བྱེད་མ། སྤྱི་གཙུག་ཏུ་ཧཱུྃ་ཧཱུྃ་ལྗང་གུ་སྐྲག་བྱེད་མ། ཡན་ལག་ཐམས་ཅད་ལ་ཕཊ་ཕཊ་དུད་ཁ་ཙཎྜི་ཀའི་ངོ་བོར་གྱུར།

Dey Ne Nam Su Da-Way Kyil-Khor Gyi Teng Du, Te-War Oṁ Vaṁ Mar-Mo Dor-Je Phag-Mo, Nying Gar Haṁ Yoṁ Ngon-Mo Shin-Je-Ma, Khar Hriṁ Moṁ Kar-Mo Mong-Je-Ma, Tel-War Hriṁ Hriṁ Ser-Mo Kyo-Je-Ma, Chi Tsug Tu Hūṁ Hūṁ Jang Khu Tag-Je-Ma, Yen-Lag Tham-Ché La Phaṭ Phaṭ Dü-Kha Chan-Di-Kay Ngo-Wo Gyur

On top of moon discs at these locations on one's body are:

red *Oṁ Vaṁ* (ཨོཾ་བཾ) on the navel,

the essence of Vārāhī;

blue *Haṁ Yoṁ* (ཧཾ་ཡོཾ) on the heart,

the essence of Yāminī;

white *Hriṁ Moṁ* (ཧྲིཾ་མོཾ) on the mouth,

the essence of Mohinī;

yellow *Hriṁ Hriṁ* (ཧྲིཾ་ཧྲིཾ) on the forehead,

the essence of Saṁcālinī;

green *Hūṁ Hūṁ* (ཧཱུཾ་ཧཱུཾ) on the crown,

the essence of Saṁtrāsinī;

smoky *Phaṭ Phaṭ* (ཕཊ་ཕཊ) on all the limbs,

the essence of Caṇḍikā.

སླར་ཡང་རང་གི་ཐུགས་ཀ་ནས་འོད་ཟེར་འཕྲོས་པས། དབང་གི་ལྷ་དཔལ་འཁོར་ལོ་བདེ་མཆོག་ལྷ་དྲུག་ཅུ་རྩ་གཉིས་ཀྱི་དཀྱིལ་འཁོར་མདུན་གྱི་ནམ་མཁར་ཨོཾ་བཛྲ་ས་མཱ་ཛཿ ཞེས་པས་སྤྱན་དྲངས།

Lar Yang Rang Gi Thug Ka Ne Ö-Zer Trö-Pe, Wang Gi Lha Pal Khor-Lo De-Chog Lha Drug Chu Tsa Nyi Kyi Kyil-Khor Dün Gyi Nam-Khar, Oṁ vajra samājaḥ She-Pé Chan-Drang

Once again, light rays shining from one's heart invite the empowerment deities, the sixty-two deities of Shrī Cakrasamvara maṇḍala into the sky in front.

Thus invite with:
Oṁ vajra samājaḥ

དེ་བཞིན་གཤེགས་པ་ཐམས་ཅད་ཀྱིས་འདི་ལ་མངོན་པར་དབང་བསྐུར་བ་སྩལ་དུ་
གསོལ། ཞེས་གསོལ་བ་བཏབ་པས།

De-Shin Sheg-Pa Tham-Ché Kyi Di La Ngön-Par Wang Kur-Wa Tsal Du Söl

Then, recite the supplication:
"May all the tathāgatas bestow the empowerment here!"

དབང་གི་ལྷ་རྣམས་ཀྱིས།
ཇི་ལྟར་བལྟམས་པ་ཙམ་གྱིས་ནི།
ལྷ་རྣམས་ཀྱིས་ནི་ཁྲུས་གསོལ་ལྟར།
ལྷ་ཡི་ཆུ་ནི་དག་པ་ཡིས།
དེ་བཞིན་བདག་གིས་དབང་བསྐུར་རོ།

Ji Tar Tam-Pa Tsam Gyi Ni,
Lha Nam Kyi Ni Tru Söl Tar,
Lha Yi Chu Ni Dag-Pa Yi
De-Shin Dag Gi Wang Kur Ro

The empowerment deities reply:
Just as he [the Buddha] was washed by the gods
at the time of his birth,
likewise, we will bestow the empowerment
with pure divine water.

ཨོཾ་སརྦ་ཏ་ཐཱ་ག་ཏ་ཨ་བྷི་ཥེ་ཀ་ཏ་ས་མ་ཡ་ཤྲཱི་ཡེ་ཧཱུྃ།

Oṁ sarvatathāgata abhiṣekata samaya shrīye hūṁ

ཞེས་གསུང་ཞིང་བུམ་ཆུས་སྤྱི་བོ་ནས་དབང་བསྐུར། སྐུ་གང་དྲི་མ་དག ཆུའི་ལྷག་མ་ཡར་ལུད་པ་ལས་རྣམ་པར་སྣང་མཛད་ཀྱིས་དབུར་བརྒྱན།

She Sung-Shing Bum-Chü Chi-Wo Ne Wang-Kur, Ku-Kang Di-Ma-Thag, Chui Lhag-Ma Yar Lu-Pa Lé Nam-Par Nang-Zé Kyi Wur-Gyen

While speaking, those deities confer the empowerment on her crown with the water from the vase, filling her body, and purifying the taints. From the overflow of the excess water, her head is adorned with Vairocana.

སླར་ཡང་ཐུགས་ཀ་ནས་འོད་ཟེར་འཕྲོས་པས། རྩ་བའི་བླ་མ་རྗེ་བཙུན་རྡོ་རྗེ་ཆོས་ཀྱི་རྣམ་པ་ཅན་ལ་བརྒྱུད་པའི་བླ་མ་དཔའ་བོ་དང་རྣལ་འབྱོར་མའི་ཚོགས་ཀྱིས་བསྐོར་བ་མཆོད་པའི་ཡུལ་དུ་མདུན་གྱི་ནམ་མཁར། ཨོཾ་བཛྲ་ས་མཱ་ཛཿ ཞེས་པས་ཚོགས་ཞིང་ཁྱད་པར་བ་སྤྱན་དྲངས།

Lar Yang Thug Ka Ne Ö-Zer To Pe, Tsa Way La-Ma Je-Tsün Dor-Je Chö Kyi Nam Pa Chan La Gyü Pay La-Ma Pa-Wo Dang Nal-Jor May Tsog Kyi Kor Wa Chö Pay Yül Du Dün Gyi Nam Khar, Oṁ vajra samājaḥ

Once again, from one's heart light rays radiate and summon the root guru in the form of Jetsun Vajradharma surrounded by the lineage gurus, hero and yoginīs into the sky in front as objects of offering.

Thus invite the special field of merit with:
Oṁ vajra samājaḥ

མདུན་གྱི་མཆོད་པ་རྣམས།
ཨོཾ་སུམྦྷ་ནི་སུམྦྷ་ཧཱུཾ་ཧཱུཾ་ཕཊ།
ཨོཾ་གྲྀཧྞ་གྲྀཧྞ་ཧཱུཾ་ཧཱུཾ་ཕཊ།
ཨོཾ་གྲྀཧྞ་པ་ཡ་གྲྀཧྞ་པ་ཡ་ཧཱུཾ་ཧཱུཾ་ཕཊ།
ཨོཾ་ཨཱ་ན་ཡ་ཧོཿ བྷ་ག་ཝཱན་བིདྱཱ་རཱ་ཛ་ཧཱུཾ་ཧཱུཾ་ཕཊ། ཀྱིས་བསང་།

Cleanse offerings in front with:
Oṁ sumbha nisumbha huṁ hūṁ phaṭ
Oṁ grihaṇa grihaṇa huṁ hūṁ phaṭ
Oṁ grihaṇapaya grihaṇapaya huṁ hūṁ phaṭ
Oṁ ānayaho bhagavān vidyārāja huṁ hūṁ phaṭ

ཨོཾ་སྭ་བྷཱ་ཝ་ཤུདྡྷཱཿ སརྦ་དྷརྨཱཿ སྭ་བྷཱ་ཝ་ཤུདྡྷོ྅ ཧཾ། གིས་སྦྱངས།

Purify with:
Oṁ svabhāva shuddhaḥ sarva dharmāḥ svabhāva shuddho' haṁ

སྟོང་པའི་ངང་ལས་ཨ་ལས་ཡེ་ཤེས་ཀྱི་ཀ་པཱ་ལ་ཡངས་ཤིང་རྒྱ་ཆེ་བ་རྣམས་ཀྱི་ནང་དུ། ཧཱུཾ་ཞུ་བ་ལས་བྱུང་བའི་ལྷ་རྫས་ལས་གྲུབ་པའི་མཆོད་ཡོན། ཞབས་བསིལ། མེ་ཏོག བདུག་སྤོས། མར་མེ། དྲི་ཆབ། ཞལ་ཟས། རོལ་མོ་རྣམས་དྭངས་ཤིང་ཐོགས་པ་མེད་པ་ནམ་མཁའི་མཐའ་དང་མཉམ་པར་གྱུར།

Tong Pay Ngang Lé Ah Lé Ye-She Kyi Ka-Pa-La Yang Shing Gya Che-Wa Nam Kyi Nang Du, Hūṁ Zhu Wa Lé Chung Way Lha Zé Lé Drub Pay Chö Yon, Shab-Sil, Me-Tog, Dug-Pö, Mar-Me, Di-Chab, Shal-Ze, Röl-Mo Nam Dang Shing Thog Pa Me Pa Nam Khay Tha Dang Nyam Par Gyur

From the state of emptiness arises an *Ah* (ཨ), from which arises wide and vast wisdom skullcups. Inside of each skullcup, from dissolving and melting of *Hūṁ* (ཧཱུྃ) arises all the offerings made from divine substances — pure and unimpeded drinking water, washing water, flowers, incense, lamps, scent, food, and music — which fill all of space.

ཨོཾ་བཛྲ་ཨརྒྷཾ་ཨཱཿ ཧཱུྃ། ཨོཾ་བཛྲ་པཱདྱཾ་ཨཱཿ ཧཱུྃ། ཨོཾ་བཛྲ་པུཥྤེ་ཨཱཿ ཧཱུྃ། ཨོཾ་བཛྲ་དྷཱུཔེ་ཨཱཿ ཧཱུྃ། ཨོཾ་བཛྲ་ཨཱ་ལོ་ཀེ་ཨཱཿ ཧཱུྃ། ཨོཾ་བཛྲ་གནྡྷེ་ཨཱཿ ཧཱུྃ། ཨོཾ་བཛྲ་ནཻ་ཝི་དྱེ་ཨཱཿ ཧཱུྃ། ཨོཾ་བཛྲ་ཤབྡ་ཨཱཿ ཧཱུྃ། བརྗོད་ཅིང་བྱིན་གྱིས་བརླབས་ལ།

Recite and bless with:

Oṁ vajra arghaṁ āḥ hūṁ
Oṁ vajra pādyaṁ āḥ hūṁ
Oṁ vajra puṣpe āḥ hūṁ
Oṁ vajra dhūpe āḥ hūṁ
Oṁ vajra āloke āḥ hūṁ
Oṁ vajra ghande āḥ hūṁ
Oṁ vajra naiwidye āḥ hūṁ
Oṁ vajra shabda āḥ hūṁ

མཆོད་པ་འབུལ་བ་ནི་ཐལ་མོ་སྦྱར་ཏེ།

སྟོང་གསུམ་འདི་འམ་སྟོང་གསུམ་གཞན་དག་ན།།

ལྷ་རྫས་མཆོད་ཡོན་ཇི་སྙེད་ཡོད་པ་རྣམས།།

བླ་མ་རྡོ་རྗེ་རྣལ་འབྱོར་མ་ལ་འབུལ།།

ཐུགས་རྗེས་འགྲོ་བའི་དོན་དུ་བཞེས་སུ་གསོལ།།

Tong Sum Di Am Tong Sum Shen Dag Na
Lha Zé Chö Yon Ji Nye Yo-Pa Nam
La-Ma Dor-Je Nal-Jor-Ma La Bül
Thug Je Dro-Way Don Du She Su Söl

Make offerings with folded hand:

The divine drinking water, as much as
in this billion worlds or in another billion worlds,
is offered to guru Jetsun Vajrayoginī.
Please accept this with compassion for the benefit of
migrating beings.

ཨོཾ་སརྦ་ཏ་ཐཱ་ག་ཏ་སརྦ་ཝཱི་ར་ཡོ་གི་ནཱི་ས་པ་རི་ཝཱ་ར་ཨརྒྷཾ་པྲ་ཏཱིཙྪ་པཱུ་ཛ་མེ་གྷ་ས་མུ་དྲ་སྥ་
ར་ཎ་ས་མ་ཡེ་ཨཱཿ ཧཱུྃ།

Oṁ sarvatathāgata sarva vīra yoginī saparivāra argham praticcha
pūja megha samudra sapharaṇa samaye āḥ hūṁ

སྟོང་གསུམ་འདི་འམ་སྟོང་གསུམ་གཞན་དག་ན།།
ལྷ་རྫས་ཞབས་བསིལ་ཇི་སྙེད་ཡོད་པ་རྣམས།།
བླ་མ་རྡོ་རྗེ་རྣལ་འབྱོར་མ་ལ་འབུལ།།
ཐུགས་རྗེས་འགྲོ་བའི་དོན་དུ་བཞེས་སུ་གསོལ།།

Tong Sum Di Am Tong Sum Shen Dag Na
Lha Zé Shab Sil Ji Nye Yo-Pa Nam
La-Ma Dor-Je Nal-Jor-Ma La Bül
Thug Je Dro-Way Don Du She Su Söl

The divine washing water, as much as
in this billion worlds or in another billion worlds,
is offered to guru Jetsun Vajrayoginī.
Please accept this with compassion for the benefit of
migrating beings.

ཨོཾ་སརྦ་ཏ་ཐཱ་ག་ཏ་སརྦ་ཝཱི་ར་ཡོ་གི་ནཱི་ས་པ་རི་ཝཱ་ར་པཱ་དྱཾ་པྲ་ཏཱིཙྪ་པཱུ་ཛ་མེ་གྷ་ས་མུ་དྲ་སྥ་
ར་ཎ་ས་མ་ཡེ་ཨཱཿ ཧཱུྃ།

Oṁ sarvatathāgata sarva vīra yoginī saparivāra pādyaṁ praticcha pūja megha samudra sapharaṇa samaye āḥ hūṁ

སྟོང་གསུམ་འདི་འམ་སྟོང་གསུམ་གཞན་དག་ན།།
ལྷ་རྫས་མེ་ཏོག་ཇི་སྙེད་ཡོད་པ་རྣམས།།
བླ་མ་རྡོ་རྗེ་རྣལ་འབྱོར་མ་ལ་འབུལ།།
ཐུགས་རྗེས་འགྲོ་བའི་དོན་དུ་བཞེས་སུ་གསོལ།།

Tong Sum Di Am Tong Sum Shen Dag Na
Lha Zé Me-Tog Ji Nye Yo-Pa Nam
La-Ma Dor-Je Nal-Jor-Ma La Bül
Thug Je Dro-Way Don Du She Su Söl

The divine flowers, as many as
in this billion worlds or in another billion worlds,
are offered to guru Jetsun Vajrayoginī.
Please accept this with compassion for the benefit of
migrating beings.

ༀ་སརྦ་ཏ་ཐཱ་ག་ཏ་སརྦ་ཝཱི་ར་ཡོ་གི་ནཱི་ས་པ་རི་ཝཱ་ར་པུཥྤེ་པྲ་ཏཱིཙྪ་པཱུ་ཛ་མེ་གྷ་ས་མུ་དྲ་སྥ་
ར་ཎ་ས་མ་ཡེ་ཨཱཿ ཧཱུྃ།

Oṁ sarvatathāgata sarva vīra yoginī saparivāra puṣpe praticcha
pūja megha samudra sapharaṇa samaye āḥ hūṁ

སྟོང་གསུམ་འདི་འམ་སྟོང་གསུམ་གཞན་དག་ན།།
ལྷ་རྫས་བདུག་སྤོས་ཇི་སྙེད་ཡོད་པ་རྣམས།།
བླ་མ་རྡོ་རྗེ་རྣལ་འབྱོར་མ་ལ་འབུལ།།
ཐུགས་རྗེས་འགྲོ་བའི་དོན་དུ་བཞེས་སུ་གསོལ།།

Tong Sum Di Am Tong Sum Shen Dag Na
Lha Zé Dug-Pö Ji Nye Yo-Pa Nam
La-Ma Dor-Je Nal-Jor-Ma La Bül
Thug Je Dro-Way Don Du She Su Söl

The divine incense, as much as
in this billion worlds or in another billion worlds,
is offered to guru Jetsun Vajrayoginī.
Please accept this with compassion for the benefit of
migrating beings.

ཨོཾ་སརྦ་ཏ་ཐཱ་ག་ཏ་སརྦ་བཱི་ར་ཡོ་གི་ནཱི་ས་པ་རི་ཝཱ་ར་དྷཱུ་པེ་པྲ་ཏཱིཙྪ་པཱུ་ཛ་མེ་གྷ་ས་མུ་དྲ་སྥ་
ར་ཎ་ས་མ་ཡེ་ཨཱཿ ཧཱུྃ།

Oṁ sarvatathāgata sarva vīra yoginī saparivāra dhūpe praticcha
pūja megha samudra sapharaṇa samaye āḥ hūṁ

སྟོང་གསུམ་འདི་འམ་སྟོང་གསུམ་གཞན་དག་ན།།
ལྷ་རྫས་སྣང་གསལ་ཇི་སྙེད་ཡོད་པ་རྣམས།།
བླ་མ་རྡོ་རྗེ་རྣལ་འབྱོར་མ་ལ་འབུལ།།
ཐུགས་རྗེས་འགྲོ་བའི་དོན་དུ་བཞེས་སུ་གསོལ།།

Tong Sum Di Am Tong Sum Shen Dag Na
Lha Zé Nang-Sel Ji Nye Yo-Pa Nam
La-Ma Dor-Je Nal-Jor-Ma La Bül
Thug Je Dro-Way Don Du She Su Söl

The divine lamps, as many as
in this billion worlds or in another billion worlds,
are offered to guru Jetsun Vajrayoginī.
Please accept this with compassion for the benefit of
migrating beings.

ཨོཾ་སརྦ་ཏ་ཐཱ་ག་ཏ་སརྦ་བཱི་ར་ཡོ་གི་ནཱི་ས་པ་རི་ཝཱ་ར་ཨཱ་ལོ་ཀེ་པྲ་ཏཱིཙྪ་པཱུ་ཛ་མེ་གྷ་ས་མུ་དྲ་
སྥ་ར་ཎ་ས་མ་ཡེ་ཨཱཿ ཧཱུྃ།

Oṁ sarvatathāgata sarva vīra yoginī saparivāra āloke praticcha
pūja megha samudra sapharaṇa samaye āḥ hūṁ

སྟོང་གསུམ་འདི་འམ་སྟོང་གསུམ་གཞན་དག་ན།།
ལྷ་རྫས་དྲི་མཆོག་ཇི་སྙེད་ཡོད་པ་རྣམས།།
བླ་མ་རྡོ་རྗེ་རྣལ་འབྱོར་མ་ལ་འབུལ།།
ཐུགས་རྗེས་འགྲོ་བའི་དོན་དུ་བཞེས་སུ་གསོལ།།

Tong Sum Di Am Tong Sum Shen Dag Na
Lha Zé Dri Chog Ji Nye Yo-Pa Nam
La-Ma Dor-Je Nal-Jor-Ma La Bül
Thug Je Dro-Way Don Du She Su Söl

The divine scented water, as much as
in this billion worlds or in another billion worlds,
is offered to guru Jetsun Vajrayoginī.
Please accept this with compassion for the benefit of
migrating beings.

ཨོཾ་སརྦ་ཏ་ཐཱ་ག་ཏ་སརྦ་བཱི་ར་ཡོ་གི་ནཱི་ས་པ་རི་ཝཱ་ར་གནྡྷེ་པྲ་ཏཱིཙྪ་པཱུ་ཛ་མེ་གྷ་ས་མུ་དྲ་སྥ་
ར་ཎ་ས་མ་ཡེ་ཨཱཿ ཧཱུྃ།

Oṁ sarvatathāgata sarva vīra yoginī saparivāra gandhe praticcha
pūja megha samudra sapharaṇa samaye āḥ hūṁ

སྟོང་གསུམ་འདི་འམ་སྟོང་གསུམ་གཞན་དག་ན།།
ལྷ་རྫས་ཞལ་ཟས་ཇི་སྙེད་ཡོད་པ་རྣམས།།
བླ་མ་རྡོ་རྗེ་རྣལ་འབྱོར་མ་ལ་འབུལ།།
ཐུགས་རྗེས་འགྲོ་བའི་དོན་དུ་བཞེས་སུ་གསོལ།།

Tong Sum Di Am Tong Sum Shen Dag Na
Lha Zé Shal Ze Ji Nye Yo-Pa Nam
La-Ma Dor-Je Nal-Jor-Ma La Bül
Thug Je Dro-Way Don Du She Su Söl

The divine food, as much as
in this billion worlds or in another billion worlds,
is offered to guru Jetsun Vajrayoginī.
Please accept this with compassion for the benefit of
migrating beings.

ཨོཾ་སརྦ་ཏ་ཐཱ་ག་ཏ་སརྦ་ཝཱི་ར་ཡོ་གི་ནཱི་ས་པ་རི་ཝཱ་ར་ནཻ་ཝི་དྱེ་པྲ་ཏཱིཙྪ་པཱུ་ཛ་མེ་གྷ་ས་མུ་དྲ་
སྥ་ར་ཎ་ས་མ་ཡེ་ཨཱཿ ཧཱུྃ།

Oṁ sarvatathāgata sarva vīra yoginī saparivāra naividye praticcha
pūja megha samudra sapharaṇa samaye āḥ hūṁ

སྟོང་གསུམ་འདི་འམ་སྟོང་གསུམ་གཞན་དག་ན།།
ལྷ་རྫས་རོལ་མོ་ཇི་སྙེད་ཡོད་པ་རྣམས།།
བླ་མ་རྡོ་རྗེ་རྣལ་འབྱོར་མ་ལ་འབུལ།།
ཐུགས་རྗེས་འགྲོ་བའི་དོན་དུ་བཞེས་སུ་གསོལ།།

Tong Sum Di Am Tong Sum Shen Dag Na
Lha Zé Röl-Mo Ji Nye Yo-Pa Nam
La-Ma Dor-Je Nal-Jor-Ma La Bül
Thug Je Dro-Way Don Du She Su Söl

The divine music, as much as
in this billion worlds or in another billion worlds,
is offered to guru Jetsun Vajrayoginī.
Please accept this with compassion for the benefit of
migrating beings.

ཨོཾ་སརྦ་ཏ་ཐཱ་ག་ཏ་སརྦ་ཝཱི་ར་ཡོ་གི་ནཱི་ས་པ་རི་ཝཱ་ར་ཤབྡ་པྲ་ཏཱིཙྪ་པཱུ་ཛ་མེ་གྷ་ས་མུ་དྲ་སྥ
ར་ཎ་ས་མ་ཡེ་ཨཱཿ ཧཱུྃ།

Oṁ sarvatathāgata sarva vīra yoginī saparivāra shabda praticcha
pūja megha samudra sapharaṇa samaye āḥ hūṁ

ཨོཾ་བཛྲ་གྷཎྚེ་ར་ཎི་ཏ། པྲ་ར་ཎི་ཏ། སཾ་པྲ་ར་ཎི་ཏ། སརྦ་བུདྡྷ་ཀྵེ་ཏྲ་པྲ་ཙ་ལི་ཏེ། པྲཛྙཱ་པཱ་
ར་མི་ཏ་ན་ད་སཾ་བྷ་ཝེ་ཏ། བཛྲ་དྷརྨ་ཧྲི་ད་ཡ་སནྟོ་ཥ་ཎི་ཧཱུྃ་ཧཱུྃ་ཧཱུྃ་ཧོ་ཧོ་ཧོ་ཨ་ཁཾ་སྭཱ་ཧཱ།
སྔགས་སོ་སོའི་ཕྱག་རྒྱ་དང་རོལ་མོ་བཅས་འབུལ།

Offer the individual mantra with the mudras and music:

Oṁ vajraghaṇḍe raṇita praraṇita saṁpraraṇita sarvabuddha kṣetra pracalite prajñāpāramitā nāda saṁbhaveta vajradharma hridaya santoṣaṇi hūṁ hūṁ hūṁ ho ho ho akhaṁ svāhā

གོས་ཟུང་ལ་དམིགས་ཏེ།

ཨོཾ་སུམྦྷ་ནི་སུམྦྷ་ཧཱུྃ་ཧཱུྃ་ཕཊ།

ཨོཾ་གྲྀཧྞ་གྲྀཧྞ་ཧཱུྃ་ཧཱུྃ་ཕཊ།

ཨོཾ་གྲྀཧྞ་པ་ཡ་གྲྀཧྞ་པ་ཡ་ཧཱུྃ་ཧཱུྃ་ཕཊ།

ཨོཾ་ཨཱ་ན་ཡ་ཧོཿ བྷ་ག་ཝཱན་བིདྱཱ་རཱ་ཛ་ཧཱུྃ་ཧཱུྃ་ཕཊ། ཀྱིས་བསང་།

Visualize the garment and cleanse with:

Oṁ sumbha nisumbha huṁ hūṁ phaṭ

Oṁ grihaṇa grihaṇa huṁ hūṁ phaṭ

Oṁ grihaṇapaya grihaṇapaya huṁ hūṁ phaṭ

Oṁ ānayaho bhagavān vidyārāja huṁ hūṁ phaṭ

ཨོཾ་སྭ་བྷཱ་ཝ་ཤུདྡྷཿ སརྦ་དྷརྨཱཿ སྭ་བྷཱ་ཝ་ཤུདྡྷོ྅ཧཾ། གིས་སྦྱངས།

Purify with:

Oṁ svabhāva shuddhaḥ sarva dharmāḥ svabhāva shuddho' haṁ

སྟོང་པའི་ངང་ལས་ཧཱུྃ་ལས་བྱུང་བའི་ལྷའི་གོས་སྲབ་པ་འཇམ་པ་ཡང་བ་དྭངས་ཤིང་། ཐོགས་པ་མེད་པ་ཟུང་དུ་སྦྱར་བ་དང་ལྡན་པར་གྱུར།

Tong-Pay Ngang-Lé Hūṁ Lé Jung-Way Lhay Go Sab Pa Jam-Pa Yang-Wa Dang-Shing Thog-Pa Me-Pa Zung-Du Jar-Wa Dang Den-Par Gyur

From the state of emptiness arises *Hūṁ* (ཧཱུྃ), from which arises divine garments, smooth, light, pure, and unimpeded, joined together into a pair.

ཁ་དོག་བཟང་ཞིང་དྲི་ཞིམ་རེག་ན་བདེ།།
སྲབ་འཇམ་ཡང་མཛེས་ལྷ་ལས་བྱུང་བ་ཡི།།
ན་བཟའ་མཆོག་འདི་རྡོ་རྗེའི་སྐུ་ལ་འབུལ།།
བགྲེས་པ་མེད་པ་རྡོ་རྗེའི་སྐུ་ཐོབ་ཤོག།

Kha Dog Zang Shing Di Shim Reg Na De
Sab Jam Yang Ze Lha Lé Jung Wa Yi
Na Za Chog Di Dor-Jey Ku La Bül
De Pa Me Pa Dor-Jey Ku Tob Shog

With excellent color, sweet smell, comfortable to touch,
the garment from the devas is smooth, soft, light, and
beautiful.
This supreme garment is offered to the vajrakāya.
May the ageless vajrakāya be attained.

ཨོཾ་སརྦ་ཏ་ཐཱ་ག་ཏ་སརྦ་ཝཱི་ར་ཡོ་གི་ནཱི་ས་པ་རི་ཝཱ་ར་བཛྲ་ཝསྟྲ་ཨཱཿ ཧཱུྃ། ཞེས་གོས་ཟུང་ཕུལ།

Offer the pair of garments with:
Oṁ sarvatathāgata sarva vīra yoginī saparivāra vajra vastra āḥ hūṁ

དེ་ནས་སྙིང་ཁ་ནས་རིག་མ་བཅུ་དྲུག་སྤྲོས་ཏེ། དཀྱིལ་འཁོར་པ་རྣམས་མཆོད་པར་བསམས་ལ།
རྡོ་རྗེ་ལྷ་མོ་པི་ཝཾ་མ།།
སྟོན་ཀའི་མདོག་མཚུངས་པི་ཝཾ་ལག།
པི་ཝཾ་སྒྲ་དང་དབྱངས་ལྡན་མ།།
ནམ་མཁའ་ཁྱབ་པས་མཆོད་པར་བགྱི།།

Dor-Je Lha-Mo Pi Vaṁ Ma
Ton-Kay Dog Tsung Pi Vaṁ Lag
Pi Vaṁ Dra Dang Yang Den Ma
Nam-Kha Khyab-Pé Chö-Par Gyi

Imagine sixteen vidyas emanating from one's heart and making offering to the deities of the maṇḍala:

Playing a vina,
Vajravinidevī has the same color as the autumn sky.
She makes offerings by filling the sky
with sound of the vina and melodies.

ཨོཾ་སརྦ་ཏ་ཐཱ་ག་ཏ་སརྦ་བཱི་ར་ཡོ་གི་ནཱི་ས་པ་རི་ཝཱ་ར་ཨོཾ་བཛྲ་བཱི་ཎེ་ཧཱུྃ་ཧཱུྃ་ཕཊ།

Oṁ sarvatathāgata sarva vīra yoginī saparivāra oṁ vajra vīṇe huṁ hūṁ phaṭ

རྡོ་རྗེ་ལྷ་མོ་གླིང་བུ་མ།།
གསེར་གྱི་མདོག་ཅན་གླིང་བུ་ལག།
གླིང་བུའི་སྒྲ་དང་དབྱངས་ལྡན་མ།།
ནམ་མཁའ་ཁྱབ་པས་མཆོད་པར་བགྱི།།

Dor-Je Lha-Mo Ling Bu Ma
Ser Gyi Dog Chen Ling Bu Lag
Ling Bui Dra Dang Yang Den Ma
Nam-Kha Khyab-Pé Chö-Par Gyi

Playing a flute,
Vajravaṃśādevī has the color of gold.

She makes offering by filling the sky
with the sound of the flute and melodies.

ཨོཾ་སརྦ་ཏ་ཐཱ་ག་ཏ་སརྦ་ཝཱི་ར་ཡོ་གི་ནཱི་ས་པ་རི་ཝཱ་ར་ཨོཾ་བཛྲ་ཝཾ་སེ་ཧཱུྃ་ཧཱུྃ་ཕཊ།

Oṁ sarvatathāgata sarva vīra yoginī saparivāra oṁ vajra vaṁse
huṁ hūṁ phaṭ

རྡོ་རྗེ་ལྷ་མོ་རྔ་ཟླུམ་མ།།
བནྡྷུའི་མདོག་ཅན་རྔ་ཟླུམ་ལག།
རྔ་ཟླུམ་སྒྲ་དང་དབྱངས་ལྡན་མ།།
ནམ་མཁའ་ཁྱབ་པས་མཆོད་པར་བགྱི།།

Dor-Je Lha-Mo Nga Dum Ma
Ban-Dhui Dog Chen Nga Dum Lag
Nga Dum Dra Dang Yang Den Ma
Nam-Kha Khyab-Pé Chö-Par Gyi

Playing a mridanga drum,
Vajramridangadevī has the color of ruby.
She makes offering by filling the sky
with the sound the mridanga drum and melodies.

ཨོཾ་སརྦ་ཏ་ཐཱ་ག་ཏ་སརྦ་ཝཱི་ར་ཡོ་གི་ནཱི་ས་པ་རི་ཝཱ་ར་ཨོཾ་བཛྲ་མྲི་དཾ་གེ་ཧཱུྃ་ཧཱུྃ་ཕཊ།

Oṁ sarvatathāgata sarva vīra yoginī saparivāra oṁ vajra mridaṇge
huṁ hūṁ phaṭ

རྡོ་རྗེ་ལྷ་མོ་ཛ་ང་མ།།
མ་རྒད་མདོག་ཅན་ཛ་ང་ལག།
ཛ་ངའི་སྒྲ་དང་དབྱངས་ལྡན་མ།།
ནམ་མཁའ་ཁྱབ་པས་མཆོད་པར་བགྱི།།

Dor-Je Lha-Mo Za Nga Ma
Ma Ge Dog Chen Za Nga Lag
Za Ngay Dra Dang Yang Den Ma
Nam-Kha Khyab-Pé Chö-Par Gyi

Playing a murajā drum,
Vajramurajādevī has the color of emerald.
She makes offering by filling the sky
with the sound of the murajā drum and melodies.

ཨོཾ་སརྦ་ཏ་ཐཱ་ག་ཏ་སརྦ་བཱི་ར་ཡོ་གི་ནཱི་ས་པ་རི་ཝཱ་ར་ཨོཾ་བཛྲ་མུཛ་ཧཱུྃ་ཧཱུྃ་ཕཊ།

Oṁ sarvatathāgata sarva vīra yoginī saparivāra oṁ vajra murajā hum̐ hūṁ phaṭ

རྡོ་རྗེ་ལྷ་མོ་བཞད་པ་མོ།།
ཀིཾ་ཤུའི་མདོག་མཚུངས་བཞད་པའི་ཞལ།།
འཛུམ་པའི་བཞིན་དང་དབྱངས་ལྡན་མ།།
ནམ་མཁའ་ཁྱབ་པས་མཆོད་པར་བགྱི།།

Dor-Je Lha-Mo She Pa Mo
Kim Shui-Dog Tsung She Pay Shal
Zum Pay Shin Dang Yang Den Ma
Nam-Kha Khyab-Pé Chö-Par Gyi

Laughing Vajrahāsedevī
has the same color as the orange flower of the parrot tree.
She makes offering by filling the sky
with her smiling face and melodious sound.

ཨོཾ་སརྦ་ཏ་ཐཱ་ག་ཏ་སརྦ་ཝཱི་ར་ཡོ་གི་ནཱི་ས་པ་རི་ཝཱ་ར་ཨོཾ་བཛྲ་ཧཱ་སེ་ཧཱུཾ་ཧཱུཾ་ཕཊ།

Oṁ sarvatathāgata sarva vīra yoginī saparivāra oṁ vajra hāse huṁ hūṁ phaṭ

རྡོ་རྗེ་ལྷ་མོ་སྒེག་པ་མོ།།
དབང་སྔོན་མདོག་མཚུངས་སྒེག་པའི་ཚུལ།།
སྙེམས་པའི་ལུས་དང་གླུ་ལྡན་མ།།
ནམ་མཁའ་ཁྱབ་པས་མཆོད་པར་བགྱི།།

Dor-Je Lha-Mo Geg Pa Ma
Wang Ngon Dog Tsung Geg Pay Tsul
Nyem Pay Lü Dang Lu Den Ma
Nam-Kha Khyab-Pé Chö-Par Gyi

Dancing flirtatiously,
Vajralāsyadevī has the same color as sapphire.
She makes offering by filling the sky
with her vanity and song.

ཨོཾ་སརྦ་ཏ་ཐཱ་ག་ཏ་སརྦ་ཝཱི་ར་ཡོ་གི་ནི་ས་པ་རི་ཝཱ་ར་ཨོཾ་བཛྲ་ལཱ་སྱེ་ཧཱུྃ་ཧཱུྃ་ཕཊ།

Oṁ sarvatathāgata sarva vīra yoginī saparivāra oṁ vajra lāsye huṁ hūṁ phaṭ

རྡོ་རྗེ་ལྷ་མོ་གླུ་དབྱངས་མ།།
འཆར་ཀའི་མདོག་མཚུངས་གླུ་ལེན་མ།།
སྙན་པའི་གླུ་དབྱངས་རོལ་མོ་བཅས།།
ནམ་མཁའ་ཁྱབ་པས་མཆོད་པར་བགྱི།།

Dor-Je Lha-Mo Lu Yang Ma
Char Kay Dog Tsung Lu Len Ma
Nyen Pay Lu Yang Röl Mo Ché
Nam-Kha Khyab-Pé Chö-Par Gyi

Singing a song,
Vajragītidevī has the same color as sunrise.
She makes offering by filling the sky
with melodious song and harmonious music.

ཨོཾ་སརྦ་ཏ་ཐཱ་ག་ཏ་སརྦ་ཝཱི་ར་ཡོ་གི་ནི་ས་པ་རི་ཝཱ་ར་ཨོཾ་བཛྲ་གཱི་ཏི་ཧཱུྃ་ཧཱུྃ་ཕཊ།

Oṁ sarvatathāgata sarva vīra yoginī saparivāra oṁ vajra gīti huṁ hūṁ phaṭ

རྡོ་རྗེ་ལྷ་མོ་གར་མཁན་མ།།
མ་རྒད་མདོག་མཚུངས་གར་སྒྱུར་ཞིང་།།

གར་དང་སྙན་པའི་དབྱངས་ལྡན་མ།།
ནམ་མཁའ་ཁྱབ་པས་མཆོད་པར་བགྱི།།

Dor-Je Lha-Mo Gar Khen Ma
Ma Ge Dog Tsung Gar Gyur Shing
Gar Dang Nyen Pay Yang Den Ma
Nam-Kha Khyab-Pé Chö-Par Gyi

Dancing and singing melodiously,
Vajranritidevī has the same color as emerald.
She makes offering by filling the sky
with dance and harmonious melodies.

ཨོཾ་སརྦ་ཏ་ཐཱ་ག་ཏ་སརྦ་བཱི་ར་ཡོ་གི་ནཱི་ས་པ་རི་ཝཱ་ར་ཨོཾ་བཛྲ་ནྲྀ་ཏི་ཧཱུྃ་ཧཱུྃ་ཕཊ།

Oṁ sarvatathāgata sarva vīra yoginī saparivāra oṁ vajra nriti hum hūṁ phaṭ

རྡོ་རྗེ་ལྷ་མོ་མེ་ཏོག་མ།།
གུར་གུམ་མདོག་མཚུངས་མེ་ཏོག་ལག།
མེ་ཏོག་ཆར་དང་རོལ་མོར་བཅས།།
ནམ་མཁའ་ཁྱབ་པས་མཆོད་པར་བགྱི།།

Dor-Je Lha-Mo Me-Tok Ma
Gur Gum Dog Tsug Me-Tog Lag
Me-Tog Char Dang Röl Mor Ché
Nam-Kha Khyab-Pé Chö-Par Gyi

Carrying flowers,
Vajrapuṣpedevī has the same color as saffron.
She makes offering by filling the sky
with a rain of flowers and music.

ཨོཾ་སརྦ་ཏ་ཐཱ་ག་ཏ་སརྦ་བཱི་ར་ཡོ་གི་ནཱི་ས་པ་རི་ཝཱ་ར་ཨོཾ་བཛྲ་པུཥྤེ་ཧཱུྃ་ཧཱུྃ་ཕཊ།

Oṁ sarvatathāgata sarva vīra yoginī saparivāra oṁ vajra puṣpe huṁ hūṁ phaṭ

རྡོ་རྗེ་ལྷ་མོ་བདུག་སྤོས་མ།།
དུ་བའི་མདོག་མཚུངས་བདུག་སྤོས་ལག།
བདུག་སྤོས་སྤྲིན་དང་རོལ་མོ་བཅས།།
ནམ་མཁའ་ཁྱབ་པས་མཆོད་པར་བགྱི།།

Dor-Je Lha-Mo Dug Pö Ma
Du Way Dog Tsung Dug Po Lag
Dug Pö Trin Dang Röl Mo Ché
Nam-Kha Khyap-Pé Chö-Par Gyi

Carrying incense,
Vajradhūpedevī has the same color as smoke.
She makes offering by filling the sky
with a cloud of incense and music.

ཨོཾ་སརྦ་ཏ་ཐཱ་ག་ཏ་སརྦ་ཝཱི་ར་ཡོ་གི་ནཱི་ས་པ་རི་ཝཱ་ར་ཨོཾ་བཛྲ་དྷཱུ་པེ་ཧུྃ་ཧཱུྃ་ཕཊ།

Oṁ sarvatathāgata sarva vīra yoginī saparivāra oṁ vajra dhūpe huṁ hūṁ phaṭ

རྡོ་རྗེ་ལྷ་མོ་མར་མེ་མ།།
གློག་འོད་མདོག་མཚུངས་མར་མེའི་ལག།
མར་མེའི་འོད་དང་རོལ་མོ་བཅས།།
ནམ་མཁའ་ཁྱབ་པས་མཆོད་པར་བགྱི།།

Dor-Je Lha-Mo Mar-Me Ma
Log Ö Dog Tsung Mar Mey Lag
Mar Mey Ö Dang Röl Mo Ché
Nam-Kha Khyab-Pé Chö-Par Gyi

Carrying a lamp,
Vajraālokedevī has the same color as a flash of lightning.
She makes offering by filling the sky
with lamplight and music.

ཨོཾ་སརྦ་ཏ་ཐཱ་ག་ཏ་སརྦ་ཝཱི་ར་ཡོ་གི་ནཱི་ས་པ་རི་ཝཱ་ར་ཨོཾ་བཛྲ་ཨཱ་ལོ་ཀེ་ཧུྃ་ཧཱུྃ་ཕཊ།

Oṁ sarvatathāgata sarva vīra yoginī saparivāra oṁ vajra āloke huṁ hūṁ phaṭ

རྡོ་རྗེ་ལྷ་མོ་དྲི་ཆབ་མ།།
ཁྲི་ཡང་མདོག་མཚུངས་དུང་ཆོས་ལག།
དྲི་ཡི་ཆར་དང་རོལ་མོ་བཅས།།
ནམ་མཁའ་ཁྱབ་པས་མཆོད་པར་བགྱི།།

Dor-Je Lha-Mo Dri Chab Ma
Tri Yang Dog Tsung Dung Chö Lag
Dri Yi Char Dang Röl Mo Ché
Nam-Kha Khyab-Pé Chö-Par Gyi

Carrying a conch,
Vajragandhedevī has same color as the blue dragonhead flower.
She makes offering by filling the sky
with scented water and music.

ཨོཾ་སརྦ་ཏ་ཐཱ་ག་ཏ་སརྦ་ཝཱི་ར་ཡོ་གི་ནཱི་ས་པ་རི་ཝཱ་ར་ཨོཾ་བཛྲ་གནྡྷེ་ཧཱུྃ་ཧཱུྃ་ཕཊ།

Oṁ sarvatathāgata sarva vīra yoginī saparivāra oṁ vajra gandhe hum hūṁ phaṭ

རྡོ་རྗེ་ལྷ་མོ་མེ་ལོང་མ།།
ཆུ་ཤེལ་མདོག་མཚུངས་མེ་ལོང་ལག།
སྣ་ཚོགས་གཟུགས་ཀྱིས་མཉེས་བྱེད་མ།།
ནམ་མཁའ་ཁྱབ་པས་མཆོད་པར་བགྱི།།

Dor-Je Lha-Mo Me long Ma
Chu Shel Dog Tsung Me Long Lag
Na Tsog Zug Kyi Nye Je Ma
Nam-Kha Khyab-Pé Chö-Par Gyi

Carrying a mirror,
Vajraādarśadevī has the same color as crystal.
She makes offering by filling the sky,
giving pleasure with various forms.

ཨོཾ་སརྦ་ཏ་ཐཱ་ག་ཏ་སརྦ་ཝཱི་ར་ཡོ་གི་ནཱི་ས་པ་རི་ཝཱ་ར་ཨོཾ་བཛྲ་རཱུ་པ་བཛྲི་ཧཱུྃ་ཧཱུྃ་ཕཊ།

Oṁ sarvatathāgata sarva vīra yoginī saparivāra oṁ vajra rūpa vajrī huṁ hūṁ phaṭ

རྡོ་རྗེ་ལྷ་མོ་ཞལ་ཟས་མ།།
ཛ་བའི་མདོག་མཚུངས་ཞལ་ཟས་ལག།
ཞལ་ཟས་བདུད་རྩིའི་ཆར་འབེབས་མ།།
ནམ་མཁའ་ཁྱབ་པས་མཆོད་པར་བགྱི།།

Dor-Je Lha-Mo Shal Ze Ma
Za Way Dog Tsung Shal Ze Lag
Shal Ze Dü-Tsiy Char Beb Ma
Nam-Kha Khyab-Pé Chö-Par Gyi

Carrying food,
Vajranaividyadevī has the same color as the yellow champaka flower.
She makes offerings by filling the sky
with a rain shower of ambrosial food.

ཨོཾ་སརྦ་ཏ་ཐཱ་ག་ཏ་སརྦ་ཝཱི་ར་ཡོ་གི་ནཱི་ས་པ་རི་ཝཱ་ར་ཨོཾ་བཛྲ་ར་ས་བཛྲཱི་ཧཱུཾ་ཧཱུཾ་ཕཊ།

Oṁ sarvatathāgata sarva vīra yoginī saparivāra oṁ vajra rasa vajrī huṁ hūṁ phaṭ

རྡོ་རྗེ་ལྷ་མོ་ན་བཟའ་མ།།
མ་ཀྱད་མདོག་མཚུངས་ན་བཟའི་ལག།
གོས་དང་རེག་དང་འཁྱུད་པ་ལྡན།།
ནམ་མཁའ་ཁྱབ་པས་མཆོད་པར་བགྱི།།

Dor-Je Lha-Mo Na Za Ma
Ma Ge Dog Tsung Na Zay Lag
Gö Dang Reg Dang Khyü-Pa Den
Nam-Kha Khyab-Pé Chö-Par Gyi

Carrying cloth,
Vajrasparṣdevī has the same color as an emerald.
She makes offerings by filling the sky
with cloth, touch and embraces.

ཨོཾ་སརྦ་ཏ་ཐཱ་ག་ཏ་སརྦ་བཱི་ར་ཡོ་གི་ནཱི་ས་པ་རི་ཝཱ་ར་ཨོཾ་བཛྲ་སྤརྴེ་བཛྲཱི་ཧཱུཾ་ཧཱུཾ་ཕཊ།

Oṁ sarvatathāgata sarva vīra yoginī saparivāra oṁ vajra sparṣhe vajrī huṁ hūṁ phaṭ

རྡོ་རྗེ་ལྷ་མོ་ཆོས་དབྱིངས་མ།།
ཀུནྡ་འི་མདོག་མཚུངས་ཆོས་འབྱུང་ལག།
ཟག་པ་མེད་པའི་བདེ་སྟེར་མ།།
ནམ་མཁའ་ཁྱབ་པས་མཆོད་པར་བགྱི།།

Dor-Je Lha-Mo Chö Ying Ma
Kün-Day Dog Tsung Chö Jung Lag
Zag Pa Me-Pay De Ter Ma
Nam-Kha Khyab-Pé Chö-Par Gyi

Carrying a dharmakara,
Vajradharmadhātudevī has the same colors as star jasmine.
She makes offerings by filling the sky,
bestowing immaculate bliss.

ཨོཾ་སརྦ་ཏ་ཐཱ་ག་ཏ་སརྦ་བཱི་ར་ཡོ་གི་ནཱི་ས་པ་རི་ཝཱ་ར་ཨོཾ་བཛྲ་དྷརྨ་དྷཱ་ཏུ་བཛྲཱི་ཧཱུཾ་ཧཱུཾ་ཕཊ།
ཞེས་མཆོད།

Oṁ sarvatathāgata sarva vīra yoginī saparivāra oṁ vajra dharmadhātu vajrī huṁ hūṁ phaṭ

Thus, make offerings.

ནམ་མཁའ་མཛོད་ཀྱི་ཕྱག་རྒྱ་དཔྲལ་བར་བཅས་ཤིང་།

ཨོཾ་སརྦ་བིཏ་པཱུ་ར་པཱུ་ར་སུ་ར་སུ་ར་ཨཱ་ཝརྟ་ཡ་ཨཱ་ཝརྟ་ཡ་ཧོཿ

Make the mudra of the treasury of space at one's forehead:

Oṁ sarvavita pūrapūra sura sura āvartaya āvartaya hoḥ

ཞེས་བརྗོད་ཅིང་། ཐལ་མོ་སྙིང་གར་སྦྱར་ལ།

བདེ་བར་གཤེགས་པ་ཐམས་ཅད་ལ།།
འཁོར་ལོ་རིན་ཆེན་འདི་ཕུལ་བས།།
སྲིད་པའི་འཁོར་ལོ་རྒྱུན་བཅད་དེ།།
ཆོས་ཀྱི་འཁོར་ལོ་བསྐོར་བར་ཤོག།

De-War Sheg-Pa Tham-Ché La
Khor-Lo Rin-Chen Di Phul-We
Si-Pay Khor-Lo Gyun Ché De
Chö-Kyi Khor-Lo Kor-War Shog

Join one's palms together at the heart and recite:

By offering this precious wheel
to all the Sugatas,
may the wheel of samsara be stopped
and the wheel of Dharma be turned.

ཨོཾ་སརྦ་ཏ་ཐཱ་ག་ཏ་སརྦ་ཝཱི་ར་ཡོ་གི་ནཱི་ས་པ་རི་ཝཱ་ར་ཨོཾ་ཙཀྲ་རཏྣ་པཱུ་ཛི་ཏེ་ཨཱཿཧཱུྃ།

Oṁ sarvatathāgata sarva vīra yoginī saparivāra oṁ chakra ratna pūjite āḥ hūṁ

རྒྱལ་བ་སྲས་དང་བཅས་རྣམས་ལ།།
ནོར་བུ་རིན་ཆེན་འདི་ཕུལ་བས།།
བཀྲེས་ཤིང་ཕོངས་པ་རྒྱུན་བཅད་དེ།།
འབྱོར་པ་ཕུན་སུམ་ཚོགས་པར་ཤོག།

Gyal-Wa Se Dang Ché Nam La
Nor-Bu Rin-Chen Di Phul-We
Tre Shing Phong Pa Gyun Ché De
Jor-Pa Phun Sum Tsog Par Shog

By offering this precious gem
to the victors with their children,
may hunger and poverty be eradicated
and abundant wealth be accumulated.

ཨོཾ་སརྦ་ཏ་ཐཱ་ག་ཏ་སརྦ་བཱི་ར་ཡོ་གི་ནཱི་ས་པ་རི་ཝཱ་ར་ཨོཾ་མ་ཎི་རཏྣ་པཱུ་ཛི་ཏེ་ཨཱཿ ཧཱུྃ།

Oṁ sarvatathāgata sarva vīra yoginī saparivāra oṁ maṇi ratna pūjite āḥ hūṁ

བཙུན་མོ་རིན་ཆེན་འདི་ཕུལ་བས།།
མ་རིག་མུན་པ་རྒྱུན་བཅད་དེ།།
ཤེས་རབ་དབྱིངས་ཀྱི་དོན་རྟོགས་ནས།།
ཐབས་དང་ཤེས་རབ་འབྲེལ་བར་ཤོག།

Tsun-Mo Rin-Chen Di Phul-We
Ma Rig Mun-Pa Gyun Ché De
She-Rab Ying Kyi Don Tog Ne
Thab Dang She-Rab Drel-War Shog

By offering this precious queen,
may the darkness of ignorance be eradicated.
Through the wisdom by realizing the meaning of
dharmadhatū,
may method and wisdom be connected.

ཨོཾ་སརྦ་ཏ་ཐཱ་ག་ཏ་སརྦ་ཝཱི་ར་ཡོ་གི་ནཱི་ས་པ་རི་ཝཱ་ར་ཨོཾ་ཝསྟི་རཏྣ་པཱུ་ཛི་ཏེ་ཨཱཿཧཱུྃ།

Oṁ sarvatathāgata sarva vīra yoginī saparivāra oṁ vasti ratna pūjite āḥ hūṁ

བློན་པོ་རིན་ཆེན་འདི་ཕུལ་བས།།
ཕྱི་ནང་གསང་གསུམ་ཐེག་གསུམ་ལྡན།།
བསམ་ཡས་བསྟན་པ་རབ་འཛིན་ཅིང་།།
ཡོན་ཏན་ཐམས་ཅད་ལྡན་པར་ཤོག།

Lon-Po Rin-Chen Di Phul-We
Chi Nang Sang Sum Theg Sum Den
Sam-Ye Ten-Pa Rab Zin Ching
Yon-Ten Tham-Ché Den-Par Shog

By offering this precious minister,
may inconceivable teachings
endowed with the outer, inner, and secret yānas be fully
upheld,
and may all qualities be possessed.

ཨོཾ་སརྦ་ཏ་ཐཱ་ག་ཏ་སརྦ་བཱི་ར་ཡོ་གི་ནཱི་ས་པ་རི་ཝཱ་ར་ཨོཾ་མ་ཧཱ་ཏ་ར་ཏྣ་པཱུ་ཛི་ཏེ་ཨཱཿ ཧཱུྃ།

Oṁ sarvatathāgata sarva vīra yoginī saparivāra oṁ mahāta ratna pūjite āḥ hūṁ

གླང་པོ་རིན་ཆེན་འདི་ཕུལ་བས།།
ལྟ་ངན་རྣམས་ནི་རབ་བསལ་ནས།།
བླ་མེད་ཐེག་པ་རབ་ཞོན་ཏེ།།
ཐམས་ཅད་མཁྱེན་གྲོང་བགྲོད་བར་ཤོག།

Lang-Po Rin-Chen Di Phul-We
Ta Ngen Nam Ni Rab Sal Ne
La-Me Theg-Pa Rab Shon Te
Tham-Ché Khyen Drong Drö-Bar Shog

By offering this precious elephant,
after fully removing evil views,
may the unsurpassed vehicle be mounted
and ridden to the city of omniscience.

ཨོཾ་སརྦ་ཏ་ཐཱ་ག་ཏ་སརྦ་བཱི་ར་ཡོ་གི་ནཱི་ས་པ་རི་བཱ་ར་ཨོཾ་ཧ་སྟི་རཏྣ་པཱུ་ཛི་ཏེ་ཨཱཿ ཧཱུྃ།

Oṁ sarvatathāgata sarva vīra yoginī saparivāra oṁ hasti ratna pūjite āḥ hūṁ

རྟ་མཆོག་རིན་ཆེན་འདི་ཕུལ་བས།།
སྲིད་པའི་གཟེབ་ལས་ངེས་གྲོལ་ཏེ།།
རྫུ་འཕྲུལ་མཆོག་གི་ཤུགས་ཐོབ་ནས།།
སངས་རྒྱས་ཞིང་དུ་འགྲོ་བར་ཤོག།

Ta Chog Rin-Chen Di Phul-We
Si-Pay Zeb Lé Nge Dröl Te
Zu Trul Chog Gi Shug Tob Ne
Sang-Gyé Shing Du Dro-War Shog

By offering this precious horse,
having become definitively free from the trap of existence,
and attained the supreme magical power,
may we travel to buddhafields.

ཨོཾ་སརྦ་ཏ་ཐཱ་ག་ཏ་སརྦ་བཱི་ར་ཡོ་གི་ནཱི་ས་པ་རི་བཱ་ར་ཨོཾ་ཏུ་རངྒ་ཨ་ཤྭ་རཏྣ་པཱུ་ཛི་ཏེ་ཨཱཿ ཧཱུྃ།

Oṁ sarvatathāgata sarva vīra yoginī saparivāra oṁ turanga ashva ratna pūjite āḥ hūṁ

དམག་དཔོན་རིན་ཆེན་འདི་ཕུལ་བས།།
ཉོན་མོངས་དགྲ་ལས་རྒྱལ་གྱུར་ནས།།

ཕས་ཀྱི་རྒོལ་བ་ཚར་བཅད་དེ།།
བསྙེངས་བྲལ་མཆོག་ཉི་ཐོབ་པར་ཤོག།

Mag Pon Rin-Chen Di Phul-We
Nyon Mong Dra Lé Gyal Gyur Ne
Phe Kyi Gol-Wa Tsar Ché De
Nyeng Dral Chog Ni Thop-Par Shog

By offering this precious general,
after becoming victorious over the enemy afflictions,
the adversary is destroyed,
may the supreme fearlessness be attained.

ༀ་སརྦ་ཏ་ཐཱ་ག་ཏ་སརྦ་ཝཱི་ར་ཡོ་གི་ཉཱི་ས་པ་རི་ཝཱ་ར་ༀ་ཁཌྒ་རཏྣ་པཱུ་ཛི་ཏེ་ཨཱཿ ཧཱུྃ།

Oṁ sarvatathāgata sarva vīra yoginī saparivāra oṁ khaḍga ratna pūjite āḥ hūṁ

ཞེས་དང་། འདོད་ཡོན་ལྔའི་མཆོད་པ་ནི།
ཁ་དོག་དབྱིབས་ལེགས་ཡིད་འོང་རྒྱན་ཕྲེང་ལྡན།།
ཕྱོགས་དུས་ཀུན་ན་གཟུགས་མཆོག་ཅི་མཆིས་པ།།
མོས་བློས་བླ་མ་རྣལ་འབྱོར་མ་ལ་འབུལ།།
བཞེས་ཤིག་བླ་མེད་གྲུབ་མཆོག་སྩོལ་དུ་གསོལ།།

Kha-Dog Yib leg Yi Ong Gyen Teng Den
Chog Dü Kün Na Zug Chog Chi Chi-Pa
Mo Lo La-Ma Nal-Jor-Ma La Pul
She Shig La-Me Drub Chog Tsal Du Söl

The offering of five desirable objects:

Existing in all directions and times, all supreme forms, ornaments and garlands possessing attractive color and perfect shape,
are offered to the guru Yoginī with a devoted mind.
Please accept this and grant me the unsurpassed siddhi.

ཨོཾ་སརྦ་ཏ་ཐཱ་ག་ཏ་སརྦ་ཝཱི་ར་ཡོ་གི་ནཱི་ས་པ་རི་ཝཱ་ར་རཱུ་པ་ཀཱ་མ་གུ་ཎ་པཱུ་ཛི་ཏེ་ཨཱཿ ཧཱུྃ།

Oṁ sarvatathāgata sarva vīra yoginī saparivāra rūpa kāma guṇa pūjite āḥ hūṁ

ཕྱོགས་དུས་ཀུན་ན་ཟིན་དང་མ་ཟིན་པའི།།
ཡོན་ཏན་ཚིག་བརྗོད་སྒྲ་སྙན་ཅི་མཆིས་རྣམས།།
མོས་བློས་བླ་མ་རྣལ་འབྱོར་མ་ལ་འབུལ།།
བཞེས་ཤིག་བླ་མེད་གྲུབ་མཆོག་སྩལ་དུ་གསོལ།།

Chog Dü Kün Na Zin Dang Ma Zin-Pay
Yon-Ten Tsig Jö Dra Nyen Chi Chi-Nam
Mo Lo La-Ma Nal-Jor-Ma La Pul
She Shig La-Me Drub Chog Tsal Du Söl

Existing in all directions and times, animate and inanimate,
all melodious sounds and praises
are offered to the guru Yoginī with a devoted mind.
Please accept this and grant me the unsurpassed siddhi.

ཨོཾ་སརྦ་ཏ་ཐཱ་ག་ཏ་སརྦ་བཱི་ར་ཡོ་གི་ནཱི་ས་པ་རི་ཝཱ་ར་ཤབྡ་ཀཱ་མ་གུ་ཎ་པཱུ་ཛི་ཏེ་ཨཱཿ ཧཱུྃ།

Oṁ sarvatathāgata sarva vīra yoginī saparivāra shabda kāma guṇa pūjite āḥ hūṁ

ཕྱོགས་དུས་ཀུན་ན་ཙནྡན་སྦྲུལ་སྙིང་དང་།།
ཨ་གར་ལ་སོགས་དབང་པོ་ཚིམ་བྱེད་རྣམས།།
མོས་བློས་བླ་མ་རྣལ་འབྱོར་མ་ལ་འབུལ།།
བཞེས་ཤིག་བླ་མེད་གྲུབ་མཆོག་སྩོལ་དུ་གསོལ།།

Chog Dü Kün Na Chan-Den Drul Nying Dang
Ah-Gar La Sog Wang-Po Tsim Je Nam
Mo Lo La-Ma Nal-Jor-Ma La Pul
She Shig La-Me Drub Chog Tsal Du Söl

Existing in all directions and times, such as snake-heart sandalwood,
agarwood and so on, all satisfying things
are offered to the guru Yoginī with a devoted mind.
Please accept this and grant me the unsurpassed siddhi.

ཨོཾ་སརྦ་ཏ་ཐཱ་ག་ཏ་སརྦ་བཱི་ར་ཡོ་གི་ནཱི་ས་པ་རི་ཝཱ་ར་གནྡྷེ་ཀཱ་མ་གུ་ཎ་པཱུ་ཛི་ཏེ་ཨཱཿ ཧཱུྃ།

Oṁ sarvatathāgata sarva vīra yoginī saparivāra gandhe kāma guṇa pūjite āḥ hūṁ

ཕྱོགས་དུས་ཀུན་ན་རོ་དང་བཅུད་ལྡན་པའི།།
ལུས་སེམས་བརྟས་བྱེད་རོ་མཆོག་ཅི་མཆིས་རྣམས།།
མོས་བློས་བླ་མ་རྣལ་འབྱོར་མ་ལ་འབུལ།།
བཞེས་ཤིག་བླ་མེད་གྲུབ་མཆོག་སྩལ་དུ་གསོལ།།

Chog Dü Kün Na Ro Dang Chü Den Pay
Lü Sem Te Je Ro Chog Chi Chi-Nam
Mo Lo La-Ma Nal-Jor-Ma La Pul
She Shig La-Me Drub Chog Tsal Du Söl

Existing in all directions and times, tasty and nutritious,
all supreme tastes building the body and mind
are offered to the guru Yoginī with a devoted mind.
Please accept this and grant me the unsurpassed siddhi.

ཨོཾ་སརྦ་ཏ་ཐཱ་ག་ཏ་སརྦ་ཝཱི་ར་ཡོ་གི་ནཱི་ས་པ་རི་ཝཱ་ར་ར་ས་ཀཱ་མ་གུ་ཎ་པཱུ་ཛི་ཏེ་ཨཱཿ ཧཱུྃ།

Oṁ sarvatathāgata sarva vīra yoginī saparivāra rasa kāma guṇa pūjite āḥ hūṁ

ཕྱོགས་དུས་ཀུན་ན་འཇམ་མཉེན་འཁྲིལ་ཆགས་པའི།།
རེག་བྱའི་ཁྱད་པར་ལུས་སེམས་ཚིམ་བྱེད་རྣམས།།
མོས་བློས་བླ་མ་རྣལ་འབྱོར་མ་ལ་འབུལ།།
བཞེས་ཤིག་བླ་མེད་གྲུབ་མཆོག་སྩལ་དུ་གསོལ།།

Chog Dü Kün Na Jam Nyen Til Chag Pay
Reg Jay Khye-Par Lü Sem Tsim Je Nam

Mo Lo La-Ma Nal-Jor-Ma La Pul
She Shig La-Me Drub Chog Tsal Du Söl

Existing in all directions and times, smooth and gentle caresses,
all special sensations satisfying body and mind
are offered to the guru Yoginī with a devoted mind.
Please accept this and grant me the unsurpassed siddhi.

ཨོཾ་སརྦ་ཏ་ཐཱ་ག་ཏ་སརྦ་ཝཱི་ར་ཡོ་གི་ནཱི་ས་པ་རི་ཝཱ་ར་སྤརྵེ་ཀཱ་མ་གུ་ཎ་པཱུ་ཛི་ཏེ་ཨཱཿ ཧཱུྃ།

Oṁ sarvatathāgata sarva vīra yoginī saparivāra sparṣhe kāma guṇa pūjite āḥ hūṁ

དེ་རྣམས་ཕྱིའི་མཆོད་པ་སྟེ། སོ་སོའི་སྔགས་དང་ཕྱག་རྒྱ་ཏིང་ངེ་འཛིན་དང་བཅས་པས་འབུལ་ལོ།

Those are the outer offerings offered with their individual mantra, mudra, and samādhi.

ནང་གི་མཆོད་པ་ནི། ཨོཾ་ཨཱཿ ཧཱུྃ་ཞེས་པས་བྱིན་གྱིས་རླབས་པ་དྲན་པར་བྱས་ལ། གཡོན་པའི་མཐེབ་སྲིན་གྱིས་ནང་མཆོད་ཀྱི་དབུས་ནས་བླང་སྟེ་ཐིགས་པ་འཐོར་ཞིང་། ཨོཾ་མཆོད་དོ།

The inner offerings: recall the blessings with Oṁ āḥ hūṁ. After taking the inner offering with the left ring finger, scatter the drops [from the ring finger with the thumb] and offer with Oṁ.

ཕྱོགས་བཅུ་དུས་གསུམ་གྱི་དེ་བཞིན་གཤེགས་པ་ཐམས་ཅད་ཀྱི་སྐུ་གསུང་ཐུགས་ཡོན་ཏན་ཕྲིན་ལས་ཐམས་ཅད་ཀྱི་ངོ་བོར་གྱུར་པ། མཁྱེན་པའི་ཡེ་ཤེས། བརྩེ་བའི་ཐུགས་རྗེ། མཛད་པའི་ཕྲིན་ལས་བསམ་གྱིས་མི་ཁྱབ་པ་མངའ་བ། དྲིན་ཆེན་རྩ་བའི་བླ་མ་རིན་པོ་ཆེའི་ཞལ་དུ་ཨོཾ་ཨཱཿ ཧཱུྃ།

Chog Chu Dü Sum Gyi De-Shin Sheg-Pa Tham-Ché Kyi Ku Sung Thug Yon-Ten Trin-Lé Tham-Ché Kyi Ngo-Wor Gyur-Pa, Khyen Pay Ye-She, Tse-Way Thug-Je, Zé-Pay Trin-Lé Sam Gyi Mi Khyab Pa Nga-Wa, Drin Chen Tsa-Way La-Ma Rin-Po-Chey Shal Du Oṁ āḥ hūṁ

To the mouth of the greatly kind root guru, the essence of the body, speech, mind, qualities, and activities of all the tathāgatas of the ten directions and three times, the one who possesses omniscient wisdom, loving compassion and inconceivable deeds.
Oṁ āḥ hūṁ

ཁྱབ་བདག་དང་པོའི་སངས་རྒྱས་རྡོ་རྗེ་ཆོས།།
རྒྱལ་བའི་ཡུམ་གྱུར་རྡོ་རྗེ་རྣལ་འབྱོར་མ།།
གྲུབ་པའི་དབང་པོ་རྡོ་རྗེ་དྲིལ་བུ་པ།།
རྣམ་དག་བདུད་རྩིའི་དམ་རྫས་མཉེས་མཆོད་འབུལ།།
ཨོཾ་ཨཱཿ ཧཱུྃ།

Khyab Dag Dang Poy Sang-Gyé Dor-Je Chö
Gyal-Way Yum Gyur Dor-Je Nal-Jor-Ma
Dub Pay Wang-Po Dor-Je Dril-Bu-Pa
Nam-Dag Dü-Tsiy Dam Zé Nye Chö Bül
Oṁ āḥ hūṁ

This offering of the pleasing samaya substance, pure amrita,
is made
to Vajradharma, the sovereign Ādibuddha,
Vajrayoginī, mother of the victors
and Vajraghantapada, the lord of siddhas.
Oṁ āḥ hūṁ

ལྷག་པའི་ལྷ་ཡིས་རྗེས་བཟུང་ཌེཾ་གི་པ།།
དོན་དམ་མཆོག་བརྙེས་གྲུབ་ཆེན་ཨནྟ་ར་པ།།
བརྩོན་པས་གྲུབ་པ་བརྙེས་པའི་ཏེ་ལོ་པ།།
རྣམ་དག་བདུད་རྩིའི་དམ་རྫས་མཉེས་མཆོད་འབུལ།།
ཨོཾ་ཨཱཿ ཧཱུྃ།

Lhag Pay Lha Yi Je Zung Deṁ-Gi-Pa
Don Dam Chog Nye Drub Chen An-Tar-Pa
Tsön Pé Drub Pa Nye-Pay Te-Lo-Pa
Nam-Dag Dü-Tsiy Dam Zé Nye Chö Bül
Oṁ āḥ hūṁ

This offering of the pleasing samaya substance, pure amrita,
is made
to Deṁgipa, taken care by the special deity,
Antarapa, the great siddha who attained the supreme
ultimate,
and Tilopa, who attained siddhi with diligence.
Oṁ āḥ hūṁ

པཎ་གྲུབ་འཁོར་ལོས་སྒྱུར་བ་ནཱ་རོ་པ།།
སྙན་བརྒྱུད་སློབ་བཤད་འཛིན་པའི་ཕམ་མཐིང་པ།།
ཟབ་ལམ་མཐར་ཕྱིན་ཀློག་སྐྱ་ཤེས་རབ་བརྩེགས།།
རྣམ་དག་བདུད་རྩིའི་དམ་རྫས་མཉེས་མཆོད་འབུལ།།
ཨོཾ་ཨཱཿ ཧཱུྃ།

Pan-Drub Khor-Lo Gyur-Wa Nā-Ro-Pa
Nyen-Gyü Lob-She Zin-Pay Pham-Ting-Pa
Zab-Lam Thar-Chin Log Kya She-Rab Tseg
Nam-Dag Dü-Tsiy Dam Zé Nye Chö Bül
Oṁ āḥ hūṁ

This offering of the pleasing samaya substance, pure amrita, is made
to Nāropa, the emperor of paṇḍitas and siddhas,
the Phaimtingpas, lineage holders of the aural lineage,
and Logkya Sherab Tsek, who reached the conclusion of the profound path.
Oṁ āḥ hūṁ

སྐད་གཉིས་སྨྲ་བའི་ལོ་ཆེན་བློ་གྲོས་གྲགས།།
བསྟན་པའི་མངའ་བདག་བླ་ཆེན་ས་སྐྱ་པ།།
དེ་སྲས་བུ་བོ་རྗེ་བཙུན་སྐུ་མཆེད་གཉིས།།
རྣམ་དག་བདུད་རྩིའི་དམ་རྫས་མཉེས་མཆོད་འབུལ།།
ཨོཾ་ཨཱཿ ཧཱུྃ།

Ke Nyi Ma-Way Lo-Chen Lo-Drö Dag
Ten-Pay Nga-Dag La-Chen Sa-Kya-Pa
De Se Tu-Wo Je-Tsün Ku Che Nyi
Nam-Dag Dü-Tsiy Dam Zé Nye Chö Bül
Oṁ āḥ hūṁ

This offering of the pleasing samaya substance, pure amrita,
is made
to the great translator Lodroe Drak, speaker of two languages,
the Mahaguru Sakyapa, lord of the doctrine,
and his powerful sons, the two Jetsun brothers.
Oṁ āḥ hūṁ

ཀུན་མཁྱེན་གཉིས་པ་ས་སྐྱ་པཎྜི་ཏ།།
སྲིད་ཞིའི་གཙུག་རྒྱན་འཕགས་པ་རིན་པོ་ཆེ།།
ཆོས་བརྒྱུད་འཛིན་པ་ཀུན་སྤངས་དཀོན་མཆོག་དཔལ།།
རྣམ་དག་བདུད་རྩིའི་དམ་རྫས་མཉེས་མཆོད་འབུལ།།
ཨོཾ་ཨཱཿ ཧཱུྃ།

Kün-Khyen Nyi-Pa Sa-Kya Paṇ-Di-Ta
Si Shiy Tsug Gyen Phag-Pa Rin-Po-Che
Chö Gye Ching-Wa Kün Pang Kon-Chog Pal
Nam-Dag Dü-Tsiy Dam Zé Nye Chö Bül
Oṁ āḥ hūṁ

This offering of the pleasing samaya substance, pure amrita, is made
to Sakya Paṇḍita, the second omniscient one,
Phagpa Rinpoche, ornament of the crown of existence and peace,
and Konchog Pal, completely free from the bondage of the eight worldly dharmas.
Oṁ āḥ hūṁ

རྩེ་གཅིག་སྒྲུབ་པ་མཐར་ཕྱིན་བྲག་ཕུག་པ།།
འགྲོ་བའི་བླ་མ་བསོད་ནམས་རྒྱལ་མཚན་དཔལ།།
བཤད་སྒྲུབ་ཆུ་བོ་ཀུན་འདུས་དཔལ་ལྡན་པར།།
རྣམ་དག་བདུད་རྩིའི་དམ་རྫས་མཉེས་མཆོད་འབུལ།།
ཨོཾ་ཨཱཿཧཱུྃ།

Tse Chig Drub Pa Thar Chin Dag-Phug-Pa
Dro-Way La-Ma Sö-Nam Gyal-Tsen Pal
She-Drub Chu-Wo Kün Dü Pal Den Par
Nam-Dag Dü-Tsiy Dam Zé Nye Chö Bül
Oṁ āḥ hūṁ

This offering of the pleasing samaya substance, pure amrita, is made
to Dragpukpa, who reached the ultimate siddhi one-pointedly,
Sonam Gyaltsen, the guru of all migrating beings,
and Paldenpa, in whom all streams of teachings and practices merged.
Oṁ āḥ hūṁ

མཐུ་སྟོབས་དབང་ཕྱུག་སེང་གེ་རྒྱལ་མཚན་ཞབས།།[4]
མཁན་ཆེན་བསོད་ནམས་རྒྱལ་བ་མཆོག་དབྱངས་དཔལ།།
ཡབ་རྗེ་འཇམ་དབྱངས་ནམ་མཁའ་རྒྱལ་མཚན་ལ།།
རྣམ་དག་བདུད་རྩིའི་དམ་རྫས་མཉེས་མཆོད་འབུལ།།
ཨོཾ་ཨཱཿ ཧཱུྃ།

Thu Tob Wang-Chug Sen-Ge Gyal-Tsen Shab
Khen-Chen Sö-Nam Gyal-Wa Chog Yang Pal
Yab Je Jam-Yang Nam-Kha Gyal-Tsen La
Nam-Dag Dü-Tsiy Dam Zé Nye Chö Bül
Oṁ āḥ hūṁ

This offering of the pleasing samaya substance, pure amrita, is made
to Senge Gyaltsen, the lord of power,
great abbot, glorious Sonam Gyalwa Chogyang,
and the esteemed father, Jamyany Namkhai Gyaltsen.
Oṁ āḥ hūṁ

མཁས་པའི་དབང་པོ་ཡེ་ཤེས་རྒྱལ་མཚན་ཞབས།།
རྒྱལ་བས་ལུང་བསྟན་དོར་ཆེན་རྡོ་རྗེ་འཆང་།།
འཁོར་ལོ་སྡོམ་པ་དཀོན་མཆོག་རྒྱལ་མཚན་ལ།།
རྣམ་དག་བདུད་རྩིའི་དམ་རྫས་མཉེས་མཆོད་འབུལ།།
ཨོཾ་ཨཱཿ ཧཱུྃ།

---

4 འདི་ནས་ཚིག་གསུམ་གསར་བསྣིགས། Three lines have been newly added after this.

Khe-Pay Wang-Po Ye-She Gyal-Tsen Shab
Gyal-We Lung-Ten Ngor-Chen Dor-Je Chang
Khor-Lo Dom-Pa Kon-Chog Gyal-Tsen La
Nam-Dag Dü-Tsiy Dam Zé Nye Chö Bül
Oṁ āḥ hūṁ

This offering of the pleasing samaya substance, pure amrita,
is made
to Yeshe Gyaltsen, lord of scholars,
Ngorchen Vajradhara, prophecied by the victor
and Chakrasamvara Konchog Gyaltsen.
Oṁ āḥ hūṁ

ཆོས་ཀྱི་རྒྱལ་པོ་བློ་གྲོས་རྒྱལ་མཚན་ཞབས།།
གྲུབ་པ་མཆོག་གི་དེད་དཔོན་རྡོ་རིང་བ།།
བསྟན་པའི་སྲོག་ཤིང་ཚར་ཆེན་རྡོ་རྗེ་འཆང་།།
རྣམ་དག་བདུད་རྩིའི་དམ་རྫས་མཉེས་མཆོད་འབུལ།།
ཨོཾ་ཨཱཿ ཧཱུྃ།

Chö-Kyi Gyal-Po Lo-Drö Gyal-Tsen Shab
Dub Pa Chog Gi De-Pon Do-Ring-Wa
Ten-Pay Sog Shing Tsar Chen Dor-Je Chang
Nam-Dag Dü-Tsiy Dam Zé Nye Chö Bül
Oṁ āḥ hūṁ

This offering of the pleasing samaya substance, pure amrita,
is made
to the Dharmaraja Lodroe Gyaltsen,

Doringpa, leader of supreme siddhi,
and Tsarchen Vajradhara, the pillar of the doctrine.
Oṁ āḥ hūṁ

ངེས་པ་ཐམས་ཅད་མཁྱེན་པ་མཁྱེན་བརྩེའི་ཞབས།།
ཐུགས་སྲས་མཁན་ཆེན་བསླབ་གསུམ་རྒྱལ་མཚན་དཔལ།།[5]
མཐུ་སྟོབས་དབང་ཕྱུག་བསོད་ནམས་ཆོས་འཕེལ་ལ།།
རྣམ་དག་བདུད་རྩིའི་དམ་རྫས་མཉེས་མཆོད་འབུལ།།
ཨོཾ་ཨཱཿ ཧཱུྃ།

Nge-Pa Tham-Ché Khyen-Pa Khyen-Tsey Shab
Thug Se Khen-Chen Lab Sum Gyal-Tsen Pal
Thu Tob Wang-Chug Sö-Nam Chö-Phel La
Nam-Dag Dü-Tsiy Dam Zé Nye Chö Bül
Oṁ āḥ hūṁ

This offering of the pleasing samaya substance, pure amrita,
is made
to the truly omniscient venerable Khyentse,
great abbot Lhapsum Gyaltsen, the heart son,
and Sonam Chophel, lord of power.
Oṁ āḥ hūṁ

---

5 ཚིག་རྐང་གཉིས་པོ་གསར་བསྒྲིགས། Two lines have been newly added after this.

ཁྱབ་བདག་བླ་མ་དབང་ཕྱུག་རབ་བརྟན་དཔལ།།
རིགས་ཀྱི་བདག་པོ་རྗེ་བཙུན་བཀའ་འགྱུར་བ།།
སྙན་བརྒྱུད་མངའ་བདག་མཁན་ཆེན་ཞ་ལུ་བར།།
རྣམ་དག་བདུད་རྩིའི་དམ་རྫས་མཉེས་མཆོད་འབུལ།།
ཨོཾ་ཨཱཿ ཧཱུྃ།

Khyab Dag La-Ma Wang-Chug Rab-Ten Pal
Rig Kyi Dag-Po Je-Tsün Kan-Gyur-Wa
Nyen-Gyü Nga Dag Khen-Chen Zha-Lu-Pa
Nam-Dag Dü-Tsiy Dam Zé Nye Chö Bül
Oṁ āḥ hūṁ

This offering of the pleasing samaya substance, pure amrita, is made
to glorious Wangchuk Rabten, the sovereign guru,
Jetsun Kangyurwa, lord of the lineage
and great abbot Zhalupa, holder of aural lineage.
Oṁ āḥ hūṁ

པཎ་ཆེན་དགེ་དབང་ཆོས་ཀྱི་གྲགས་པ་དང་།།
གྲུབ་པའི་རྣལ་འབྱོར་བུདྡྷ་རཏྣའི་ཞབས།།
སེམས་དཔའ་ཆེན་པོ་མཁྱེན་རབ་བསྟན་འཛིན་བཟང་།།
རྣམ་དག་བདུད་རྩིའི་དམ་རྫས་མཉེས་མཆོད་འབུལ།།
ཨོཾ་ཨཱཿ ཧཱུྃ།

Pan-Chen Nga-Wang Chö-Kyi Drak-Pa Dang
Be-Pay Nal-Jor Bu-Dha Rat-Nay Shab
Sem-Pa Chen-Po Khyen-Rab Ten-Zin Sang
Nam-Dag Dü-Tsiy Dam Zé Nye Chö Bül
Oṁ āḥ hūṁ

This offering of the pleasing samaya substance, pure amrita,
is made
to the mahapaṇḍita, Ngawang Choekyi Drakpa,
venerable Buddha Ratna, the hidden yogi,
and Khyenrab Tenzin, the great bodhisattva.
Oṁ āḥ hūṁ

སྔགས་འཆང་ཐམས་ཅད་མཁྱེན་པ་ཀུན་དགའི་མཚན།།
འཇམ་དཔལ་རྡོ་རྗེ་བསོད་ནམས་དབང་ཕྱུག་ཞབས།།
རིགས་ཀུན་ཁྱབ་བདག་མངྒའི་མཚན་ཅན་ལ།།
རྣམ་དག་བདུད་རྩིའི་དམ་རྫས་མཉེས་མཆོད་འབུལ།།
ཨོཾ་ཨཱཿ ཧཱུྃ།

Ngag Chang Tham-Ché Khyen-Pa Kün-Gay Tsen
Jam-Pal Dor-Je Sö-Nam Wang-Chug Shab
Rig Kün Khyab Dag Mang-Gay Tsen Chen La
Nam-Dag Dü-Tsiy Dam Zé Nye Chö Bül
Oṁ āḥ hūṁ

This offering of the pleasing samaya substance, pure amrita,
is made
to Kunga, the omniscient mantradhara,
venerable Sonam Wangchuk, the real Manjuvajra,
and Manga, the master of all lineages.
Oṁ āḥ hūṁ

དཀྱིལ་འཁོར་རྒྱ་མཚོའི་རིགས་བདག་རྡོ་རྗེ་འཆང་།།
ངུར་སྨིག་གར་གྱིས་རྣམ་རོལ་ཐམས་ཅད་མཁྱེན།།
མཁྱེན་རབ་བྱམས་པ་ངག་དབང་ལྷུན་གྲུབ་ཞབས།།
རྣམ་དག་བདུད་རྩིའི་དམ་རྫས་མཉེས་མཆོད་འབུལ།།
ཨོཾ་ཨཱཿ ཧཱུྃ།

Kyil-Khor Gya-Tsoy Rig Dag Dor-Je Chang
Ngur Mig Gar Gyi Nam Röl Tham-Ché Khyen
Khyen-Rab Jam-Pa Nga Wang Lhun-Drub Shab
Nam-Dag Dü-Tsiy Dam Zé Nye Chö Bül
Oṁ āḥ hūṁ

This offering of the pleasing samaya substance, pure amrita,
is made
to Vajradhara, master of the lineages of oceanic maṇḍalas,
the omniscient one manifesting with saffron robes,
venerable Khyenrab Jampa Ngawang Lhundrup.
Oṁ āḥ hūṁ

བླ་མ་གསུང་གི་ཐུགས་ལས་འཁྲུངས་པའི་སྲས།།
སྙན་བརྒྱུད་གདམས་པའི་མངའ་བདག་རྡོ་རྗེ་འཆང་།།
ངག་དབང་ཀུན་དགའ་ལྷུན་གྲུབ་མོར་ཆེན་ཞབས།།
རྣམ་དག་བདུད་རྩིའི་དམ་རྫས་མཉེས་མཆོད་འབུལ།།
ཨོཾ་ཨཱཿ ཧཱུྃ།

La-Ma Sung Gi Thug Lé Trung-Pay Se
Nyen-Gyü Dam-Pay Nga Dag Dor-Je Chang
Nga-Wang Kün-Ga Lhun-Drub Mor-Chen Shab
Nam-Dag Dü-Tsiy Dam Zé Nye Chö Bül
Oṁ āḥ hūṁ

This offering of the pleasing samaya substance, pure amrita,
is made
to the son born from the heart of the guru's speech,
Vajradhara, who owns the instructions of the aural lineage,
venerable Morchen Ngawang Kunga Lhundrup.
Oṁ āḥ hūṁ

སྙན་བརྒྱུད་གདམས་པའི་ཆུ་བོ་ཀུན་འདུས་པ།།
གསང་ཆེན་བསྟན་པའི་མངའ་བདག་རྡོ་རྗེ་སེམས།།
དྲིན་ཆེན་བླ་མ་ཀུན་དགའི་མཚན་ཅན་ལ།།
རྣམ་དག་བདུད་རྩིའི་དམ་རྫས་མཉེས་མཆོད་འབུལ།།
ཨོཾ་ཨཱཿ ཧཱུྃ།

Nyen-Gyü Dam-Pay Chu-Wo Kün Dü-Pa
Sang Chen Ten-Pay Nga Dag Dor-Je Sem
Drin-Chen La-Ma Kün-Gay Tsen-Chen La
Nam-Dag Dü-Tsiy Dam Zé Nye Chö Bül
Oṁ āḥ hūṁ

This offering of the pleasing samaya substance, pure amrita, is made
to whom all streams of instructions of the aural lineage merged,
Vajrasattva, the owner of the great secret teachings,
the kind guru, Kunga.
Oṁ āḥ hūṁ

ཁྱབ་བདག་བླ་མ་ཀུན་དགའ་བློ་གྲོས་དང་།།
གྲུབ་རིགས་གཙུག་རྒྱན་རིགས་བདག་ཐར་རྩེ་བ།།
བཀའ་དྲིན་མཉམ་མེད་ནམ་མཁའི་མཚན་ཅན་ལ།།
རྣམ་དག་བདུད་རྩིའི་དམ་རྫས་མཉེས་མཆོད་འབུལ།།
ཨོཾ་ཨཱཿ ཧཱུྃ།

Khyab Dag La-Ma Kün-Ga Lo-Drö Dang
Drub Rig Tsug Gyen Rig Dag Thar-Tse-Wa
Ka-Drin Nyam Me Nam-Khay Tsen-Chen La
Nam-Dag Dü-Tsiy Dam Zé Nye Chö Bül
Oṁ āḥ hūṁ

This offering of the pleasing samaya substance, pure amrita,
is made
to Kunga Lodroe, the sovereign guru,
Thartsewa, the master of the lineage, crown ornament of a
family of siddhas,
and Namkha, the peerlessly kind one.
Oṁ āḥ hūṁ

གཞན་ཡང་སྨིན་བྱེད་དབང་དང་གྲོལ་བྱེད་ལམ།།
ཟབ་མོའི་ལམ་གྱི་མན་ངག་སྟོན་མཛད་པ།།
དངོས་བརྒྱུད་དཔལ་ལྡན་བླ་མའི་ཚོགས་རྣམས་ལ།།
རྣམ་དག་བདུད་རྩིའི་དམ་རྫས་མཉེས་མཆོད་འབུལ།།
ཨོཾ་ཨཱཿཧཱུཾ།

Shen Yang Min-Je Wang Dang Dröl-Je Lam
Zab-Moy Lam Gyi Men Ngag Ton Zé-Pa
Ngö Gyü Pal-Den La-May Tsog Nam La
Nam-Dag Dü-Tsiy Dam Zé Nye Chö Bül
Oṁ āḥ hūṁ

This offering of the pleasing samaya substance, pure amrita,
is made
to the assembly of actual and lineage gurus,
who teach the ripening empowerments, the liberating path,
and the intimate instructions of the profound path.
Oṁ āḥ hūṁ

ཨོཾ་ཨོཾ་ཨོཾ་སརྦ་བུདྡྷ་ཌཱ་ཀི་ནཱི་ཡེ། བཛྲ་ཝརྞྞ་ནཱི་ཡེ།བཛྲ་བཻ་རོ་ཙ་ནཱི་ཡེ། ཧཱུྃ་ཧཱུྃ་ཧཱུྃ། ཕཊ་ཕཊ་ཕཊ་སྭཱ་ཧཱ།

Oṁ oṁ oṁ sarvabuddhaḍākinīye vajra varṇṇanīye vajra vairocanīye hūṁ hūṁ hūṁ phaṭ phaṭ phaṭ svāhā

མཁའ་ཁྱབ་ཆོས་ཀྱི་དབྱིངས་ལས་མ་གཡོས་ཀྱང་།།
སྣ་ཚོགས་སྤྲུལ་པས་འགྲོ་བའི་དོན་མཛད་མ།།
བདག་གི་ཡི་དམ་རྡོ་རྗེ་རྣལ་འབྱོར་མར།།
རྣམ་དག་བདུད་རྩིའི་དམ་རྫས་མཉེས་མཆོད་འབུལ།།
ཨོཾ་ཨཱཿཧཱུྃ།

Kha Khyab Chö-Kyi Ying Lé Ma Yö Kyang
Na Tsog Trül-Pé Dro-Way Don Zé-Ma
Dag Gi Yi-Dam Dor-Je Nal-Jor-Mar
Nam-Dag Dü-Tsiy Dam Zé Nye Chö Bül
Oṁ āḥ hūṁ

This offering of the pleasing samaya substance, pure amrita, is made
to my yidam, Vajrayoginī,
who performs the benefit of migrating beings with various emanations
while never leaving the dharmadhatū that pervades the space.
Oṁ āḥ hūṁ

གཞན་ཡང་གསང་སྔགས་བྱ་སྤྱོད་རྣལ་འབྱོར་རྒྱུད།།
རྣལ་འབྱོར་བླ་མེད་རྒྱུད་སྡེ་ཆེན་པོ་བཞི།།
རྗེས་འབྲེལ་ཡི་དམ་དཀྱིལ་འཁོར་ལྷ་ཚོགས་ལ།།
རྣམ་དག་བདུད་རྩིའི་དམ་རྫས་མཉེས་མཆོད་འབུལ།།
ཨོཾ་ཨཱཿ ཧཱུྃ། ཞེས་པས་མཆོད།

Zhen Yang Sang Ngag Ja Chö Nal-Jor Gyü
Nal-Jor La-Me Gyü De Chen-Po Shi
Je Drel Yi-Dam Kyil-Khor Lha Tsog La
Nam-Dag Dü-Tsiy Dam Zé Nye Chö Bül

Oṁ āḥ hūṁ

Thus make offering.

This offering of the pleasing samaya substance, pure amrita, is made
to the assembled deities of the maṇḍalas, the yidams associated
with the four major division of tantras of secret mantras,
Kriya, Charya, Yoga and Anuttarayoga.

Oṁ āḥ hūṁ

དེ་ནས་མཐེབ་སྲིན་གྱིས་རང་གི་ལྕེ་རྩེ་སྨིན་འཚམས་སྤྱི་གཙུག་ཏུ་བདུད་རྩིའི་ཐིག་ལེ་རེ་བྱ།
ཨོཾ་ཨཱཿ ཧཱུྃ། ཞེས་བརྗོད་པས་ཕུང་ཁམས་སྐྱེ་མཆེད་ལྷའི་ངོ་བོར་གསལ་བ་བདེ་བས་ཚོམས་པར་གྱུར་པར་
བསམ་ཞིང་། བདུད་རྩིའི་བར་ཕུད་གཏོར་མ་ལ་ཕུལ་ལ།

Next, place a drop of amrita on the tip of one's tongue, at the brow and on the crown with the thumb and ring finger. Imagine that the skandha, dhātu, and āyatana manifesting as the essence of deities are satisfied with bliss by saying:

Oṁ āḥ hūṁ

ཨོཾ་ཤྲཱི་མཧཱ་ཀཱ་ལཱ་ཡ།

དཔལ་མགོན་ལྷ་མཆོག་རྡོ་རྗེ་ནག་པོ་ཆེ།།

གུར་གྱི་མགོན་པོ་འདོད་ཁམས་དབང་ཕྱུག་མ།།

ལྕམ་དྲལ་བྲན་གཡོག་བཀའ་སྡོད་འཁོར་བཅས་ལ།།

རྣམ་དག་བདུད་རྩིའི་དམ་རྫས་མཉེས་མཆོད་འབུལ།།

ཨོཾ་ཨཱཿ ཧཱུྃ།

Oṁ shrī mahākālāya

Pal Gon Lha Chog Dor-Je Nag-Po Che

Gur Gyi Gon-Po Dö Kham Wang-Chug Ma

Cham Drel Den Yog Ka Dö Khor Ché La

Nam-Dag Dü-Tsiy Dam Zé Nye Chö Bül

Oṁ āḥ hūṁ

Oṁ shrī mahākālāya

This offering of the pleasing samaya substance, pure amrita, is made

to the glorious protector, the supreme deity,

Vajramahākālā Pañjaranatha, Kamadhatesvari

and the siblings with the retinue of servants and attendants.

Oṁ āḥ hūṁ

ཨོཾ་ཤྲཱི་ཀྲྀཥྞ་པཱ་ལ་ཙ་ཏུརྨུ་ཁཱ་ཡ།

མཐུ་སྟོབས་དབང་ཕྱུག་དཔལ་མགོན་ཞལ་བཞི་པ།།

ཡུམ་ཆེན་རྣམ་བཞི་ཞིང་སྐྱོང་འབྲུམ་སྟེ་དང་།།

དྲེགས་བྱེད་སྡེ་བརྒྱད་བཀའ་ཉན་འཁོར་ཚོགས་ལ།།
རྣམ་དག་བདུད་རྩིའི་དམ་རྫས་མཉེས་མཆོད་འབུལ།།
ཨོཾ་ཨཱཿཧཱུཾ།

Oṁ shrī dharmāpāla chaturmukhāya
Thu Tob Wang-Chug Pal Gon Shal Shi-Pa
Yum Chen Nam-Shi Shing Kyong Bum De Dang
Dreg Je De Gye Ka Nyen Khor Tsog La
Nam-Dag Dü-Tsiy Dam Zé Nye Chö Bül
Oṁ āḥ hūṁ

Oṁ shrī dharmāpāla chaturmukhāya
This offering of the pleasing samaya substance, pure amrita,
  is made
to the lord of power, the glorious protector Chaturmukhā
with his four great mothers, army of one hundred thousand
  Kṣetrapālas,
and retinue of obedient eight classes of arrogant ones.
Oṁ āḥ hūṁ

ཨོཾ་ཤྲཱི་རེ་མ་ཏི།
མི་འགྱུར་ལྷུན་གྲུབ་བདེ་ཆེན་ཆོས་དབྱིངས་ན།།
གྲངས་མེད་འཁའ་འགྲོའི་གཙོ་མོ་རབ་བརྟན་མ།།
ཀླུ་སྲིན་གདོང་སོགས་གྲངས་མེད་འཁོར་བཅས་ལ།།
རྣམ་དག་བདུད་རྩིའི་དམ་རྫས་མཉེས་མཆོད་འབུལ།།
ཨོཾ་ཨཱཿཧཱུཾ།

Oṁ shrī remati

Mi Gyur Lhun-Drub De-Chen Chö Ying Na

Dang Me Khan-Droy Tso-Mo Rab-Ten-Ma

Chu Sin Dong Sog Drang Me Khor Ché La

Nam-Dag Dü-Tsiy Dam Zé Nye Chö Bül

Oṁ āḥ hūṁ

Oṁ shrī remati

This offering of the pleasing samaya substance, pure amrita, is made

to the queen of countless ḍākinīs, Rabtenma

with a countless retinue such as Crocodile-face and so on,

in the unchanging and naturally perfect dharmadhatū of great bliss.

Oṁ āḥ hūṁ

ཨོཾ་བཻ་ཤྲཱ་ཝ་ཎཱ་ཡ།

བྱང་ཕྱོགས་རིན་ཆེན་མང་སྤྲུལ་རྣམ་ཐོས་སྲས།།

ཡབ་ཡུམ་བཙུན་མོ་སྲས་ཀྱི་ཚོགས་རྣམས་དང་།།

གནོད་སྦྱིན་ནོར་ལྷའི་འཁོར་ཚོགས་རྒྱ་མཚོ་ལ།།

རྣམ་དག་བདུད་རྩིའི་དམ་རྫས་མཉེས་མཆོད་འབུལ།།

ཨོཾ་ཨཱཿཧཱུྃ།

Oṁ vaishrāvanāya

Jang Chog Rin-Chen Mang Trül Nam Thö Se

Yab Yum Tsun-Mo Se Kyi Tsog Nam Dang

Nö Jin Nor Lhay Khor Tsog Gya-Tso La
Nam-Dag Dü-Tsiy Dam Zé Nye Chö Bül
Oṁ āḥ hūṁ

Oṁ vaishrāvanāya
This offering of the pleasing samaya substance, pure amrita,
is made
to Vaisravana who emanates many jewels in the north,
the assembly of the father and mother with the queen and son,
and the oceanic retinue of yaksha wealth gods.
Oṁ āḥ hūṁ

ཨོཾ་གྷྲི་རཱ་ཛ་གྷྲི་རཱ་ཛ་ཀུ་མ་ཀུ་མ་ཁུམ་ཐིས་སྭཱ་ཧཱ།
ཨོ་རྒྱན་ཡུལ་གྱི་ཞིང་སྐྱོང་གསང་ཆེན་གཉེར།།
མཐུ་སྟོབས་དབང་ཕྱུག་ནོར་སྐྱོང་དུར་ཁྲོད་བདག།
ཡབ་ཡུམ་བཀའ་ཉན་ཤ་ཟ་འབུམ་སྡེ་ལ།།
རྣམ་དག་བདུད་རྩིའི་དམ་རྫས་མཉེས་མཆོད་འབུལ།།
ཨོཾ་ཨཱཿཧཱུྃ།

Oṁ ghrirāja ghrirāja kuma kuma khumthis svāhā
O-Gyen Yül-Gyi Shing Kyong Sang Chen Nyer
Thu Tob Wang-Chug Nor Kyong Dur Trö Dag
Yab Yum Ka Nyen Sha Za Bum De La
Nam-Dag Dü-Tsiy Dam Zé Nye Chö Bül
Oṁ āḥ hūṁ

Oṁ ghrirāja ghrirāja kuma kuma khumthis svāhā

This offering of the pleasing samaya substance, pure amrita, is made
to the Kṣetrapala of the Oḍḍiyāna, caretaker of the great secret,
the lords of power, the wealth gaurdians, lords of the charnel ground,
father and mother with an army of a hundred thousand obedient pishācīs.

Oṁ āḥ hūṁ

ཆོས་འཁོར་སྐྱོང་ཞིང་བསྟན་པ་སྲུང་བ་དང་།།
སྒྲུབ་པོ་འཁོར་བཅས་སྐྱོང་བའི་དམ་ཅན་ཚོགས།།
བཀའ་སྡོད་ཆོས་སྐྱོང་སྲུང་མ་འཁོར་བཅས་ལ།།
རྣམ་དག་བདུད་རྩིའི་དམ་རྫས་མཉེས་མཆོད་འབུལ།།
ཨོཾ་ཨཱཿ ཧཱུྃ།

Chö-Khor Kyong Shing Ten-Pa Sung-Wa Dang
Drub Po Khor Ché Kyong-Way Dam-Chen Tsog
Ka Dö Chö Kyong Sung-Ma Khor Ché La
Nam-Dag Dü-Tsiy Dam Zé Nye Chö Bül

Oṁ āḥ hūṁ

This offering of the pleasing samaya substance, pure amrita, is made

to the assembly of samaya-bound protectors
with their retinue of obedient guardian Dharmapālas,
who guard the wheel of Dharma, protect the teachings, and
guard the practitioners together with their retinues.
Oṁ āḥ hūṁ

གནས་མཆོག་བཞི་དང་ཉེ་བའི་གནས་མཆོག་བཞི།།
མཁའ་སྤྱོད་ཐུགས་ཀྱི་འཁོར་ལོའི་བདག་ཉིད་ཅན།།
དཔའ་བོ་མཁའ་འགྲོའི་འཁོར་ཚོགས་མ་ལུས་ལ།།
རྣམ་དག་བདུད་རྩིའི་དམ་རྫས་མཉེས་མཆོད་འབུལ།།
ཨོཾ་ཨཱཿཧཱུྃ།

Ne Chog Shi Dang Nye-Way Ne Chog Shi
Kha-Chö Thug Kyi Khor-Loy Dag Nyi Chen
Pa-Wo Khan-Droy Khor Tsog Ma Lü la
Nam-Dag Dü-Tsiy Dam Zé Nye Chö Bül
Oṁ āḥ hūṁ

This offering of the pleasing samaya substance, pure amrita,
is made
to the assembly of the vīrās and ḍākinīs with their retinue,
the embodiments of the mind wheel of Khecarī,
in the four supreme Pīṭha, and the four supreme Upapīṭhas.
Oṁ āḥ hūṁ

ཞིང་མཆོག་གཉིས་དང་ཉེ་བའི་ཞིང་མཆོག་གཉིས།།
ཚནྡོ་ཧ་ཟུང་ཉེ་བའི་ཚནྡོ་གཉིས།།
ས་སྤྱོད་གསུང་གི་འཁོར་ལོའི་རང་བཞིན་གྱི།།
དཔའ་བོ་རྣལ་འབྱོར་མ་ཚོགས་ཐམས་ཅད་ལ།།
རྣམ་དག་བདུད་རྩིའི་དམ་རྫས་མཉེས་མཆོད་འབུལ།།
ཨོཾ་ཨཱཿཧཱུྃ།

Shing Chog Nyi Dang Nye-Way Shing Chog Nyi
Chan-Do Ha Zung Nye-Way Chan-Do Nyi
Sa Chö Sung Gi Khor-Loy Rang-Shin Gyi
Pa-Wo Nal-Jor-Ma Tsog Tham-Ché La
Nam-Dag Dü-Tsiy Dam Zé Nye Chö Bül
Oṁ āḥ hūṁ

This offering of the pleasing samaya substance, pure amrita, is made
to the assembly of the vīrās and ḍākinīs with their retinue,
the nature of the speech wheel of the Bhūmichara,
in the two supreme Kṣetras, the two supreme Upakṣetras,
the two Chandohas and the two Upachandohas.
Oṁ āḥ hūṁ

འདུ་བ་གཉིས་དང་ཉེ་བའི་འདུ་བ་གཉིས།།
དུར་ཁྲོད་ཟུང་དང་ཉེ་བའི་དུར་ཁྲོད་གཉིས།།

ས་འོག་ལེགས་སྤྱོད་སྐུ་འཁོར་ངོ་བོ་ཉིད།།
དཔའ་བོ་རྣལ་འབྱོར་སྤྲུལ་སྐུ་ཐམས་ཅད་ལ།།
རྣམ་དག་བདུད་རྩིའི་དམ་རྫས་མཉེས་མཆོད་འབུལ།།
ཨོཾ་ཨཱཿ ཧཱུྃ།

Du-Wa Nyi Dang Nye-Way Du-Wa Nyi
Dur Trö Zung Dang Nye-Way Dur Trö Nyi
Sa Og Leg-Chö Ku-Khor Ngo-Wo Nyi
Pa-Wo Nal-Jor Trül-Ku Tham-Ché La
Nam-Dag Dü-Tsiy Dam Zé Nye Chö Bül
Oṁ āḥ hūṁ

This offering of the pleasing samaya substance, pure amrita, is made
to the assembly of the vīrās and ḍākinīs with their retinue,
the nature of the body wheel of the Adhobhūmichara,
in the two Melāpakas, the two Upamelāpakas,
the two Shmashānas, and the two Upashmashānas.
Oṁ āḥ hūṁ

འཐུང་སྤྱོད་ཉེ་བའི་འཐུང་སྤྱོད་ཞེས་པ་སོགས།།
ངོ་མཚར་མཁའ་འགྲོའི་གནས་ན་བཞུགས་པ་ཡི།།
འགྲོ་བ་སེམས་ཅན་དོན་མཛད་མ་ཚོགས་ལ།།
རྣམ་དག་བདུད་རྩིའི་དམ་རྫས་མཉེས་མཆོད་འབུལ།།
ཨོཾ་ཨཱཿ ཧཱུྃ།

Thung Chö Nye-Way Thung Chö She-Pa Sog
Ngo Tsa Khan-Droy Ne Na Shug-Pa Yi
Dro-Wa Sem-Chen Don Zé Ma Tsog La
Nam-Dag Dü-Tsiy Dam Zé Nye Chö Bül
Oṁ āḥ hūṁ

This offering of the pleasing samaya substance, pure amrita,
is made
to all assembly of females benefiting all migrating beings
who live in the amazing land of ḍākinīs,
such as the Pīlavaṃ, Upapīlavaṃ, and so on.
Oṁ āḥ hūṁ

སོ་གཉིས་ཡུལ་དང་ཉི་ཤུ་རྩ་བཞིའི་གནས།།
དུར་ཁྲོད་ཆེན་པོ་བརྒྱད་ན་ལེགས་བཞུགས་པའི།།
བསམ་གྱིས་མི་ཁྱབ་དཔའ་བོ་རྣལ་འབྱོར་མར།།
རྣམ་དག་བདུད་རྩིའི་དམ་རྫས་མཉེས་མཆོད་འབུལ།།
ཨོཾ་ཨཱཿ ཧཱུྃ།

So Nyi Yül Dang Nyi Shu Tsa Shiy Ne
Dur Trö Chen-Po Gye Na Leg Shug Pay
Sam Gyi Mi Khyab Pa-Wo Nal-Jor-Mar
Nam-Dag Dü-Tsiy Dam Zé Nye Chö Bül
Oṁ āḥ hūṁ

This offering of the pleasing samaya substance, pure amrita,
is made
to the inconceivable vīrās and yoginīs

living well in the thirty-two lands,
the twenty-four places, and the eight charnel grounds.
Oṁ āḥ hūṁ

ཞིང་སྐྱོང་བཞི་བཅུ་རྩ་བརྒྱད་ཕོ་ཉའི་ཚོགས།།
གནས་རིགས་སྔགས་དང་ལས་ལས་སྐྱེས་པ་ཡི།།
གནས་གསུམ་རྡོ་རྗེ་མཁའ་འགྲོའི་ཚོགས་རྣམས་ལ།།
རྣམ་དག་བདུད་རྩིའི་དམ་རྫས་མཉེས་མཆོད་འབུལ།།
ཨོཾ་ཨཱཿཧཱུྃ།

Shing Kyong Shi Chu Tsa Gye Pho Nye Tsog
Ne Rig Ngag Dang Lé Lé Kye-Pa Yi
Ne Sum Dor-Je Khan-Droy Tsog Nam La
Nam-Dag Dü-Tsiy Dam Zé Nye Chö Bül
Oṁ āḥ hūṁ

This offering of the pleasing samaya substance, pure amrita,
is made
to the assembly of messengers of the forty-eight Kṣetrapala
and the assembly of Vajrayoginīs of the three places,
those born from place, race, mantra, and karma.
Oṁ āḥ hūṁ

གནོད་སྦྱིན་སྲིན་པོ་འབྱུང་པོ་ཡི་དྭགས་ཚོགས།།
ཤ་ཟ་སྨྱོ་བྱེད་བརྗེད་བྱེད་པོ་ཉའི་ཚོགས།།
འཕྲོག་མ་གྲུབ་པ་རིག་འཛིན་མ་ལུས་པར།།

རྣམ་དག་བདུད་རྩིའི་དམ་རྫས་མཉེས་མཆོད་འབུལ།།
ཨོཾ་ཨཱཿ ཧཱུྃ།

Nö-Jin Sin-Po Jung-Po Yi-Dag Tsog
Sha-Za Nyo-Je Je Je Pho Nyay Tsog
Trog-Ma Drup Pa Rig Zin Ma-Lü Par
Nam-Dag Dü-Tsiy Dam Zé Nye Chö Bül
Oṁ āḥ hūṁ

This offering of the pleasing samaya substance, pure amrita, is made
to the assembly of yakshas, rakshas, bhūtas, and pretas,
and the assembly of pishācīs, apasmāras, unmādas and dūtas,
hārītis, siddhas, and vidyādharas
Oṁ āḥ hūṁ

བོད་ཁམས་ཉེར་སྐྱོང་བརྟན་མ་བཅུ་གཉིས་པོ།།
བཀའ་ཉན་བྲན་གཡོག་གཞན་ཡང་གནས་ཡུལ་གྲོང་།།
གཞི་བདག་གཉུག་མར་གནས་པ་འཁོར་བཅས་ལ།།
རྣམ་དག་བདུད་རྩིའི་དམ་རྫས་མཉེས་མཆོད་འབུལ།།
ཨོཾ་ཨཱཿཧཱུྃ།

Bö-Kham Nyer Kyong Ten Ma Chu Nyi Po
Ka Nyen Dren Yog Shen Yang Ne Yül Dong
Shi Dag Nyug Mar Ne-Pa Khor Ché La
Nam-Dag Dü-Tsiy Dam Zé Nye Chö Bül
Oṁ āḥ hūṁ

This offering of the pleasing samaya substance, pure amrita, is made
to the twelve Tenma, the guardians of Tibetan region,
with their obedient servants and attendants, furthermore,
to the native local guardians with their retinue, residing permanently in the place, region, and town.
Oṁ āḥ hūṁ

འགྲོ་བ་རིགས་དྲུག་ལམ་རྒྱུད་རྣམ་པ་ལྔ།།
སྐྱེ་གནས་བཞིས་བསྡུས་ཁམས་གསུམ་སེམས་ཅན་རྣམས།།
ཚིམ་ཞིང་ཟག་མེད་བདེ་བས་རྒྱུད་གང་ནས།།
མྱུར་དུ་བླ་མེད་བྱང་ཆུབ་ཐོབ་གྱུར་ཅིག།
ཨོཾ་ཨཱཿཧཱུྃ། ཞེས་བརྗོད་ཅིང་།

Dro-Wa Rig Drug Lam Gyü Nam-Pa Nga
Kye-Ne Shi-Du Kham-Sum Sem-Chen Nam
Tsim Shing Zag Me De-We Gyü Gang Ne
Nyur-Du La-Me Jang-Chub Thob Gyur Chig
Oṁ āḥ hūṁ

To all migrating beings of the six classes, circling on the five paths
with four types of birth in the three realms,
may you be satisfied and your continuums filled with undefiled bliss;
may you swiftly attain the unsurpassed awakening.
Oṁ āḥ hūṁ

དེ་ནས་རང་གི་ལྗེ་རྩེས་བདུད་རྩི་མྱང་ལ། ཨོཾ་ཨཱཿ ཧཱུྃ། བརྗོད་པས་གསུང་རྡོ་རྗེ་མཉེས་པར་བསམ་ལ།

Then taste the amrita with one's tongue. Imagine the vajra of speech is pleased by reciting:

Oṁ āḥ hūṁ

ཡིད་འབྱུང་གི་མཆོད་པ་ནི།

ན་མོ་ཆོས་ཀྱི་དབྱིངས་ཀྱི་བྱིན་རླབས་དང་། སངས་རྒྱས་དང་བྱང་ཆུབ་སེམས་དཔའ་
ཐམས་ཅད་ཀྱི་ཐུགས་རྗེ་རྣམ་པར་དག་པའི་བྱིན་རླབས་དང་། གསང་སྔགས་དང་ཕྱག་
རྒྱའི་ནུས་མཐུ་དང་བདག་གི་མོས་པ་དང་། ཏིང་ངེ་འཛིན་དང་། སྨོན་ལམ་གྱི་དབང་གིས་
འཇིག་རྟེན་གྱི་ཁམས་ན་བདག་པོས་ཡོངས་སུ་མ་བཟུང་བའི་མཆོད་པའི་བྱེ་བྲག་ཇི་སྙེད་
ཡོད་པ་དང་། གཞན་ཡང་བྱང་ཆུབ་སེམས་དཔའ་ཀུན་ཏུ་བཟང་པོའི་རྣམ་པར་ཐར་པ་
ལས་བྱུང་བའི་མཆོད་སྤྲིན་གྱི་ཕུང་པོ་ལྟ་བུ་བསམ་གྱི་མི་ཁྱབ་པ་ཞིག་བླ་མ་དང་རྗེ་བཙུན་
རྡོ་རྗེ་རྣལ་འབྱོར་མའི་ལྷ་ཚོགས་སངས་རྒྱས་དང་བྱང་ཆུབ་སེམས་དཔའ་ཐམས་ཅད་ཀྱི་
སྤྱན་ལམ་དུ་འབྱུང་ཞིང་རྒྱས་པར་གྱུར་ཅིག།

Na-Mo Chö-Kyi Ying Kyi Jin-Lab Dang, Sang-Gyé Dang Jang-Chub Sem-Pa Tham-Ché Kyi Thug Je Nam-Par Dag-Pay Jin-Lab Dang, Sang Ngag Dang Chag-Gyay Nu Thu Dang Dag Gi Mo-Pa Dang, Ting Nge Zin Dang, Mon-Lam Gyi Wang Gi Jig-Ten Gyi Kham Na Dag-Pö Yong Su Ma Zung Way Chö-Pay Je-Drag Jin-Ye Yö-Pa Dang, Shen Yang Jang-Chub Sem-Pa Kün-Tu Zang-Poy Nam-Par Tar-Pa Lé Jung-Way Chö Trin Gyi Phung-Po Ta-Bu Sam Gyi Mi Khyab Pa Shig La-Ma Dang Je-Tsün Dor-Je Nal-Jor-May Lha Tsog Sang-Gyé Dang Jang-Chub Sem-Pa Tham-Ché Kyi Chen Lam Du Jung Shing Gye-Par Gyur Chig

The mentally produced offerings:

Namo, by the power of the blessings of the dharmadhātu and the blessings of the compassion of all buddhas and bodhisattvas, by the power of secret mantra, the mudra, one's devotion, samādhi, and aspirations, may as many offerings as there are in the universe that are not owned, and moreover, the inconceivable cloud-like offerings that come from the biography of Bodhisattva Samantabhadra, arise and increase in the sight of the guru, the assembly of deities of Jetsun Vajrayoginī, and all the buddhas and bodhisattvas.

ཨོཾ་སརྦ་བིཏ་པཱུ་ར་པཱུ་ར་སུ་ར་སུ་ར་ཨཱ་བརྟ་ཡ་ཨཱ་བརྟ་ཡ་ཧོཿ ན་མཿ ས་མནྟ་བུདྡྷཱ་ནཱཾ། ཨ་བྷི་སྨ་ར་ཡེ་སྥ་ར་ཎ་ཨི་མཱཾ་ག་ག་ན་ཁཾ་དྷརྨ་དྷཱ་ཏུ་ཨཱ་ཀཱ་ཤ་ས་མནྟ་མཱཾ། སརྦ་ཏ་ཐཱ་ག་ཏ་ཨ་པ་རི་ཤོ་དྷ་ཡེ་མཎྜ་ལེ་མ་མ་པྲ་ཎི་དྷི་པུཎྱེ་ཛྙཱ་ན་བཱ་ལེ་ན། སརྦ་ཏ་ཐཱ་ག་ཏ་བ་ལེནྡྷ་བནྡྷ་སྭཱ་སྠཾ་ན་བ་ལེན་ཙ་ཡེ་སྭཱ་ཧཱ། ཞེས་པས་ཕྱག་རྒྱ་དང་བཅས་པ་བྱ།

Oṁ sarvavita pūrapūra sura sura āvartaya āvartaya hoḥ Namaḥ samanta buddhānāṁ, abhismaraye spharaṇa imāṁ gagana khaṁ, dharmadhātu ākāsha samantamāṁ, sarva tathāgata aparishodhaye maṇḍale mamapraṇidhi punye jñāna bālena, sarva tathāgata balendha bhandha svāsthanaṁ balenacaye svāhā

Thus, perform with the mudra.

དེ་ནས་བསྟོད་པ་ནི། རོལ་ཆེན་བྱ་ཞིང་།

ཨོཾ་ན་མོ་བྷ་ག་ཝ་ཏི་བཛྲ་ཝཱ་རཱ་ཧཱི་ཝཾ་ཧུཾ་ཧཱུཾ་ཕཊ།

ཨོཾ་ན་མཿ ཨཱརྱ་ཨ་པ་རཱ་ཛི་ཏེ་ཏཻ་ལོ་ཀྱཱ་མ་ཏེ།མ་ཧཱ་བི་དྱེ་ཤྭ་རི་ཧུཾ་ཧཱུཾ་ཕཊ།

ཨོཾ་ན་མསྶརྦ་བྷཱུ་ཏ་བྷ་ཡཱ་ཝ་ཧེ་མ་ཧཱ་བཛྲེ་ཧུཾ་ཧཱུཾ་ཕཊ།

ཨོཾ་ན་མོ་བཛྲ་ཨཱ་ས་ནེ་ཨ་ཛི་ཏེ་ཨ་པ་རཱ་ཛི་ཏེ། བ་ཤྱཾ་ཀ་རི་ནེ་ཏྲ་བྷྲ་མ་ཎི་ཧུཾ་ཧཱུཾ་ཕཊ།

ཨོཾ་ན་མཿ བི་ཥ་ཎི་ཤོ་ཥ་ཎི། རོ་ཥ་ཎི། ཀྲོ་དྷི་ཀ་རཱ་ལི་ནི་ཧུཾ་ཧཱུཾ་ཕཊ།

ཨོཾ་ན་མསྟྲ་ས་ནི། མཱ་ར་ཎི། པྲ་བྷེ་ད་ནི། ཨ་པ་རཱ་ཛི་ཏེ་ཧུཾ་ཧཱུཾ་ཕཊ།

ཨོཾ་ན་མོ་བི་ཛ་ཡེ། ཛམྦྷ་ནི། སྟམྦྷ་ནི། མོ་ཧ་ནི་ཧུཾ་ཧཱུཾ་ཕཊ།

ཨོཾ་ན་མོ་བཛྲ་ཝཱ་རཱ་ཧི་མ་ཧཱ་ཡོ་གི་ནི་ཀཱ་མེ་ཤྭ་རི་ཁ་གེ་ཧུཾ་ཧཱུཾ་ཕཊ། ཞེས་བྱ་བ་དང་།

Next recite the praises with music:

Oṁ namo bhagavate vajravārāhī vaṁ huṁ hūṁ phaṭ

Oṁ namaḥ ārya aparājite trailokyamāte mahāvidyeśvari huṁ hūṁ phaṭ

Oṁ namas sarva bhūtabhayāvahe mahāvajre huṁ hūṁ phaṭ

Oṁ namo vajra āsane ajite aparājite vaśayaṁkarinetra bhrāmaṇi huṁ hūṁ phaṭ

Oṁ namaḥ viśaṇi śoṣaṇi roṣaṇi kṛodhikarālini huṁ hūṁ phaṭ

Oṁ namas trāsani māraṇi prabhedani aparājaye huṁ hūṁ phaṭ

Oṁ namo vijaye jambhani staṁbhani mohani huṁ hūṁ phaṭ

Oṁ namo vajravārāhī mahāyoginī kāmeśvarikhage huṁ hūṁ phaṭ

དཔལ་ལྡན་རྡོ་རྗེ་མཁའ་འགྲོ་མ།།
མཁའ་འགྲོ་མ་ཡི་འཁོར་ལོས་སྒྱུར།།

ཡེ་ཤེས་ལྔ་དང་སྐུ་གསུམ་བརྙེས།།
འགྲོ་བ་སྐྱོབ་ལ་ཕྱག་འཚལ་ལོ།།

Pal-Den Dor-Je Khan-Dro-Ma
Khan-Dro-Ma Yi Khor-Lo Gyur
Ye-She Nga Dang Ku Sum Nye
Dro-Wa Kyob La Chag Tsal Lo

The glorious Vajraḍākinī,
the empress of all ḍākinīs,
the one who has attained the five wisdoms and three kāyas,
I pay homage to the protector of migrating beings.

ཇི་སྙེད་རྡོ་རྗེ་མཁའ་འགྲོ་མ།།
ཀུན་ཏུ་རྟོག་པའི་འཆིང་གཅོད་ཅིང་།།
འཇིག་རྟེན་བྱ་བར་རབ་འཇུག་མ།།
དེ་སྙེད་རྣམས་ལ་ཕྱག་འཚལ་ལོ།།

Ji Nye Dor-Je Khan-Dro-Ma
Kün-Tu Tog-Pay Ching Chö Ching
Jig-Ten Ja-War Rab Jug Ma
De Nye Nam La Chag Tsal Lo

I pay homage to Vajraḍākinī,
who eliminates the bondage of all concepts,
those who attain
full engagement in the activities of the world.

ཞེས་ཤློ་ཀ་གཉིས་དང་སྟོད་པ་ལ་དགའ་ན་རྡོ་རྗེ་འཆང་ཀུན་དགའ་བཟང་པོས་མཛད་པའི་རྡོ་རྗེ་རྣལ་འབྱོར་མའི་བསྟོད་པ་ནི། རྡོ་རྗེ་དྲིལ་བུ་འཛིན་པས་ཚིགས་བཅད་རྣམས་ལ་གཡས་པའི་རྡོ་རྗེའི་ཕྱག་འཚལ་བའི་སྟང་ཀས་སྙིང་གར་བཟུང་ཞིང་། གཡོན་པས་དྲིལ་བུ་ཤློ་ཀ་རེ་རེའི་མཚམས་སུ་གསིལ་ལ།

Recite the above two verses and the praise of Vajrayoginī composed by Vajradhara Kunga Zangpo if one likes to elaborate. Holding the vajra and bell for all verses, the vajra is held in the right hand at the heart with the manner of a prostration. Ring the bell in between every verse with the left hand.

ཡེ་ཤེས་ཆེན་པོའི་མཛོད་འཛིན་ཆོས་ཀྱི་རྗེ།།
དཔལ་ལྡན་བླ་མའི་ཞབས་ལ་གུས་བཏུད་ནས།།
རྒྱལ་བའི་ཡུམ་གྱུར་རྡོ་རྗེ་རྣལ་འབྱོར་མ།།
དྭངས་བའི་སེམས་ཀྱིས་ཆུང་ཟད་བསྟོད་པར་བགྱི།།

Ye-She Chen-Poy Zö Zin Chö Kyi Je
Pal-Den La-May Shab La Gü Tu Ne
Gyal-Way Yum Gyur Dor-Je Nal-Jor-Ma
Dang-Way Sem Kyi Chung Zé Tö-Par Gyi

I bow with devotion to the feet of the glorious guru,
holder of treasury of great wisdom, the lord of Dharma.
With a pure mind, I shall offer a brief praise
to the mother of the victors, Vajrayoginī.

འདབ་བརྒྱ་ལྟེ་བར་ཉིན་མོར་བྱེད་པའི་དབུས།།
ཞལ་གཅིག་ཕྱག་གཉིས་འབར་བའི་སྤྱན་གསུམ་གཡོ།།

པདྨ་རཱ་ག་ལྟར་དམར་རྗེ་བཙུན་མ།།
མཁའ་སྤྱོད་ལོངས་སྤྱོད་རྫོགས་ལ་ཕྱག་འཚལ་ལོ།།

Dab Gya Te-War Nyin Mor Je-Pay Wü
Shal Chig Chag Nyi Bar-Way Chen Sum Yo
Pad-Ma Ra-Ga Tar Mar Je-Tsün-Ma
Kha-Chö Long-Chö Zog La Chag Tsal Lo

In the middle of a sun on the center of one hundred petalled lotus,
she has one face, two hands, and three rolling blazing eyes.
Jetsunma, red like a ruby,
I prostrate to the saṃbhoga[kāya] of Khecarī.

ཆགས་ཆེན་སྐྱེས་བུ་འདུལ་བར་བྱ་བའི་ཕྱིར།།
བརྟན་གཡོའི་བདག་པོ་ཧེ་རུ་ཀ་དཔལ་དང་།།
གཉིས་མེད་ལྷན་སྐྱེས་གར་གྱིས་རོལ་མཛད་མ།།
མཁའ་སྤྱོད་ཁ་སྦྱོར་ཆེ་ལ་ཕྱག་འཚལ་ལོ།།

Chag Chen Kye-Bu Dul-War Ja-Way Chir
Ten Yoy Dag-Po He-Ru-Ka Pal Dang
Nyi-Me Lhen Kye Gar Gyi Röl Zé Ma
Kha-Chö Kha-Jor Che La Chag Tsal Lo

In order to tame passionate people,
she displays the innate dance, non-dual with
Heruka, the lord of the animate and inanimate.
I prostrate to the great union of Khecarī.

ཉིད་ཐུགས་ཟག་པ་མེད་པའི་བདེ་བ་ཆེ།།
འགྱུར་མེད་དགའ་བ་རྒྱ་ནོམ་བླ་ན་མེད།།
རྒྱུན་མི་ཆད་པའི་བདེ་བའི་རོལ་གང་བ།།
མཁའ་སྤྱོད་བདེ་བ་ཆེ་ལ་ཕྱག་འཚལ་ལོ།།

Nyi Thug Zag-Pa Me-Pay De-Wa Che
Gyur-Me Ga-Wa Gya-Nom La Na Me
Gyun Mi Ché-Pay De-Way Röl Gang-Wa
Kha-Chö De-Wa Che La Chag Tsal Lo

The great bliss of the immaculate mind,
the unsurpassed sublime unchanging joy
filled with the taste of uninterrupted bliss,
I prostrate to the great bliss of Khecarī

རྣམ་དག་ཆོས་དབྱིངས་སྤྲོས་བྲལ་ནམ་མཁའི་དབྱིངས།།
མཐའ་ཡས་ཡོན་ཏན་མང་པོས་ཉེར་མཛེས་པའི།།
རྣམ་པ་ཀུན་གྱི་མཆོག་དང་རབ་ལྡན་མ།།
མཁའ་སྤྱོད་རང་བཞིན་མེད་ལ་ཕྱག་འཚལ་ལོ།།

Nam-Dag Chö-Ying Trö-Dral Nam-Khay Ying
Tha-Ye Yon-Ten Mang-Po Nyer Ze-Pay
Nam-Pa Kün Gyi Chog Dang Rab Den Ma
Kha-Chö Rang Shin Me La Chag Tsal Lo

The spacious expanse of the pure dharmadhatū free from
proliferation,
beautified with many limitless qualities,
supremely endowed with all aspects,
I prostrate to the Khecarī without inherent nature,

གང་གི་རང་བཞིན་རྣམ་པར་མི་རྟོག་ཀྱང་།།
ཐུགས་རྗེ་ཆེན་པོས་སེམས་ཅན་མ་ལུས་པར།།
ཡིད་བཞིན་ནོར་ལྟར་དགོས་འདོད་ཀུན་སྩོལ་མ།།
མཁའ་སྤྱོད་སྙིང་རྗེས་ཡོངས་གང་ལ་ཕྱག་འཚལ།།

Gang Gi Rang Shin Nam-Par Mi Tog Kyang
Thug-Je Chen-Po Sem-Chen Ma Lü Par
Yi Shin Nor Tar Gö Dö Kün Tsöl-Ma
Kha Chö Nying-Je Yong Gang La Chag Tsal

Without a concept of any nature,
to all sentient beings with her compassion,
she grants all needs and wants like a wish fulfilling gem.
I prostrate to compassion-filled Khecarī.

སྲིད་དང་ཞི་བའི་མཐའ་དང་བྲལ་བ་ཡི།།
མི་གནས་མྱ་ངན་འདས་པའི་ས་བརྙེས་ནས།།
རྒྱུན་ཆད་མེད་པར་འགྲོ་བའི་དོན་མཛད་མ།།
མཁའ་སྤྱོད་རྒྱུན་ཆད་མེད་ལ་ཕྱག་འཚལ་ལོ།།

Si Dang Shi-Way Tha Dang Dral-Wa Yi
Mi Ne Nya Ngen Dé-Pay Sa Nye Ne
Gyun Ché Me-Par Dro-Way Don Zé-Ma
Kha Chö Gyun Ché Me La Chag Tsal Lo

Free from the extremes of existence and peace,
having attained the stage of non-abiding nirvana,
she benefits sentient beings without interruption.
I prostrate to ceaseless Khecarī.

དམིགས་མེད་སྙིང་རྗེའི་གཞན་གྱི་དབང་བསྒྱུར་ནས།།
འཁོར་བ་ཇི་སྲིད་གནས་པ་དེ་སྲིད་དུ།།
མྱ་ངན་མི་འདའ་རྟག་པར་རབ་བཞུགས་མ།།
མཁའ་སྤྱོད་འགོགས་པ་མེད་ལ་ཕྱག་འཚལ་ལོ།།

Mig-Me Nying-Jey Shen Gyi Wang Gyur Ne
Khor-Wa Ji-Si Ne-Pa De Si Du
Nya Ngen Mi Da Tag-Par Rab Shug-Ma
Kha Chö Gog-Pa Me La Chag Tsal Lo

Having transformed others with objectless compassion
for however long samsara remains,
she always dwells without passing into nirvana.
I prostrate to endless Khecarī.

དབང་བཞིའི་དོན་ལྡན་བསྐྱེད་རིམ་ཟབ་མོའི་ལམ།།
ཐུན་བཞིར་བསྒོམ་ཞིང་གུས་པས་གསོལ་བཏབ་པས།།
སྐུ་བཞི་དབྱེར་མེད་ཟུང་འཇུག་རྡོ་རྗེའི་སྐུ།།
མཁའ་སྤྱོད་སྐུ་ཡི་བྱིན་གྱིས་བརླབ་ཏུ་གསོལ།།

Wang Shiy Don Den Kye-Rim Zab-Moy Lam
Thun Shir Gom Shing Gü-Pé Söl Tab Pe
Ku Shi Yer-Me Zung-Jug Dor-Jey Ku
Kha-Chö Ku Yi Jin Gyi Lab-Tu Söl

Through the profound path of the generation stage with the
meaning of four empowerments,
meditating and offering supplications devotedly in four
sessions,
please grant blessings with the body of Khecarī,
the vajrakāya of the inseparable union of the four kāyas

ཨོཾ་གསུམ་ལྡན་པའི་གསང་སྔགས་ཡི་གེའི་ཚོགས།།
དུས་གསུམ་ངག་དང་ཡིད་ཀྱིས་རབ་བཟླས་པས།།
སྲིད་གསུམ་སྒྲ་དབྱངས་རྣམ་སྤངས་བརྗོད་བྲལ་གསུངས།།
མཁའ་སྤྱོད་གསུང་གིས་བྱིན་གྱིས་བརླབ་ཏུ་གསོལ།།

Oṁ Sum Den-Pay Sang Ngag Yi-Gey Tsog
Dü Sum Ngag Dang Yi Kyi Rab De-Pe
Si Sum Da Yang Nam Pang Jö-Dral Sung
Kha-Chö Sung Gi Jin Gyi Lab-Tu Söl

By always verbally and mentally reciting the assembly
of the syllables of the secret mantra endowed with three *Oṁs*
in the three times,
please grant blessings with the speech of Khecarī,
the inexpressible speech free from the sounds and tones of the three realms.

བདེན་གཉིས་རྣམ་དག་རྫོགས་རིམ་དབུ་མའི་ལམ།།
སྒྲིབ་གཉིས་སྦྱང་ཕྱིར་བརྩོན་པས་ལེགས་བསྒོམས་པས།།
དོན་གཉིས་ལྷུན་གྲུབ་འགྱུར་མེད་བདེ་བའི་ཐུགས།།
མཁའ་སྤྱོད་ཐུགས་ཀྱིས་བྱིན་གྱིས་བརླབ་ཏུ་གསོལ།།

Den Nyi Nam-Dag Zog Rim Wu-May Lam
Dib Nyi Jang Chir Tsön-Pé Leg Gom-Pe
Don Nyi Lhun Drub Gyur-Me De-Way Thug
Kha-Chö Thug Kyi Jin Gyi Lab-Tu Söl

Through the path of the central channel, the completion stage of pure two truths,
diligently meditating in order to purify the two obscurations,
please grant blessings with the mind of Khecarī,
the mind of unchanging great bliss accomplishing two purposes effortlessly

དེ་ལྟར་བསྟོད་ཅིང་གསོལ་བ་བཏབ་པའི་མཐུས།།
ཉིད་ཐུགས་བརྩེ་བ་ཆེན་པོས་རྗེས་བཟུང་ནས།།
ཚེ་འདི་ཉིད་དམ་བར་དོ་ལ་སོགས་པར།།
མཁའ་སྤྱོད་ཆེན་མོའི་གོ་འཕང་ཐོབ་པར་ཤོག། ཅེས་པས་བསྟོད།

De-Tar Tö Ching Söl-Wa Tab Pay Thü
Nyi Thug Tse-Wa Chen-Po Je Zung Ne
Tse Di Nyi Dam Bar-Do La Sog Par
Kha-Chö Chen-Moy Go-Phang Thop-Par Shog

Taken care by her great compassionate mind
through the power of such praise and supplication,
may the stage of great Khecarī be attained
either in this life, the bardo, and so on.

The Vase Sādhana

དེ་ནས་བུམ་པ་བསྒྲུབ་པ་ནི།

ཨོཾ་སུམྦྷ་ནི་སུམྦྷ་ཧུྃ་ཧཱུྃ་ཕཊ།
ཨོཾ་གྲྀཧྞ་གྲྀཧྞ་ཧུྃ་ཧཱུྃ་ཕཊ།
ཨོཾ་གྲྀཧྞ་པ་ཡ་གྲྀཧྞ་པ་ཡ་ཧུྃ་ཧཱུྃ་ཕཊ།
ཨོཾ་ཨཱ་ན་ཡ་ཧོཿ བྷ་ག་ཝཱན་བིདྱ་རཱ་ཛ་ཧུྃ་ཧཱུྃ་ཕཊ། ཀྱིས་བསང་།

Cleanse with:
Oṁ sumbha nisumbha huṁ hūṁ phaṭ
Oṁ grihaṇa grihaṇa huṁ hūṁ phaṭ
Oṁ grihaṇapaya grihaṇapaya huṁ hūṁ phaṭ
Oṁ ānayaho bhagavān vidyārāja huṁ hūṁ phaṭ

ཨོཾ་སྭ་བྷཱ་ཝ་ཤུདྡྷཿསརྦ་དྷརྨཱཿ སྭ་བྷཱ་ཝ་ཤུདྡྷོ྅ ཧཾ། གིས་ སྦྱང་།

Purify with:
Oṁ svabhāva shuddhaḥ sarva dharmāḥ svabhāva shuddho' haṁ

སྟོང་པའི་ངང་ལས་པཾ་ལས་པདྨ་དང་ཨ་ལས་ཟླ་བའི་སྟེང་དུ་ཧཱུྃ་ལས་རིན་པོ་ཆེའི་བུམ་པ་ཡངས་ཤིང་རྒྱ་ཆེ་བ། ཞབས་ཞུམ་པ། ལྟོ་བ་ལྡིར་བ། མགྲིན་པ་ཕྲ་བ། ཁ་གཡེལ་བ། མཆུ་འཕྱང་བ། ལྷའི་གོས་ཀྱི་མགུལ་པ་དཀྲིས་པ། དཔག་བསམ་གྱི་ཤིང་གི་ཁ་བརྒྱན་པ། ནང་ཆུ་དང་བཅུད་ཐམས་ཅད་ཀྱིས་ཡོངས་སུ་གང་བའི་བུམ་པའི་ནང་དུ། ཨེ་ཨེ་ལས་ཆོས་འབྱུང་དམར་པོ་གྲུ་གསུམ་ཉིས་བརྩེགས་ཀྱི་ནང་དུ་ཟླ་བའི་དཀྱིལ་འཁོར་གྱི་དབུས་སུ་བཾ་ཡིག་དམར་པོའི་མཐར་གཡོན་བསྐོར་དུ། ཨོཾ་ཨོཾ་ཨོཾ་སརྦ་བུདྡྷ་ཌཱ་ཀི་ནཱི་ཡེ་

བཛྲ་ཝརྞ་ནཱི་ཡེ། བཛྲ་བཻ་རོ་ཙ་ནཱི་ཡེ། ཧཱུྃ་ཧཱུྃ་ཧཱུྃ། ཕཊ་ཕཊ་ཕཊ་སྭཱ་ཧཱ། ཞེས་པའི་སྔགས་ཕྲེང་ཁ་དོག་དམར་པོས་བསྐོར་བ་ལས་འོད་ཟེར་འཕྲོས། འཕགས་པ་མཆོད། སེམས་ཅན་གྱི་དོན་བྱས། ཚུར་འདུས་ཡིག་འབྲུ་རྣམས་ལ་ཐིམ་པ་ཡོངས་སུ་གྱུར་པ་ལས་རྗེ་བཙུན་རྡོ་རྗེ་རྣལ་འབྱོར་མའི་སྐུར་གྱུར་པ་ནི།

Tong-Pay Ngang Lé Paṁ Lé Pad-Ma Dang Ah Lé Da-Way Teng Du Bhruṁ Lé Rin-Po-Chey Bum-Pa Yang Shing Gya-Che-Wa, Shab Shum Pa, To-Wa Dir-Wa, Drin-Pa Tra-Wa, Kha Yel-Wa, Chu Chang-Wa, Lhay Gö Kyi Gul-Pa Tri-Pa, Pag-Sam Gyi Shing Gi Kha Gyen-Pa, Nang Chu Dang Chü Tham-Ché Kyi Yong Su Gang-Way Bum-Pay Nang Du, E E Lé Chö-Jung Mar-Po Tu Sum Nyi Tseg Kyi Nang Du Da-Way Kyil-Khor Gyi Wü-Su Vaṁ Yig Mar-Poy Thar Yön Kor-Du, Oṁ oṁ oṁ sarvabuddhaḍākinīye vajra varṇṇanīye vajra vairocanīye hūṁ hūṁ hūṁ phaṭ phaṭ phaṭ svāhā, She-Pay Ngag Treng Kha-Dog Mar-Po Kor-Wa Lé Ö-Zer Trö, Phag-Pa Chö, Sem-Chen Gyi Don Je, Tsur Dü Yig Tru Nam La Thim-Pa Yong Su Gyur-Pa Lé Je-Tsün Dor-Je Nal-Jor-May Kur Gyur Pa Ni

From the state of emptiness, a *Paṁ* (པཾ) arises and turns into a lotus; from *Ah* (ཨ) arises a moon. Upon this is a *Bhruṁ* (བྷྲཱུྃ); from which arises a precious vase, vast and wide, with narrow base, round belly, and wide mouth. Its long neck is thin and draped with a divine cloth. It has a mouth ornament of a wish-fulfilling tree. It is totally filled with water and all essences. Inside of this vase, from *E E* (ཨེ ཨེ) arises a doubled dharmakara. Inside that, a moon maṇḍala arises from *Ah* (ཨ). In the center of which, there is a red *Vaṁ* (བཾ) surrounded by the red mantra garland circling to the left:

Oṁ oṁ oṁ sarvabuddhaḍākinīye vajra varnanīye vajra vairocanīye hūṁ hūṁ hūṁ phaṭ phaṭ phaṭ svāhā.

Light shines from the mantra rosary, making offerings to the nobles, benefiting all sentient beings, and then returning and absorbing into the syllables. From the complete transformation of that, the syllables turn into Vajrayoginī.

སྣ་ཚོགས་པདྨ་དང་ཉི་མའི་གདན་ལ་ཞབས་གཡས་བརྐྱང་པས་དུས་མཚན་མ་དམར་མོའི་ནུ་མའི་སྟེང་ནས་མནན་པ། གཡོན་བསྐུམ་པས་འཇིགས་བྱེད་ནག་པོའི་མགོ་བོ་རྒྱབ་ཏུ་བལྟབས་ནས་མནན་པ། སྐུ་མདོག་དམར་མོ་བསྐལ་པའི་མེ་ལྟ་བུའི་གཟི་བརྗིད་ཅན། ཞལ་གཅིག་ཕྱག་གཉིས་སྤྱན་གསུམ་དག་པ་མཁའ་སྤྱོད་དུ་གཟིགས་པ། ཕྱག་གཡས་པས་རྡོ་རྗེས་མཚན་པའི་གྲི་གུག་ཐུར་དུ་བརྐྱང་ནས་འཛིན་པ། གཡོན་པས་ཐོད་པ་ཁྲག་གིས་གང་བ་སྟེང་ཕྱོགས་སུ་བཟུང་ནས་ཞལ་ཕྱིན་དུ་ཕྱོགས་པས་གསོལ་བ། ཕྲག་པ་གཡོན་པར་རྡོ་རྗེས་མཚན་པའི་ཁ་ཊྭཱཾ་ག་ལ་ཌཱ་མ་རུ་དང་། དྲིལ་བུ་དང་འཕན་རྩེ་གསུམ་པ་འཕྱང་བཞིན་པ་བསྣམས་པ། དབུ་སྐྲ་ནག་པོ་སིལ་བུར་གྲོལ་པས་སྐུ་སྨད་ཡན་ཆད་ཁེབས་པ། །ལང་ཚོ་དར་ལ་བབ་ཅིང་འདོད་པའི་ནུ་འབུར་རྒྱས་པ། བདེ་བ་བསྐྱེད་པའི་ཉམས་ཅན་མི་མགོ་སྐམ་པོ་ལྔའི་དབུ་རྒྱན་དང་། སྐམ་པོ་ལྔ་བཅུའི་དོ་ཤལ་ཅན། གཅེར་བུ་ཕྱག་རྒྱ་ལྔས་བརྒྱན་པ། ཡེ་ཤེས་ཀྱི་མེ་འབར་བའི་དབུས་ན་བཞུགས་པའོ།

Na Tsog Pad-Ma Dang Nyi-May Den La Shab Yé Kyang-Pé Dü-Tsen-Ma Mar-Poy Nu-May Teng Ne Nen-Pa, Yön Kum-Pé Jig-Je Nag-Poy Go-Wo Gyab Tu Tab Ne Nen-Pa, Ku Dog Mar-Mo Kal-Pay Me Ta-Bui Zi Ji Chen, Shal Chig Chag Nyi Chen Sum Dag-Pa Kha-Chö Du Zig-Pa, Chag Yé-Pé Dor-Jé Tsen-Pay Tri Gug Thur Du Kyang Ne Zin-Pa, Yön-Pé Thö-Pa Trag Gi Gang-Wa Teng Chog Su Zung Ne

Shal Gyen Du Chog-Pé Söl-Wa, Tag-Pa Yön-Par Dor-Jé Tsen-Pay Kha-Tam-Ga La Da-Ma-Ru Dang, Dril-Bu Dang Phen-Tse Sum-Pa Chang Shin-Pa Nam-Pa, Wu-Tra Nag-Po Sil Bur Gyur-Pé Ku Ke Yen-Ché Kheb Pa, Lang Tso Dar La Bab Ching Dö-Pay Nu-Bur Gye-Pa, De-Wa Kye-Pay Nyam Chen Mi Go Kam-Po Ngay Wu-Gyen Dang, Kam-Po Nga Chui Do Shal Chen, Cher-Bu Chag-Gya Nge Gyen-Pa, Ye-She Kyi Me Bar-Way Wü-Na Shug-Pa'o

She stands on a multicolored lotus and sun seat. Her extended right leg presses down on red Kālarātri's breasts; her contracted left leg presses down on black Bhairava's head which is bent backwards. She is red in color, brilliant as the fire at the end of the eon. She has one face, two hands, and three eyes which gaze into the Khecarī realm. Her right hand extends downwards holding a curved knife marked with a vajra. Her left hand holds aloft a skull filled with blood from which she drinks with her upturned face. On her left shoulder is a khaṭvāṅga staff marked with a vajra, from which hang a damaru, a bell, and three banners. Her black hair is loose and falls to her waist. She has reached the fullness of youth, her breasts swelling with passion. She has an expression that generates bliss. She has a diadem of five dried human heads and a necklace of fifty dried ones. She is naked, adorned with five bone ornaments. She stands in the center of the blazing fire of wisdom.

དེ་ནས་འབར་བའི་ཕྱག་རྒྱ་སྨིན་མཚམས་སུ་གཡོན་བསྐོར་དུ་ལན་གསུམ་བསྐོར་ཞིང་དག་ཏུ།
ཕཻཾ།

Rotate the blazing mudra in the center of the forehead three times and recite:

Phaiṁ

རང་གི་ཐུགས་ཀའི་བཾ་ཡིག་ལས་འོད་ཟེར་འཕྲོས་པས་འོག་མིན་ནས་རྗེ་བཙུན་རྡོ་རྗེ་རྣལ་འབྱོར་མ་ལ་སངས་རྒྱས་དང་བྱང་ཆུབ་སེམས་དཔའ་དཔའ་བོ་དང་རྣལ་འབྱོར་མའི་ཚོགས་དཔག་ཏུ་མེད་པས་བསྐོར་བ་ཨོཾ་བཛྲ་ས་མ་ཛཿ སྤྱན་དྲངས།

Rang Gi Tuk Kay Vaṁ Yig Lé Ö-Zer Trö Pé, Og-Min Ne Je-Tsün Dor-Je Nal-Jor-Ma La Sang-Gyé Jang-Chup Sem-Pa Pa-Wo Dang Nal-Jor-May Tsog Pak Tu Me Pé Kor-Wa, Oṁ vajra samājaḥ

Light rays shining from the *Vaṁ* (བཾ) syllable within one's heart summon Jetsun Vajrayoginī from the realm of Akanishta, surrounded by an assembly of immeasurable buddhas, bodhisattvas, heroes, and yoginīs, *Oṁ vajra samājaḥ.*

ཛཿ ཧཱུྃ་བཾ་ཧོཿ གཉིས་སུ་མེད་པར་ཐིམ། པད་ཀོར་གྱི་མཐར་འཁྱུད་པའི་ཕྱག་རྒྱ་བཅས་ལ།
ཨོཾ་ཡོ་ག་ཤུདྡྷཿ སརྦ་དྷརྨཱཿ ཡོ་ག་ཤུདྡྷོ྅ ཧཾ།

With *Jaḥ hūṁ vaṁ hoḥ*, they are absorbed nondually.

At the end of lotus rolls, make the mudra of embrace with:
Oṁ yogaśuddhaḥ sarva dharmāḥ yogaśuddho'haṁ

དེའི་གནས་རྣམས་སུ་ཟླ་བའི་དཀྱིལ་འཁོར་གྱི་སྟེང་དུ། ལྟེ་བར་ཨོཾ་བཾ་དམར་མོ་རྡོ་རྗེ་ཕག་མོ། སྙིང་གར་ཧཾ་ཡོཾ་སྔོན་མོ་གཤིན་རྗེ་མ། ཁར་ཧྲིཾ་མོཾ་དཀར་མོ་རྨོངས་བྱེད་མ། དཔྲལ་བར་ཧྲིཾ་ཧྲིཾ་སེར་མོ་སྐྱོད་བྱེད་མ། སྤྱི་གཙུག་ཏུ་ཧཱུྃ་ཧཱུྃ་ལྗང་གུ་སྐྲག་བྱེད་མ། ཡན་ལག་ཐམས་ཅད་ལ་ཕཊ་ཕཊ་དུད་ཁ་ཙཎྜི་ཀའི་ངོ་བོ་གྱུར།

Dey Ne Nam Su Da-Way Kyil-Khor Gyi Teng Du, Te-War Oṁ Vaṁ Mar-Mo Dor-Je Phag-Mo, Nying Gar Haṁ Yoṁ Ngon-Mo Shin-Je-Ma, Khar Hriṁ Moṁ Kar-Mo Mong-Je-Ma, Tel-War Hriṁ Hriṁ Ser-Mo Kyo-Je-Ma, Chi Tsug Tu Hūṁ Hūṁ Jang Khu Tag-Je-Ma, Yen-Lag Tham-Ché La Phaṭ Phaṭ Dü-Kha Chan-Di-Kay Ngo-Wo Gyur

On top of moon discs at these locations on one's body are:

red *Oṁ Vaṁ* (ཨོྃ་བྃ) on the navel,

the essence of Vārāhī;

blue *Haṁ Yoṁ* (ཧྃ་ཡོྃ) on the heart,

the essence of Yāminī;

white *Hriṁ Moṁ* (ཧྲིྃ་མོྃ) on the mouth,

the essence of Mohinī;

yellow *Hriṁ Hriṁ* (ཧྲིྃ་ཧྲིྃ) on the forehead,

the essence of Saṁcālinī;

green *Hūṁ Hūṁ* (ཧཱུྃ་ཧཱུྃ) on the crown,

the essence of Saṁtrāsinī;

smoky *Phaṭ Phaṭ* (ཕཊ྄་ཕཊ྄) on all the limbs,

the essence of Caṇḍikā.

སླར་ཡང་རང་གི་ཐུགས་ཀ་ནས་འོད་ཟེར་འཕྲོས་པས། དབང་གི་ལྷ་དཔལ་འཁོར་ལོ་བདེ་མཆོག་ལྷ་དྲུག་ཅུ་རྩ་གཉིས་ཀྱི་དཀྱིལ་འཁོར་མདུན་གྱི་ནམ་མཁར་ཨོྃ་བཛྲ་ས་མ་ཛཿ ཞེས་པས་སྤྱན་དྲངས།

Lar Yang Rang Gi Thug Ka Ne Ö-Zer Trö-Pe, Wang Gi Lha Pal Khor-Lo De-Chog Lha Drug Chu Tsa Nyi Kyi Kyil-Khor Dün Gyi Nam-Khar, Oṁ vajra samājaḥ

Once again, light rays shining from one's heart invite the empowerment deities, the sixty-two deities of Shrī Chakrasamvara maṇḍala into the sky in front.

Thus invite with:
Oṁ vajra samājaḥ

དེ་བཞིན་གཤེགས་པ་ཐམས་ཅད་ཀྱིས་འདི་ལ་མངོན་པར་དབང་བསྐུར་བ་སྩལ་དུ་གསོལ། ཞེས་གསོལ་བ་བཏབ་པས།

De-Shin Sheg-Pa Tham-Ché Kyi Di La Ngön-Par Wang Kur-Wa Tsal Du Söl

Then, recite the supplication:
"May all the tathāgatas bestow the empowerment here!"

དབང་གི་ལྷ་རྣམས་ཀྱིས།
ཇི་ལྟར་བལྟམས་པ་ཙམ་གྱིས་ནི།
ལྷ་རྣམས་ཀྱིས་ནི་ཁྲུས་གསོལ་ལྟར།
ལྷ་ཡི་ཆུ་ནི་དག་པ་ཡིས།
དེ་བཞིན་བདག་གིས་དབང་བསྐུར་རོ།

Ji Tar Tam-Pa Tsam Gyi Ni,
Lha Nam Kyi Ni Tru Söl Tar,

Lha Yi Chu Ni Dag-Pa Yi
De-Shin Dag Gi Wang Kur Ro

The empowerment deities reply:
Just as he [the Buddha] was washed by the gods
at the time of his birth,
likewise, we will bestow the empowerment
with pure divine water.

ཨོཾ་སརྦ་ཏ་ཐཱ་ག་ཏ་ཨ་བྷི་ཥེ་ཀ་ཏ་ས་མ་ཡ་ཤྲཱི་ཡེ་ཧཱུྃ།

Oṁ sarvatathāgata abhiṣekata samaya shrīye hūṁ

ཞེས་གསུང་ཞིང་བུམ་ཆུས་སྤྱི་བོ་ནས་དབང་བསྐུར། སྐུ་གང་དྲི་མ་དག ཆུའི་ལྷག་མ་
ཡར་ལུད་པ་ལས་རྣམ་པར་སྣང་མཛད་ཀྱིས་དབུར་བརྒྱན།

She Sung-Shing Bum-Chü Chi-Wo Ne Wang-Kur, Ku-Gang Di-Ma-Thag, Chui Lhag-Ma Yar Lu-Pa Lé Nam-Par Nang-Zé Kyi Wur-Gyen

While speaking, those deities confer the empowerment on her crown with the water from the vase, filling her body, and purifying the taints. From the overflow of the excess water, her head is adorned with Vairocana.

ཨོཾ་སརྦ་ཏ་ཐཱ་ག་ཏ་བཛྲ་ཡོ་གི་ནཱི་ས་པ་རི་ཝཱ་ར་ཨརྒྷཾ་པྲ་ཏཱིཙྪ་པཱུ་ཛ་མེ་གྷ་ས་མུ་དྲ་སྥ་ར་ཎ་
ས་མ་ཡེ་ཨཿ ཧཱུྃ།

Oṁ sarvatathāgata vajrayoginī saparivāra arghaṁ praticcha pūja megha samudra spharaṇa samaye āḥ hūṁ

ཨོཾ་སརྦ་ཏ་ཐཱ་ག་ཏ་བཛྲ་ཡོ་གི་ནཱི་ས་པ་རི་ཝཱ་ར་པཱདྱཾ་པྲ་ཏཱིཙྪ་པཱུ་ཛ་མེ་གྷ་ས་མུ་དྲ་སྥ་ར་ཎ་ས་མ་ཡེ་ཨཱཿ ཧཱུྃ།

Oṁ sarvatathāgata vajrayoginī saparivāra pādyaṁ praticcha pūja megha samudra spharaṇa samaye āḥ hūṁ

ཨོཾ་སརྦ་ཏ་ཐཱ་ག་ཏ་བཛྲ་ཡོ་གི་ནཱི་ས་པ་རི་ཝཱ་ར་པུཥྤེ་པྲ་ཏཱིཙྪ་པཱུ་ཛ་མེ་གྷ་ས་མུ་དྲ་སྥ་ར་ཎ་ས་མ་ཡེ་ཨཱཿ ཧཱུྃ།

Oṁ sarvatathāgata vajrayoginī saparivāra puṣpe praticcha pūja megha samudra spharaṇa samaye āḥ hūṁ

ཨོཾ་སརྦ་ཏ་ཐཱ་ག་ཏ་བཛྲ་ཡོ་གི་ནཱི་ས་པ་རི་ཝཱ་ར་དྷཱུ་པེ་པྲ་ཏཱིཙྪ་པཱུ་ཛ་མེ་གྷ་ས་མུ་དྲ་སྥ་ར་ཎ་ས་མ་ཡེ་ཨཱཿ ཧཱུྃ།

Oṁ sarvatathāgata vajrayoginī saparivāra dhūpe praticcha pūja megha samudra spharaṇa samaye āḥ hūṁ

ཨོཾ་སརྦ་ཏ་ཐཱ་ག་ཏ་བཛྲ་ཡོ་གི་ནཱི་ས་པ་རི་ཝཱ་ར་ཨཱ་ལོ་ཀེ་པྲ་ཏཱིཙྪ་པཱུ་ཛ་མེ་གྷ་ས་མུ་དྲ་སྥ་ར་ཎ་ས་མ་ཡེ་ཨཱཿ ཧཱུྃ།

Oṁ sarvatathāgata vajrayoginī saparivāra āloke praticcha pūja megha samudra spharaṇa samaye āḥ hūṁ

ཨོཾ་སརྦ་ཏ་ཐཱ་ག་ཏ་བཛྲ་ཡོ་གི་ནཱི་ས་པ་རི་ཝཱ་ར་གནྡྷེ་པྲ་ཏཱིཙྪ་པཱུ་ཛ་མེ་གྷ་ས་མུ་དྲ་སྥ་ར་ཎ་ས་མ་ཡེ་ཨཱཿ ཧཱུྃ།

Oṁ sarvatathāgata vajrayoginī saparivāra ghande praticcha pūja megha samudra spharaṇa samaye āḥ hūṁ

ཨོཾ་སརྦ་ཏ་ཐཱ་ག་ཏ་བཛྲ་ཡོ་གི་ནཱི་ས་པ་རི་ཝཱ་ར་ནཻ་ཝི་དྱེ་པྲ་ཏཱི་ཙྪ་པཱུ་ཛ་མེ་གྷ་ས་མུ་དྲ་སྥ་ར་ཎ་ས་མ་ཡེ་ཨཱཿ ཧཱུྃ།

Oṁ sarvatathāgata vajrayoginī saparivāra naividye praticcha pūja megha samudra spharaṇa samaye āḥ hūṁ

ཨོཾ་སརྦ་ཏ་ཐཱ་ག་ཏ་བཛྲ་ཡོ་གི་ནཱི་ས་པ་རི་ཝཱ་ར་ཤབྡ་པྲ་ཏཱི་ཙྪ་པཱུ་ཛ་མེ་གྷ་ས་མུ་དྲ་སྥ་ར་ཎ་ས་མ་ཡེ་ཨཱཿ ཧཱུྃ།

Oṁ sarvatathāgata vajrayoginī saparivāra shabda praticcha pūja megha samudra spharaṇa samaye āḥ hūṁ

ཞེས་རོལ་མོ་དང་བཅས་པས་མཆོད།
ཨོཾ་བཛྲ་གྷཎྜེ་ར་ཎི་ཏ། པྲ་ར་ཎི་ཏ། སཾ་པྲ་ར་ཎི་ཏ། སརྦ་བུདྡྷ་ཀྵེ་ཏྲ་པྲ་ཙ་ལི་ཏེ། པྲཛྙཱ་པཱ་ར་མི་ཏ་ནཱ་ད་སཾ་བྷ་ཝེ་ཏ། བཛྲ་དྷརྨ་ཧྲི་ད་ཡ་སནྟོ་ཥ་ཎི་ཧཱུྃ་ཧཱུྃ་ཧཱུྃ་ཧོ་ཧོ་ཧོ་ཨ་ཁཾ་སྭཱ་ཧཱ།

Make offerings with music:

Oṁ vajraghaṇḍe raṇita praraṇita saṁpraraṇita sarvabuddha kṣetra pracalite prajñāpāramitā nāda saṁbhaveta vajradharma hridaya santoṣaṇi hūṁ hūṁ hūṁ ho ho ho akhaṁ svāhā

ཨོཾ་སརྦ་ཏ་ཐཱ་ག་ཏ་བཛྲ་ཡོ་གི་ནཱི་ས་པ་རི་ཝཱ་ར་ཨོཾ་ཨཱཿ ཧཱུྃ། ཞེས་ནང་མཆོད་ཕུལ་ལ་རྡོ་རྗེ་དྲིལ་བུ་འཛིན་པས།

Make inner offering and hold the vajra and bell:

Oṁ sarvatathāgata vajrayoginī saparivāra oṁ āḥ hūṁ

དཔལ་ལྡན་རྡོ་རྗེ་མཁའ་འགྲོ་མ།།
མཁའ་འགྲོ་མ་ཡི་འཁོར་ལོས་སྒྱུར།།
ཡེ་ཤེས་ལྔ་དང་སྐུ་གསུམ་བརྙེས།།
འགྲོ་བ་སྐྱོབ་ལ་ཕྱག་འཚལ་ལོ།།

Pal-Den Dor-Je Khan-Dro-Ma
Khan-Dro-Ma Yi Khor-Lo Gyur
Ye-She Nga Dang Ku Sum Nye
Dro-Wa Kyob La Chag Tsal Lo

The glorious Vajraḍākinī,
the empress of all ḍākinīs,
the one who has attained the five wisdoms and three kāyas,
I pay homage to the protector of migrating beings.

ཇི་སྙེད་རྡོ་རྗེ་མཁའ་འགྲོ་མ།།
ཀུན་ཏུ་རྟོག་པའི་འཆིང་གཅོད་ཅིང་།།
འཇིག་རྟེན་བྱ་བར་རབ་འཇུག་མ།།
དེ་སྙེད་རྣམས་ལ་ཕྱག་འཚལ་ལོ།།

Ji Nye Dor-Je Khan-Dro-Ma
Kün-Tu Tog-Pay Ching Chö Ching
Jig-Ten Ja-War Rab Jug Ma
De Nye Nam La Chag Tsal Lo

I pay homage to Vajraḍākinī,
who eliminates the bondage of all concepts,
those who attain
full engagement in the activities of the world.

ཅེས་བསྟོད་ལ་པད་ཀོར་སྔོན་དུ་འགྲོ་བའི་གཟུངས་ཐག་བཟུང་ལ།

Hold the dharani cord with a lotus roll as a preliminary.

རང་གི་ཐུགས་ཀ་ནས་སྔགས་ཀྱི་ཕྲེང་བ་བྱུང་སྟེ་གཟུངས་ཐག་ལ་འཁྲིལ་ནས་སོང་། རྗེ་བཙུན་མའི་སྐུ་ལ་ཕོག་པས་བ་སྤུའི་བུ་ག་ནས་བདུད་རྩིའི་ཆུ་རྒྱུན་བྱུང་བས་བུམ་པ་གང་བར་གྱུར་པར་བསམས་ལ།

Rang Gi Thug Ka Ne Ngag Kyi Teng Wa Jung Te Zung Tag La Til Ne Song, Je-Tsün-May Ku La Phog Pé Ba-Puy Bu-Ga Ne Dü-Tsiy Chu Gyun Jung-We Bum-Pa Gang-War Gyur Par Sam La

Imagine that the mantra garland arises from one's heart and curls around the dharani cord. Since it touches Jetsunma's body, a stream of amrita water comes out from her pores and fills the vase.

ཨོཾ་ཨོཾ་ཨོཾ་སརྦ་བུདྡྷ་ཌཱ་ཀི་ནཱི་ཡེ། བཛྲ་ཝརྞྞ་ནཱི་ཡེ།བཛྲ་བཻ་རོ་ཙ་ནཱི་ཡེ། ཧཱུཾ་ཧཱུཾ་ཧཱུཾ། ཕཊ་ཕཊ་ཕཊ་སྭཱ་ཧཱ། བརྒྱ་རྩ་དང་།

Recite 100 times:

Oṁ oṁ oṁ sarvabuddhaḍākinīye vajra varṇṇanīye vajra vairocanīye hūṁ hūṁ hūṁ phaṭ phaṭ phaṭ svāhā

ཨོཾ་སུམྦྷ་ནི་སུམྦྷ་ཧུྃ་ཧཱུྃ་ཕཊ།
ཨོཾ་གྲྀཧྞ་གྲྀཧྞ་ཧུྃ་ཧཱུྃ་ཕཊ།
ཨོཾ་གྲྀཧྞ་པ་ཡ་གྲྀཧྞ་པ་ཡ་ཧུྃ་ཧཱུྃ་ཕཊ།
ཨོཾ་ཨཱ་ན་ཡ་ཧོཿ བྷ་ག་ཝཱན་བིདྱཱ་རཱ་ཛ་ཧུྃ་ཧཱུྃ་ཕཊ། ཉེར་གཅིག

Recite 21 times:

Oṁ sumbha nisumbha huṁ hūṁ phaṭ

Oṁ grihaṇa grihaṇa huṁ hūṁ phaṭ

Oṁ grihaṇapaya grihaṇapaya huṁ hūṁ phaṭ

Oṁ ānayaho bhagavān vidyārāja huṁ hūṁ phaṭ

ཨོཾ་སརྦ་ཏ་ཐཱ་ག་ཏ་ཨ་བྷི་ཥེ་ཀ་ཏ་ས་མ་ཡ་ཤྲཱི་ཡེ་ཧཱུྃ། ཉེར་གཅིག་ལ་སོགས་པ་ཅི་ལྟར་རིགས་པ་བཟླས།

Recite 21 times or whatever is reasonable:

Oṁ sarvatathāgata abhiṣekata samaya shrīye hūṁ

མཆོད་བསྟོད་ནི།
ཨོཾ་སརྦ་ཏ་ཐཱ་ག་ཏ་བཛྲ་ཡོ་གི་ནཱི་ས་པ་རི་ཝཱ་ར་ཨརྒྷཾ་པྲ་ཏཱིཙྪ་པཱུ་ཛ་མེ་གྷ་ས་མུ་དྲ་སྥ་ར་ཎ་ས་མ་ཡེ་ཨཱཿ ཧཱུྃ།

The praises and offerings:

Oṁ sarvatathāgata vajrayoginī saparivāra arghaṁ praticcha pūja megha samudra spharaṇa samaye āḥ hūṁ

ཨོཾ་སརྦ་ཏ་ཐཱ་ག་ཏ་བཛྲ་ཡོ་གི་ནཱི་ས་པ་རི་ཝཱ་ར་པཱདྱཾ་པྲ་ཏཱིཙྪ་པཱུ་ཛ་མེ་གྷ་ས་མུ་དྲ་སྥ་ར་ཎ་ས་མ་ཡེ་ཨཱཿ ཧཱུྃ།

Oṁ sarvatathāgata vajrayoginī saparivāra pādyaṁ praticcha pūja megha samudra spharaṇa samaye āḥ hūṁ

ཨོཾ་སརྦ་ཏ་ཐཱ་ག་ཏ་བཛྲ་ཡོ་གི་ནཱི་ས་པ་རི་ཝཱ་ར་པཱདྱཾ་པྲ་ཏཱིཙྪ་པཱུ་ཛ་མེ་གྷ་ས་མུ་དྲ་སྥ་ར་ཎ་
ས་མ་ཡེ་ཨཱཿ ཧཱུྃ།

Oṁ sarvatathāgata vajrayoginī saparivāra puṣpe praticcha pūja megha samudra spharaṇa samaye āḥ hūṁ

ཨོཾ་སརྦ་ཏ་ཐཱ་ག་ཏ་བཛྲ་ཡོ་གི་ནཱི་ས་པ་རི་ཝཱ་ར་པུཥྤེ་པྲ་ཏཱིཙྪ་པཱུ་ཛ་མེ་གྷ་ས་མུ་དྲ་སྥ་ར་ཎ་
ས་མ་ཡེ་ཨཱཿ ཧཱུྃ།

Oṁ sarvatathāgata vajrayoginī saparivāra dhūpe praticcha pūja megha samudra spharaṇa samaye āḥ hūṁ

ཨོཾ་སརྦ་ཏ་ཐཱ་ག་ཏ་བཛྲ་ཡོ་གི་ནཱི་ས་པ་རི་ཝཱ་ར་དྷཱུ་པེ་པྲ་ཏཱིཙྪ་པཱུ་ཛ་མེ་གྷ་ས་མུ་དྲ་སྥ་
ར་ཎ་ས་མ་ཡེ་ཨཱཿ ཧཱུྃ།

Oṁ sarvatathāgata vajrayoginī saparivāra āloke praticcha pūja megha samudra spharaṇa samaye āḥ hūṁ

ཨོཾ་སརྦ་ཏ་ཐཱ་ག་ཏ་བཛྲ་ཡོ་གི་ནཱི་ས་པ་རི་ཝཱ་ར་ཨཱ་ལོ་ཀེ་པྲ་ཏཱིཙྪ་པཱུ་ཛ་མེ་གྷ་ས་མུ་དྲ་སྥ་ར་ཎ་
ས་མ་ཡེ་ཨཱཿ ཧཱུྃ།

Oṁ sarvatathāgata vajrayoginī saparivāra ghande praticcha pūja megha samudra spharaṇa samaye āḥ hūṁ

ༀ་སརྦ་ཏ་ཐཱ་ག་ཏ་བཛྲ་ཡོ་གི་ནཱི་ས་པ་རི་ཝཱ་ར་ནཻ་ཝི་དྱེ་པྲ་ཏཱི་ཙྪ་པཱུ་ཛ་མེ་གྷ་ས་མུ་དྲ་སྥ་ར་ཎ་ས་མ་ཡེ་ཨཱཿ ཧཱུྃ།

Oṁ sarvatathāgata vajrayoginī saparivāra naividye praticcha pūja megha samudra spharaṇa samaye āḥ hūṁ

ༀ་སརྦ་ཏ་ཐཱ་ག་ཏ་བཛྲ་ཡོ་གི་ནཱི་ས་པ་རི་ཝཱ་ར་ཤབྡ་པྲ་ཏཱི་ཙྪ་པཱུ་ཛ་མེ་གྷ་ས་མུ་དྲ་སྥ་ར་ཎ་ས་མ་ཡེ་ཨཱཿ ཧཱུྃ།

Oṁ sarvatathāgata vajrayoginī saparivāra shabda praticcha pūja megha samudra spharaṇa samaye āḥ hūṁ

ༀ་བཛྲ་གྷཎྚེ་ར་ཎི་ཏ། པྲ་ར་ཎི་ཏ། སཾ་པྲ་ར་ཎི་ཏ། སརྦ་བུདྡྷ་ཀྵེ་ཏྲ་པྲ་ཙ་ལི་ཏེ། པྲཛྙཱ་པཱ་ར་མི་ཏཱ་ནཱ་ད་སཾ་བྷ་ཝེ་ཏ། བཛྲ་དྷརྨ་ཧྲི་ད་ཡ་སནྟོ་ཥ་ཎི་ཧཱུྃ་ཧཱུྃ་ཧཱུྃ་ཧོ་ཧོ་ཧོ་ཨ་ཁཾ་སྭཱ་ཧཱ།
ཞེས་རོལ་མོ་དང་བཅས་པས་མཆོད།

Make offerings with music:
Oṁ vajraghaṇḍe raṇita praraṇita saṁpraraṇita sarvabuddha kṣetra pracalite prajñāpāramitā nāda saṁbhaveta vajradharma hridaya santoṣaṇi hūṁ hūṁ hūṁ ho ho ho akhaṁ svāhā

ༀ་སརྦ་ཏ་ཐཱ་ག་ཏ་བཛྲ་ཡོ་གི་ནཱི་ས་པ་རི་ཝཱ་ར་ༀ་ཨཱཿ ཧཱུྃ། གིས་ནང་མཆོད།

Make the inner offering with:
Oṁ sarvatathāgata vajrayoginī saparivāra oṁ āḥ hūṁ

དཔལ་ལྡན་རྡོ་རྗེ་མཁའ་འགྲོ་མ།།
མཁའ་འགྲོ་མ་ཡི་འཁོར་ལོས་སྒྱུར།།

ཡེ་ཤེས་ལྔ་དང་སྐུ་གསུམ་བརྙེས།།
འགྲོ་བ་སྐྱོབ་ལ་ཕྱག་འཚལ་ལོ།།

Pal-Den Dor-Je Khan-Dro-Ma
Khan-Dro-Ma Yi Khor-Lo Gyur
Ye-She Nga Dang Ku Sum Nye
Dro-Wa Kyob La Chag Tsal Lo

The glorious Vajraḍākinī,
the empress of all ḍākinīs,
the one who has attained the five wisdoms and three kāyas,
I pay homage to the protector of migrating beings.

ཇི་སྙེད་རྡོ་རྗེ་མཁའ་འགྲོ་མ།།
ཀུན་ཏུ་རྟོག་པའི་འཆིང་གཅོད་ཅིང་།།
འཇིག་རྟེན་བྱ་བར་རབ་འཇུག་མ།།
དེ་སྙེད་རྣམས་ལ་ཕྱག་འཚལ་ལོ།།

Ji Nye Dor-Je Khan-Dro-Ma
Kün-Tu Tog-Pay Ching Chö Ching
Jig-Ten Ja-War Rab Jug Ma
De Nye Nam La Chag Tsal Lo

I pay homage to Vajraḍākinī,
who eliminates the bondage of all concepts,
those who attain
full engagement in the activities of the world.

རྗེ་བཙུན་རྡོ་རྗེ་རྣལ་འབྱོར་མས་བདག་དང་སེམས་ཅན་ཐམས་ཅད་དག་པ་མཁའ་སྤྱོད་
དུ་འཁྲིད་པར་མཛད་དུ་གསོལ། འཇིག་རྟེན་དང་འཇིག་རྟེན་ལས་འདས་པའི་དངོས་གྲུབ་
མ་ལུས་པ་སྩལ་དུ་གསོལ། ཞེས་གསོལ་བ་བཏབ།

Je-Tsün Dor-Je Nal-Jor-Mé Dag Dang Sem-Chen Tham-Ché Dag-Pa Kha-Chö Du Ti-Par Zé Du Söl, Jig-Ten Dang Jig-Ten Lé Dé-Pay Ngö-Drup Ma Lü Pa Tsal Du Söl

Jetsun Vajrayoginī, please lead myself and all sentient beings to Khecarī and please grant all mundane and transcendent siddhis.

Thus Supplicate.

ཨོཾ་ཤྲཱི་བཛྲ་ཧེ་རུ་ཀ་ས་མ་ཡ་མ་ནུ་པཱ་ལ་ཡ། ཧེ་རུ་ཀ་ཏྭེ་ནོ་པ་ཏིཥྛ། དྲྀ་ཌྷོ་མེ་བྷ་ཝ། སུ་ཏོ་
ཥྱོ་མེ་བྷ་ཝ། ཨ་ནུ་རཀྟོ་མེ་བྷ་ཝ། སུ་པོ་ཥྱོ་མེ་བྷ་ཝ། སརྦ་སིདྡྷི་མྨེ་པྲ་ཡཙྪ། སརྦ་ཀརྨ་
སུ་ཙ་མེ་ཙིཏྟཾ་ཤྲི་ཡཾ་ཀུ་རུ་ཧཱུཾ། ཧ་ཧ་ཧ་ཧ་ཧོཿ བྷ་ག་ཝཱན། བཛྲ་ཧེ་རུ་ཀ་མཱ་མེ་མུཉྩ། ཧེ་
རུ་ཀོ་བྷ་ཝ། མ་ཧཱ་ས་མ་ཡ་ས་ཏྭ་ཨཱཿ ཧཱུཾ་ཕཊ། ཞེས་ལན་གསུམ་བརྗོད།

Recite three times:

Oṁ shrī vajraheruka samayamanupālaya heruka tvenopatiṣṭha dṛiḍho me bhava sutosyo me bhava anurakto me bhava suposyo me bhava sarva sidhhim me prayaccha sarva karmasu ca me cittaṁ shriyaṁ kuru hūṁ ha ha ha ha hoḥ bhagavān vajraheruka mā me muñca heruko' bhava mahāsamayasattva āḥ hūṁ phaṭ

མ་འབྱོར་པ་དང་ཉམས་པ་དང་།།
གང་ཡང་བདག་རྨོངས་བློ་ཡིས་ནི།།
བགྱིས་པ་དང་ནི་བགྱིད་སྐུལ་པ།།
དེ་ཀུན་མགོན་པོས་བཟོད་པར་གསོལ།

Ma Jor-Pa Dang Nyam-Pa Dang
Gang-Yang Dag Mong Lo Yi Ni
Gyi-Pa Dang Ni Gyi Tsal-Pa
De Kün Gon-Po Zö-Par Söl

Whatever was not prepared or was damaged,
or that I did with a confused mind,
or asked [others] to do,
protector, please be patient with it all.

དུང་ཆོས་ཀྱིས་མཆོད་ཡོན་འབུལ།
ཨོཾ་ཨཱཿ ཧཱུྃ། བུམ་ནང་གི་ལྷ་ཞུ་བ་ལས་བྱུང་བའི་བུམ་པའི་ཆུ་ནུས་པ་དང་ལྡན་པར་གྱུར་
ཞེས་བརྗོད།

Oṁ āḥ hūṁ, Bum Nang Gi Lha Shu-Wa Lé Jung-Way Bum-Pay Chu Nü-Pa Dang Den Par Gyur

Make a water offering with the conch shell:
Oṁ āḥ hūṁ

The potent water of the vase arises from the melting of the deities inside the vase.
Thus recite.

Self-Initiation

དེ་ནས་བདག་འཇུག་ལ་མདུན་བསྐྱེད་ཀྱི་རྡོ་རྗེ་རྣལ་འབྱོར་མ་དང་། རྩ་བའི་བླ་མ་གཉིས་སུ་མེད་པ་ལ་དཔའ་བོ་དང་རྣལ་འབྱོར་མའི་ཚོགས་དཔག་ཏུ་མེད་པས་བསྐོར་བ་མངོན་སུམ་ལྟར་དམིགས་ལ། དེ་ལྟར་དགོངས་པ་རྩེ་གཅིག་པས་བདག་ལ་དགོངས་པར་བསམ་སྟེ།

After that, for the self-initiation, visualize the front generated Vajrayoginī inseparable with one's root guru as if they are there in person, surrounded by an immeasurable assembly of heroes and yoginīs. As such, imagine their one-pointed intention is focusing on yourself.

ཇི་ལྟར་བལྟམས་པ་ཙམ་གྱིས་ནི།
ལྷ་རྣམས་ཀྱིས་ནི་ཁྲུས་གསོལ་ལྟར།
ལྷ་ཡི་ཆུ་ནི་དག་པ་ཡིས།
དེ་བཞིན་བདག་གིས་དབང་བསྐུར་རོ།

Ji Tar Tam-Pa Tsam Gyi Ni,
Lha Nam Kyi Ni Tu Söl Tar,
Lha Yi Chu Ni Dag-Pa Yi
De-Shin Dag Gi Wang Kur Ro

Just as he [the Buddha] was washed by the gods
at the time of his birth,
likewise, we will bestow the empowerment
with pure divine water.

ༀ་སརྦ་ཏ་ཐཱ་ག་ཏ་ཨ་བྷི་ཥེ་ཀ་ཏ་ས་མ་ཡ་ཤྲཱི་ཡེ་ཧཱུྃ། ཞེས་པས་བུམ་ཆུ་ཅུང་ཟད་སྦྱང་།

Oṁ sarvatathāgata abhiṣekata samaya shrīye hūṁ

Taste a little of the vase water.

རང་གི་ལུས་ལོངས་སྤྱོད་དུས་གསུམ་གྱི་དགེ་བའི་རྩ་བ་དང་བཅས་པ་ཡོན་དུ་ཕུལ་བར་བསམ་ནས།
ཨོཾ་བཛྲ་བྷཱུ་མི་ཨཱཿ ཧཱུྃ། གཞི་ཡོངས་སུ་དག་པ་དབང་ཆེན་གསེར་གྱི་ས་གཞི། ཨོཾ་བཛྲ་རེ་
ཁེ་ཨཱཿ ཧཱུྃ། ཕྱི་ལྕགས་རི་འཁོར་ཡུག་གིས་བསྐོར་བའི་དབུས་སུ་ཧཱུྃ། རིའི་རྒྱལ་པོ་རི་རབ།
ཤར་ལུས་འཕགས་པོ། ལྷོ་འཛམ་བུ་གླིང་། ནུབ་བ་གླང་སྤྱོད། བྱང་སྒྲ་མི་སྙན། ཉི་མ། ཟླ་
བ། དབུས་སུ་ལྷ་དང་མིའི་དཔལ་འབྱོར་ཕུན་སུམ་ཚོགས་པ་མ་ཚང་བ་མེད་པ་འདི་ཉིད་
བླ་མ་དང་རྗེ་བཙུན་རྡོ་རྗེ་རྣལ་འབྱོར་མ་ཐ་མི་དད་པ་ལ་བྱིན་རླབས་ཟབ་མོ་ཞུ་བའི་ཡོན་དུ་
འབུལ་བར་བགྱིའོ། ཐུགས་རྗེས་འགྲོ་བའི་དོན་དུ་བཞེས་སུ་གསོལ། བཞེས་ནས་བྱིན་
གྱིས་བརླབ་ཏུ་གསོལ།

Oṁ vajra bhumi āḥ hūṁ, Shi Yong Su Dag-Pa Wang Chen Ser Gyi Sa Shi, Oṁ vajra rekhe āḥ hūṁ, Chi Chag Ri Khor Yug Gi Kor-Way Wü-Su Hūṁ, Ri Gyal-Po Ri-Rab, Shar Lü-Phag-Po, Lho Zam-Bu-Ling, Nub Ba-Lang-Chö, Jang Dra-Mi-Nyen, Nyi-Ma, Da-Wa, Wü-Su Lha Dang Miy Pal-Jor Phun-Sum Tsog-Pa Ma Tsang-Wa Me-Pa Di Nyi La-Ma Dang Je-Tsün Dor-Je Nal-Jor-Ma Tha Mi Dé-Pa La Jin-Lab Zab-Mo Zhu-Way Yon Du-Bül-War Gyi'o, Thug-Jey Dro-Way Don Du She Su Söl, She-Ne Jin-Gyi-Lap Tu Söl

Then, imagine offering one's body, enjoyments, along with the roots of virtue of the three times:

Oṁ vajra bhumi āḥ hūṁ

The totally pure foundation is the mighty golden ground.

Oṁ vajra rekhe āḥ hūṁ

The outside is circled by a range of iron mountains. In the center of that is *Hūm* (ཧཱུྃ), the king of mountains, Sumeru. In the east is Pūrvavideha. In the south is Jambudvīpa. In the west is Godānīya. In the north is Kurava. There is the sun and the moon. In the center is the abundant prestige and wealth of devas and humans in no way incomplete. This is offered to the guru inseparable with Jetsun Vajrayoginī to request blessings. Please accept this with compassion for the benefit of migrating beings. Having accepted it, please bless me.

ཞེས་པས་ཡོན་ཕུལ་ནས། གསོལ་བ་གདབ་པ་ནི།
གང་གི་དྲིན་གྱིས་བདེ་ཆེན་ཉིད།།
སྐད་ཅིག་ཉིད་ལ་འཆར་བ་གང་།།
བླ་མ་རིན་ཆེན་ལྟ་བུའི་སྐུ།།
རྡོ་རྗེ་ཅན་ཞབས་པད་ལ་འདུད།།

Gang Gi Drin Gyi De-Chen Nyi
Ke-Chig Nyi La Char-Wa Gang
La-Ma Rin-Chen Ta-Bu Ku
Dor-Je Chen Shab Pe La Dü

After making the offerings is the supplication. Recite the supplication three times:

I bow to the lotus feet of the guru,
whose body is like a jewel, endowed with the three vajras,[6]
by whose kindness great bliss
arises in an instant.

---

[6] Following Chogyal Phagpa's explanation of this verse in Sa skya bka' 'bum, vol pa, pg. 110

སངས་རྒྱས་ཀུན་གྱི་རང་བཞིན་སྐུ།།
སློབ་དཔོན་ལ་ནི་བདག་སྐྱབས་མཆི།།
དཔལ་ལྡན་རྡོ་རྗེ་མཁའ་འགྲོ་མ།།
མཁའ་འགྲོ་མ་ཡི་འཁོར་ལོས་སྒྱུར།།
ཡེ་ཤེས་ལྔ་དང་སྐུ་གསུམ་བརྙེས།།
འགྲོ་བ་སྐྱོབ་ལ་ཕྱག་འཚལ་ལོ།།
དཔལ་ལྡན་རྡོ་རྗེ་མཁའ་འགྲོ་མས།།
བདག་ལ་བྱིན་གྱིས་བརླབ་ཏུ་གསོལ།།
ཞེས་ལན་གསུམ་གྱིས་གསོལ་བ་བཏབ།

Sang-Gyé Kün Gyi Rang-Shin Ku
Lob-Pon La Ni Dag Kyab Chi
Pal-Den Dor-Je Khan-Dro-Ma
Khan-Dro-Ma Yi Khor-Lo Gyur
Ye-She Nga Dang Ku Sum Nye
Dro-Wa Kyob La Chag Tsal Lo
Pal-Den Dor-Je Khan-Dro-Mé
Dag La Jin Gyi Lab-Tu Söl

I go for refuge to the guru,
the embodiment of all the Buddhas,
the glorious Vajraḍākinī,
the empress of all ḍākinīs,
the one who has attained the five wisdoms and three kāyas,
I pay homage to the protector of migrating beings.
Glorious Vajraḍākinī
please bless me.

དེ་ནས་རྡོ་རྗེ་རྣལ་འབྱོར་མས་མཛད་པར་བསམས་ལ།
ཨ་ཁཾ་ཝཱི་ར་ཧཱུྃ་གིས་གདོང་བཅིངས།

Imagine that Vajrayoginī is acting, tie the blindfold while reciting:
Ah khaṁ vīra hūṁ

ཨཱཿ ཁཾ་ཝཱི་ར་ཧཱུྃ་གིས་མེ་ཏོག་གི་ཕྲེང་བ་བླང་།

Take the garland of flowers while reciting:
Āḥ khaṁ vīra hūṁ

སིནྡྷུ་རའི་དཀྱིལ་འཁོར་ལས་ཁྲོ་མོ་ཁཎྜ་རོ་ཧཱ་དཔག་ཏུ་མེད་པ་འཕྲོས་ཏེ། བྱིན་རླབས་ཟབ་མོ་ཞུ་བ་ལ་བར་དུ་གཅོད་པའི་བགེགས་དང་ལོག་འདྲེན་ཐམས་ཅད་རྒྱང་རིང་དུ་བསྐྲད་པར་གྱུར་པར་བསམས་ལ།

Sin-Dhu-Ray Kyil-Khor Lé Tro-Mo Khan-Da-Ro-Ha Pag Tu Me-Pa Trö Te, Jin Lab Zab-Mo Shu-Wa La Bar-Du Chö-Pay Geg Dang Log Dren Tham-Ché Gyang Ring Du Tre-Par Gyur Par Sam La

To request profound blessings, imagine that countless Khaṇḍarohās arise from the sindhura maṇḍala, frighten all of the obstructors and false guides who cause obstacles to be far away.

ཀུ་ཤས་ཕྲུམ་ཀྱུ་རང་ལ་འཕོར་ཞིང་།
ཨོཾ་སུམྦྷ་ནི་སུམྦྷ་ཧཱུྃ་ཧཱུྃ་ཕཊ།
ཨོཾ་གྲྀཧྞ་གྲྀཧྞ་ཧཱུྃ་ཧཱུྃ་ཕཊ།

ཨོཾ་གྲྀཧྞ་པ་ཡ་གྲྀཧྞ་པ་ཡ་ཧཱུྃ་ཧཱུྃ་ཕཊ།
ཨོཾ་ཨཱ་ན་ཡ་ཧོཿ བྷ་ག་ཝཱན་བིདྱཱ་རཱ་ཛ་ཧཱུྃ་ཧཱུྃ་ཕཊ་ཅེས་བརྗོད།

Sprinkle vase water using kusha grass on oneself and recite:

Oṁ sumbha nisumbha huṁ hūṁ phaṭ

Oṁ grihaṇa grihaṇa huṁ hūṁ phaṭ

Oṁ grihaṇapaya grihaṇapaya huṁ hūṁ phaṭ

Oṁ ānayaho bhagavān vidyārāja huṁ hūṁ phaṭ

ཨོཾ་ཨཱཿ ཧཱུྃ། གིས་ནང་མཆོད་ལྕེ་ལ་མྱངས་པས་སེམས་བདེ་བས་གང་། ནང་གི་བག་ཆགས་ཐམས་ཅད་དག་པར་མོས།

Oṁ āḥ hūṁ, Gi Nang Chö Che-La Nyang-Pé Sem De-We Gang, Nang Gi Bag Chag Tham-Ché Dag-Par Mö

Feel that the mind is filled with bliss by tasting the inner offering on the tongue and that all internal traces[7] are purified, *Oṁ āḥ hūṁ*

བུ་ཁྱོད་སུ་ཡིན་ཅི་ལ་དགའ། སྐལ་བཟང་བདག་བདེ་བ་ཆེན་པོ་ལའོ། དེ་ཡིས་བུ་ལ་ཅི་ཞིག་བྱ། སངས་རྒྱས་མཆོག་གི་དམ་ཚིག་གོ། ཞེས་པས་རིགས་དང་འདུན་པ་ཆེད་དུ་བྱ་བ་དྲིས་ཤིང་ངེས་པར་བྱས།

Bu Khyö Su Yin Chi La Ga, Kel-Zang Dag De-Wa Chen Po La'o, De Yi Bu La Chi Shig Ja, Sang-Gyé Chog Gi Dam-Tsig Go

---

7 That refers to habitual patterns, karmic imprints, latent tendencies, and so on.

The inquiry and ascertainment of one's family and motivation:

"Child, who are you and what will please you?"

"I am the fortunate one, pleased by great bliss."

"Child, what is the use of that?"

"It is the supreme commitment of the Buddha."

རང་གི་སྙིང་གའི་ནང་དུ་ཟླ་བ་ལ་གནས་པའི་རྡོ་རྗེ་དཀར་པོ་ཀུན་རྫོབ་དང་། དོན་དམ་པའི་བྱང་ཆུབ་སེམས་ཀྱི་ངོ་བོར་གྱུར་པར་བསམས་ལ། དེ་ཉིད་རྗེ་བཙུན་མས་རྡོ་རྗེ་སྙིང་ཁར་བཞག་ནས་བརྟན་པར་བྱིན་གྱིས་བརླབ་པར་བསམ་ཞིང་།

Rang Gi Nying Gay Nang Du Da-Wa La Ne-Pay Dor-Je Kar-Po Kün-Zob Dang, Don-Dam-Pay Jang-Chub Sem Kyi Ngo-Wor Gyur Par Sam-La De-Nyi Je-Tsün-Mé Dor-Je Nying-Khar Shag-Ne Ten-Par Jin-Gyi Lab-Par Sam-Shing

Imagine that the vajra existing on a moon inside of one's heart becomes the essence of relative and ultimate bodhicitta. Imagine that Jetsuma blesses those to become stable through placing a vajra on one's heart.

ཨོཾ་སརྦ་ཡོ་ག་ཙིཏྟ་ཨུཏྤཱ་ད་ཡཱ་མི་ཞེས་དང་།

Recite:

Oṁ sarva yoga chitta utpādayāmi

སུ་ར་ཏེ་ས་མ་ཡ་སྟྭཾ་ཧོཿ་སིདྡྷི་བཛྲ་ཡ་ཐཱ་སུ་ཁཾ་ཞེས་བརྗོད།

Recite:

Surate samaya stvaṁ hoḥ siddhi vajra yathā sukhaṁ

རྣལ་འབྱོར་མས་གསང་བར་དམ་པར་བསམས་ལ་རྡོ་རྗེ་སྤྱི་བོར་བཞག་ལ།

Nal-Jor-Mé Sang-War Dam-Par Sam-La Dor-Je Chi-Wor Shag-La

Imagine that Yoginī gives advice about secrecy and places a vajra on one's crown.

དེང་ཁྱོད་རྣལ་འབྱོར་མ་ཐམས་ཅད་ཀྱི་རིགས་སུ་ཞུགས་ཀྱིས། རྣལ་འབྱོར་མ་ཐམས་ཅད་ཀྱི་གསང་ཆེན་དམ་པ་འདི་རྣལ་འབྱོར་མ་ཐམས་ཅད་ཀྱི་དཀྱིལ་འཁོར་དུ་མ་ཞུགས་པ་རྣམས་ཀྱི་མདུན་དུ་སྨྲ་བར་མི་བྱ་སྟེ། མ་དད་པ་རྣམས་ལ་ཡང་མ་ཡིན་ནོ། ཞེས་རྣལ་འབྱོར་མའི་ཕྱག་ན་གནས་པའི་རྡོ་རྗེ་ལ་འཛུས་ཏེ་དཀྱིལ་འཁོར་གྱི་དབུས་ན་རྣལ་འབྱོར་མ་བཞུགས་པའི་དྲུང་དུ་སླེབ་པར་མོས་ལ

Deng Khyo Nal-Jor-Ma Tham-Ché Kyi Rig Su Shug kyi, Nal-Jor-Ma Tham-Ché Kyi Sang Chen Dam-Pa Di Nal-Jor-Ma Tham-Ché Kyi Kyil-Khor Du Ma Shug-Pa Nam Kyi Dün Du Ma-War Mi Ja Te, Ma Dé-Pa Nam La Yang Ma Yin No, She Nal-Jor-May Chag-Na Ne-Pay Dor-Je-La Ju-Te Kyil-Khor-Gyi Wü-Na Nal-Jor-Ma Shug-Pay Drung-Du Leb-Par Mo-La

Now you have entered into the family of all yoginīs. This sublime great secret of all yoginīs must not be uttered in the presence of those who have not entered into the maṇḍala of all the yoginīs nor to those who lack faith.

Think that one takes the vajra that is in Yoginī's hand, and one arrives in the presence of the Yoginī residing in the center of the maṇḍala.

ཛཿ ཧཱུྃ་བཾ་ཧོཿ ཞེས་བརྗོད་པ་ནི་ཕྱི་འཇུག་གོ

Jaḥ hūṁ vaṁ hoḥ

Reciting this is outer admission.

ནང་འཇུག་གི་དོན་དུ་རྣལ་འབྱོར་མའི་དྲུང་དུ་ཡན་ལག་བདུན་པ་དང་ལྡན་པའི་སྒོ་ནས་
བྱང་ཆུབ་མཆོག་ཏུ་སེམས་བསྐྱེད་པར་མོས་ནས།

Nang-Jug Gi Don-Du Nal-Jor-May Drung-Du Yen-Lag Dun-Pa Dang Dan-Pay Go-Ne Jang-Chub Chog-Tu Sem-Kye Par Mö Ne

Think that one has generated the supreme bodhicitta through the seven limbs in the presence of Yoginī for the purpose of the inner admission.

དཀོན་མཆོག་གསུམ་ལ་བདག་སྐྱབས་མཆི།།
སྡིག་པ་ཐམས་ཅད་སོ་སོར་བཤགས།།
འགྲོ་བའི་དགེ་ལ་རྗེས་ཡི་རང་།།
སངས་རྒྱས་བྱང་ཆུབ་ཡིད་ཀྱིས་བཟུང་།།

Kon-Chog Sum La Dag Kyab Chi
Dig-Pa Tham-Ché So Sor Shag
Dro-Way Ge La Je Yi Rang
Sang-Gyé Jang-Chub Yi Kyi Zung

Thus, recite [the following] three times:

I go for refuge to the Three Jewels
and individually confess each misdeed.

I rejoice in the virtue of beings
and bear in mind the bodhicitta of the Buddhas

སངས་རྒྱས་ཆོས་དང་ཚོགས་མཆོག་ལ།།
བྱང་ཆུབ་བར་དུ་སྐྱབས་སུ་མཆི།།
རང་གཞན་དོན་ནི་རབ་བསྒྲུབ་ཕྱིར།།
བྱང་ཆུབ་སེམས་ནི་བསྐྱེད་པར་བགྱི།།

Sang-Gyé Chö Dang Tsog Chog La
Jang-Chub Bar-Du Kyab Su Chi
Rang Shen Don Ni Rab Drub Chir
Jang-Chub Sem Ni Kye-Par Gyi

I go for refuge until awakening
to the Buddha, the Dharma, and the Supreme Sangha.
In order to truly accomplish my own and other's benefit,
I generate bodhicitta.

བྱང་ཆུབ་མཆོག་གི་སེམས་ནི་བསྐྱེད་བགྱིས་ནས།།
སེམས་ཅན་ཐམས་ཅད་བདག་གི་མགྲོན་དུ་གཉེར།།
བྱང་ཆུབ་སྤྱོད་མཆོག་ཡིད་འོང་སྤྱད་པར་བགྱི།།
འགྲོ་ལ་ཕན་ཕྱིར་སངས་རྒྱས་འགྲུབ་པར་ཤོག། ཅེས་ལན་གསུམ་བརྗོད།

Jang-Chub Chog Gi Sem Ni Kye Gyi Ne
Sem-Chen Tham-Ché Dag Gi Dron Du Nyer
Jang-Chub Chö Chog Yi Ong Che-Par Gyi
Dro La Phen Chir Sang-Gyé Drub Par Shog

Having created supreme bodhicitta,
I invite all sentient beings
to engage in the appealing supreme conduct of awakening.
May I accomplish Buddhahood in order to benefit migrating beings.

རིགས་ལྔ་སྤྱི་དང་ཁྱད་པར་གྱི་དམ་ཚིག་གོང་འཕེལ་དུ་བཟུང་བར་བསམས་ལ།

Rig-Nga Chi Dang Khye-Par Gyi Dam-Tsig Gong Phel Du Zung War Sam-La

In order to increase, imagine that general and specific
samayas of the five families are taken.

སྲས་བཅས་སངས་རྒྱས་ཐམས་ཅད་དང་།།
དཔའ་བོ་རྣལ་འབྱོར་མ་རྣམས་ཀུན།།
ཐམས་ཅད་བདག་ལ་དགོངས་སུ་གསོལ།།

Se Ché Sang-Gyé Tham-Ché Dang
Pa-Wo Nal-Jor-Ma Nam Kün
Tham-Ché Dag La Gong Su Söl

Recite [the following] three times:

All Buddhas with their children,
all vīrās and yoginīs,
please heed me!

རིག་པ་འཛིན་པ་བདག་གིས་ནི།།
དུས་འདི་ནས་ནི་བཟུང་ནས་སུ།།

ཇི་སྲིད་བྱང་ཆུབ་སྙིང་པོའི་བར།།
ཇི་ལྟར་དུས་གསུམ་མགོན་པོ་རྣམས།།
བྱང་ཆུབ་ཏུ་ནི་ངེས་མཛད་པའི།།
བྱང་ཆུབ་སེམས་ནི་བླ་ན་མེད།།
དམ་པ་བདག་གིས་བསྐྱེད་པར་བགྱི།།

Rig-Pa Zin-Pa Dag Gi Nï
Dü Di Ne Nï Zung Ne Su
Ji-Si Jang-Chub Nying-Poy Bar
Ji-Tar Dü Sum Gon-Po Nam
Jang-Chub Tu Nï Nge Zé-Pay
Jang-Chub Sem Nï La-Na-Me
Dam-Pa Dag Gi Kye-Par Gyi

Beginning from now
until the seat of awakening,
I, the vidyādhara,
will generate sublime
unsurpassed bodhicitta
just as the protectors of the three times
actualizing awakening.

ཚུལ་ཁྲིམས་ཀྱི་ནི་བསླབ་པ་དང་།།
དགེ་བའི་ཆོས་ནི་སྡུད་པ་དང་།།
སེམས་ཅན་དོན་བྱེད་ཚུལ་ཁྲིམས་གསུམ།།
སོ་སོར་བརྟན་པོར་གཟུང་བར་བགྱི།།

Tsul-Tim Kyi Ni Lab-Pa Dang
Ge-Way Chö Ni Dü-Pa Dang
Sem-Chen Don-Je Tsul-Tim Sum
So-Sor Ten-Por Zung-War Gyi

The training of discipline,
gathering virtuous qualities,
and benefiting sentient beings
are three disciplines I will individually hold firmly.

སངས་རྒྱས་ཆོས་དང་དགེ་འདུན་ཏེ།།
བླ་ན་མེད་པའི་དཀོན་མཆོག་གསུམ།།
སངས་རྒྱས་རྣལ་འབྱོར་ལས་སྐྱེས་པའི།།
སྡོམ་པ་དེང་ནས་བརྟན་པོར་གཟུང་།།

Sang-Gyé Chö Dang Gen-Dun Te
La Na Me-Pay Kon-Chog Sum
Sang-Gyé Nal-Jor Lé Kye-Pay
Dom-Pa Deng Ne Ten-Por Zung

The Buddha, Dharma, and Sangha,
the unsurpassed Three Jewels,
the vow arising from the Buddha's yoga,
I will hold firmly from now on.

རྡོ་རྗེའི་རིགས་མཆོག་ཆེན་པོ་ལ།།
རྡོ་རྗེ་དྲིལ་བུ་ཕྱག་རྒྱ་ཡང་།།

ཡང་དག་ཉིད་དུ་གཟུང་བར་བགྱི།།
སློབ་དཔོན་དག་ཀྱང་གཟུང་བར་བགྱི།།

Dor-Jey Rig-Chog Chen-Po La
Dor-Je Dril-Bu Chag-Gya Yang
Yang-Dag Nyi Du Zung-War Gyi
Lob-Pon Dag Kyang Zung-War Gyi

In the great supreme vajra family,
the vajra, bell, and mudra
must be upheld correctly.
The master must also be upheld.

རིན་ཆེན་རིགས་མཆོག་ཆེན་པོ་ཡི།།
དམ་ཚིག་ཡིད་དུ་འོང་བ་ལ།།
ཉིན་རེ་བཞིན་དུ་དུས་དྲུག་ཏུ།།
སྦྱིན་པ་རྣམ་བཞི་རྟག་ཏུ་སྦྱིན།།

Rin-Chen Rig-Chog Chen-Po Yi
Dam-Tsig Yi Du Ong-Wa La
Nyin Re Shin-Du Dü Drug Tu
Jin-Pa Nam Shi Tag-Tu Jin

For the pleasant samaya
of the great supreme jewel family,
always give the four kinds of generosity
six times every day.

བྱང་ཆུབ་ཆེན་པོ་ལས་བྱུང་བའི།།
པདྨའི་རིགས་ཆེན་དག་པ་ལ།།
ཕྱི་ནང་གསང་བ་ཐེག་པ་གསུམ།།
དམ་པའི་ཆོས་ནི་མ་ལུས་གཟུང་།།

Jang-Chub Chen-Po Lé Jung-Way
Pad-May Rig-Chen Dag-Pa La
Chi Nang Sang-Wa Theg-Pa Sum
Dam-Pay Chö Ni Ma-Lü Zung

In the pure great lotus family
arising from great awakening,
all of the sublime Dharma is upheld,
the outer, inner, and secret, three yānas.

ལས་ཀྱི་རིགས་མཆོག་ཆེན་པོ་ལ།།
སྡོམ་པ་ཐམས་ཅད་ལྡན་པར་ནི།།
ཡང་དག་ཉིད་དུ་གཟུང་བར་བགྱི།།
མཆོད་པའི་ལས་ཀྱང་ཅི་ནུས་བགྱི།།

Lé Kyi Rig-Chog Chen-Po La
Dom-Pa Tham-Ché Den-Par Ni
Yang-Dag Nyi Du Zung-War Gyi
Chö-Pay Lé Kyang Chi Nu Gyi

In the great supreme karma family,
possession of all the vows

should be maintained correctly
and engage in the activity of offerings as much as possible.

བྱང་ཆུབ་སེམས་ནི་བླ་མེད་མཆོག།
དམ་པ་བདག་གིས་བསྐྱེད་བགྱིས་ནས།།
སེམས་ཅན་ཀུན་གྱི་དོན་གྱི་ཕྱིར།།
བདག་གིས་སྡོམ་པ་མ་ལུས་གཟུང་།།

Jang-Chub Sem Ni La-Me Chog
Dam-Pa Dag Gi Kye Gyi Ne
Sem-Chen Kün Gyi Don Gyi Chir
Dag Gi Dom-Pa Ma-Lü Zung

After I generate
sublime unsurpassed bodhicitta,
I will hold all the vows
in order to benefit sentient beings.

མ་བསྒྲལ་བ་རྣམས་བདག་གིས་བསྒྲལ།།
མ་གྲོལ་བ་རྣམས་བདག་གིས་དགྲོལ།།
དབུགས་མ་ཕྱུང་བ་དབུགས་དབྱུང་ཞིང་།།
སེམས་ཅན་མྱ་ངན་འདས་ལ་དགོད། ཞེས་ལན་གསུམ་བརྗོད།

Ma Dral-Wa Nam Dag Gi Dral
Ma Dröl-Wa Nam Dag Gi Dröl
Wug-Ma Chug-Wa Wug Yung Shing
Sem-Chen Nya Ngen Dé La Gö

I will free those who are not free;
I will release those who are not liberated;
I will give solace to those without solace;
and place all sentient beings in nirvana.

ཁྱད་པར་དུ་གཡོན་པའི་ཀུན་སྤྱོད་ཀྱི་དམ་ཚིག་ཕྱིར་བུད་མེད་ལ་མི་སྨོད་པ་དང་། ཁྱད་པར་ཤེས་རབ་མ་ལ་བརྟེན་པའི་དམ་ཚིག་བརྒྱད་པོ་བཟུང་སྙམ་པས།

In particular, think that one takes the samaya of the constant practice of left-handedness, not disparaging women in general and specifically the eight samayas that depend on the Prajñā.

སངས་རྒྱས་ཆོས་དང་དགེ་འདུན་ལ།།
རྟག་པར་བདག་ནི་སྐྱབས་སུ་མཆི།།
རྣལ་འབྱོར་གསང་སྔགས་མཁའ་འགྲོ་མ།།
འཁོར་ལོ་གསུམ་གྱི་བདག་ཉིད་ཅན།།
ཀུན་ལ་རྟག་ཏུ་སྐྱབས་སུ་མཆི།།

Sang-Gyé Chö Dang Gen-Dun La
Tag-Par Dag Ni Kyab Su Chi
Nal-Jor Sang Ngag Khan-Dro-Ma
Khor-Lo Sum Gyi Dag Nyi Chen
Kün La Tag-Tu Kyab Su Chi

Recite [the following] three times:

I always go for refuge to
the Buddha, Dharma and Sangha.

I always go for refuge to
the ḍākinīs of secret mantra's yoga,
the embodiment of the three cakras.

དཔའ་བོ་དཔའ་མོ་དབང་ལྷ་མོ།།
བྱང་ཆུབ་སེམས་དཔའ་བདག་ཉིད་ཆེ།།
ཁྱད་པར་དུ་ཡང་སློབ་དཔོན་ལ།།
རྟག་པར་བདག་ནི་སྐྱབས་སུ་མཆི།།

Pa-Wo Pa-Mo Wang Lha-Mo
Jang-Chub Sem-Pa Dag Nyi Che
Khye Par Du Yang Lob Pon La
Tag-Par Dag Nï Kyab Su Chi

I always go for refuge to
the heroes, heroines, the goddesses of the empowerment,
and the great ones, the bodhisattvas,
and in particular to the masters.

དཔལ་ལྡན་ཁྲག་འཐུང་སོགས་དཔའ་བོ།།
རྣལ་འབྱོར་མ་དང་སྣང་མཛད་སོགས།།
བྱང་ཆུབ་སེམས་དཔའ་དཔག་མེད་པ།།
ཐམས་ཅད་བདག་ལ་དགོངས་སུ་གསོལ།།

Pal-Den Trag Thung Sog Pa-Wo
Nal-Jor-Ma Dang Nang-Zé Sog
Jang-Chub Sem-Pa Pag Me-Pa
Tham-Ché Dag La Gong Su Söl

Heroes such as Shrī Heruka and so on,
Yoginī, Vairocana, and so on,
countless bodhisattvas,
please heed me.

བདག་གིས་དུས་འདི་ནས་བཟུང་སྟེ།།
ཇི་སྲིད་གཉིས་མེད་ལ་གནས་པར།།
དེ་ཡི་ཚངས་སྤྱོད་གཉིས་མེད་པ།།
ཉི་ཤུ་རྩ་གཉིས་ལེགས་པར་བཟུང་།། ཞེས་ལན་གསུམ་བརྗོད།

Dag-Gi Dü Di-Ne Zung-Te
Ji-Si Nyi-Me La-Ne-Par
De-Yi Tsang Chö Nyi-Me-Pa
Nyi-Shu Tsa-Nyi Leg-Par Zung

Beginning from now
until dwelling in nonduality,
I will perfectly hold the twenty-two samayas
of the nondual brahmacarya.

དེ་ནས་བཅོམ་ལྡན་འདས་མའི་ཐུགས་ཀ་ནས་འོད་ཟེར་དཔག་ཏུ་མེད་པ་འཕྲོས། རང་གི་ལུས་ལ་ཕོག་པས་ཚེ་ཐོག་མ་མེད་པ་ནས་བསགས་པའི་སྡིག་སྒྲིབ་བག་ཆགས་དང་བཅས་པ་དང་རྣམ་སྨིན་ཤ་རུས་ཀྱི་བར་དུ་སྦྱངས་ཏེ་མི་དམིགས་པ་སྟོང་པ་ཉིད་དུ་གྱུར།

De Ne Chom Den Dé May Thug-Ka Ne Ö-Zer Pag-Tu Me-Pa Trö, Rang Gi Lü La Phog-Pé Tse Thog-Ma Me-Pa Ne Sag-Pay Dig Drib Bag Chag Dang Ché-Pa Dang Nam Min Sha Ru Kyi Bar Du Jang Te Mi Mig Pa Tong Pa Nyi Du Gyur

Then, countless light rays shine from the heart of the Bhagavatī, striking one's body; the misdeeds and obscurations gathered without beginning along with their traces are purified down to the flesh and bones on one's karmically ripened body, disappearing and becoming empty.

སྟོང་པའི་ངང་ལས་ཨེ་ཨེ་ལས་ཆོས་འབྱུང་དམར་པོ་གྲུ་གསུམ་ཉིས་བརྩེགས་ཀྱི་དབུས་སུ་བཾ་ཡིག་དམར་པོའི་མཐར་ཨོཾ་ཨོཾ་ཨོཾ་སརྦ་བུདྡྷ་ཌཱ་ཀི་ནཱི་ཡེ་བཛྲ་ཝརྞྞི་ནཱི་ཡེ། བཛྲ་བཻ་རོ་ཙ་ནཱི་ཡེ། ཧཱུྃ་ཧཱུྃ་ཧཱུྃ། ཕཊ་ཕཊ་ཕཊ་སྭཱ་ཧཱ། ཞེས་པས་བསྐོར་བ་ལས་འོད་ཟེར་འཕྲོས། འཕགས་པ་མཆོད། སེམས་ཅན་ཐམས་ཅད་ཀྱི་སྡིག་སྒྲིབ་བག་ཆགས་དང་བཅས་པ་སྦྱངས། རྣལ་འབྱོར་མའི་སྐུར་གྱུར། དེ་རྣམས་འོད་དུ་ཞུ་ནས་ཚུར་འདུས་ཡིག་འབྲུ་རྣམས་ལ་ཐིམ་པ་ཡོངས་སུ་གྱུར་པ་ལས་རང་ཉིད་རྗེ་བཙུན་རྡོ་རྗེ་རྣལ་འབྱོར་མའི་སྐུར་གྱུར་པ་ནི། སྣ་ཚོགས་པདྨ་དང་ཉི་མའི་གདན་ལ་ཞབས་གཡས་བརྐྱང་བས་དུས་མཚན་མ་དམར་མོའི་ནུ་མའི་སྟེང་ནས་མནན་པ། གཡོན་བསྐུམ་པས་འཇིགས་བྱེད་ནག་པོའི་མགོ་བོ་རྒྱབ་ཏུ་བལྟབས་ནས་མནན་པ། སྐུ་མདོག་དམར་མོ་བསྐལ་པའི་མེ་ལྟ་བུའི་གཟི་བརྗིད་ཅན། ཞལ་གཅིག་ཕྱག་གཉིས་སྤྱན་གསུམ་དག་པ་མཁའ་སྤྱོད་དུ་གཟིགས་པ། ཕྱག་གཡས་པས་རྡོ་རྗེས་མཚན་པའི་གྲི་གུག་ཐུར་དུ་བརྒྱངས་ནས་འཛིན་པ། གཡོན་པས་ཐོད་པ་ཁྲག་གིས་གང་བ་སྟེང་ཕྱོགས་སུ་བཟུང་ནས་ཞལ་ཕྱིན་དུ་ཕྱོགས་པས་གསོལ་བ། ཕྲག་པ་གཡོན་པར་རྡོ་རྗེས་མཚན་པའི་ཁ་ཊྭཾ་ག་ལ་ཌཱ་མ་རུ་དང་དྲིལ་བུ་དང་། འཕན་རྩེ་གསུམ་པ་འཕྱང་བཞིན་པ་བསྣམས་པ། དབུ་སྐྲ་ནག་པོ་སིལ་བུར་གྱུར་པས་སྐུ་སྨད་ཡན་ཆད་ཁེབས་པ། ལང་ཚོ་དར་ལ་བབ་ཅིང་འདོད་པའི་ནུ་འབུར་རྒྱས་པ། བདེ་བ་སྐྱེད་པའི་ཉམས་ཅན། མི་མགོ་སྐམ་པོ་ལྔའི་དབུ་རྒྱན་དང་། སྐམ་པོ་ལྔ་བཅུའི་དོ་ཤལ་ཅན་གཅེར་བུ་ཕྱག་རྒྱ་ལྔས་བརྒྱན་པ། ཡེ་ཤེས་ཀྱི་མེ་འབར་བའི་དབུས་ན་བཞུགས་པའི་

ལྟེ་བར་ཨེ་ཨེ་ལས་ཆོས་འབྱུང་དམར་པོ་གྲུ་གསུམ་ཉིས་བརྩེགས་ཀྱི་དབུས་སུ་བཾ་ཡིག་དམར་པོ། མདུན་རྒྱབ་གཉིས་སྤངས་པའི་གྲྭ་བཞིར་དགའ་བ་འཁྱིལ་པ་རེ་ཡོད་པར་གྱུར་པར་བསམ།

Tong-Pay Ngang Lé E E Lé Chö-Jung Mar-Po Tru Sum Nyi Tseg Kyi Wü-Su Vaṁ Yig Mar Po Thar Oṁ oṁ oṁ sarvabuddhaḍākinīye vajra varṇṇanīye, vajra vairocanīye, hūṁ hūṁ hūṁ, phaṭ phaṭ phaṭ svāhā, She-Pé Kor-Wa Lé Ö-Zer Trö, Phag-Pa Chö, Sem-Chen Tham-Ché Kyi Dig Dib Bag Chag Dang Ché-Pa Jang, Nal-Jor-May Kur Gyur, De Nam Ö-Du Shu Ne Tsur Dü Yig Tru-Nam La Thim-Pa Yong-Su Gyur-Pa Lé Rang Nyi Je-Tsün Dor-Je Nal-Jor-May Kur Gyur Pa Ni, Na Tsog Pad-Ma Dang Nyi-May Den La Shab Yé Kyang-We Dü-Tsen-Ma Mar-Poy Nu-May Teng Ne Nen-Pa, Yön Kum-Pé Jig-Je Nag-Poy Go-Wo Gyab Tu Tab Ne Nen-Pa, Ku Dog Mar-Mo Kal-Pay Me Ta-Bui Zi Ji Chen, Shal Chig Chag Nyi Chen Sum Dag-Pa Kha-Chö Du Zig-Pa, Chag Yé-Pé Dor-Je Tsen-Pay Tri Gug Thur Du Kyang Ne Zin-Pa, Yön-Pé Thö-Pa Trag Gi Gang-Wa Teng Chog Su Zung Ne Shal Gyen Du Chog-Pé Söl-Wa, Trag-Pa Yön-Par Dor-Je Tsen-Pay Kha-Tam-Ga La Da-Ma-Ru Dang Dril-Bu Dang, Phen-Tse Sum-Pa Chang Shin-Pa Nam-Pa, Wu-Tra Nag-Po Sil Bur Gyur-Pé Ku Ke Yen-Ché Kheb Pa, Lang Tso Dar La Bab Ching Dö-Pay Nu-Bur Gye-Pa, De-Wa Kye-Pay Nyam Chen, Mi Go Kam-Po Ngay Wu-Gyen Dang, Kam-Po Nga Chui Do Shal Chen Cher-Bu Chag-Gya Nge Gyen-Pa, Ye-She Kyi Me Bar-Way Wü-Na Shug-Pay Te-War E E Lé Chö-Jung Mar-Po Tru Sum Nyi Tseg Kyi Wü-Su Vaṁ Yig Mar-Po, Dün Gyab Nyi Pang-Way Tra Shir Ga-Wa Khyil-Pa Re Yö-Par Gyur Par Sam

Imagine that from the state of emptiness arises a double dharmakara from *E E* (ཨེ་ཨེ་). Inside that, a moon maṇḍala arises from *Ah* (ཨ). In the center of which, there is a red *Vaṁ* (བྃ) surrounded by the red mantra garland circling to the left:

Oṁ oṁ oṁ sarvabuddhaḍākinīye vajra varṇṇanīye vajra vairocanīye hūṁ hūṁ hūṁ phaṭ phaṭ phaṭ svāhā

Rays of light shine from the *Vaṁ* (བྃ) encircled by the mantra garland filling the entire body. The misdeeds and obscurations of body, voice, and mind are purified. The body is transformed into a ball of light.

From the complete transformation of that, one turns into form of Vajrayoginī standing on a multicolored lotus and a sun seat. Her extended right leg presses down on red Kalaratri's breasts; her contracted left leg presses down on black Bhairava's head which is bent backwards. She is red in color, brilliant as the fire at the end of the eon. She has one face, two hands, and three eyes which gaze into the Khecari realm. Her right hand extends downwards holding a curved knife marked with a vajra. Her left hand holds aloft a skull filled with blood, from which she drinks with her upturned face. On her left shoulder is a khaṭvāṅga staff marked with a vajra, from which hang a damaru, a bell, and three banners. Her black hair is loose and falls to her waist. She has reached the fullness of youth, her breasts swelling with passion. She has an expression that generates bliss. She has a diadem of five dried human heads and a necklace of fifty dried ones.

She is naked, adorned with five bone ornaments. She stands in the center of the blazing fire of wisdom.

At her navel is a double dharmakara; in the center is a red syllable *Vaṁ* (བཾ); there are four wheels of bliss in the four corners, the front and back being empty.

བླ་མ་རྡོ་རྗེ་རྣལ་འབྱོར་མ་ཐ་མི་དད་པ་ལ་མོས་གུས་ཆེན་པོས་གསོལ་བ་འདེབས་པ་ནི།

The supplication with great devotion to the guru inseparable with Vajrayoginī:

སློབ་དཔོན་རིན་པོ་ཆེས། བདག་ལ་དེ་བཞིན་གཤེགས་པ་ཐམས་ཅད་ཀྱི་སྐུ་དང་གསུང་དང་ཐུགས་དང་ཡོན་ཏན་དང་ཕྲིན་ལས་ཐམས་ཅད་ཀྱི་དངོས་གྲུབ་དང་འཇིག་རྟེན་དང་འཇིག་རྟེན་ལས་འདས་པའི་དངོས་གྲུབ་མ་ལུས་པ་སྩལ་ཞིང་བརྟན་པར་མཛད་དུ་གསོལ། ཞེས་ལན་གསུམ་གསོལ་བ་བཏབ་པས།

Lob-Pon Rin-Po-Che, Dag La De-Shin Sheg-Pa Tham-Ché Kyi Ku Dang Sung Dang Thug Dang Yon-Ten Dang Trin-Lé Tham-Ché Kyi Ngö-Drub Dang Jig-Ten Dang Jig-Ten Lé Dé-Pay Ngö-Drub Ma Lü Pa Tsal Shing Ten-Par Zé-Du Söl

Offer [the supplication with great devotion to the guru inseparable with Vajrayoginī] three times:

Precious guru, please grant me all the siddhis of the body, speech, mind, qualities, and activities of all the Tathāgatas, as well as all mundane and transcendent siddhis and stabilize them.

སིནྡྷུ་རའི་དཀྱིལ་འཁོར་གྱི་དབུས་ན་བཞུགས་པའི་རྗེ་བཙུན་མའི་ཐུགས་ཀ་ནས་དེ་འདྲ་བའི་རྗེ་བཙུན་མ་མཐེབ་སོར་གྱི་ཚད་ཙམ་པ་ཞིག་དམར་ཧྲིལ་གྱིས་བྱོན་ནས་རང་གི་ཁར་ཐོགས་མེད་དུ་ཞུགས་པར་གྱུར་པར་བསམས་ལ་ཏིང་ལོའི་མར་མེ་ཡོད་ན་དེ་ཉིད།

Sin-Dhu-Ray Kyil-Khor Gyi Wü-Na Shug-Pay Je-Tsün-May Thug-Ka Ne De Dra-Way Je-Tsün-Ma Theb Sor Gyi Tse Tsam-Pa Shig Mar Hril Gyi Jon Ne Rang Gi Khar Thog-Me Du Shug-Par Gyur-Par Sam-La Ting-Lö Mar-Me Yö-Na Di-Nyi

Imagine that a red Jetsunma, about the size of one's thumb, emerges from the heart of the Jetsunma existing in the center of the sindhura maṇḍala and enters into one's mouth without impediment.

ཨོཾ་ཨོཾ་ཨོཾ་སརྦ་བུདྡྷ་ཌཱ་ཀི་ནཱི་ཡེ། བཛྲ་ཝརྞྞ་ནཱི་ཡེ།བཛྲ་བཻ་རོ་ཙ་ནཱི་ཡེ། ཧཱུྃ་ཧཱུྃ་ཧཱུྃ། ཕཊ་ཕཊ་ཕཊ་སྭཱ་ཧཱ། ཞེས་བརྗོད་ཅིང་རང་གི་ཁར་བཙུག་པར་བསམས་ལ།

Recite the following and imagine that fire ball enters into one's mouth:

Oṁ oṁ oṁ sarvabuddhaḍākinīye vajra varṇṇanīye vajra vairocanīye hūṁ hūṁ hūṁ phaṭ phaṭ phaṭ svāhā

རྣལ་འབྱོར་མ་དེ་ཉིད་རང་གི་སྤྱི་བོ་ནས་རྐང་མཐིལ་གྱི་བར་ལ་གར་སྟབས་མཛད་ཅིང་ཡར་འཕྲུག་མར་འཕྲུག་མཛད་པའི་མཐར་ལྟེ་བའི་བཾ་ཡིག་ལ་ཐིམ་པས་དེ་ཉིད་རྣལ་འབྱོར་མའི་སྐུ་གྱུར་བ་ནི། སྣ་ཚོགས་པདྨ་དང་ཉི་མའི་གདན་ལ་ཞབས་གཡས་བརྐྱང་བས་དུས་མཚན་མ་དམར་མོའི་ནུ་མའི་སྟེང་ནས་མནན་པ། གཡོན་བསྐུམ་པས་འཇིགས་བྱེད་ནག་པོའི་མགོ་བོ་རྒྱབ་ཏུ་བལྟབས་ནས་མནན་པ། སྐུ་མདོག་དམར་མོ་བསྐལ་པའི་

མེ་ལྟ་བུའི་གཟི་བརྗིད་ཅན། ཞལ་གཅིག་ཕྱག་གཉིས་སྤྱན་གསུམ་དགའ་བ་མཁའ་སྤྱོད་དུ་
གཟིགས་པ། ཕྱག་གཡས་པས་རྡོ་རྗེས་མཚན་པའི་གྲི་གུག་ཐུར་དུ་བརྐྱངས་ནས་འཛིན་
པ། གཡོན་པས་ཐོད་པ་ཁྲག་གིས་གང་བ་སྟེང་ཕྱོགས་སུ་བཟུང་ནས་ཞལ་གྱེན་ལ་
ཕྱོགས་པས་གསོལ་བ། ཕྲག་པ་གཡོན་པར་རྡོ་རྗེས་མཚན་པའི་ཁ་ཊྭཱཾ་ག་ལ་ཌཱ་མ་རུ་དང་
དྲིལ་བུ་དང་། འཕན་རྩེ་གསུམ་པ་འཕྱང་བཞིན་པ་བསྣམས་པ། དབུ་སྐྲ་ནག་པོ་སིལ་བུར་
གྱུར་པས་སྐུ་སྨད་ཡན་ཆད་ཁེབས་པ། ལང་ཚོ་དར་ལ་བབ་ཅིང་འདོད་པའི་ནུ་འབུར་
རྒྱས་པ། བདེ་བ་སྐྱེད་པའི་ཉམས་ཅན། མི་མགོ་སྐམ་པོ་ལྔའི་དབུ་རྒྱན་དང་། སྐམ་པོ་ལྔ་
བཅུའི་དོ་ཤལ་ཅན་གཅེར་བུ་ཕྱག་རྒྱ་ལྔས་བརྒྱན་པ། ཡེ་ཤེས་ཀྱི་མེ་འབར་བའི་དབུས་
ན་བཞུགས་པའོ།

Nal-Jor-Ma De Nyi Rang Gi Chi-Wo Ne Kang Thil Gyi Bar La Gar Tab Zé Ching Yar Khyug Mar Khyug Zé-Pay Thar Te-Way Vaṁ Yig La Thim-Pé De Nyi Nal-Jor-May Ku Gyur-Wa Ni, Na Tsog Pad-Ma Dang Nyi-May Den La Shab Yé Kyang-We Dü-Tsen-Ma Mar-Poy Nu-May Teng Ne Nen-Pa, Yön Kum-Pé Jig-Je Nag-Poy Go-Wo Gyab Tu Tab Ne Nen-Pa, Ku Dog Mar-Mo Kal-Pay Me Ta-Bui Zi Ji Chen, Shal Chig Chag Nyi Chen Sum Dag-Pa Kha-Chö Du Zig-Pa, Chag Yé-Pé Dor-Jé Tsen-Pay Ti Gug Thur Du Kyang Ne Zin-Pa, Yön-Pé Thö-Pa Trag Gi Gang-Wa Teng Chog Su Zung Ne Shal Gyen La Chog-Pé Söl-Wa, Tag-Pa Yön-Par Dor-Jé Tsen-Pay Kha-Tam-Ga La Da-Ma-Ru Dang Dril-Bu Dang, Phen-Tse Sum-Pa Chang Shin-Pa Nam-Pa, Wu-Tra Nag-Po Sil Bur Gyur-Pé Ku Ke Yen-Ché Kheb Pa, Lang Tso Dar La Bab Ching Dö-Pay Nu-Bur Gye-Pa De-Wa Kye-Pay Nyam Chen, Mi Go Kam-Po Ngay Wu-Gyen Dang Kam-Po Nga Chui Do Shal Chen, Cher-Bu Chag-Gya Nge Gyen-Pa, Ye-She Kyi Me Bar-Way Wü-Na Shug-Pa'o

That yoginī dances between the head and crown and races up and down. Finally, she dissolves into the *Vaṁ* (བྃ) syllable of the navel. It turns into the form of Vajrayoginī standing on a multicolored lotus and a sun seat. Her extended right leg presses down on red Kālarātri's breasts; her contracted left leg presses down on black Bhairava's head which is bent backwards. She is red in color, brilliant as the fire at the end of the eon. She has one face, two hands, and three eyes which gaze into the Khecarī realm. Her right hand extends downwards holding a curved knife marked with a vajra. Her left hand holds aloft a skull filled with blood from which she drinks with her upturned face. On her left shoulder is a khaṭvāṅga staff marked with a vajra, from which hang a damaru, a bell, and three banners. Her black hair is loose and falls to her waist. She has reached the fullness of youth, her breasts swelling with passion. She has an expression that generates bliss. She has a diadem of five dried human heads and a necklace of fifty dried ones. She is naked, adorned with five bone ornaments. She stands in the center of the blazing fire of wisdom.

རང་ཉིད་ཕྱིའི་རྣལ་འབྱོར་མར་གསལ་བའི་གནས་རྣམས་སུ་ཟླ་བའི་དཀྱིལ་འཁོར་གྱི་སྟེང་དུ་ལྟེ་བར་ཨོཾ་བཾ་དམར་མོ་རྡོ་རྗེ་ཕག་མོ། སྙིང་གར་ཧཾ་ཡོཾ་སྔོན་མོ་གཤིན་རྗེ་མ། ཁར་ཧྲིཾ་མོཾ་དཀར་མོ་རྨོངས་བྱེད་མ། དཔྲལ་བར་ཧྲིཾ་ཧྲིཾ་སེར་མོ་སྐྱོད་བྱེད་མ། སྤྱི་གཙུག་ཏུ་ཧཱུྃ་ཧཱུྃ་ལྗང་གུ་སྐྲག་བྱེད་མ། ཡན་ལག་ཐམས་ཅད་ཕཊ་ཕཊ་དུད་ཁ་ཙཎྜི་ཀའི་ངོ་བོ་སྒྱུར་ཞེས་བརྗོད་ཅིང་བསམ་ལ།

Rang Nyi Chiy Nal-Jor-Mar Sal-Way Ne Nam Su Da-Way Kyil-Khor Gyi Teng Du Te-War Oṁ Vaṁ Mar-Mo Dor-Je Phag-Mo, Nying Gar Haṁ Yoṁ Ngon-Mo Shin-Je-Ma, Khar Hriṁ Moṁ Kar-Mo Mong-Je-Ma, Tel-War Hriṁ Hriṁ Ser-Mo Kyo-Je-Ma, Chi Tsug Tu Hūṁ Hūṁ Jang Khu Tag-Je-Ma, Yen-Lag Tham-Ché La Phaṭ Phaṭ Dü-Kha Chan-Di-Kay Ngo-Wo Gyur She Jö-Ching Sam-La

Imagine that oneself manifesting as the outer Yoginī, on top of moon discs at these locations on one's body are:

red *Oṁ Vaṁ* (ཨོཾ་བཾ) on the navel,

the essence of Vārāhī;

blue *Haṁ Yoṁ* (ཧཾ་ཡོཾ) on the heart,

the essence of Yāminī;

white *Hriṁ Moṁ* (ཧྲིཾ་མོཾ) on the mouth,

the essence of Mohinī;

yellow *Hriṁ Hriṁ* (ཧྲིཾ་ཧྲིཾ) on the forehead,

the essence of Saṁcālinī;

green *Hūṁ Hūṁ* (ཧཱུཾ་ཧཱུཾ) on the crown,

the essence of Saṁtrāsinī;

smoky *Phaṭ Phaṭ* (ཕཊ྄་ཕཊ྄) on all the limbs,

the essence of Caṇḍikā.

ལྟེ་བའི་བཾ་ཡིག་དེ་ཉིད་གདོད་མ་ནས་ནང་གི་རྡོ་རྗེ་རྣལ་འབྱོར་མ་ཡིན་པ་དེ་ཐབས་འདིས་གསལ་བཏབ་པ་ཡིན་ནོ། དེ་ནས་མདུན་བསྐྱེད་ཀྱི་རྡོ་རྗེ་རྣལ་འབྱོར་མ་ལ་དཔའ་བོ་དང་རྣལ་འབྱོར་མའི་ཚོགས་ཀྱིས་བསྐོར་བ་རྣམས་ཀྱིས་དགེས་པའི་གར་མཛད། སྔགས་ཀྱི་སྒྲ་ཆེན་པོ་སྒྲོག་ཅིང་། གཙོ་མོའི་ཐུགས་ཀ་ནས་འོད་ཟེར་ཕྱོགས་བཅུར་འཕྲོས་པས་ཕྱོགས་བཅུའི་སངས་རྒྱས་དང་བྱང་ཆུབ་སེམས་དཔའ་དཔའ་བོ་དང་རྣལ་འབྱོར་མ་ཐམས་ཅད་རྗེ་བཙུན་རྡོ་རྗེ་རྣལ་འབྱོར་མའི་རྣམ་པར་བྱོན་ཏེ་རང་གི་སྤྱི་བོ་ནས་ཐིམ་པར་གྱུར་པར་བསམས་ལ།

Te-Way Vaṁ Yig Di-Nyi Dö-Ma Ne Nang Gi Dor-Je Nal-Jor-Ma Yin-Pa De Thab Di Sal-Tab-Pa Yin-No, De-Ne Dün-Kye Kyi Dor-Je Nal-Jor-Ma La Pa-Wo Dang Nal-Jor-May Tsog Kyi Kor-Wa Nam-Kyi Ge-Pay Gar-Ze Ngag-Kyi Dra Chen-Po Drog-Ching, Tso-Moy Thug-Ka-Ne Ö-Zer Chok Chur Trö-Pé Chog-Chui Sang-Gyé Dang Jang-Chub Sem-Pa Pa-Wo Dang Nal-Jor-Ma Tham-Ché Je-Tsün Dor-Je Nal-Jor-May Nam-Par Jon-Te Rang Gi Chi-Wor Ne Thim-Par Gyur-Par Sam-La

This is the method to visualize that the *Vaṁ* (བཾ) syllable at the navel has been the inner Vajrayoginī from the beginning. Next, imagine that the Vajrayoginī generated in front, surrounded by all the heroes and yoginīs, dances with joy and utters a great sound of mantras. Since light rays shine to the ten directions from the heart of the main deity, all of the Buddhas, Bodhisattvas, heroes, and yoginīs from the ten directions arrive in the form of Vajrayoginī and dissolve into one's crown.

ཨོཾ་ཨོཾ་ཨོཾ་སརྦ་བུདྡྷ་ཌཱ་ཀི་ནཱི་ཡེ། བཛྲ་ཝརྞྞ་ནཱི་ཡེ།བཛྲ་བཻ་རོ་ཙ་ནཱི་ཡེ། ཧཱུྃ་ཧཱུྃ་ཧཱུྃ། ཕཊ་ཕཊ་ཕཊ་སྭཱ་ཧཱ། དྲག་ཏུ་བརྗོད་ཅིང་ཌཱ་དྲིལ་དཀྲོལ། གུ་གུལ་གྱི་དུད་པས་བདུག

Recite loudly, play the damaru and bell, and burn gugul to make incense smoke:

Oṁ oṁ oṁ sarvabuddhaḍākinīye vajra varṇṇanīye vajra vairocanīye hūṁ hūṁ hūṁ phaṭ phaṭ phaṭ svāhā

སླར་ཡང་བདུན་བསྐྱེད་ཀྱི་ཐུགས་ཀ་ནས་ཀྱང་རྗེ་བཙུན་མའི་སྐུ་དཔག་ཏུ་མེད་པ་བྱུང་སྟེ་རང་གི་སྤྱི་བོ་ནས་ཐིམ་པར་གྱུར་པར་བསམས་ལ། སྔར་བཞིན་སྔགས་དང་སྤོས་རོལ་བྱ་བ་ནི་ཕྱིའི་རྣལ་འབྱོར་མ་སྤྱན་དྲངས་པའི་སྒོ་ནས་དབབ་པ་ཡིན།

Lar Yang Dun Kye Kyi Thug-Ka Ne Kyang Je-Tsün-May Ku Pag-Tu Me-Pa Jung Te Rang Gi Chi-Wo Ne Thim-Par Gyur Par Sam-La, Ngar-Shin Ngag Dang Pö-Röl Ja-Wa-Ni Chiy Nal-Jor-Ma Chen Trang-Pay Go-Ne Wab-Pa Yin

As before, reciting the mantra with incense and music to invite the outer Yoginī decently:

Once again, imagine that countless Jetsunmas emanate from the heart of the front generated deity and dissolve into one's crown.

རང་ཉིད་རྡོ་རྗེ་རྣལ་འབྱོར་མར་གསལ་བའི་སྨིན་མཚམས་ནས་གསང་གནས་ཀྱི་བར་དུ་རྩ་དབུ་མ་ཁ་དོག་དམར་པོ་སྦུབ་སྟོང་སྦོམ་ཕྲ་མདའ་སྨྱུག་འབྲིང་པོ་ཙམ་པའི་མས་སྣར་དགའ་བ་འཁྱིལ་པ་ཁ་དོག་དམར་པོ་གཡོན་བསྐོར་དུ་ཤུགས་དྲག་ཏུ་འཁོར་བས། དབུ་མའི་ནང་ནས་ཡར་བྱ་འཕུར་བ་བཞིན་སྙིང་གའི་ཐད་དུ་སོང་བས་ལུས་སེམས་ཐམས་ཅད་བདེ་བས་ཁྱབ་པར་གྱུར་པར་བསམས།

Rang Nyi Dor-Je Nal-Jor-Mar Sal-Way Min Tsam Ne Sang Ne Kyi Bar-Du Tsa Wu-Ma Kha-Dog Mar-Po Bub Tong Bom Tra Da Nyug Dring-Po Tsam-Pay Mé Nar Ga-Wa Khyil-Pa Kha-Dog Mar-Po Yön Kor-Du Shug Drag-Tu Khor-We, Wu-May Nang Ne Yar Ja Phur-Wa Shin Nyin-Gay The-Du Song-We Lü Sem Tham-Ché De-We Khyab-Par Gyur-Par Sam

Imagine that oneself appearing as Vajrayoginī, from one's forehead to the secret place is the central channel, red, hollow, about the size of medium bamboo arrow shaft. At the lower tip is a red bliss swirl spinning rapidly to the left. Since it moves upward inside the central channel to the level of the heart like a bird, bliss spreads through one's body and mind.

དབུ་མའི་ཡས་སྣར་དགའ་བ་འཁྱིལ་པ་ཁ་དོག་དཀར་པོ་གཡོན་བསྐོར་དུ་ཤུགས་དྲག་ཏུ་འཁོར་བས། དབུ་མའི་ནང་ནས་མར་འཁོར་བཞིན་པས་སྙིང་གའི་ཐད་དུ་བྱུང་བས་སྣང་བ་ཐམས་ཅད་སྟོང་ཉིད་ཀྱི་ངང་དུ་ཐིམ་ཞིང་དགའ་འཁྱིལ་དེ་གཉིས་སྙིང་གར་རོ་གཅིག་ཏུ་འདྲེས་པས་བདེ་སྟོང་གཉིས་མེད་ཀྱི་ཡེ་ཤེས་ཀྱི་ངོ་བོ་དགའ་བ་འཁྱིལ་བ་དམར་སྐྱ་ཤུགས་དྲག་ཏུ་འཁོར་བ་དང་། མཐར་དེ་ཉིད་ཀྱང་ནམ་མཁའ་ལ་འཇའ་ཡལ་བ་བཞིན་དུ་གྱུར་པར་བསམས་ལ། བརྗོད་མེད་ཀྱི་ངང་ལ་ཇི་ཙམ་གནས་ཀྱི་བར་དུ་མཉམ་པར་བཞག་ཅིང་སྨོས་རོལ་བྱ་བ་ནི་གསང་བ་བདེ་སྟོང་དབྱེར་མེད་ཀྱི་རྣལ་འབྱོར་མདོ་སྒྲུད་པ་ཡིན།

Wu-May Ye Nar Ga-Wa Kyil-Pa Kha-Dog Kar-Po Yön Kor-Du Shug Drag-Tu Khor-We, Wu-May Nang Ne Mar Khor Shin-Pé Nyin-Gay The-Du Jung-We Nang-Wa Tham-Ché Tong Nyi Kyi Ngang Du Thim

Shing Ga Khyil De Nyi Nying-Gar Ro Chig Tu Dre-Pé De-Tong Nyi Me Kyi Ye-She Kyi Ngo-Wo Ga-Wa Khyil-Wa Mar Kya Shug Drag-Tu Khor-Wa Dang, Thar De-Nyi Kyang Nam-Kha La Ja Yal-Wa Shin Du Gyur-Par Sam-La, Jö-Me Kyi Ngang La Ji-Tsam Ne Kyi Bar-Du Nyam-Par Shag-Ching Pö-Röl Ja-Wa-Ni Sang-Wa De-Tong Yir-Me Kyi Nal-Jor-Ma Ngo Tre-Pa Yin

At the upper tip of the central channel, there is a white bliss swirl spinning rapidly to the left. Since it descends down inside the central channel arriving at the level of the heart, all appearances dissolve into the state of emptiness. Those two bliss swirls merged into one taste become a rapidly spinning pink bliss swirl with the nature of bliss and emptiness. Finally, imagine that it becomes like a rainbow disappearing in space.

With music and incense, remaining in this inexpressible state, that introduces the inseparable bliss and emptiness of the secret yoginī.

ཅེས་གསང་བར་གདམས་པ་ནི།

ཌྷུ་ཌྷུ་ར་གུ་ཧྱ་ས་མ་ཡཿ དེ་ལྟར་བྱིན་རླབས་ཞུགས་པ་དེ་མི་འབྲལ་ཞིང་བརྟན་པར་བསམ་ལ།

Dhu dhu ra guhya samayaḥ De-Tar Jin-Lab Shug-Pa De Mi-Tral Shing Ten-Par Sam-La

The instruction on secrecy:

Dhu dhu ra guhya samayaḥ

As such, imagine that the blessing enters; one is never parted from them; and they are stabilized.

ལུས་ཀྱི་གོ་ཆའི་ལྷ་རྣམས་དྲན་པས།
ཨོཾ་བཾ། ཧཾ་ཡོཾ། ཧྲཱིཾ་མོཾ། ཧྲིཾ་ཧྲིཾ། ཧཱུཾ་ཧཱུཾ། ཕཊ་ཕཊ།

Recall the deities of the body armor:

Oṁ Vaṁ (ཨོཾ་བཾ), *Haṁ Yoṁ* (ཧཾ་ཡོཾ), *Hrīṁ Moṁ* (ཧྲཱིཾ་མོཾ), *Hriṁ Hriṁ* (ཧྲིཾ་ཧྲིཾ), *Hūṁ Hūṁ* (ཧཱུཾ་ཧཱུཾ), *Phaṭ Phaṭ* (ཕཊ་ཕཊ)

ཅེས་ཚར་གཅིག་བརྗོད་ཅིང་སྤྱི་བོར་རྡོ་རྗེ་རྒྱ་གྲམ་དུ་བཞག་ལ།
ཏིཥྛ་བཛྲ། ཞེས་བརྗོད་ཅིང་བྱིན་རླབས་ཀྱི་ཉམས་མྱོང་ལ་ཅུང་ཟད་མཉམ་པར་བཞག

Place the crossed vajra on one's head and recite this once:

Tistha vajra

Remain in equipoise for a little while on the experience of the blessing.

མེ་ཏོག་གི་ཕྲེང་བ་རྗེ་བཙུན་མའི་ཐུགས་ཀར་ཕུལ་བར་བསམ་ཞིང་། ཨོཾ་པྲ་ཏཱིཙྪ་བཛྲ་ཧོཿ ཞེས་པས་སིནྡྷུ་རའི་མཎྜལ་གྱི་དབུས་ཀྱི་དབུས་སུ་ཕུལ་བའི་སྟངས་ཀ་ཙམ་བྱས། མེ་ཏོག་གི་ཕྲེང་བ་དེ་ཉིད་སྔགས་ཀྱི་ཕྲེང་བར་བྱིན་གྱིས་བརླབས་ནས། རྗེ་བཙུན་མས་རང་གི་སྤྱི་བོར་བཞག་པར་མོས་ལ།

Me-Tog Gi Treng-Wa Je-Tsün-May Thug-Kar Phul-War Sam-Shing, Oṁ pratīccha vajra hoḥ She-Pé Sin-Dhu-Ray Maṇ-Da-La Gyi Wü Gyi Wü Su Phul-Way Tang-Ka Tsam Je, Me-Tog Gi Treng-Wa Di-Nyi Ngag-Kyi Treng-War Jin-Gyi Lab Ne, Je-Tsün-Mé Rang Gi Chi-Wor Shag-Par Mö-La

Imagine one offers a garland of flowers to the heart of Jetsunma.

Oṁ pratīccha vajra hoḥ, make a gesture of offering it to the center of the sindhura maṇḍala. Imagine that Jetsunma blesses that flower garland into a mantra garland to place it on one's crown.

ཨོཾ་པྲ་ཏི་གྲྀཧྞ་སྟྭཾ། ཨི་མཾ་སཏྭ་མ་ཧཱ་བ་ལ་ཞེས་གསུང་བར་བསམས་ཤིང་སྤྱི་བོར་བཞག
དེ་ལྟར་སེམས་དང་བཾ་ལྷན་ཅིག་སྐྱེས་པའི་ཕག་མོར་ཡེ་ནས་གནས་པ་ཆོ་ག་དེ་དག་གིས་
གསལ་བར་བྱས་པས། དཀྱིལ་འཁོར་མཐོང་བ་ལ་སྒྲིབ་བྱེད་བསལ་བའི་མཚོན་བྱེད་དུ།
རྣལ་འབྱོར་མས་གདོང་གཡོགས་དཀྲོལ་བར་མོས་ཏེ།

Oṁ prati grihana stvaṁ, imaṁ sattva mahā bala She Sung-War Sam-Shing Chi-Wor Shag The-Tar Sem Dang Vaṁ Lhen-Chig Khye-Pay Phag-Mor Ye-Ne Ne-Pa Cho-Ga The-Thag Gi Sal-War Je-Pe, Kyil-Kor Thong-Wa-La Drib-Je Sal-Way Tson-Je Du, Nal-Jor-Mé Dong-Yog Trol-War Mö-Te

Imagine that she says, *"Oṁ prati grihana stvam, imam sattva mahā bala"*, and places the mantra garland on the crown. Through that procedure, the mind and *Vaṁ* (བཾ) that have been always existing as the connate Vārāhī is revealed. As a symbol of removing the obstruction to see the maṇḍala, Yoginī releases the blindfold.

རྣལ་འབྱོར་མ་དཔལ་དེང་ཁྱོད་ཀྱི།།
མིག་འབྱེད་པར་ནི་བརྩོན་པར་མཛད།།

ཕྱེ་བས་ཐམས་ཅད་མཐོང་གྱུར་པ།།
རྡོ་རྗེའི་མིག་ནི་བླ་ན་མེད།།

Nal-Jor-Ma Pal Deng Khyö-Kyi
Mig Je-Par Ni Tsön-Par Ze
Che-We Tham-Ché Thong Gyur-Pa
Dor-Jey Mig Ni La Na Me

Glorious Yoginī, today
be diligent to open your eyes!
The vajra eye is unsurpassed,
seeing everything when opened.

ཨོཾ་བཛྲ་ནཻ་ཏྲ་ཨ་པ་ཧཱ་ར་པཊ་ལཾ་ཧྲཱིཿ པྲཾ། ཅེས་དང་། ཁྱེད་རྣམས་རྡོ་རྗེ་རྣལ་འབྱོར་མའི་དཀྱིལ་འཁོར་ལ་ལྟོས་ཞེས་གསུངས་ཤིང་། བལྟས་པས་རྟེན་དང་བརྟེན་པར་བཅས་པའི་དཀྱིལ་འཁོར་ཐམས་ཅད་མངོན་སུམ་དུ་མཐོང་བར་གྱུར་པར་མོས། དེ་དག་ནི་འཇུག་པའི་ཆོས་འཁོར་དང་བཅས་པའོ།

Oṁ vajra naitra apahāra phaṭ laṁ hrīḥ praṁ, Che Dang, Khye-Nam Dor-Je Nal-Jor-May Kyil-Khor La Tö She Sung Shing, Te-Pé Ten Dang Ten-Par Ché-Pay Kyil-Khor Tham-Ché Ngön-Sum Du Thong-War Gyur Par Mö

She says, "*Oṁ vajra naitra apahāra phaṭ laṁ hrīḥ praṁ*, you all should look at the maṇḍala of Vajrayoginī!"

Imagine that the whole maṇḍala with its support and supported is seen in person.

These conclude the dharma wheel of the admission.

The Main Part

དངོས་གཞི་དབང་བཞི་བྱིན་རླབས་ཀྱི་ཚུལ་དུ་བསྐུར་བ་ལ།

The main section is conferring the four empowerments in the form of a blessing.

མཎྜལ་བཤམས་ལ། མཎྜལ་རི་རབ་གླིང་བཞི་ཉི་ཟླ་ཟུང་གཅིག་ལྷ་མིའི་དཔལ་འབྱོར་ཕུན་སུམ་ཚོགས་པ་མ་ཚང་བ་མེད་པ་འདི་ཉིད་བླ་མ་དང་རྡོ་རྗེ་རྣལ་འབྱོར་མ་ཐ་མི་དད་པ་ལ་བྱིན་རླབས་ཟབ་མོ་ཞུ་བའི་ཡོན་དུ་འབུལ་བར་བགྱིའོ། ཐུགས་རྗེས་འགྲོ་བའི་དོན་དུ་བཞེས་སུ་གསོལ། བཞེས་ནས་བྱིན་གྱིས་བརླབ་ཏུ་གསོལ། ཞེས་པས་ཡོན་འབུལ།

Man-Da-La Ri-Rab Ling Shi Nyi Da Zung Chig Lha Miy Pal-Jor Phun Sum Tsog-Pa Ma-Tsang-Wa Me-Pa Di Nyi La-Ma Dang Dor-Je Nal-Jor-Ma Tha Mi Dé-Pa La Jin Lab Zab-Mo Zhu-Way Yon Du-Bül-War Gyi'o, Thug-Jey Dro-Way Don-Du She Su Söl, She Ne Jin Gyi Lab-Tu Söl

Arrange a maṇḍala offering. Then, make the offering:

A maṇḍala of Sumeru, the four continents, the sun and the moon, the abundant prestige and wealth of devas and humans in no way incomplete is offered to the guru inseparable with Jetsun Vajrayoginī to request blessings. Please accept this with compassion for the benefit of migrating beings. Having accepted it, please bless me.

རྣལ་འབྱོར་མ་དཔལ་དབང་བསྐུར་བ།།
འགྲོ་བ་སྐྱོབ་པའི་གཞི་བརྗོད་ཅན།།

ཇི་ལྟར་ཡོན་ཏན་འབྱུང་གནས་གཙོ།།
དེ་བཞིན་བདག་ལ་དེང་སྩོལ་ཅིག།
ཅེས་པའམ། ཡང་ན།
བྱང་ཆུབ་རྡོ་རྗེ་སངས་རྒྱས་ལ།།
མཆོག་ཆེན་ཇི་ལྟར་སྩལ་བ་ལྟར།།
བདག་ཀྱང་སྐྱོབ་པའི་དོན་གྱི་ཕྱིར།།
ནམ་མཁའི་རྡོ་རྗེ་དེང་བདག་སྩོལ།། ཞེས་ལན་གསུམ་གྱིས་གསོལ་བ་བཏབ།

Nal-Jor-Ma Pal Wang Kur-Wa
Dro-Wa Kyob-Pay Zi Ji Chen
Ji-Tar Yon-Ten Jung Ne Tso
De Shin Dag La Deng Tsöl Chig

[Or:]
Jang-Chub Dor-Je Sang-Gyé La
Chog Chen Ji-Tar Tsal-Wa Tar
Dag Kyang Kyob-Pay Don Gyi Chir
Nam-Khay Dor-Je Deng Dag Tsöl

Offer this supplication three times:

Just as the empowerment conferred by Shrī Yoginī,
the brilliant protector of migrating beings,
the chief source of all qualities,
likewise, now bestow it upon me!

Or, [offer the following supplication three times:]

Just as Bodhivajra conferred
the most supreme upon the Buddha,
in order to protect me, also
confer the vajra of space now upon me!

རང་ཉིད་སིནྡྷུ་རའི་དཀྱིལ་འཁོར་གྱི་མདུན་དུ་སེང་གེས་བཏེགས་པའི་རིན་པོ་ཆེའི་ཁྲི་སྣ་ཚོགས་པདྨ་དང་ཉི་མ་འཇིགས་བྱེད་དུས་མཚན་གྱི་གདན་ལ་སྐད་ཅིག་གིས་རྡོ་རྗེ་རྣལ་འབྱོར་མར་གསལ་བའི་སྟེང་དུ་གདུགས་དཀར་པོ་གསེར་གྱི་ཡུ་བ་ཅན། མཐའ་བསྐོར་དུ་མཆོད་པའི་སྤྲིན་ཕུང་བསམ་གྱིས་མི་ཁྱབ་པས་བསྐོར་བར་གྱུར།

Rang Nyi Sin-Dhu-Ray Kyil-Khor Gyi Dün Du Seng-Gey Teg-Pay Rin-Po-Chey Ti Na Tsog Pad-Ma Dang Nyi-Ma Jig-Je Dü-Tsen Gyi Den La Ke Chig Gi Dor-Je Nal-Jor-Mar Sal-Way Teng-Du Dug Kar-Po Ser Gyi Yu-Wa Chen, Tha Kor-Du Chö-Pay Trin Phum Sam Gyi Mi Khyab-Pé Kor-War Gyur

In front of the sindhura maṇḍala, in an instant one appears as Vajrayoginī on a jeweled throne supported by lions, standing upon a multicolored lotus, sun, Kālarātri and Bhairava; above is a white parasol with a golden handle. One is surrounded by oceanic cloud of offerings, inconceivable and all around.

ཡཾ། ཞེས་བརྗོད་པས། རྗེ་བཙུན་མའི་ཐུགས་ཀ་ནས་འོད་ཟེར་འཕྲོས་པས་རང་བཞིན་གྱི་གནས་ནས་དབང་གི་ལྷ་དཔལ་འཁོར་ལོ་བདེ་མཆོག་ལྷ་དྲུག་ཅུ་རྩ་གཉིས་ཀྱི་དཀྱིལ་འཁོར་མདུན་གྱི་ནམ་མཁར་བཀྲ་ལམ་གྱིས་བྱོན་པའི་ཧེ་རུ་ཀ་ཡབ་ཡུམ་གྱིས་དབང་བསྐུར་བའི་དགོངས་པ་མཛད། སྙིང་པོའི་རྣལ་འབྱོར་མ་བཞིས་རྡོ་རྗེའི་གླུ་ལེན། ཁཎྜ་ཀ་པཱ་ལི་ལ་སོགས་པའི་དཔའ་བོ་རྣམས་ཀྱིས་ཤིས་པ་བརྗོད། རབ་ཏུ་གཏུམ་མོ་ལ་སོགས་པའི་རྣལ་འབྱོར་མ་རྣམས་ཀྱིས་མཆོད་པའི་ལས་བརྩམ། སྒོ་མཚམས་མ་བརྒྱད་ཀྱིས་བགེགས་དང་ལོག་པར་འདྲེན་པའི་ཚོགས་རྣམས་རྒྱང་རིང་དུ་བསྐྲད་པར་གྱུར་པར་བསམས་ལ།

Phaiṁ, Ze Jö Pe, Je-Tsün-May Thug-Ka Ne Ö-Zer Trö-Pé Rang-Shin Gyi Ne Ne Wang Gi Lha Pal Khor-Lo De-Chog Lha Drug Chu Tsa Nyi Kyi Kyil-Khor Dün Gyi Nam-Khar Tra Lam Gyi Jon-Pay He-Ru-Ka Yab Yum Gyi Wang Kur-Way Gong-Pa Ze, Nying-Poy Nal-Jor-Ma Shi Dor-Jey Lu Len, Khan-Da Ka-Pa-Li La Sog Pay Pa-Wo Nam Kyi Shi-Pa Jö, Rab-Tu Tum-Mo La Sog Pay Nal-Jor-Ma Nam Kyi Chö-Pay Lé Tsam, Go Tsam Ma Gye Kyi Geg Dang Log-Par Dren-Pay Tsog Nam Gyang Ring-Du Tre-Par Gyur-Par Sam-La

By reciting *Phaiṁ*, light rays shine from the heart of Jetsunma, inviting the empowerment deities, the sixty-two deities of Shrī Chakrasamvara maṇḍala from their natural abode into the sky in front. The Heruka father and mother intend to bestow the empowerment. Imagine that four yoginīs from the [Heruka's] heart sing vajra songs. The heroes such as Khaṇḍakapāli and so on recite benedictions. Yoginīs such as Pracaṇḍā and so on begin the activity of offerings. The eight-door female guardians frighten the entire assembly of the obstructors and false guides to be far away.

མེ་ཏོག་འཐོར་ཞིང་དྲིལ་བུ་གསིལ་བས།
ཧེ་རུ་ཀ་དཔལ་འབར་བའི་སྐུ་མངའ་བ།།
ཧ་ཧའི་གད་རྒྱངས་ས་གསུམ་གཡོ་བར་བྱེད།།
ཧཱུྃ་ཧཱུྃ་ཕཊ་ཕཊ་བདུད་ཀྱི་ཀླད་འགེམས་པའི།།
བདེ་མཆོག་འཁོར་ལོའི་བཀྲ་ཤིས་དེང་འདིར་སྩོལ།།

He-Ru-Ka Pal Bar-Way Ku Nga-Wa
Ha Hay Ge Gyang Sa Sum Yo-War Je

Hūṁ Hūṁ Phaṭ Phaṭ Dü-Kyi Le Gem-Pay
De-Chog Khor-Loy Ta-Shi Deng Dir Tsöl

Ring bell and scatter flowers while reciting:

Heruka possesses a glorious, blazing body,
shaking the three realms with his laugh, *Ha Ha!*
Smashing the brain of Mara with *Hūṁ Hūṁ Phaṭ Phaṭ*,
Chakrasamvara grants good fortune here and now.

ཨེ་ཝཾ་མཉམ་པར་སྦྱོར་བ་སྔགས་ཀྱི་སྐུ།།
ཨཱ་ལི་ཀཱ་ལི་གཉིས་མེད་རོལ་པའི་གསུང་།།
ཨོཾ་གྱི་ངོ་བོར་སོན་པའི་ཐུགས་མངའ་བ།།
རྡོ་རྗེ་ཕག་མོའི་བཀྲ་ཤིས་དེང་འདིར་སྩོལ།། ཞེས་བརྗོད།

E Vaṁ Nyam-Par Jor-Wa Ngag Kyi Ku
Ah-Li Ka-Li Nyi-Me Röl-Pay Sung
Oṁ Gyi Ngo-Wor Son-Pay Thug Nga-Wa
Dor-Je Phag-Moy Ta-Shi Deng Dir Tsöl

Recite:

With the mantra body in union with *E* (ཨེ) and *Vaṁ* (ཝཾ),
the speech expressing the vowels and consonants nondually,
and the mind encountering the nature of *Oṁ* (ཨོཾ),
Vajravārāhī grants good fortune here and now.

དེ་ནས་གཙོ་བོའི་ཐུགས་ཀ་ནས་སྤྲུལ་པའི་སྒོ་མཚམས་མ་བརྒྱད་ཀྱིས་ཟླ་བ་ལྟར་དཀར་
བའི་བུམ་པ་བྱང་ཆུབ་སེམས་ཀྱི་བདུད་རྩི་ལྷས་ཡོངས་སུ་གང་བ་ཡལ་འདབ་དང་བཅས་

པ་ཅུང་ཟད་ཡོ་བར་འཛིན་པས་བྱང་ཆུབ་སེམས་ཀྱི་ཆུ་རྒྱུན་གྱིས་སྤྱི་བོ་ནས་དབང་བསྐུར་བར་གྱུར་པར་བསམས་ལ།

De-Ne Tso-Woy-Thug-Ka Ne Trül-Pay Go Tsam Ma Gye Kyi Da-Wa Tar Kar-Way Bum-Pa Jang-Chub Sem Kyi Dü-Tsi Nge Yong Su Gang-Wa Yal Dab Dang Ché-Pa Chung Zé Yo-War Zin Pé Jang-Chub Sem Kyi Chu Gyun Gyi Chi-Wo Ne Wang Kyur-War Gyur-Par Sam-La

Then, imagine that from the heart of the main deity emanates the eight-door guardians. With a sprig, they fill up the vase, white like the moon, with the five amritas of bodhicitta. By slightly tilting the vase, they confer the empowerment on the crown with a stream of bodhicitta.

ཇི་ལྟར་བལྟམས་པ་ཙམ་གྱིས་ནི།།
ལྷ་རྣམས་ཀྱིས་ནི་ཁྲུས་གསོལ་ལྟར།།
ལྷ་ཡི་ཆུ་ནི་དག་པ་ཡིས།།
དེ་བཞིན་བདག་གིས་དབང་བསྐུར་རོ།།

Ji-Tar Tam-Pa Tsam Gyi Ni
Lha Nam Kyi Ni Tru Söl Tar
Lha Yi Chu Ni Dag-Pa Yi
De-Shin Dag Gi Wang Kur Ro

Just as he [the Buddha] was washed by the gods
at the time of his birth,
likewise, we will bestow the empowerment
with pure divine water.

ༀ་སརྦ་ཏ་ཐཱ་ག་ཏ་ཨ་བྷི་ཥེ་ཀ་ཏ་ས་མ་ཡ་ཤྲཱི་ཡེ་ཧཱུྃ། ཙཀྲ་བཱི་ར་སྟྭཾ། ཨ་བྷི་ཥིཉྩ་མཾ། ཀཱ་ཀཱ་སྱ། ཨཱུ་ལཱུ་ཀཱ་སྱ། ཤྭ་ན་ཀ་སྱ། སཱུ་ཀ་རཱ་སྱ། ཡ་མ་དཱ་ཌྷཱི། ཡ་མ་དུ་ཏཱི། ཡ་མ་དཾ་ཥྚི་ཎཱི། ཡ་མ་མ་ཐཱ་ནི། ༀ་བཛྲཱི་བྷ་ཝ་ཨ་བྷི་ཥིཉྩ་ཧཱུྃ།

Oṁ sarvatathāgata abhiṣekata samaya shrīye hūṁ, chakra vīra stvaṁ, abhishiñcamaṁ, kākāsya, ūlukāsya, shvanakasya, sūkarāsya, yamadādhī, yamadutī, yamadaṁshtinī, yamamathāni, oṁ vajrī bhava abhishiñca hūṁ

ཞེས་གསུང་ཞིང་བུམ་པའི་ཆུས་སྤྱི་བོ་ནས་དབང་བསྐུར་བས་སྐུ་གང་། དྲི་མ་དག་ཆུའི་ལྷག་མ་ཡར་ལུད་པ་ལས་རྣམ་པར་སྣང་མཛད་ཀྱིས་དབུར་བརྒྱན། དབང་ལྷ་རྣམས་ཛཿ ཧཱུྃ་བཾ་ཧོཿ ཞེས་པས་རང་གི་སྤྱི་བོ་ནས་ཐིམ། རང་ཉིད་ཁམས་གསུམ་ཆོས་ཀྱི་རྒྱལ་པོར་དབང་བསྐུར་བ་ལ་རྗེ་བཙུན་མ་འཁོར་བཅས་ཀྱིས་རབ་གནས་མཛད་པར་གྱུར་པར་བསམས་ལ།

She Sung Shing Bum-Pay Chü Chi-Wo Ne Wang Kur-We Ku Gang, Dri-Ma Dag Chui Lhag Ma Yar Lü-Pa Lé Nam-Par Nang-Zé Kyi Wur-Gyen, Wang Lha Nam Jaḥ hūṁ vaṁ hoḥ She-Pé Rang Gi Chi-Wo Ne Thim, Rang Nyi Kham Sum Chö Kyi Gyal-Por Wang Kur-Wa La Je-Tsün-Ma Khor Ché Kyi Rab-Ne Zé-Par Gyur Par Sam La

They confer the empowerment on the crown, one's body is filled, the taints are purified; and from the overflow of the excess water, Vairocana adorns one's crown.

With *Jaḥ hūṁ vaṁ hoḥ*, the empowerment deities dissolve into one's crown. Imagine that one is empowered and consecrated to be the ruler of the three realms by Jetsunma and her retinue.

ༀ་སུ་པྲ་ཏིཥྛ་བཛྲ་ཡེ་སྭཱ་ཧཱ། ཞེས་བརྗོད་ཅིང་མེ་ཏོག་གཏོར་བ་ནི་དབང་གི་དངོས་གཞི་འོ།

Reciting [the following] and scattering flowers is the main part of the empowerment:
Oṁ supratistha vajraye svāhā

མདུན་གྱི་རྗེ་བཙུན་མའི་ཐུགས་ཀའི་བཾ་ཡིག་ལས་སྔགས་ཀྱི་ཕྲེང་བ་ཁ་དོག་དམར་པོ་ཆུ་ལས་ཆུ་བུར་རྡོལ་བའི་ཚུལ་དུ་ཐོལ་ཐོལ་བྱུང་། རྗེ་བཙུན་མའི་ཞལ་ནས་འཐོན། རང་གི་ཁར་ཞུགས་སྙིང་གའི་བཾ་ཡིག་ལ་ཐིམ་པར་གྱུར་པར་བསམས་ལ།

Dün Gyi Je-Tsün-May Thug-Kay Vaṁ Yig Lé Ngag Kyi Treng-Wa Kha-Dog Mar-Po Chu Lé Chu-Bur Dol-Way Tsul Du Thol Thol Jung, Je-Tsün-May Shal Ne Thon, Rang Gi Khar Shug Nyin-Gay Vaṁ Yig La Thim-Par Gyur Par Sam-La

Imagine that a mantra garland bubbles out from the *Vaṁ* (བཾ) syllable in the heart of the Jetsunma in front just like water bubbles out of a spring. It leaves Jetsunma's mouth, enters into one's own mouth, and dissolves into the *Vaṁ* (བཾ) syllable at one's heart.

ༀ་ༀ་ༀ་སརྦ་བུདྡྷ་ཌཱ་ཀི་ནཱི་ཡེ། བཛྲ་ཝརྞྞ་ནཱི་ཡེ།བཛྲ་བཻ་རོ་ཙ་ནཱི་ཡེ། ཧཱུྃ་ཧཱུྃ་ཧཱུྃ། ཕཊ་ཕཊ་ཕཊ་སྭཱ་ཧཱ། ཞེས་ལན་གསུམ་བརྗོད།

Recite three times:
Oṁ oṁ oṁ sarvabuddhaḍākinīye vajra varṇṇanīye vajra vairocanīye hūṁ hūṁ hūṁ phaṭ phaṭ phaṭ svāhā

དེ་ནས་རྡོ་རྗེ་རྣལ་འབྱོར་མ་མཁའ་སྤྱོད་སྒྲུབ་པའི་ཡི་དམ་གྱི་ལྷར་བཟུང་སྙམ་པས་མེ་ཏོག་འཐོར་ཞིང༌། བཅོམ་ལྡན་བདག་ལ་སྩོལ་ལགས་ཀྱིས། །བཅོམ་ལྡན་བདག་ལ་བྱིན་གྱི་རློབས། ཞེས་ལན་གསུམ་བརྗོད།

De-Ne Dor-Je Nal-Jor-Ma Kha-Chö Drup-Pay Yi-Dam Gyi Lhar Zung Nyam-Pé Me-Tog Thor-Shing, Chom-Den Dag La Tsel Lag Kyi, Chom-Den Dag La Jin Gyi Lob

Next, think that one will take Vajrayoginī as one's yidam for accomplishing Khecarī and scatter flowers.

Recite three times:

Bhagavatī, please bestow it on me.
Bhagavatī, bless me.

རྗེ་བཙུན་མས་མེ་ཏོག་གི་ཕྲེང་བ་དེ་ཉིད་སྔགས་ཀྱི་ཕྲེང་བར་བྱིན་གྱིས་རླབས་ཏེ། རང་གི་སྤྱི་གཙུག་ཏུ་བཞག་ཅིང་གསུངས་པར་བསམས་ལ། བཅོམ་ལྡན་འདི་ལ་སྩོལ་ལགས་ཀྱིས། །བཅོམ་ལྡན་འདི་ལ་བྱིན་གྱིས་རློབས། ཞེས་ལན་གསུམ་བརྗོད།

Je-Tsün-Mé Me-Tog Gi Treng-Wa De-Nyi Ngag Kyi Treng-War Jin-Gyi Lab-Te Rang Gi Chi Tsug Tu Shag Ching Sung-Par Sam-La, Chom-Den Di La Tsal Lag Kyi, Chom-Den Di La Jin Gyi Lob

Jetsunma blesses that flower garland into a mantra garland and places it on one's crown.

Imagine she says three times:

"The Bhagavatī will bestow this."
"The Bhagavatī will bless this."

སིནྡྷུ་རའི་རྡུལ་ཚོན་ནས་གཡོན་པའི་མཐེབ་སྲིན་གྱིས་བླངས་ཏེ། དཔྲལ་བ་མགྲིན་པ་སྙིང་ཁ་རྣམས་སུ་ཐིག་ལེ་བྱ་ཞིང་།

Take sindhura powder with the left ring finger, and make dots on the forehead, throat and heart.

ༀ་ༀ་ༀ་སརྦ་བུདྡྷ་ཌཱ་ཀི་ནཱི་ཡེ། བཛྲ་ཝརྞྞ་ནཱི་ཡེ།བཛྲ་བཻ་རོ་ཙ་ནཱི་ཡེ། ཧཱུྃ་ཧཱུྃ་ཧཱུྃ། ཕཊ་ཕཊ་ཕཊ་སྭཱ་ཧཱ། ཞེས་ལན་གསུམ་བརྗོད།

Recite three times:

Oṁ oṁ oṁ sarvabuddhaḍākinīye vajra varṇṇanīye vajra vairocanīye hūṁ hūṁ hūṁ phaṭ phaṭ phaṭ svāhā

སྐུ་ཚོམ་བུའི་དཀྱིལ་འཁོར་ལ་བརྟེན་ནས་བུམ་པའི་དབང་ཐོབ། ལུས་ཀྱི་དྲི་མ་དག་རྣལ་འབྱོར་མའི་སྐུ་བསྒོམ་པ་ལ་དབང་ཞིང་སྐུའི་བྱིན་རླབས་དང་དངོས་གྲུབ་ཐམས་ཅད་ཐོབ་པ་ཡིན་ནོ། ཞེས་བརྗོད་ཅིང་རྗེ་བཙུན་མས་གསུངས་པར་བསམ།

Ku Tsom-Bui Kyil-Khor La Ten Ne Bum-Pay Wang Thob, Lü-Kyi Dri-Ma Dag Nal-Jor-May Ku Gom-Pa La Wang Shing Kui Jin-Lab Dang Ngö-Drub Tham-Ché Thọb-Pa Yin No

Recite with imagining that Jetsunma says:

"You have obtained the vase empowerment based on the pile maṇḍala of the body; the taints of the body have been purified. You are empowered to meditate on the form of Yoginī, and have obtained all the blessings and siddhis of the body."

གསང་དབང་གི་དོན་དུ་དམིགས་པ་འདི་ལྟར་བྱ་ཞིང་། ཕྱོགས་བཅུའི་དེ་བཞིན་གཤེགས་པ་ཐམས་ཅད་དང་། རྡོ་རྗེ་རྣལ་འབྱོར་མ་སྙོམས་པར་ཞུགས་པའི་བྱང་ཆུབ་སེམས་ཀྱི་ཐིག་ལེ་ཐོད་པའི་ནང་དུ་ལྷུང་བ། རྗེ་བཙུན་མས་རང་གི་ལྕེ་ཐོག་ཏུ་བཞག་པར་གྱུར་པར་བསམ།

Chog Chui De-Shin Sheg-Pa Tham-Ché Dang, Dor-Je Nal-Jor-Ma Nyom-Par Shug-Pay Jang-Chub Sem Kyi Thig-Le Thö-Pay Nang Du Lhung-Wa, Je-Tsün-Mé Rang Gi Che Thog-Tu Shag-Par Gyur Par Sam

For the sake of the secret empowerment, imagine the following:

A drop of bodhicitta from the union of all the Tathāgatas of the ten directions with Vajrayoginī falls into the skull. Imagine that Jetsunma places that on one's tongue.

ཨོཾ་ཨོཾ་ཨོཾ་སརྦ་བུདྡྷ་ཌཱ་ཀི་ནཱི་ཡེ། བཛྲ་ཝརྞྞ་ནཱི་ཡེ།བཛྲ་བཻ་རོ་ཙ་ནཱི་ཡེ། ཧཱུྃ་ཧཱུྃ་ཧཱུྃ། ཕཊ་ཕཊ་ཕཊ་སྭཱ་ཧཱ།

Oṁ oṁ oṁ sarvabuddhaḍākinīye vajra varṇṇanīye vajra vairocanīye hūṁ hūṁ hūṁ phaṭ phaṭ phaṭ svāhā

ཞེས་བརྗོད་ཅིང་གཡོན་པའི་མཐེབ་སྲིན་གྱིས་ཐོད་པའི་ནང་ནས་བདུད་རྩི་བླངས་ཏེ་ལྕེ་ཐོག་ཏུ་བཞག་མགྲིན་པའི་ལམ་ནས་མྱང་བས། ལུས་ཀྱི་རྩ་ནང་གི་བྱང་སེམས་དམ་ཚིག་པའི་ཚུལ་དང་དབྱེར་མེད་རོ་གཅིག་ཏུ་འདྲེས་པས་རང་བཞིན་བརྒྱད་ཅུའི་རྟོག་པ་དབྱིངས་སུ་དག་ཅིང་གསལ་སྟོང་བདེ་བས་བརྒྱན་པའི་ཏིང་ངེ་འཛིན་རྒྱུད་ལ་སྐྱེས་པར་གྱུར་པར་བསམ་ལ་ཙུང་ཟད་མཉམ་པར་བཞག

Drin-Pay Lam Ne Nyang-We, Lü-Kyi Tsa Nang Gi Jang-Sem Dam-Tsig-Pay Tsul Dang Yer-Me Ro Chig-Tu Dre-Pé Rang-Shin Gye-Chui

Tog-Pa Ying Su Dag Ching Sal Tong De-We Gyen-Pay Ting Nge-Zin Gyü La Kye-Par Gyur

With the left ring finger, take a drop of amrita from the skullcup and place it on the tip of one's tongue:

Tasting it through the pathway of the throat, since this drop merges as one taste inseparable with bodhicitta inside one's body in the form of a samayasattva, eighty natural concepts are purified into the dharmadhatū and a samādhi adorned with clarity, emptiness, and bliss arising in one's continuum.

Imagine and remain in equipoise for a little while.

དེ་ལྟར་ན་གསུང་བདུད་རྩིའི་དཀྱིལ་འཁོར་དུ་གསང་བའི་དབང་ཐོབ། ངག་གི་དྲི་མ་
དག་རྣལ་འབྱོར་མའི་གསུང་གསང་བ་སྔགས་ཀྱི་བཟླས་བརྗོད་བྱེད་པ་ལ་དབང་ཞིང་།
གསུང་གི་བྱིན་རླབས་དང་དངོས་གྲུབ་ཐམས་ཅད་ཐོབ་པ་ཡིན་ནོ། ཞེས་བརྗོད་ཅིང་རྗེ་བཙུན་
མས་གསུང་བར་བསམ།

De-Tar Na Sung Dü-Tsiy Kyil-Khor Du Sang-Way Wang Thob, Ngag Gi Dri-Ma Dag Nal-Jor-May Sung Sang-Wa Ngag Kyi De Jö Je-Pa La Wang Shing, Sung Gi Jin-Lab Dang Ngö-Drub Tham-Ché Thob-Pa Yin No

Recite with imagining that Jetsunma says:

"As such, you have obtained the secret empowerment based on the amrita maṇḍala of the speech; the taints of the voice have been purified. You are empowered to recite the secret mantra, the speech of Yoginī, and have obtained all blessings and siddhis of speech."

ཤེས་རབ་ཡེ་ཤེས་ཀྱི་དབང་ནི།

ཕྱོགས་བཅུའི་དཔའ་བོ་ཐམས་ཅད་གཅིག་ཏུ་འདུས་པ་དཔལ་ཧེ་རུ་ཀར་གྱུར་པ་དང་། རྗེ་བཙུན་རྡོ་རྗེ་རྣལ་འབྱོར་མ་སྙོམས་པར་ཞུགས་པའི་བྱང་ཆུབ་ཀྱི་སེམས་རང་ཉིད་རྡོ་རྗེ་རྣལ་འབྱོར་མར་གསལ་བའི་མཁའ་ནང་དུ་བྱིན་པར་གྱུར་པར་བསམ་ལ། སིནྡྷུ་རའི་དཀྱིལ་འཁོར་ནས་གཡོན་པའི་སྲིན་ལག་གི་རྩེས་བླངས་ལ།

Chog Chui Pa-Wo Tham-Ché Chig-Tu Dü-Pa Pal He-Ru-Kar Gyur-Pa Dang, Je-Tsün Dor-Je Nal-Jor-Ma Nyom-Par Shug-Pay Jang-Chub Kyi Sem Rang Nyi Dor-Je Nal-Jor-Mar Sal-Way Kha Nang Du Jin-Par Gyur Par Sam-La Sin-Du-Ray Khyil-Kor Ne Yön-Pay Sin-Lag Gi Tse Lang-La

The wisdom empowerment of the Prajñā:

Imagine that all the tathāgatas of the ten directions combine into Heruka, who is in union with Jetsun Vajrayoginī; the bodhicitta [from the union] arrives in the space of oneself appearing as Vajrayoginī. Take the sindhura from the mandala with the tip of the left ring finger and recite:

ཨོཾ་ཨོཾ་ཨོཾ་སརྦ་བུདྡྷ་ཌཱ་ཀི་ནཱི་ཡེ། བཛྲ་ཝརྞྞ་ནཱི་ཡེ།བཛྲ་བཻ་རོ་ཙ་ནཱི་ཡེ། ཧཱུྃ་ཧཱུྃ་ཧཱུྃ། ཕཊ་ཕཊ་ཕཊ་སྭཱ་ཧཱ། ལྟེ་བ། སྙིང་ག མགྲིན་པ། དཔྲལ་བ་རྣམས་སུ་མས་ནས་ཡར་ཐིག་ལེ་བྱ།

Oṁ oṁ oṁ sarvabuddhaḍākinīye vajra varṇṇanīye vajra vairocanīye hūṁ hūṁ hūṁ phaṭ phaṭ phaṭ svāhā

Make dots from below to above on the navel, heart, throat and forehead.

མཁའ་ནང་གི་བྱང་ཆུབ་ཀྱི་སེམས་དེ་ཉིད་ལྟེ་བར་དྲངས་པས་ལྟེ་བའི་རྩ་འཁོར་ཐམས་ཅད་བྱང་ཆུབ་སེམས་ཀྱིས་གང་བས་དགའ་བའི་ཡེ་ཤེས་ཉམས་སུ་མྱོང་། དེ་བཞིན་དུ་སྙིང་གར་དྲངས་པས་སྙིང་གའི་རྩ་འཁོར་ཐམས་ཅད་གང་བས་མཆོག་དགའི་ཡེ་ཤེས་ཉམས་སུ་མྱོང་། མགྲིན་པར་དྲངས་པས་མགྲིན་པའི་རྩ་འཁོར་གང་བས་དགའ་བྲལ་གྱི་ཡེ་ཤེས་ཉམས་སུ་མྱོང་། སྤྱི་བོར་དྲངས་པས་རྩ་འཁོར་གང་། དེའི་ཚེ་ལུས་ཐམས་ཅད་ལ་རྩས་ཁྱབ། རྩ་ཐམས་ཅད་ལ་བྱང་ཆུབ་སེམས་ཀྱིས་ཁྱབ། བྱང་ཆུབ་ཀྱི་སེམས་ལ་བདེ་བས་ཁྱབ། བདེ་བ་ལ་སྟོང་པས་ཁྱབ། བདེ་སྟོང་ཟུང་འཇུག་ལྷན་ཅིག་སྐྱེས་པའི་དགའ་བ་ཉམས་སུ་མྱོང་བར་གྱུར་པར་བསམས་ལ་ཅུང་ཟད་མཉམ་པར་བཞག

Kha-Nang Gi Jang-Chub Kyi Sem De Nyi Te-War Drang-Pé Te-Way Tsa Khor Tham-Ché Jang-Chub Sem Kyi Gang-We Ga-Way Ye-She Nyam-Su Nyang, De Shin Du Nying-Gar Drang-Pé Nying-Gay Tsa-Khor Tham-Ché Gang-We Chog Gay Ye-She Nyam-Su Nyang, Drin-Par Drang-Pé Drin-Pay Tsa-Khor Gang-We Ga-Drel Gyi Ye-She Nyam-Su Nyang, Chi-Wor Drang-Pé Tsa-Khor Gang, Dey Tse Lü Tham-Ché La Tsé Khyab, Tsa Tham-Ché Jang-Chub Sem-Kyi Khyab, Jang-Chub Kyi Sem La De-We Khyab, De-Wa La Tong-Pé Khyab, De-Tong Zung-Jug Lhen Chig Kye-Pay Ga-Wa Nyam-Su Nyang-War Gyur

Imagine that since the bodhicitta inside the space is drawn up to the navel, all the channels of the navel cakra are filled with bodhicitta. One experiences the wisdom of joy.

In the same way, since the bodhcitta is drawn to the heart, all the channels of the heart cakra are filled with bodhicitta. One experiences the wisdom of supreme joy.

Since the bodhcitta is drawn to the throat, all the channels of the throat cakra are filled with bodhicitta. One experiences the wisdom of joyless joy.

Since the bodhicitta is drawn to the crown, all the channels of the crown cakra are filled with bodhicitta. At that time, amrita spreads throughout the whole body; bodhicitta spreads throughout all the channels; bliss spreads throughout bodhicitta; and emptiness spreads throughout bliss. Imagine that one experiences the connate joy of the union of the bliss and emptiness.

Imagine and remain in equipoise for a little while.

དེ་ལྟར་ན་ཐུགས་སིནྡྷུ་རའི་དཀྱིལ་འཁོར་ལ་བརྟེན་ནས་ཤེས་རབ་ཡེ་ཤེས་ཀྱི་དབང་ཐོབ་སེམས་ཀྱི་དྲི་མ་དག ཐུགས་གཉིས་མེད་ཀྱི་ཡེ་ཤེས་བསྒོམས་པ་ལ་དབང་ཞིང་ཐུགས་ཀྱི་བྱིན་རླབས་དང་དངོས་གྲུབ་ཐམས་ཅད་ཐོབ་པ་ཡིན་ནོ། ཞེས་བརྗོད་ཅིང་གསུང་བར་བསམ།

De-Tar Na Thug Sin-Dhu-Ray Kyil-Khor La Ten Ne She-Rab Ye-She Kyi Wang Thob Sem Kyi Dri-Ma Dag, Thug Nyi-Me Kyi Ye-She Gom-Pa La Wang Shing Thug Kyi Jin-Lab Dang Ngö-Drub Tham-Ché Thob-Pa Yin No

Recite with imagining that Jetsunma says:

"As such, you have obtained the wisdom empowerment of the Prajñā based on the sindhura maṇḍala of mind; the taints of mind have been purified. You are empowered to meditate on the wisdom of nondual mind, and have obtained all the blessings and siddhis of mind."

དབང་བཞི་པ་ནི། མདུན་བསྐྱེད་རྗེ་བཙུན་མའི་ཞལ་ནས་གསུངས་པར་བསམས་ལ།

དངོས་པོ་མེད་པའི་ཆོས་ཉིད་ཆོས།།

ནམ་མཁའ་ལྟ་བུ་དྲི་མ་མེད།།

སྟོང་ཉིད་ཡེ་ཤེས་རྡོ་རྗེ་ཡི།།

སྟོང་པ་ཉིད་དུ་རྣམ་པར་བསྒོམ།།

Ngö-Po Me-Pay Chö-Nyi Chö
Nam-Kha Ta-Bu Dri-Ma Me
Tong Nyi Ye-She Dor-Je Yi
Tong-Pa Nyi Du Nam-Par Gom

The fourth initiation, imagine that the Jetsunma generated in front says:

"The dharmatā of phenomena is insubstantial,
undefiled like space.
Meditate on the emptiness
with the wisdom-vajra of emptiness."

ཞེས་གསུང་བར་བསམ། དེའི་དོན་ནི། བདེན་པའི་དངོས་པོ་ཙམ་ཙམ་ཡང་ཡེ་ནས་ཡོད་མ་མྱོང་བ་ཆོས་ཐམས་ཅད་ཀྱི་ཆོས་ཉིད་ཅེས་བྱ་བ་ནི་ཡོད་མེད་རྟག་ཆད་སྲིད་ཞིའི་མཐའ་ཐམས་ཅད་དང་བྲལ་བས་ནམ་མཁའི་དཀྱིལ་ལྟ་བུ། དེའི་ངོ་བོ་གཟུང་འཛིན་གྱི་སྒྲིབ་པའི་དྲི་མས་གདོད་མ་ནས་གོས་མ་མྱོང་བས་དྲི་མ་མེད་པ་དེ་ལྟ་བུའི་ཡུལ་སྟོང་པ་ཉིད་དང་ཡུལ་ཅན་གཉིས་སྣང་ཐམས་ཅད་ནུབ་པའི་གཉིས་མེད་ཡེ་ཤེས་ཀྱི་རྡོ་རྗེའི་སྟོང་ཉིད་དུ་རྣམ་པར་བསྒོམ་ཞེས་པས་ཟུང་འཇུག་བདེ་བ་ཆེན་པོ་རྒྱུད་ལ་སྐྱེས་པར་གྱུར། དེའི་ངང་དུ་ཙུང་ཟད་མཉམ་པར་བཞག

Den-Pay Ngö-Po Chung-Zé Tsam Yang Ye Ne Yö Ma Nyong Wa Chö Tham-Ché Kyi Chö-Nyi Che Ja Wa Nï Yö Me Tag-Ché Si Shiy Tha Tham-Ché Dang Dral-We Nam-Khay Kyil Ta-Bu, Dey Ngo-Wo Zung Zin Gyi Trö-Pay Dri-Mé Dö-Ma Ne Go Ma Nyong-We Dri-Ma Me-Pa De-Ta-Bui Yül Tong-Pa-Nyi Dang Yül-Chen Nyi Nang Tham-Ché Nub-Pay Nyi Me Ye-She Kyi Dor-Jey Tong-Nyi Du Nam-Par Gom She-Pé Zung-Jug De-Wa Chen-Po Gyü La Kye-Par Gyur

Having imagined what she said, the meaning is:

The so-called "dharmatā" of all phenomena is free from all extremes of existence and nonexistence, permanence and annihilation, as well as saṃsāra and nirvāṇa; it is like in the middle of space. From the very beginning, that [dharmatā] is undefiled because its nature has never been covered with taints of the proliferation of grasper and the grasped. It is said that one should meditate on the emptiness, the nondual wisdom-vajra. Since in emptiness, all appearances such as both an object and the subject have subsided, the great bliss of union arises in one's continuum.

Remain in that state of equipoise for a while.

དེ་ལྟར་ན་རྡོ་རྗེ་རྣལ་འབྱོར་མའི་སྐུ་གསུང་ཐུགས་ཡོན་ཏན་ཕྲིན་ལས་དང་བཅས་པའི་སྒོ་ནས་དབང་བཞི་པ་ཐོབ། སྒོ་གསུམ་གྱི་དྲི་མ་བག་ཆགས་དང་བཅས་པ་དག་སྐུ་གསུང་ཐུགས་ཀྱི་གསང་བ་མཐའ་དག་བསྒོམ་པ་ལ་དབང་། རྡོ་རྗེ་རྣལ་འབྱོར་མའི་སྐུ་གསུང་ཐུགས་ཡོན་ཏན་ཕྲིན་ལས་དང་བཅས་པའི་བྱིན་རླབས་དང་དངོས་གྲུབ་ཐམས་ཅད་ཐོབ་པ་ཡིན་ནོ། །ཞེས་གསུངས་པར་བསམས་ལ་ཞིང་བརྗོད།

De-Tar-Na Dor-Je Nal-Jor-May Ku Sung Thug Yon-Ten Trin-Lé Dang Ché-Pay Go Ne Wang Shi-Pa Thob, Go Sum Gyi Dri-Ma Bag Chag Dang Ché-Pa Dag Ku Sung Thug Kyi Sang-Wa Tha-Dag Gom-Pa La Wang, Dor-Je Nal-Jor-May Ku Sung Thug Yon-Ten Trin-Lé Dang Ché-Pay Jin-Lab Dang Ngö-Drub Tham-Ché Thob-Pa Yin No

Imagine she says the following and recite:

"You have obtained the empowerment through the body, speech, mind, qualities, and activities of Vajrayoginī; the taints of the three doors along with their traces are purified. You are empowered to meditate on all the secrets of body, speech, and mind, and have obtained all the blessings and siddhis of the body, speech, mind, qualities, and activities of Vajrayoginī."

དེ་ལྟར་ཁས་བླངས་པའི་དམ་ཚིག་དང་སྡོམ་པ་བསྲུང་སྙམ་པས། གཙོ་བོས་ཇི་ལྟར་བཀའ་སྩལ་བ། དེ་དག་ཐམས་ཅད་བདག་གིས་བགྱི། །ཞེས་ལན་གསུམ་བརྗོད།

Tso-Wö Ji-Tar Ka-Tsal-Wa, De-Dag Tham-Ché Dag-Gi Gyi

As such, thinking that one will guard the samayas and vows one has promised, recite three times:

Whatever the guru commands,
all of that I will do.

བྱིན་རླབས་ཐོབ་པའི་བཀའ་དྲིན་གྱི་ཡོན་དུ།

ཨོཾ་བཛྲ་ཧྲ་མི་ཨཱཿ ཧཱུྃ། གཞི་ཡོངས་སུ་དག་པ་དབང་ཆེན་གསེར་གྱི་ས་གཞི། ཨོཾ་བཛྲ་རེ་ཁེ་ཨཱཿ ཧཱུྃ། ཕྱི་ལྕགས་རི་འཁོར་ཡུག་གིས་བསྐོར་བའི་དབུས་སུ་ཧཱུྃ། རིའི་རྒྱལ་པོ་རི་རབ།

-ཤར་ལུས་འཕགས་པོ། ལྷོ་འཛམ་བུ་གླིང་། ནུབ་བ་གླང་སྤྱོད། བྱང་སྒྲ་མི་སྙན། ཉི་མ། ཟླ་བ། དབུས་སུ་ལྷ་དང་མིའི་ཡི་དཔལ་འབྱོར་ཕུན་སུམ་ཚོགས་པ་མ་ཚང་བ་མེད་པ་འདི་ཉིད་བླ་མ་དང་རྗེ་བཙུན་རྡོ་རྗེ་རྣལ་འབྱོར་མ་ཐ་མི་དད་པ་ལ་བྱིན་རླབས་ཟབ་མོ་ལེགས་པར་ཐོབ་པའི་བཀའ་དྲིན་གཏང་རག་གི་ཡོན་དུ་འབུལ་བར་བགྱིའོ། ཐུགས་རྗེས་འགྲོ་བའི་དོན་དུ་བཞེས་སུ་གསོལ། བཞེས་ནས་བྱིན་གྱིས་བརླབ་ཏུ་གསོལ།

Oṁ vajra bhumi āḥ hūṁ, Shi Yong Su Dag-Pa Wang Chen Ser Gyi Sa Shi, Oṁ vajra Rekhe āḥ hūṁ, Chi Chag Ri Khor Yug Gi Kor-Way Wü-Su Hūṁ, Ri Gyal-Po Ri-Rab, Shar Lü-Phag-Po, Lho Zam-Bu-Ling, Nub Ba-Lang-Chö, Jang Dra-Mi-Nyen, Nyi-Ma, Da-Wa, Wü-Su Lha Dang Miy Pal-Jor Phun-Sum Tsog-Pa Ma Tsang-Wa Me-Pa Di Nyi La-Ma Dang Je-Tsün Dor-Je Nal-Jor-Ma Tha Mi Dé-Pa La Jin-Lab Zab-Mo Leg-Par Thob-Pay Ka-Drin Tang Rag Gi Yon-Du-Bül-War Gyi'o, Thug-Jey Dro-Way Don Du She Su Söl She Ne Jin-Gyi Lab-Tu Söl

Make a maṇḍala offering as an appreciation for receiving this blessing:

Oṁ vajra bhumi āḥ hūṁ

The totally pure foundation is the mighty golden ground.

Oṁ vajra Rekhe āḥ hūṁ

The outside is circled by a range of iron mountains. In the center of that is Hūṁ, the king of mountains, Sumeru. In the east is Pūrvavideha. In the south is Jambudvīpa. In the west is Godānīya. In the north is Kurava. There is the sun and the moon. In the center is the abundant prestige and wealth of devas and humans in no way incomplete. This is offered to the guru inseparable with Jetsun Vajrayoginī as an appreciation for receiving this blessing. Please accept this with compassion for the benefit of migrating beings. Having accepted it, please bless me.

ལུས་ལོངས་སྤྱོད་རྣམས་ཀྱང་འབུལ་ཞིང་ཆ་ཤས་ནས་ལོངས་སྤྱོད་དུ་གསོལ་སྙམ་པས།

དེང་ནས་བརྩམས་སྟེ་བདག་བྲན་དུ།

ཁྱེད་ལ་བདག་ནི་འབུལ་ལགས་ན།

ཁྱེད་ཀྱིས་སློབ་མར་བཟུང་བ་དང་།

ཆ་ཡིས་ཀྱང་ནི་སྤྱད་དུ་གསོལ། ལན་གསུམ་བརྗོད།

Deng Ne Tsam Te Dag Dren Du
Khye La Dag Ni Bül Lag Na
Khye Kyi Lob-Mar Zung-Wa Dang
Cha Yi Kyang Ni Ché Du Söl

Thus, imagine that one is offering one's body and all of one's possessions, requesting the lama to use every portion of them. Recite three times:

Starting from now, I offer myself
to you as a servant.
Please take me as a disciple
and use me as necessary.

Torma Offering to Vajrayoginī

དེ་ནས་གཏོར་མ་རྣམས་ནང་མཆོད་ཆུ་ཆང་གིས་སྦྱངས་ལ

ཨོཾ་སུམྦྷ་ནི་སུམྦྷ་ཧུྃ་ཧཱུྃ་ཕཊ།

ཨོཾ་གྲྀཧྞ་གྲྀཧྞ་ཧུྃ་ཧཱུྃ་ཕཊ།

ཨོཾ་གྲྀཧྞ་པ་ཡ་གྲྀཧྞ་པ་ཡ་ཧུྃ་ཧཱུྃ་ཕཊ།

ཨོཾ་ཨཱ་ན་ཡ་ཧོཿ བྷ་ག་ཝཱན་བིདྱཱ་རཱ་ཛ་ཧུྃ་ཧཱུྃ་ཕཊ། ཀྱིས་བསངས།

Purify the torma with water and alcohol from the inner offerings cleansing them with:

Oṁ sumbha nisumbha huṁ hūṁ phaṭ

Oṁ grihaṇa grihaṇa huṁ hūṁ phaṭ

Oṁ grihaṇapaya grihaṇapaya huṁ hūṁ phaṭ

Oṁ ānayaho bhagavān vidyārāja huṁ hūṁ phaṭ

ཨོཾ་སྭ་བྷཱ་ཝ་ཤུདྡྷཿ སརྦ་དྷརྨཱཿ སྭ་བྷཱ་ཝ་ཤུདྡྷོ྅ ཧཾ། གིས་སྦྱངས།

Purify with:

Oṁ svabhāva shuddhaḥ sarva dharmāḥ svabhāva shuddho' haṁ

སྟོང་པའི་ངང་ལས་ཨ་ལས་བྱུང་བའི་ཐོད་པ་ཡངས་ཤིང་རྒྱ་ཆེ་བའི་ནང་དུ་ཤ་ལྔ་བདུད་རྩི་ལྔ་ཡེ་ཤེས་ལྔ་རྣམས་ཞུ་བ་ལས་བྱུང་བའི་ཡེ་ཤེས་ཀྱི་བདུད་རྩིའི་རྒྱ་མཚོ་ཆེན་པོར་གྱུར་པར་བསམས་ལ།

Tong-Pay Ngang Lé Ah Lé Jung-Way Thö-Pa Yang Shing Gya Che Way Nang Du Sha Nga Dü-Tsi Nga Ye-She Nga Nam Shu-Wa Lé Jung-Way Ye-She Kyi Dü-Tsiy Gya-Tso Chen-Por Gyur Par Sam-La

Imagine that an *Ah* (ཨ) arises out of the state of emptiness. That *Ah* (ཨ) turns into a vast and wide skull, in which is a great ocean of wisdom amrita that comes from the melting of the five meats, five amritas, and five wisdoms.

ཨོཾ་ཨཱཿ ཧཱུྃ་ཧ་ཧོཿ ཧྲཱིཿ ཞེས་པ་ཕྱག་རྒྱ་དང་བཅས་པ་ལན་གསུམ་སོགས་བརྗོད་ཅིང་བྱིན་གྱིས་བརླབས་ལ།

Recite three times with the mudra and so on, and bless with:

Oṁ āḥ hūṁ ha hoḥ hrīḥ

ཕཻཾ་ཞེས་བརྗོད་པས།

Recite:

Phaiṁ

རང་གི་སྙིང་ག་ནས་འོད་ཟེར་འཕྲོས་པས་འོག་མིན་གྱི་གནས་ནས་རྗེ་བཙུན་རྡོ་རྗེ་རྣལ་འབྱོར་མ་ལ་སངས་རྒྱས་དང་བྱང་ཆུབ་སེམས་དཔའ་དཔའ་བོ་དང་རྣལ་འབྱོར་མ་ཆོས་སྐྱོང་བ་དང་འཇིག་རྟེན་སྐྱོང་བའི་ཚོགས་ཀྱིས་བསྐོར་བ་མདུན་གྱི་ནམ་མཁར་ཨོཾ་བཛྲ་ས་མཱ་ཛཿ ཅེས་པས་སྤྱན་དྲངས།

Rang Gi Nyin-Ga Ne Ö-Zer Trö-Pé Og-Min Gyi Ne Ne Je-Tsün Dor-Je Nal-Jor-Ma La Sang-Gyé Dang Jang-Chub Sem-Pa Pa-Wo Dang Nal-Jor-Ma Chö-Kyong-Wa Dang Jig-Ten Kyong-Way Tsog Kyi Kor-Wa Dün Gyi Nam-Khar Oṁ vajra samājaḥ Che-Pé Chan-Drang

Light rays shining from one's heart summon Vajrayoginī and an assembly of buddhas, bodhisattvas, heroes, yoginīs, dharmapālas and lokapalas into the sky in front, *Oṁ vajra samājaḥ*

པད་ཀོར་སྟོན་དུ་འགྲོ་བའི་རྡོ་རྗེ་ཐལ་མོ་ཁ་ཕྱེན་དུ་ཕྱེ་བའི་མཐར་སེ་གོལ་གཏོགས་པ་དང་བཅས་པ་བྱ་ཞིང་།
ཨོཾ་ཨོཾ་ཨོཾ་སརྦ་བུདྡྷ་ཌཱ་ཀི་ནཱི་ཡེ། བཛྲ་ཝརྞྞ་ནཱི་ཡེ།བཛྲ་བཻ་རོ་ཙ་ནཱི་ཡེ། ཧཱུྃ་ཧཱུྃ་ཧཱུྃ། ཕཊ་ཕཊ་ཕཊ་སྭཱ་ཧཱ། ཨོཾ་ཨ་ཀཱ་རོ་མུ་ཁཾ་སརྦ་དྷརྨཱ་ཎཾ་ཨཱདྱ་ནུཏྤནྣ་ཏྭཱ་ཏ་ཨོཾ་ཨཱཿཧཱུྃ་ཕཊ་སྭཱ་ཧཱ། ཞེས་
ལན་གསུམ་མམ་ལྔའམ་བདུན་གྱིས་ཕུལ་ལ།

Starting with lotus rolls, opening the vajra folded palms, face up at the end, and snap one's fingers. Make the offering by reciting three, five or seven times:

Oṁ oṁ oṁ sarvabuddhaḍākinīye vajravarṇṇanīye vajravairocanīye hūṁ hūṁ hūṁ phaṭ phaṭ phaṭ svāhā, oṁ akāro mukhaṁ sarva dharmāṇāṁ ādyan utpanna tvata oṁ āḥ hūṁ phaṭ svāhā

ཨོཾ་བཛྲ་ཡོ་གི་ནཱི་ས་པ་རི་ཝཱ་ར་ཨརྒྷཾ། པཱ་དྱཾ། པུཥྤེ། དྷཱུ་པེ། ཨཱ་ལོ་ཀེ། གནྡྷེ། ནཻ་ཝི་དྱེ།
ཤབྡ་ཨཱཿ ཧཱུྃ་གིས་ཕྱི་མཆོད་འབུལ།

The outer offering is made with:

Oṁ Vajrayoginī saparivāra arghaṁ, pādyaṁ, puṣpe, dhūpe, āloke, gandhe, naividye, shabda āḥ hūṁ

ཨོཾ་བཛྲ་ཨཱ་ར་ལི་ཧོཿ ཨོཾ་ཨཱཿ ཧཱུྃ་རྗེ་བཙུན་རྡོ་རྗེ་རྣལ་འབྱོར་མ་དཔའ་བོ་དང་མཁའ་
འགྲོའི་ལྷ་ཚོགས་རྣམས་ཀྱི་ཞལ་དུ་མཆོད་པ་དམ་པ་འབུལ་ལོ། །ཞེས་ནང་མཆོད་གཏོར།

Oṁ vajra ārali hoḥ, oṁ āḥ hūṁ, Je-Tsün Dor-Je Nal-Jor-Ma Pa-Wo Dang Khan-Droy Lha Tsog Nam Kyi Shal Du Chö-Pa Dam-Pa Bül Lo

Oṁ vajra ārali hoḥ, oṁ āḥ hūṁ, this sublime offering is made to the mouths of Jetsun Vajrayoginī and the assembly of heroes and yoginīs.

Thus, scatter the inner offerings.

བསྟོད་པ་ནི། ཌ་མ་རུས་མགོ་འདྲེན་གྱིས་རོལ་ཆེན་བྱ་ཞིང་།
དཔལ་ལྡན་རྡོ་རྗེ་མཁའ་འགྲོ་མ།།
མཁའ་འགྲོ་མ་ཡི་འཁོར་ལོས་སྒྱུར།།
ཡེ་ཤེས་ལྔ་དང་སྐུ་གསུམ་བརྙེས།།
འགྲོ་བ་སྐྱོབ་ལ་ཕྱག་འཚལ་ལོ།།

Pal-Den Dor-Je Khan-Dro-Ma
Khan-Dro-Ma Yi Khor-Lo Gyur
Ye-She Nga Dang Ku Sum Nye
Dro-Wa Kyob La Chag Tsal Lo

For the praise, make loud music with the assistance of the damaru:

The glorious Vajraḍākinī,
the empress of all ḍākinīs,
the one who has attained the five wisdoms and three kāyas,
I pay homage to the protector of migrating beings.

ཇི་སྙེད་རྡོ་རྗེ་མཁའ་འགྲོ་མ།།
ཀུན་ཏུ་རྟོག་པའི་འཆིང་གཅོད་ཅིང་།།
འཇིག་རྟེན་བྱ་བར་རབ་འཇུག་མ།།
དེ་སྙེད་རྣམས་ལ་ཕྱག་འཚལ་ལོ།། ཞེས་བསྟོད་ལ།

Ji Nye Dor-Je Khan-Dro-Ma
Kün-Tu Tog-Pay Ching Chö Ching
Jig-Ten Ja-War Rab Jug Ma
De Nye Nam La Chag Tsal Lo

I pay homage to Vajradakinī
who eliminates the bondage of all concepts,
those who attain
full engagement in the activities of the world.

འཆི་ཚེ་མགོན་དང་དཔའ་བོ་མ་ཚོགས་ཀྱིས།།
མེ་ཏོག་གདུགས་དང་རྒྱལ་མཚན་ཐོགས་ནས་སུ།།
རོལ་མོ་གླུ་དབྱངས་སྒྲ་སྙན་སོགས་མཆོད་ཅིང་།།
མཁའ་ལ་སྤྱོད་པའི་གནས་སུ་ཁྲིད་པར་ཤོག།

Chi Tse Gon Dang Pa-Wo Ma Tsog Kyi
Me-Tog Dug Dang Gyal-Tsen Thog Ne Su
Röl-Mo Lu Yang Dra Nyen Sog Chö Ching
Kha La Chö-Pay Ne Su Ti-Par Shog

At the time of death, may the protector with an assembly of heroes and heroines,
bearing flowers, parasols and victory banners,
making offerings of music and melodious songs pleasing to hear and so on,
guide us to the Khecarī realm.

དགེ་བ་འདི་ཡིས་མྱུར་དུ་བདག།
མཁའ་སྤྱོད་མ་དངོས་འགྲུབ་གྱུར་ནས།།
འགྲོ་བ་གཅིག་ཀྱང་མ་ལུས་པ།།
དེ་ཡི་ས་ལ་འགོད་པར་ཤོག།

Ge-Wa Di Yi Nyur Du Dag
Kha-Chö-Ma Ngö-Drub Gyur Ne
Dro-Wa Chig Kyang Ma-Lü-Pa
De Yi Sa La Go-Par Shog

By the virtue of this,
after I swiftly attain the siddhi of Khecarī,
may all migrating beings
be placed on Her stage.

Torma Offering to Mahākāla

དེ་ནས་མགོན་པོ་ཆེ་ཆུང་གི་གཏོར་མ་རྒྱས་པར་སྒྲོན་གཏོར་ཆོག་ཕྱག་ལེན་ལྟར་དང་། མདོར་བསྡུ་ན་གཏོར་མ། ཨོཾ་ཨཱཿཧཱུྃ་ཧ་ཧོཿཧྲཱིཿ ས་བྱིན་གྱིས་བརླབས་ལ།

Next, if one wishes to do elaborate tormas of the major and minor Mahākālas, it should be done according to the practice of the torma rite. If one wishes to do it concisely, bless the torma with:

Oṁ āḥ hūṁ ha hoḥ hrīḥ

རྡོར་དྲིལ་འཛིན་པས།

ཧཱུྃ་འོག་མིན་བདེ་ཆེན་དག་པའི་ཕོ་བྲང་ནས།།
རྣམ་སྣང་ཐུགས་ལས་སྤྲུལ་པའི་མཐུ་བོ་ཆེ།།
བསྟན་སྲུང་ཀུན་གྱི་གཙོ་བོ་རྡོ་རྗེ་གུར།།
དཔལ་ལྡན་མགོན་པོ་འདིར་བྱོན་མཆོད་གཏོར་བཞེས།།

Hūṁ
Og-Min De-Chen Dag-Pay Pho-Trang Ne
Nam Nang Thug Lé Trül-Pay Thu-Wo Che
Ten Sung Kün Gyi Tsowo Dor-Je Gur
Pal-Den Gon-Po Dir Jon Chö Tor She

Holding the vajra and bell:

Hūṁ
From the palace of the pure great bliss of Akaniṣṭha,
the powerful one who emanated from the mind of Vairocana,
the chief of all guardians of the teachings, Vajrapañjara,
Shrinatha, come here and accept this torma offering.

ཡོངས་འདུའི་ཚལ་དང་གཤིན་རྗེའི་ཕོ་བྲང་དང་།།
འཛམ་གླིང་དེ་ཝི་ཀོ་ཊའི་གནས་མཆོག་ནས།།
འདོད་ཁམས་གཙོ་མོ་ནམ་གྲུ་རེ་མ་ཏི།།
དཔལ་ལྡན་ལྷ་མོ་འདིར་གཤེགས་མཆོད་གཏོར་བཞེས།།

Yong Dui Tsal Dang Shin-Jey Pho-Trang Dang
Zam-Ling De-Vi Ko-Tay Ne Chog Ne
Dö Kham Tso-Mo Nam-Tru Re-Ma-Te
Pal-Den Lha-Mo Dir Sheg Chö Tor She

From the grove of wishfulfilling trees, Yama's palace
and the supreme place of Devīkota in Jambudvīpa,
queen of the desire realm, Rematī,
Shridevi come here and accept this torma offering.

སྣང་སྲིད་བྷ་ག་དབྱིངས་ཀྱི་དཀྱིལ་འཁོར་ནས།།
འཁོར་འདས་ཀུན་གྱི་བདག་མོ་དབྱིངས་ཕྱུག་ཡུམ།།
སྔགས་སྲུང་དྲག་མོ་མ་མོ་མཁའ་འགྲོའི་གཙོ།།
ཡུམ་ཆེན་རལ་གཅིག་འདིར་བྱོན་མཆོད་གཏོར་བཞེས།།

Nang Si Bha-Ga Ying Kyi Kyil-Khor Ne
Khor Dé Kün Gyi Dag-Mo Ying-Chug Yum
Ngag Sung Drag-Mo Ma-Mo Khan-Droy Tso
Yum Chen Rel Chig Dir Jon Chö Tor She

From the maṇḍala of the dharmadhatu, the womb of the universe, the mistress of saṃsāra and nirvana, Dhatesvari,
the fierce guardian of mantra, the queen of the mamos and ḍākinīs,
great mother Ekajati come to this place
and accept this torma offering!

བསིལ་བའི་ཚལ་དང་ཧ་ཧ་དགོད་པ་དང་།།
སིངྒ་གླིང་དང་ཏི་སེ་གངས་རི་དང་།།
དར་ལུང་གནས་དང་ཁའུའི་བྲག་རྫོང་ནས།།
ཞིང་སྐྱོང་དབང་པོ་འདིར་བྱོན་མཆོད་གཏོར་བཞེས།།

Sil-Way Tsal Dang Ha Ha Go-Pa Dang
Sin-Ga-Ling Dang Ti-Se Gang Ri Dang
Dar Lung Ne Dang Ka'u Dag Zong Ne
Shing Kyong Wang-Po Dir Jon Chö Tor She

From the Shitavana, Aṭṭaṭṭahāsa,
Siṃhaladvīpa, Kailash,
Darlung and Ka'u Drag Dzong,
powerful Kṣetrapāla come here and accept this torma offering.

དུར་ཁྲོད་བརྒྱད་དང་ལྷོ་ཕྱོགས་རི་སྲུལ་དང་།།
རྡོ་རྗེ་གདན་དང་དཔལ་གྱི་བསམ་ཡས་དང་།།
ན་ལ་ཙེ་དང་དཔལ་ལྷུན་ས་སྐྱ་ནས།།
ལས་མགོན་པོ་མོ་འདིར་བྱོན་མཆོད་གཏོར་བཞེས།།

Dur Tro Gye Dang Lho Chog Ri Sul Dang
Dor-Je Den Dang pel Gyi Sam-Ye Dang
NalaTse Dang Pal-Den Sa-Kya Ne
Lé Gon Pho Mo Dir Jon Chö Tor She

From the eight charnel grounds and southern mountain valleys,
Vajrasana and Glorious Samye,
Nalatse, and glorious Sakya,
male and female Karmanathas come here and accept this torma offering.

བྱང་ཤར་མ་རུ་རྩེ་ཡི་དུར་ཁྲོད་དང་།།
རྒྱ་གར་བང་སོ་དམར་པོའི་བྲག་རི་དང་།།
དར་ལུང་བྲག་ཧྲམ་ལ་སོགས་གནས་མཆོག་ནས།།
གནོད་སྦྱིན་ལྕམ་དྲལ་འདིར་བྱོན་མཆོད་གཏོར་བཞེས།།

Jang Shar Ma-Ru-Tse Yi Du To Dang
Gya-Gar Bang-So Mar-Poy Drag Ri Dang
Dar Lung Drag Hram La Sog Ne-Chog Ne
Nö-Jin Cham-Dral Dir Jon Chö Tor She

From the Marutse charnel ground in the north east,
The cliff of the red tomb in India,
Draghram of Darlung and so on,
Yaksa siblings come here and accept this torma offering.

གསོལ་ལོ་མཆོད་དོ་རྒྱལ་བའི་བསྟན་སྲུང་ཚོགས།།
བསྒྲུབ་བོ་བརྟན་ནོ་བླ་མའི་བཀའ་སྲུང་ཆེ།།
འབོད་དོ་བསྐུལ་ལོ་རྣལ་འབྱོར་དགྲ་ལྷའི་ཚོགས།།
རིངས་པའི་ཚུལ་གྱིས་འདིར་བྱོན་མཆོད་གཏོར་བཞེས།།

Söl-Lo Chö-Do Gyal-Way Ten-Sung Tsog
Drub-Bo Ten-No La-May Ka-Sung Che
Bö-Do Kul-Lo Nal-Jor Dra Lhay Tsog
Ring-Pay Tsul Gyi Dir Jon Chö Tor She

Assembly of guardians of the teachings of the victor, I supplicate you! I make offerings!
Great guardians of the words of commands of the guru, accomplish them! Be dependable!
Assembly of wargods of the yogin, I call you! I urge you!
Come here with haste and accept this torma offering

ཤ་ཁྲག་དམར་གྱིས་བརྒྱན་པའི་གཏོར་མས་མཆོད།།
ཛ་གད་སྨན་ཕུད་རཀྟའི་བཏུང་བས་མཆོད།།
ང་ཆེན་ཀང་གླིང་རོལ་མོའི་སྒྲ་ཡིས་མཆོད།།
དར་ནག་འཕན་ཆེན་སྤྲིན་ལྟར་གཏིབས་པས་མཆོད།།

Sha Trag Mar Gyi Gyen-Pay Tor-Mé Chö
Za-Ge Smen Phu Rak-Tay Tung-We Chö
Nga-Chen Kang Ling Röl-Moy Dra Yi Chö
Dar Nag Phen-Chen Trin Tar Tib-Pé Chö

I make offerings adorned with red flesh and blood,
I make offerings with the the first portions of beer and medicine, and drinks of blood,
I make offerings with the sound of great drums and bone trumpets,
I make offerings with streamers of black silk as thick as a cloud.

ཡིད་འཕྲོག་སྤྱན་གཟིགས་ནམ་མཁའ་མཉམ་པས་མཆོད།།
རབ་བརྗིད་སྙན་པའི་དབྱངས་ཀྱི་ང་རོས་མཆོད།།
ཕྱི་ནང་གསང་བའི་དམ་རྫས་རྒྱ་མཚོས་མཆོད།།
བདེ་སྟོང་དབྱེར་མེད་ཡེ་ཤེས་རོལ་པས་མཆོད།།

Yi-Trog Chen-Zig Nam-Kha Nyam-Pé Chö
Rab-Ji Nyen-Pay Yang Kyi Nga-Rö Chö
Chi Nang Sang-Way Dam Zé Gya-Tsö Chö
De-Tong Yer-Me Ye-She Röl-Pé Chö

I make offerings with beautiful presents equal with space,
I make offerings with chants of magnificent melodious tones,
I make offerings with an ocean of inner, outer and secret offerings,
I make offerings with the play of the wisdom of inseparable bliss and emptiness.

སངས་རྒྱས་བསྟན་པ་གཉེན་པོ་ཁྱེད་ཀྱིས་སྲུངས།།
དཀོན་མཆོག་དབུ་འཕང་གཉེན་པོ་ཁྱེད་ཀྱིས་བསྟོད།།
དཔལ་ལྡན་བླ་མའི་ཕྲིན་ལས་ཁྱེད་ཀྱིས་སྤེལ།།
རྣལ་འབྱོར་བཅོལ་པའི་ཕྲིན་ལས་ཁྱེད་ཀྱིས་སྒྲུབས།།
བསྟོད་བསྐུལ་འདི་ཡང་རྡོ་རྗེ་འཆང་བློ་གསལ་རྒྱ་མཚོས་མཛད་པའོ།།

Sang-Gyé Ten-Pa Nyen-Po Khyö Kyi Sung
Kon-Chog Wu-Phang Nyen-Po Khye Kyi Tö
Pal-Den La-May Trin-Lé Khye Kyi Pel
Nal-Jor Chol-Pay Trin-Lé Khye Kyi Drub

You must protect the remedy, the teachings of the Buddha,
you must praise the remedy, the majestic Jewels,
you must increase the activities of the glorious guru,
and you must accomplish the activities of yogins.

This praise and request was composed by Vajradhara Losal Gyatso.

Torma Offering to the Charnel Ground Lords

མུས་ཆེན་སངས་རྒྱས་རིན་ཆེན་གྱིས་མཛད་པ་དུར་ཁྲོད་བདག་པོ་ལ་གཏོར་མ་འབུལ་བ་ནི།

The torma offering of the Charnel Ground Lords composed by Muchen Sangye Rinchen

གཏོར་མ། ཨོཾ་ཨཱཿ ཧཱུྃ་ཧ་ཧོཿ ཧྲཱིཿ ས་བྲིན་གྱིས་རླབས་ལ།

Bless the torma with:

Oṁ āḥ hūṁ ha hoḥ hrīḥ

མདུན་གྱི་ནམ་མཁར་ཧཱུྃ་ཡིག་ལས་ཨེ་ཆད་པས་ནམ་མཁར་རླུང་གི་དཀྱིལ་འཁོར། རཾ་ལས་རཀྟའི་རྒྱ་མཚོ། སུཾ་ལས་ཞིང་ཆེན་གྱི་ས་གཞི། ཀཾ་ལས་ཀེང་རུས་ཀྱི་རི་རབ། རཾ་ལས་ཉི་མའི་དཀྱིལ་འཁོར། སུཾ་ལས་ཐོད་མཁར་གྱི་གཞལ་ཡས་ཁང་མི་མགོ་སྐམ་པོ་ལས་གྲུབ་པའི་གྲུ་བཞི་པ། མི་རུས་ཀྱི་ཀང་དང་། རྐེད་རུས་སྣ་ཚོགས་ཀྱིས་སྟེང་ཐོག་ཕུབ་པ། ཐོད་སྐམ་གྱི་མདའ་ཡབ་དང་པུ་ཤུས་བརྒྱན་ཅིང་། རྒྱུ་ལྟོན་གྱི་དྲྭ་བ་དང་དྲྭ་ཕྱེད་པ་འཕྱང་བ། འོག་ཏུ་རུས་པ་དང་ཤ་ཁྲག་སྣ་ཚོགས་ཀྱིས་གཅལ་དུ་བཀྲམ་པ། དེའི་སྟེང་དུ་པཾ་པདྨ་མཉལ་ཧཱུྃ་གིས་པདྨའི་གདན། མ་སུརྻ་མཉལ་ལ་ཧཱུྃ་གིས་ཉི་མའི་གདན། ཨ་ཙནྡྲ་མཉལ་ལ་ཧཱུྃ་གིས་ཟླ་བའི་གདན་གཉིས་སུ་གྱུར། གདན་གྱི་སྟེང་དུ་ས་བོན་ཧཱུྃ་དང་ཨཱཾ་ལས་དུང་དང་འགྲོན་བུ་ཧཱུྃ་དང་ཨཾ་གིས་མཚན་པ་ལས་དཔལ་དུར་ཁྲོད་ཀྱི་བདག་པོ་ཡབ་ཡུམ་གཉིས་སྐུ་མདོག་དཀར་ཞིང་འོད་ཟེར་འཕྲོ་བ་ཀེང་རུས་ཤིན་ཏུ་འཇིགས་པའི་གཟུགས་ཅན་ཞལ་གཅིག་ཕྱག་གཉིས་པ། སྤྱན་བགྲད་ཅིང་ལྗགས་འདྲིལ་བ། མཆེ་བ་གཙིགས་པ། ཕྱག་གཡས་ཀྱིས་ཐོད་སྐམ་གྱི་དབྱུག་པ་ནམ་མཁའ་ལ་འཕྱར་ཞིང་གཡོན་

པས་ཐོད་པ་ཁྲག་གིས་གང་བ་ཐུགས་ཀར་བསྣམས་ཞིང་ཞལ་དུ་གསོལ་བ། ཞབས་གཡས་བསྐུམ་པས་གཡོན་པའི་བརྐྱ་ལ་བརྟེན་པའི་སྐྱིལ་ཀྲུང་ཕྱེད་པའི་གར་སྟབས་ཀྱིས་བཞུགས་པ། དར་སྣ་ཚོགས་ཀྱི་ཤམ་ཐབས་དང་རིན་པོ་ཆེའི་དབུ་རྒྱན་དང་སྙན་ཆས་བརྒྱན་པ། ཡེ་ཤེས་ཀྱི་མེ་འབར་བའི་དབུས་ན་བཞུགས་པའི་ཡབ་ཡུམ་ལ་འཁོར་འཇིག་རྟེན་དང་འཇིག་རྟེན་ལས་འདས་པའི་མཁའ་འགྲོ་དཔག་ཏུ་མེད་པས་བསྐོར་བར་གྱུར།

Dün Gyi Nam-Khar Hūṁ Yig Lé E Ché-Pé Nam-Khar Lung Gi Kyil-Khor, Ram Lé Rak-Tay Gya-Tso, Suṁ Lé Shing Chen Gyi Sa Shi, Keṁ Lé Keng Ru Kyi Ri-Rab, Raṁ Lé Nyi-May Kyil-Khor, Suṁ Lé Thö Khar Gyi Shel-Ye Khang Mi Go Kam-Po Lé Drub-Pay Dru Shi-Pa, Mi Ru Kyi Kang Dang, Tsib Ru Na-Tsog Kyi Teng Thog Phub-Pa, Thö Kam Gyi Da Yab Dang Pu-Shü Gyen Ching, Gyu Lon Gyi Dra-Wa Dang Dra-Wa Che-Pa Chang-Wa, Og-Tu Ru-Pa Dang Sha Trag Na-Tsog Kyi Chel-Du Tram-Pa, Dey Teng Du Paṁ Pad-Ma Man-Da-La Hūṁ Gi Pad-May Den, Ma Sur-Ya Man-Da-La La Hūṁ Gi Nyi-May Den, Ah Chan-Dra Man-Da-La La Hūṁ Gi Da-Way Den Nyi Su Gyur, Den Gyi Teng Du Sa-Bon Hūṁ Dang Aṁ Lé Dung Dang Dron-Bu Hūṁ Dang Aṁ Gi Tsen-Pa Lé Pal Du Trö Kyi Dag-Po Yab Yum Nyi Ku Dog Kar Shing Ö-Zer Tro-Wa Keng Ru Shin-Tu Jig-Pay Zug-Chen Shal Chig Chag Nyi-Pa, Chen Tre Ching Jag Dril-Wa, Che-Wa Tsig-Pa, Chag Yé Kyi Thö Kam Gyi Yug-Pa Nam-Kha La Char Shing Yön-Pé Thö-Pa Trag Gi Gang-Wa Thug-Kar Nam Shing Shel-Du Söl-Wa, Shab Yé Kum-Pé Yön-Pay La La Ten-Pay Kyil Trung Che-Pay Gar Tab Kyi Shug-Pa, Dar Na-Tsog Kyi Sham Thab Dang Rin-Po-Chey Wu-Gyen Dang Nyen-Ché Gyen-Pa, Ye-She Kyi Me Bar-Way Wü-Na Shug-Pay Yab Yum La Khor Jig-Ten Dang Jig-Ten Lé Dé-Pay Khan-Dro Pag-Tu-Me-Pé Kor-War Gyur

In the sky in front, an *E* (ཨེ) syllable separates from *Hūṁ* (ཧཱུྃ) syllable, there is a maṇḍala of air in the sky. There is an ocean of blood from *Raṁ* (རཾ). There is a ground of human corpses from *Suṁ* (སུཾ). There is a mountain of skeletons from *Keṁ* (ཀེཾ). From Suṁ there is a skull palace made from a dried human skull. It has four corners, it has an upper pavilion of human thigh bones and various ribs. Adorned with a parapet and railing of dried human skulls. It is hung with nets and has nets of fresh intestines. Below there is a floor strewn with various bone, flesh and blood. Above this is lotus maṇḍala from *Paṁ* (པཾ), a lotus seat marked with a *Hūṁ* (ཧཱུྃ)[8]. From *Ma* (མ), a sun maṇḍala, a sun seat marked with a *Hūṁ*[9]. From *Ah* (ཨ) is a moon maṇḍala, a moon seat marked with a *Hūṁ*, which becomes doubled[10]. On top of the seat there are seed syllables of *Hūṁ* (ཧཱུྃ) and *Aṁ* (ཨཾ) from which arises a conch and cowric shell marked with *Hūṁ* and *Aṁ*. From these arise the glorious Charnel Ground Lord father and mother. Their bodies are white, shining with light, having the form of a very terrifying skeleton. They have one face and two hands. Their eyes are wide, and their tongues are curled. Their fangs are bared. With their right hands they raise skull batons to the sky. Their left hands hold skulls full of blood to their hearts to serve to their mouths. Since their right legs are contracted and resting on the left thigh, they stand in the half-lotus dancing posture. They are adorned with silk skirts, jeweled crowns and earrings. They stand in the midst of the blazing fire of wisdom. The father and mother are surrounded by immeasurable worldly and transcendent ḍākinīs.

---

8 On top of that, with *Paṃ Padma Maṇḍla Hūṃ,* there is a lotus seat.

9 With *Ma Surya Maṇḍala Hūṃ,* there is a sun seat.

10 With *Ah Candra Maṇḍala Hūṃ*, there are two moon seats.

དེ་གཉིས་ཀྱི་དཔྲལ་བར་ཨོཾ། མགྲིན་པར་ཨཱཿ ཐུགས་ཀར་ཧཱུྃ། ཐུགས་ཀའི་ཧཱུྃ་ལས་འོད་ཟེར་འཕྲོས་པས་རང་བཞིན་གྱི་གནས་དང་ཨུ་རྒྱན་མཁའ་འགྲོའི་ཡུལ་ནས་དཔལ་དུར་ཁྲོད་ཀྱི་བདག་པོ་ཡབ་ཡུམ་ལ་འཁོར་འཇིག་རྟེན་དང་འཇིག་རྟེན་ལས་འདས་པའི་མཁའ་འགྲོ་དཔག་ཏུ་མེད་པས་བསྐོར་བ་ཨོཾ་བཛྲ་ས་མ་ཛཿ ས་སྤྱན་དྲངས།

De Nyi Kyi Trel-War Oṁ, Trin-Par Ah, Thug-Kar Hūṁ, Thug-Kay Hūṁ Lé Ö-Zer Trö-Pé Rang-Shin Gyi Ne Dang Wu-Gyen Khan-Droy Yül Ne Pal Dur Trö Kyi Dag-Po Yab Yum La Khor Jig-Ten Dang Jig-Ten Lé Dé-Pay Khan-Dro Pag Tu Me-Pé Kor-Wa Oṁ vajra samājaḥ

They have *Oṁ* (ཨོཾ) at the forehead, *Āḥ* (ཨཱཿ) at the throat, and *Hūṁ* (ཧཱུྃ) at the heart. Light rays shine from the *Hūṁ* (ཧཱུྃ) at the heart, and summon the Charnel Ground Lord father and mother from their natural place and Oḍḍiyāna, the land of ḍākinīs, surrounded by immeasurable worldly and transcendent ḍākinīs, *Oṁ vajra samājaḥ*

Thus invite.

ཧཱུྃ། དཔལ་ལྡན་མཐུ་སྟོབས་དབང་ཕྱུག་ཆེ།།
ཕྲིན་ལས་རྣམ་བཞིའི་དོན་མཛད་པ།།
དང་ལྡན་དམ་ཚིག་ཆེན་པོ་ཡི།།
གནས་འདི་ཉིད་དུ་གཤེགས་སུ་གསོལ།།

Hūṁ
Pal-Den Thu Tob Wang-Chug Che
Trin-Lé Nam Shiy Don Zé-Pa

Dé-Den Dam-Tsig Chen-Po Yi
Ne Di Nyi Du Sheg Su Söl

Hūṁ
Glorious powerful lords,
one who benefits with the four activities,
please come to this place
of the great samaya of the faithful.

ཤྲཱི་ཤྨ་ཤཱ་ན་ཨ་དྷི་པ་ཏ་ཡེ་ཨེ་ཧྱེ་ཧི། ཛཿ ཧཱུྃ་བཾ་ཧོཿ པདྨ་ཀ་མ་ལཱ་ཡ་སྟྭཾ་ཅེས་དང་།

Shrī shmashana adhipataye eh hye hi, jaḥ hūṁ vaṁ hoḥ, padma kamalāya stvaṁ

ཨོཾ་བཛྲ་ཨ་རྒྷཾ། པཱ་དྱཾ། པུཥྤེ། དྷཱུ་པེ། ཨཱ་ལོ་ཀེ། གནྡྷེ། ནཻ་ཝི་དྱེ། ཤབྡ་ཨཱཿ ཧཱུྃ་གིས་མཆོད།

Offer with:
Oṁ vajra arghaṁ, pādyaṁ, puṣpe, dhūpe, āloke, gandhe, naiwidye, shabda āḥ hūṁ

ཛཿ ཧཱུྃ་བཾ་ཧོཿ

Jaḥ hūṁ vaṁ hoḥ

གཉིས་སུ་མེད་པར་ཐིམ། བཅོམ་ལྡན་འདས་འཁོར་ལོ་སྡོམ་པའི་ལྷ་ཚོགས་ཀྱིས་དབང་བསྐུར། སྐུ་གང་། དྲི་མ་དག་ཆུའི་ལྷག་མ་ཡར་ལུད་པ་ལས་འཁོར་ལོ་སྡོམ་པ་ལྷན་ཅིག་སྐྱེས་པས་དབུར་བརྒྱན།

Nyi Su Me-Par Thim, Chom-Den-Dé Khor-Lo Dom-Pay Lha Tsog Kyi Wang Kur, Ku Gang, Dri-Ma Dag Chui Lhag-Ma Yar Lü-Pa Lé Khor-Lo Dom-Pa Lhen-Chig Kye-Pé Wur-Gyen

They dissolve nondually. Bhagavan Chakrasamavara confers empowerment, their body is filled, the taints are purified and from the overflow of the excess water, their heads are adorned with Sahaja Chakrasamvara.

ཨོཾ་བཛྲ་ཨརྒྷཾ། པཱ་དྱཾ། པུཥྤེ། དྷཱུ་པེ། ཨཱ་ལོ་ཀེ། གནྡྷེ། ནཻ་ཝི་དྱེ། ཤབྡ་ཨཱཿ ཧཱུྃ།

Oṁ vajra arghaṁ, pādyaṁ, puṣpe, dhūpe, āloke, gandhe, naiwidye, shabda āḥ hūṁ

རྒྱལ་བའི་ཐུགས་ཀྱི་ཕྲིན་ལས་ཀུན།།
མ་ལུས་གདུག་པ་འདུལ་བའི་ཕྱིར།།
འཇིགས་པའི་སྐུར་སྟོན་འདོད་དོན་སྟེར།།
དུར་ཁྲོད་གནས་ཀྱི་བདག་པོར་བསྟོད།། ཞེས་པས་བསྟོད།

Gyal-Way Thug Kyi Trin-Lé Kün
Ma-Lü Dug-Pa Dul-Way Chir
Jig-Pay Kur Ton Dö-Don Ter
Du Trö Ne Kyi Dag Por Tö

Then praise:

I praise the lords of the Charnel Grounds
who grant what one wants, showing a terrifying form
in order to tame malicious beings with
all the activities of the minds of the victors

ཨོཾ་བཛྲ་ས་མ་ཡ་སྟྭཾ། ས་མ་ཡ་ཧོཿ

Oṁ vajra samaya stvaṁ
Samaya hoḥ

དཔལ་དུར་ཁྲོད་ཀྱི་བདག་པོ་འཁོར་དང་བཅས་པས་མཆོད་སྦྱིན་གྱི་གཏོར་མ་འདི་བཞེས་ལ། དཔལ་འཁོར་ལོ་བདེ་མཆོག་གི་ལྷ་ཚོགས་རྣམས་དང་། བླ་མ་དམ་པ་རྣམས་ཀྱི་བཀའ་དང་དམ་ལས་མ་འདའ་བར་རྣལ་འབྱོར་པ་བདག་ཅག་འཁོར་དང་བཅས་པ་དང་སེམས་ཅན་ཐམས་ཅད་ལ་གནོད་ཅིང་འཚེ་བའི་གདོན་བགེགས་ལོག་འདྲེན་ཐམས་ཅད་ཚར་གཅོད་པ་དང་། ཚེ་རིང་ནད་མེད་ལོངས་སྤྱོད་འཕེལ་ཞིང་ཆོམ་རྐུན་ཐམས་ཅད་བཅིང་བའི་ཕྲིན་ལས་མཛད་དུ་གསོལ། ཞེས་པའི་ཕྲིན་ལས་བཅོལ།

Pal Dur-Trö Kyi Dag-Po Khor Dang Ché-Pé Chö-Jin Gyi Tor-Ma Di She La, Pal Khor-Lo De-Chog Gi Lha Tsog Nam Dang, La-Ma Dam-Pa Nam Kyi Ka Dang Dam Lé Ma Da-War Nal-Jor-Pa Dag-Chag Khor Dang Ché-Pa Dang Sem-Chen Tham-Ché La Nö Ching Tse-Way Don-Geg Log-Dren Tham-Ché Tsar Chö-Pa Dang, Tse-Ring Ne Me Long-Chö Phel Shing Chom-Kün Tham-Ché Ching-Way Trin-Lé Zé Du Söl

The entrustment of activities:

Glorious Charnel Ground Lords with your retinues, accept this torma offering. Do not transgress the commands of the assembly of Sri Chakrasamvara deities and the sublime gurus. Destroy all spirits, obstructors and false guides who harm and injure we yogins with our retinues and all sentient beings. Increase our longevity, health and enjoyments, and please act to bind all thieves.

ལྗགས་རྡོ་རྗེའི་སྦུ་གུས་གཏོར་མ་གསོལ་བར་བསམས་ལ།

ཨོཾ་གྷྲི་རཱ་ཛ་གྷྲི་རཱ་ཛ། ཀུ་མ་ཀུ་མ་ཁུམ་ཐིས་སྭཱ་ཧཱ། ཤྲཱི་ཤྨ་ཤཱ་ན་ཨ་དྷི་པ་ཏི་མཧཱ་པི་ཤཱ་ཙི་བ་ལིཾ་ཏ་ཁ་ཁ་ཁཱ་ཧི་ཁཱ་ཧི། ཅེས་པ་གསུམ་མམ་བདུན་གྱིས་ཕུལ་བས་གསོལ་ཏེ་དགྱེས་པར་བསམས་ལ།

Imagine that they drink the torma with vajra tube tongues and they are pleased. Offers three or seven times:

Oṁ ghrirāja ghrirāja kuma kuma khumthis svāhā
shrī shmashana adhipati mahā pishāci baliṁta khakha khāhi khāhi

ཨོཾ་བཛྲ་ཨརྒྷཾ། པཱ་དྱཾ། པུཥྤེ། དྷཱུ་པེ། ཨཱ་ལོ་ཀེ། གནྡྷེ། ནཻ་ཝི་དྱེ། ཤབྡ་ཨཱཿ ཧཱུྃ་གིས་མཆོད།

Offer with:

Oṁ vajra arghaṁ, pādyaṁ, puṣpe, dhūpe, āloke, gandhe, naividye, shabda āḥ hūṁ

ནང་མཆོད་གཏོར་ཞིང་། ཨོཾ་གྷྲི་རཱ་ཛ་གྷྲི་རཱ་ཛ་ཀུ་མ་ཀུ་མ་ཁུམ་ཐིས་སྭཱ་ཧཱ། ཨོཾ་ཨཿ ཧཱུྃ།

Then recite and sprinkle the inner offering:

Oṁ ghrirāja ghrirāja kuma kuma khumthis svāhā
Oṁ āḥ hūṁ

དཔལ་དུར་ཁྲོད་ཀྱི་བདག་པོ་འཁོར་དང་བཅས་པས་མཆོད་སྦྱིན་གྱི་གཏོར་མ་འདི་བཞེས་ལ། དཔལ་འཁོར་ལོ་བདེ་མཆོག་གི་ལྷ་ཚོགས་རྣམས་དང་བླ་མ་དམ་པ་རྣམས་ཀྱི་བཀའ་དང་དམ་ལས་མ་འདའ་བར་རྣལ་འབྱོར་པ་བདག་ཅག་འཁོར་དང་བཅས་པ་དང་། སེམས་ཅན་ཐམས་ཅད་ལ་གནོད་ཅིང་འཚེ་བའི་གདོན་བགེགས་ལོག་འདྲེན་རྣམས་ཚར་གཅོད་པ་དང་། ཚེ་རིང་ནད་མེད་ལོངས་སྤྱོད་འཕེལ་ཞིང་ཆོམ་རྐུན་ཐམས་ཅད་བཅིང་བའི་ཕྲིན་ལས་མཛད་དུ་གསོལ། ཅེས་ཕྲིན་ལས་བཅོལ།

Pal Dur Trö Kyi Dag-Po Khor Dang Ché-Pé Chö-Jin Gyi Tor-Ma Di She La, Pal Khor-Lo De-Chog Gi Lha Tsog Nam Dang La-Ma Dam-Pa Nam Kyi Ka Dang Dam Lé Ma Da-War Nal-Jor-Pa Dag-Chag Khor Dang Ché-Pa Dang, Sem-Chen Tham-Ché La Nö Ching Tse-Way Don Geg Log Dren Nam Tsar Chö-Pa Dang, Tse-Ring Ne Me Long-Chö Phel Shing Chom Kün Tham-Ché Ching-Way Trin-Lé Zé Du Söl

The entrustment of activities:

Glorious Charnel Ground Lords with your retinues, accept this torma offering. Do not transgress the commands of the assembly of Sri Chakrasamvara deities and the sublime gurus. Destroy all spirits, obstructors and false guides who harm and injure we yogins with our retinues and all sentient beings. Increase our longevity, health and enjoyments, and please act to bind all thieves.

ཧཱུྃ་རྒྱལ་བའི་ཐུགས་ཀྱི་ཕྲིན་ལས་ཀུན།།
མ་ལུས་གདུག་པ་འདུལ་བའི་ཕྱིར།།
འཇིགས་པའི་སྐུར་སྟོན་འདོད་དོན་སྟེར།།
དུར་ཁྲོད་གནས་ཀྱི་བདག་པོར་བསྟོད།།

Hūṁ
Gyal-Way Thug Kyi Trin-Lé Kün
Ma-Lü Dug-Pa Dul-Way Chir
Jig-Pay Kur Ton Dö Don Ter
Dur Trö Ne Kyi Dag-Por Tö

Hūṁ

I praise the lords of the Charnel Grounds
who grant what one wants, showing a terrifying form
in order to tame malicious beings with
all the activities of the minds of the victors.

རྣམ་དཀར་ཀེང་རུས་དག་པའི་གཟུགས།།
ཕྲིན་ལས་རྣམ་བཞི་ཐོགས་མེད་པར།།
གང་ལ་ཅི་འདོད་དངོས་གྲུབ་ཀུན།།
ཉེ་བར་སྩོལ་མཛད་ཁྱོད་ལ་བསྟོད།།

Nam-Kar Keng Ru Dag-Pay Zug
Trin-Lé Nam-Shi Thog-Me-Par
Gang La Chi Dö Ngö-Drub Kün
Nye-War Tsöl Zé Khyö La Tö

With the form of a pure white skeleton,
I praise you, the one who bestows
all siddhis one could desire,
since the four activities are without impediment.

ཡང་དག་ལམ་ལ་ཉེར་གནས་ཏེ།།
ལུས་ཅན་བདེ་ལ་བཀོད་མཛད་པའི།།
སྲིད་པའི་འཆིང་བ་ཀུན་ལས་སྒྲོལ།།
ཕན་བདེ་ཀུན་སྩོལ་ཁྱོད་ལ་བསྟོད།།

Yang-Dag Lam La Nyer Ne Te
Lü-Chen De La Kö Zé-Pay
Si-Pay Ching-Wa Kün Lé Kyob
Phen De Kün Tsöl Khyö La Tö

Abiding on the right path,
I praise you, granter of all wellbeing and happiness,
the one who protects from all the bonds of existence,
placing embodied beings in happiness.

གང་གིས་ཁྱེད་བསྒྲུབ་ཁྱེད་མཆོད་ན།།
དམ་བཅས་བཞིན་དུ་ཉེར་དགོངས་ནས།།
ཇི་ལྟར་གསོལ་བ་བཏབ་པ་བཞིན།།
བདག་ལ་དངོས་གྲུབ་མ་ལུས་སྩོལ།།

Gang Gi Khye Drub Khye Chö Na
Dam-Ché Shin-Du Nyer Gong Ne
Ji-Tar Söl-Wa Tab-Pa Shin
Dag La Ngö-Drub Ma-Lü Tsöl

If someone practices you and makes offerings to you,
having thought of them according to your promises,
you act according to whatever is petitioned,
please grant me all siddhis.

མཆོད་སྦྱིན་གཏོར་མ་རྒྱ་མཚོ་དང་།།
དངོས་གྲུབ་ཀུན་འབྱུང་དམ་རྫས་ཀྱིས།།
དཔལ་ལྡན་བསྟན་སྲུང་འཁོར་བཅས་མཆོད།།
ཕྲིན་ལས་གང་བཅོལ་འགྲུབ་པར་མཛོད།། ཅེས་པས་བསྟོད།

Chö-Jin Tor-Ma Gya-Tso Dang
Ngö-Drub Kün Jung Dam-Zé Kyi
Pal-Den Ten-Sung Khor Ché Chö
Trin-Lé Gang Chol Drub-Par Zö

An offering is made to the glorious guardians of the teachings
with an ocean of torma offerings
and samaya substances, the source of all siddhis:
accomplish whatever activities are entrusted!

Thus praise.

Torma Offering to All Ḍākinīs

མཁའ་འགྲོ་སྤྱི་གཏོར་ནི།

ཨོཾ་ཨཱཿ ཧཱུྃ་ཧ་ཧོཿ ཧྲཱིཿ ལན་གསུམ་གྱིས་གཏོར་མ་བྱིན་གྱིས་བརླབས་ལ། འབར་བའི་ཕྱག་རྒྱ་དཔྲལ་བར་བཅས་ལ། ཕཻཾ། ཨོཾ་བཛྲ་ཨཱ་ར་ལླི་ཧོཿ ཛཿ ཧཱུྃ་བཾ་ཧོཿ བཛྲ་ཌཱ་ཀི་ནཱི་ས་མ་ཡ་སྟྭཾ་དྲྀ་ཤྱ་ཧོཿ

ཅེས་གཏོར་མགྲོན་སྤྱན་དྲངས་ལ་གཏོར་མ་ཕུལ་བར་བསམས་ཏེ།

Bless the torma by reciting the following three times:

Oṁ āḥ hūṁ ha hoḥ hrīḥ

Perform the blazing mudra at the forehead and say:

Phaiṁ, oṁ vajra āralli hoḥ, jaḥ hūṁ vaṁ hoḥ, vajradākinī samaya stvaṁ drishya hoḥ

The torma guests are invited.

རྡོ་རྗེ་ཐལ་མོ་ཁ་ཕྱེན་དུ་ཕྱེ་བའི་མཐར་སེ་གོལ་གཏོགས་ཤིང་།

ཨོཾ་ཁ་ཁ་ཁཱ་ཧི་ཁཱ་ཧི་སརྦ་ཡཀྵ་རཱཀྵ་ས་བྷུ་ཏ་པྲེ་ཏ་པི་ཤཱ་ཙོ། ཨུནྨཱ་ད། ཨ་པསྨཱ་ར། ཌཱ་ཀ་ཌཱ་ཀི་ནྱ་ད་ཡ། ཨི་མཾ་བ་ལིཾ་གྲྀ་ཧྞནྟུ། ས་མ་ཡ་རཀྵནྟུ་མ་མ་སརྦ་སིདྡྷི་མྨེ་པྲ་ཡ་ཙྪནྟུ། ཡ་ཐེ་བཾ། ཡ་ཐེཥྚཾ། བྷུཉྫ་ཐ། ཛི་གྷྲ་ཐ། པི་བ་ཐ། མཱ་ཏི་ཀྲ་མ་ཐ། མ་མ་སརྦ་ཀཱཪྻ། སུ་ཁཾ་བི་ཤུདྡྷེ་ཡ། ས་ཧ་ཡི་ཀཱ་བྷ་ཝནྟུ་ཧཱུྃ་ཧཱུྃ་ཕཊ་ཕཊ་སྭཱ་ཧཱ། ཞེས་ལན་གསུམ་གྱིས་ཕུལ།

Imagine that the torma is offered. At the end of opening the vajra folded palms, face up and snap one's fingers. Offer three times:

Oṁ kha kha khāhi khāhi, sarva yaksha rākshasa bhuta preta pishāci, unmāda, apasmāra, ḍāka ḍākinyā daya imaṁ baliṁ ghrihaṇantu, samaya rakshantu mama sarva siddhim me prayacchantu, yathaivaṁ, yathaishtaṁ, bhujñatha, jighatha, pipatha, mātikramatha, mama sarva karya, satsukhaṁ vishuddhaya, sahayika bhavantu huṁ hūṁ phaṭ phaṭ svāhā

ཨོཾ་བཛྲ་ཨརྒྷཾ་ཨཱཿ ཧཱུྃ། ཨོཾ་བཛྲ་པཱ་དྱཾ་ཨཱཿ ཧཱུྃ། ཨོཾ་བཛྲ་པུཥྤེ་ཨཱཿ ཧཱུྃ། ཨོཾ་བཛྲ་དྷཱུ་པེ་ཨཱཿ ཧཱུྃ། ཨོཾ་བཛྲ་ཨཱ་ལོ་ཀེ་ཨཱཿ ཧཱུྃ། ཨོཾ་བཛྲ་གནྡྷེ་ཨཱཿ ཧཱུྃ། ཨོཾ་བཛྲ་ནཻ་ཝི་དྱེ་ཨཱཿ ཧཱུྃ། ཨོཾ་བཛྲ་ཤབྡ་ཨཱཿ ཧཱུྃ། ཞེས་ཕྱི་མཆོད་དང་།

Oṁ vajra arghaṁ āḥ hūṁ
Oṁ vajra pādyaṁ āḥ hūṁ
Oṁ vajra puṣpe āḥ hūṁ
Oṁ vajra dhūpe āḥ hūṁ
Oṁ vajra āloke āḥ hūṁ
Oṁ vajra ghande āḥ hūṁ
Oṁ vajra naividye āḥ hūṁ
Oṁ vajra shabda āḥ hūṁ

ཨོཾ་ཨཱཿ ཧཱུྃ་གིས་ནང་མཆོད་ཕུལ་ལ།

Thus make inner offering:

Oṁ āḥ hūṁ

སངས་རྒྱས་མཁའ་འགྲོ། རྡོ་རྗེ་མཁའ་འགྲོ། རིན་ཆེན་མཁའ་འགྲོ། པདྨ་མཁའ་འགྲོ། སྣ་ཚོགས་མཁའ་འགྲོ་ལ་སོགས་པ་གནས་གསུམ་གྱི་དཔའ་བོ་དང་མཁའ་འགྲོའི་

ཚོགས་རྣམས་མཆོད་སྦྱིན་གྱི་གཏོར་མ་རྒྱ་ཆེན་པོ་འདི་བཞེས་ལ་སངས་རྒྱས་ཀྱི་བསྟན་པ་སྲུངས། དཀོན་མཆོག་གི་དབུ་འཕང་བསྟོད། དགེ་འདུན་གྱི་སྡེ་སྐྱོངས། དཔལ་ལྡན་བླ་མ་དམ་པའི་སྐུ་ཚེ་སྲིངས། རྣལ་འབྱོར་པ་བདག་ཅག་དཔོན་སློབ་ཡོན་མཆོད་འཁོར་དང་བཅས་པའི་འགལ་རྐྱེན་བར་ཆད་མི་མཐུན་པའི་ཕྱོགས་ཐམས་ཅད་ཞི་བ་དང་། བསམ་སྦྱོར་ཆོས་མཐུན་ཡིད་བཞིན་དུ་འགྲུབ་པ་དང་། བྱང་ཆུབ་མ་ཐོབ་ཀྱི་བར་དུ་སྲུང་སྐྱོབ་སྦ་བའི་ཕྲིན་ལས་སྡོང་གྲོགས་རྒྱ་ཆེན་པོ་མཛད་དུ་གསོལ།།

Sang-Gyé Khan-Dro, Dor-Je Khan-Dro, Rin-Chen Khan-Dro, Pad-Ma Khan-Dro, Na-Tsog Khan-Dro La Sog Pa Ne Sum Gyi Pa-Wo Dang Khan-Droy Tsog Nam Chö-Jin Gyi Tor-Ma Gya Chen-Po Di She La Sang-Gyé Kyi Ten-Pa Sung, Kon-Chog Gi Wu-Pang Tö, Gen-Dun Gyi De Kyong, Pal-Den La-Ma Dam-Pay Ku-Tse Sing, Nal-Jor-Pa Dag-Chag Pon-Lob Yon-Chö Khor Dang Ché-Pay Gal Kyen Bar-Ché Mi-Thün-Pay Chog Tham-Ché Shi-Wa Dang, Sam Jor Chö Thün Yi-Shin Du Drub-Pa Dang, Jang-Chub Ma Thob Kyi Bar-Du Sung Kyob Ba-Way Trin-Lé Dong Drog Gya-Chen-Po Zé Du Söl

Buddha ḍākinī, Vajra ḍākinī, Ratna ḍākinī, Padma ḍākinī, Viśva ḍākinī and so on, all the heroes and ḍākinīs of the three places, accept this vast torma offering. Guard the teachings of the Buddha. Praise the majestic Jewels. Support the Sangha. Prolong the longevity of the sublime glorious Guru. For we yogins, masters, students, patrons and retinues, pacify all opposing conditions, obstacles and negativities, accomplish our plans just as we wish in accordance with the Dharma, be our great companion for the activities of guarding, protecting and concealing us until we reach awakening!

Torma Offering to the Bhūmipatis

གཞི་བདག་གཏོར་མ་ནི།

ཨོཾ་ཨཱཿ ཧཱུྃ་ཧ་ཧོཿ ཧྲཱིཿ ས་བྱིན་གྱིས་བརླབས།

Bless with:

Oṁ āḥ hūṁ ha hoḥ hrīḥ

ཧཱུྃ་མཛད་ཀྱི་ཕྱག་རྒྱ་བཅས་ལ།
ཨོཾ་བྷཱུ་མི་པ་ཏི་ཨཱ་ཀརྵ་ཡ་ཛཿ ཞེས་པས་སྤྱན་དྲངས་ལ་མགྲོན་འགུགས།

With the Humkara mudra, invite and summon the guests:

Oṁ bhūmi pati ākarshaya jaḥ

ཨོཾ་ཨཱཿ ཀཱ་རོ་མུ་ཁཾ་སརྦ་དྷརྨཱ་ཎཱཾ་ཨཱདྱ་ནུཏྤནྣ་ཏྭ་ཏ་ཨོཾ་ཨཿཧཱུྃ་ཕཊ་སྭཱ་ཧཱ། ཞེས་ལན་གསུམ་གྱིས་ཕུལ།

Make the offering three times:

Oṁ akāro mukhaṁ sarva dharmāṇāṁ adyanutpanna tvata oṁ āḥ hūṁ phaṭ svāhā

ཨོཾ་བཛྲ་ཨ་རྒྷཾ། པཱ་དྱཾ། པུཥྤེ། དྷཱུ་པེ། ཨཱ་ལོ་ཀེ། གནྡྷེ། ནཻ་ཝི་དྱེ། ཤབྡ་ཨཱཿ ཧཱུྃ། ཞེས་ཕྱི་མཆོད།

The outer offerings:

Oṁ vajra arghaṁ, pādyaṁ, puṣpe, dhūpe, āloke, gandhe, naividye, shabda āḥ hūṁ

ཨོཾ་ཨཱཿཧཱུྃ་གིས་ནང་མཆོད་ཕུལ།

The inner offerings:

Oṁ āḥ hūṁ

མཆོད་སྦྱིན་གཏོར་མ་གཟུགས་སྒྲ་དྲི་རོ་རེག་བྱ་འདོད་པའི་ཡོན་ཏན་ལྔ་དང་ལྡན་པ་འདི་
ཉིད་སའི་ལྷ་མོ་བརྟན་མ། བོད་ཁམས་སྐྱོང་བའི་བརྟན་མ་བཅུ་གཉིས་ལ་སོགས་པའི་
གནས་བདག་གཞི་བདག་གྲོང་བདག་ཡུལ་བདག་གཉུག་མར་གནས་པ་རྣམས་དང་།
མ་ལྟར་བྱམས་ཤིང་སྲིང་ལྟར་ཉེ་བ་རྣམས་ལ་འབུལ་ལོ། སངས་རྒྱས་ཀྱི་བསྟན་པ་དར་
ཞིང་འཇིག་རྟེན་དུ་དགེ་ལེགས་རྒྱ་ཆེན་པོ་འབྱུང་བ་དང་། གནས་མགྲོན་གྱི་དམ་ཚིག་
སྲུངས། བདག་ཅག་དཔོན་སློབ་ཡོན་མཆོད་འཁོར་དང་བཅས་པ་རྣམས་ཀྱི་བྱ་བ་དང་
སྤྱོད་པ་ཉེས་པ་ལ་ཀོ་ལོང་རུ་ང་ཕྲག་དོག་མ་མཛད་པར་བསམ་སྦྱོར་ཆོས་མཐུན་ཡིད་
བཞིན་དུ་འགྲུབ་པའི་ཕྲིན་ལས་སྟོང་གྲོགས་རྒྱ་ཆེན་པོ་མཛད་དུ་གསོལ།

Chö-Jin Tor-Ma Zug Dra Dri Ro Reg-Ja Dö-Pay Yon-Ten Nga Dang Den-Pa Di Nyi Say Lha-Mo Ten-Ma, Bö-Kham Kyong-Way Ten-Ma Chu Nyi La Sog-Pay Ne Dag Shi Dag Drong Dag Yül Dag Nyug-Mar Ne-Pa Nam Dang, Ma Tar Jam Shing Sing Tar Nye-Wa Nam La Bül-Lo, Sang-Gyé Kyi Ten-Pa Dar Shing Jig-Ten Du Ge-Leg Gya-Chen-Po Jung-Wa Dang, Ne Dron Gyi Dam-Tsig Sung, Dag-Chag Pon-Lob Yon-Chö Khor Dang Ché-Pa Nam Kyi Ja-Wa Dang Chö-Pa Nye-Pa La Ko-Long Ru-Nga Trag-Dog Ma Zé-Par Sam Jor Chö Thün Yi-Shin-Du Drub-Pay Trin-Lé Tong Drog Gya-Chen-Po Zé Du Söl

This torma offering with the five desirable qualities of form, sound, scent, taste and texture is offered to owners of the places, owners of the land, owners of the towns, the owners of the regions living in their native places such as the goddess of the earth, the twelve Tenma of Tibetan region and so on, those who love us like mothers and care for us like sisters. Spread the teaching of the Buddha, produce vast prosperity for the world and guard the samaya of guests in your place. Don't be annoyed, angry or jealous at our mistaken actions and conducts, master, disciples, patrons and retinues, be our great companion for the activities of accomplishing our plans in accordance with the Dharma!

ན་མོ་བདག་གི་བསམ་པའི་སྟོབས་དག་དང་།།
དེ་བཞིན་གཤེགས་པའི་བྱིན་སྟོབས་དང་།།
ཆོས་ཀྱི་དབྱིངས་ཀྱི་སྟོབས་རྣམས་ཀྱིས།།
དོན་རྣམས་གང་དག་བསམས་པ་ཀུན།།
དེ་དག་ཐམས་ཅད་ཅི་རིགས་པ།།
འཇིག་རྟེན་ཁམས་འདིར་མ་ལུས་པར།།
ཐོགས་པ་མེད་པར་འབྱུང་གྱུར་ཅིག། ཅེས་བརྗོད།

Na-Mo
Dag Gi Sam-Pay Tob Dag Dang
De-Shin Sheg-Pay Jin Tob Dang
Chö-Kyi Ying Kyi Tob Nam Kyi
Don Nam Gang Dag Sam-Pa Kün

De-Dag Tham-Ché Chi Rig-Pa
Jig-Ten Kham Dir Ma-Lü-Par
Thog-Pa Me-Par Jung Gyur Chig

Recite:

Homage!
By the power of my intention,
the power of the generosity of the tathagatas
and the power of the dharmadhātu,
may all of any wished for goals,
however many of them,
which are here in the world,
arise without impediment.

[To perform "Concise Daily Ganapūjā", go to page 310 then continue with "Conclusion Ritual" on page 260.]

Ganapūjā

དེ་ནས་ཚོགས་མཆོད་ནི། ཚོགས་ཀྱི་ཡོ་བྱད་ཅི་འབྱོར་པ་དང་། ཁྱད་པར་ཐོད་པའི་སྣོད་དུ་མ་ད་ན་ཞེས་ཆང་དང་། བ་ལ་ཞེས་ཤ་རྣམས་བཀོད་པ་མཛེས་པར་བཤམས་པའི་ཚོགས་རྫས་རྣམས་ནང་མཆོད་ཆུ་ཆང་གིས་སྦྱངས། ཚོགས་པ་མང་པོ་ཡོད་ན་ལས་ཀྱི་རྡོ་རྗེས་ཕྱག་གསུམ་བཙལ་ནས།

Next, for the Ganapūjā, set up whatever Ganapūjā articles one has, in particular, alcohol named as "madana" and meat named as "bala" inside the skullcup. Purify beautifully arranged Ganapūjā substances with the inner offering of the alcohol water. If there are many participants, the karmavajra prostrates three times to request.

ཚོགས་ཀྱི་ཡོ་བྱད་ལ་བྱིན་རླབས་གནང་བར་ཞུ། ཞེས་བརྗོད།

Tsog Kyi Yo-Je La Jin-Lab Nang-War Shu

Then he [karmavajra] says:

Please bless the articles of the Ganapūjā.

སློབ་དཔོན་གྱིས་རྡོ་རྗེའི་རྩེས་ནང་མཆོད་གཏོར་ལ།
ཨོཾ་སུམྦྷ་ནི་སུམྦྷ་ཧཱུྃ་ཧཱུྃ་ཕཊ།
ཨོཾ་གྲྀཧྞ་གྲྀཧྞ་ཧཱུྃ་ཧཱུྃ་ཕཊ།
ཨོཾ་གྲྀཧྞ་པ་ཡ་གྲྀཧྞ་པ་ཡ་ཧཱུྃ་ཧཱུྃ་ཕཊ།
ཨོཾ་ཨཱ་ན་ཡ་ཧོཿ བྷ་ག་ཝཱན་བིདྱཱ་རཱ་ཛ་ཧཱུྃ་ཧཱུྃ་ཕཊ། ཞེས་པས་བསང་།

The master sprinkles the inner offering with the tip of his vajra, cleansing them with:

Oṁ sumbha nisumbha huṁ hūṁ phaṭ
Oṁ grihaṇa grihaṇa huṁ hūṁ phaṭ
Oṁ grihaṇapaya grihaṇapaya huṁ hūṁ phaṭ
Oṁ ānayaho bhagavān vidyārāja huṁ hūṁ phaṭ

ཨོཾ་སྭ་བྷཱ་ཝ་ཤུདྡྷཿ སརྦ་དྷརྨཱཿ སྭ་བྷཱ་ཝ་ཤུདྡྷོ྅ ཧཾ། གིས་སྦྱང་།

Purify them with:

Oṁ svabhāva shuddhaḥ sarva dharmāḥ svabhāva shuddho' haṁ

སྟོང་པའི་ངང་ལས་ཨ་ལས་བྱུང་བའི་ཐོད་པ་ཡངས་ཤིང་རྒྱ་ཆེ་བའི་ནང་དུ་ཤ་ལྔ་བདུད་རྩི་ལྔ་ཡེ་ཤེས་ལྔ་རྣམས་ཞུ་བ་ལས་བྱུང་བའི་ཡེ་ཤེས་ཀྱི་བདུད་རྩིའི་རྒྱ་མཚོ་ཆེན་པོར་གྱུར།

Tong-Pay Ngang Lé Ah Lé Jung-Way Thö-Pa Yang Shing Gya-Che-Way Nang Du Sha Nga Dü-Tsi Nga Ye-She Nga Nam Shu-Wa Lé Jung-Way Ye-She Kyi Dü-Tsiy Gya-Tso Chen-Por Gyur

An *Ah* (ཨ) arises out of the state of emptiness. That *Ah* (ཨ) turns into a vast and wide skull, in which is a great ocean of wisdom amrita that comes from the melting of the five meats, five amritas, and five wisdoms.

ཨོཾ་ཨཱཿ ཧཱུྃ་ཧ་ཧོཿ ཧྲཱིཿ ཟན་མང་དུ་བརྗོད་པའི་ཡེ་ཤེས་ཀྱི་བདུད་རྩིའི་རྒྱ་མཚོ་ཟད་མི་ཤེས་པར་གྱུར་པར་བསམ་པ་ནི་ཤིན་ཏུ་གལ་ཆེ་བས་དམིགས་པ་མ་ཡེངས་པར་བྱ།

Since it is extremely important to imagine that it becomes an inexhaustible ocean of wisdom amrita, one must visualize this without distraction to recite many times:

Oṁ āḥ hūṁ ha hoh hrih

དེ་ནས་ཚོགས་ཀྱི་ཕུད་སྣོད་གཉིས་སུ་བླུགས་པ་དང་། མེད་ན་སྣོད་གཅིག་ཏུ་བླུགས་ལ་དཀྱིལ་འཁོར་གྱི་མདུན་དུ་ཕུལ། སྤྲོ་ན། གཏོར་མ་རྣམས་ལའང་ཕུད་ཐམས་ཅད་ནས་མ་ལུས་པར་ཕུལ། སླར་ཡང་ཐམས་ཅད་ལ་ནང་མཆོད་ཆུ་ཆང་གིས་བྲན།

Next, pour the first portion of the Ganapūjā into two containers, or if there are not two, pour it into one and offer it in front of the maṇḍala. If one wishes to elaborate, offer the first portions from all the tormas. Sprinkles all with the inner offering of the alcohol water again.

ལས་ཀྱི་རྡོ་རྗེས་ཕྱག་གསུམ་བཙལ་ལ།

བླ་མ་དང་དཀོན་མཆོག་གི་དྲུང་དུ་སྨན་ཕུད་འབུལ་བར་ཞུ། ཞེས་བརྗོད།

La-Ma Dang Kon-Chog Gi Drung Du Men Phü-Bül-War Shu

The karmavajra prostrates three times and says:

In the presence of the guru and the Jewels, please offer the first portion of the medicine.

དཔོན་སློབ་རྣམས་ཀྱིས།

དམན་པའི་ཡུལ་ལས་རབ་འདས་ཤིང་།།
རྒྱལ་བ་ཀུན་གྱི་དམ་ཚིག་མཆོག།
དངོས་གྲུབ་ཀུན་གྱི་གཞིར་གྱུར་པ།།
བདུད་རྩི་མཆོག་གིས་མཆོད་པར་བགྱི།།

Men-Pay Yül Lé Rab Dé Shing
Gyal-Wa Kün Gyi Dam-Tsig Chog
Ngö-Drub Kün Gyi Shir Gyur-Pa
Dü-Tsi Chog Gi Chö-Par Gyi

The master and disciples say:

Totally beyond inferior objects,
the supreme samaya of the victors,
this offering of supreme amrita
is the foundation of all siddhis.

སྒྲིབ་པའི་དྲི་མ་ཀུན་བསལ་ནས།།
རྟོག་པ་ཀུན་ལས་རྣམ་གྲོལ་བ།།
བླ་ན་མེད་པའི་བྱང་ཆུབ་སེམས།།
བདེ་བ་ཆེན་པོས་མཉེས་གྱུར་ཅིག། ཅེས་བརྗོད།

Drib-Pay Dri-Ma Kün Sal Ne
Tog-Pa Kün-Lé Nam Dröl-Wa
La-Na Me-Pay Jang-Chub Sem
De-Wa Chen-Pö Nye Gyur Chig

Having removed all taints of obscuration,
completely free from all thought,
may you be pleased with the great bliss
of unsurpassed bodhicitta.

ཡང་ཕྱག་གསུམ་བཙལ་ལ།
བླ་མ་དང་དཀོན་མཆོག་གི་དྲུང་དུ་ཚོགས་ཕུད་འབུལ་བར་ཞུ། ཞེས་བརྗོད།

La-Ma Dang Kon-Chog Gi Drung Du Tsog Phü-Bül-War Shu

Again, the karmavajra prostrates three times and says:

In the presence of the guru and the Jewels, please offer the first portion of the Ganapūjā.

དཔོན་སློབ་རྣམས་ཀྱིས།

ཞལ་ཟས་རོ་བརྒྱ་ལྡན་པའི་ཡིད་འཕྲོག་པ།།
ལེགས་སྦྱར་འདི་ནི་རྒྱལ་བ་སྲས་བཅས་ལ།།
དད་པས་ཕུལ་བས་འགྲོ་བ་འདི་དག་ཀུན།།
འབྱོར་ལྡན་ཏིང་འཛིན་ཟས་ལ་སྤྱོད་པར་ཤོག། ཅེས་བརྗོད།

Shel-Ze Ro Gya Den-Pay Yi-Trog-Pa
Leg-Jar Di Ni Gyal-Wa Se Ché La
Dé-Pé Phul-We Dro-Wa Di-Dag Kün
Jor-Den Ting Zin Ze La Chö-Par Shog

The master and disciples say:
The first portion of this well prepared food
enchanting with one hundred flavors
is offered with faith to the victors and their children;
may all migrating beings enjoy the abundant food of samādhi.

ཡང་ཕྱག་གསུམ་བཙལ།

མཁའ་འགྲོ་དང་ཆོས་སྐྱོང་གི་དྲུང་དུ་ཚོགས་ཕུད་འབུལ་བར་ཞུ། ཞེས་བརྗོད།

Khan-Dro Dang Chö Khong Gi Drung Du Tsog Phü-Bül-War Shu

Again, the karmavajra prostrates three times and says:
In the presence of the ḍākinīs and the dharmapālas, please offer the first portion of the Ganapūjā.

དཔོན་སློབ་རྣམས་ཀྱིས།

ཨོཾ་ཨོཾ་ཨོཾ་སརྦ་བུདྡྷ་ཌཱ་ཀི་ནཱི་ཡེ། བཛྲ་ཝརྞ་ནཱི་ཡེ། བཛྲ་བཻ་རོ་ཙ་ནཱི་ཡེ། ཧཱུྃ་ཧཱུྃ་ཧཱུྃ། ཕཊ་ཕཊ་ཕཊ་སྭཱ་ཧཱ། ཨོཾ་ཨ་ཀཱ་རོ་མུ་ཁཾ་སརྦ་དྷརྨཱ་ཎཱཾ་ཨཱ་དྱ་ནུཏྤནྣ་ཏྭ་ཏ་ཨོཾ་ཨཱཿ ཧཱུྃ་ཕཊ་སྭཱ་ཧཱ། ཅེས་རྗེ་བཙུན་མ་ལ་ཕུལ།

Master and disciples offer to Jetsunma and say:

Oṁ oṁ oṁ sarvabuddhaḍākinīye vajravarṇanīye vajravairocanīye hūṁ hūṁ hūṁ phaṭ phaṭ phaṭ svāhā, oṁ akāro mukhaṁ sarva dharmāṇāṁ ādyan utpanna tvata oṁ āḥ hūṁ phaṭ svāhā

དེ་ནས་གུར་མགོན་ལྕམ་དྲལ་སོགས་ཀྱི་གཏོར་མ་ཡོད་ན་སོ་སོར་གཏོར་སྔགས་ཀྱིས་རྒྱས་པར་ཕུལ་བའམ། མདོར་བསྡུ་ན། ཨོཾ་ཤྲཱི་མཧཱ་ཀཱ་ལ་ཡ་ས་པ་རི་ཝཱ་ར་ཨི་དཾ་བ་ལིཾ་ཏ་ཁ་ཁ་ཁཱ་ཧི་ཁཱ་ཧི། ཞེས་དང་།

Next, if one has the torma of Vajrapanjaranatha brother and sister, etc., one can offer extensively with their individual torma mantras. Or, offer in brief:

Oṁ Shrī Mahākālaya saparivāra idaṁ baliṁta kha kha khāhi khāhi

ཨོཾ་ཤྲཱི་དྷརྨ་པཱ་ལ་ཙ་ཏུརྨུ་ཁཾ་ས་པ་རི་ཝཱ་ར་ཨི་དཾ་བ་ལིཾ་ཏ་ཁ་ཁ་ཁཱ་ཧི་ཁཱ་ཧི་ཞེས་དང་།

Oṁ Shrī dharmāpāla chaturmukhaṁ saparivara idaṁ baliṁta kha kha khāhi khāhi

ཨོཾ་གྷྲི་རཱ་ཛ་གྷྲི་རཱ་ཛ་ཀུ་མ་ཀུ་མ་ཁུམ་ཐིས་སྭཱ་ཧཱ། ཤྲཱི་ཤྨ་ཤཱ་ན་ཨ་དྷི་པ་ཏི་མཧཱ་པི་ཤཱ་ཙི་བ་ལིཾ་ཏ་ཁ་ཁ་ཁཱ་ཧི་ཁཱ་ཧི་ཞེས་མཐར།

Oṁ ghrirāja ghrirāja kuma kuma khumthis svāhā
shrī shmashana adhipati mahā pishāci baliṁta khakha khāhi khāhi

ཨོཾ་ཁ་ཁ་ཁཱ་ཧི་ཁཱ་ཧི་སརྦ་ཡཀྵ་རཱཀྵ་ས་བྷུ་ཏ་པྲེ་ཏ་པི་ཤཱ་ཙི། ཨུནྨཱ་ད། ཨ་པསྨཱ་ར། ཌཱ་ཀ་ཌཱ་ཀི་ནྱཱ་ད་ཡ། ཨི་མཾ་བ་ལིཾ་གྲི་ཧྞནྟུ། ས་མ་ཡ་རཀྵནྟུ། མ་མ་སརྦ་སིདྡྷི་མྨེ་པྲ་ཡ་ཙྪནྟུ། ཡ་ཐེ་བཾ། ཡ་ཐེཥྚཾ། བྷུཉྫ་ཐ། ཛིགྷྲ་ཐ། པི་བ་ཐ། མ་ཏི་ཀྲ་མ་ཐ། མ་མ་སརྦ་ཀཱརྻ། སཏྶུ་ཁཾ་བི་ཤུདྡྷ་ཡ། ས་ཧ་ཡི་ཀཱ་བྷ་བནྟུ་ཧུཾ་ཧཱུཾ་ཕཊ་ཕཊ་སྭཱ་ཧཱ།

Oṁ kha kha khāhi khāhi, sarva yaksha rākshasa bhuta preta pishāci, unmāda, apasmāra, ḍāka ḍākinyā daya imaṁ baliṁ ghrihaṇantu, samaya rakshantu mama sarva siddhim me prayacchantu, yathaivaṁ, yathaishtaṁ, bhujñatha, jighatha, pipatha, mātikramatha, mama sarva karya, satsukhaṁ vishuddhaya, sahayika bhavantu huṁ hūṁ phaṭ phaṭ svāhā

ཨོཾ་ཨ་ཀཱ་རོ་མུ་ཁཾ་སརྦ་དྷརྨཱ་ཎཱཾ་ཨཱ་དྱ་ནུཏྤནྣ་ཏྭཱ་ཏ་ཨོཾ་ཨཱཿ ཧཱུྂ་ཕཊ་སྭཱ་ཧཱ། ཞེས་པ་རྣམས་ཕྱག་རྒྱ་དང་བཅས་པས་ཕུལ།

Make the offerings with the mudra:

Oṁ akāro mukhaṁ sarva dharmāṇāṁ adyanutpanna tvata oṁ āḥ hūṁ phaṭ svāhā

ཨོཾ་བཛྲ་ཨརྒྷཾ་ཨཱཿ ཧཱུྂ། ཨོཾ་བཛྲ་པཱདྱཾ་ཨཱཿ ཧཱུྂ། ཨོཾ་བཛྲ་པུཥྤེ་ཨཱཿ ཧཱུྂ། ཨོཾ་བཛྲ་དྷཱུ་པེ་ཨཱཿ ཧཱུྂ། ཨོཾ་བཛྲ་ཨཱ་ལོ་ཀེ་ཨཱཿ ཧཱུྂ། ཨོཾ་བཛྲ་གནྡྷེ་ཨཱཿ ཧཱུྂ། ཨོཾ་བཛྲ་ནཻ་ཝི་དྱེ་ཨཱཿ ཧཱུྂ། ཨོཾ་བཛྲ་ཤབྡ་ཨཱཿ ཧཱུྂ། རྣམས་ཀྱིས་ཕྱི་མཆོད་འབུལ།

The outer offerings:

Oṁ vajra arghaṁ āḥ hūṁ

Oṁ vajra pādyaṁ āḥ hūṁ

Oṁ vajra puṣpe āḥ hūṁ
Oṁ vajra dhūpe āḥ hūṁ
Oṁ vajra āloke āḥ hūṁ
Oṁ vajra ghande āḥ hūṁ
Oṁ vajra naividye āḥ hūṁ
Oṁ vajra shabda āḥ hūṁ

ཨོཾ་ཨཱཿ ཧཱུྃ་གིས་ནང་མཆོད་ཕུལ།

The inner offerings:
Oṁ āḥ hūṁ

དྲིན་ཆེན་རྩ་བ་དང་བརྒྱུད་པར་བཅས་པའི་དཔལ་ལྡན་བླ་མ་དམ་པ་རྣམས་དང་། ཡི་དམ་དཀྱིལ་འཁོར་གྱི་ལྷ་ཚོགས་ཆོས་སྐྱོང་བའི་སྲུང་མ་གནས་གསུམ་གྱི་དཔའ་བོ་མཁའ་འགྲོའི་ཚོགས་དང་བཅས་པ་རྣམས་ཀྱི་ཞལ་དུ་མཆོད་པ་དམ་པ་འབུལ་ལོ། །སངས་རྒྱས་ཀྱི་བསྟན་པ་དར་ཞིང་འཇིག་རྟེན་དུ་དགེ་ལེགས་རྒྱ་ཆེན་པོ་འབྱུང་བ་དང་། བདག་ཅག་དཔོན་སློབ་འཁོར་དང་བཅས་པའི་ཆོས་སྒྲུབ་པའི་འགལ་རྐྱེན་བར་ཆད་ཐམས་ཅད་ཞི་ཞིང་། མཐུན་རྐྱེན་ཐམས་ཅད་ཡིད་བཞིན་དུ་འགྲུབ་པར་མཛད་དུ་གསོལ། ཅེས་ཕུད་ཀྱིས་དཀོན་མཆོག་མཆོད།

Drin-Chen Tsa-Wa Dang Gyü-Par Ché-Pay Pal-Den La-Ma Dam-Pa Nam Dang, Yi-Dam Kyil-Khor Gyi Lha Tsog Chö Kyong-Way Sung-Ma Ne Sum Gyi Pa-Wo Khan-Droy Tsog Dang Ché-Pa Nam Kyi Shal-Du Chö-Pa Dam-Pa Bül-Lo, Sang-Gyé Kyi Ten-Pa Dar Shing Jig-Ten Du Ge-Leg Gya-Chen-Po Jung-Wa Dang, Dag-Chag Pon-Lob Khor Dang Ché-Pay Chö Drub-Pay Gal Kyen Bar-Ché Tham-Ché Shi Shing, Thün-Kyen Tham-Ché Yi Shin-Du Drub-Par Zé Du Söl

Make the offering to the supreme Jewels:

This supreme offering is made to the mouths of the sublime gurus, the kind root guru and the lineage gurus, the assembed deities of the yidam's maṇḍala, the guardian dharmapālas, the assembly of heroes and heroines of the three places. Please spread the teaching of the Buddha, produce vast prosperity for the world. For we yogins, masters, students, patrons and retinues, pacify all opposing conditions and obstacles to practice the Dharma, and please accomplish all positive conditions just as we wish.

དེ་ནས་དམ་ཚིག་བསྐྱོལ་བའི་ཕྱིར་རྡོ་རྗེ་སློབ་དཔོན་གྱི་དྲུང་དུ་མ་ད་ནའི་སྣོད་པདྨ་བྷཉྫ་དཔྲལ་བ་ནང་ལ་བསྟན་པ་བཞག །དེའི་སྟེང་དུ་བ་ལ་ཙུང་ཞིག་བཞག་པ་ལས་ཀྱི་རྡོ་རྗེ་ཕྱག་གསུམ་བཙལ། པད་གོར་བྱས་ལ།

In order to develop samaya, place the Padmabhañja, the container of madana, before the vajramaster with the forehead facing inwards. On top of that place a small piece of bala. The karmavajra should make three prostrations, a lotus rolls, and recites:

རྡོ་རྗེ་འཛིན་སོགས་དགོངས་སུ་གསོལ།།
བདག་གི་ཚོགས་ཀྱི་ཁྱད་པར་འདི།།
དད་པའི་སེམས་ཀྱི་འབུལ་ལགས་ཀྱི།།
ཅི་བདེ་བར་ནི་བཞེས་སུ་གསོལ།། ཅེས་བརྗོད།

Dor-Je Zin Sog Gong Su Söl
Dag Gi Tsog Kyi Khye-Par Di
Dé-Pay Sem Kyi Bül Lag Kyi
Chi De-War Ni She Su Söl

Vajraholder and so on, heed me!
This special Ganapūjā of mine
is offered with a mind of faith,
please accept this as it pleases you!

དཔོན་སློབ་རྣམས་ཀྱིས།
ཨེ་མ་ཞི་བ་ཆེན་པོ་ཀྱེ།།
ཚོགས་ཆེན་འབར་བས་ཉོན་མོངས་སྲེག།
འདི་འདྲའི་བདེ་བ་ཆེན་པོ་སྟེ།།
ཀུན་ཀྱང་ཨ་ཧོ་སུ་ཁ་ཆེ།།
ཨ་ཧོ་མཧཱ་སུ་ཁ་ཧོཿ ཞེས་བརྗོད།

E Ma Shi-Wa Chen-Po Kye
Tsog Chen Bar-We Nyon-Mong Seg
Di Dray De-Wa Chen-Po Te
Kün Kyang Ah Ho Su-Kha Che
Ah ho mahā sukha hoḥ

The master and disciples say:

Amazing! What a great peace!
Afflictions are burned with the great Ganapūjā.
The great bliss is just like this.
Also, everything is amazingly great bliss.
Ah ho mahā sukha hoḥ

ཡང་ཕྱག་གསུམ་དང་པད་ཀོར་བྱས་ལ།

འདིར་ནི་ཆོས་རྣམས་བཟང་པོར་ལྟོས།།
འདུས་པ་ལ་ནི་ཐེ་ཚོམ་མེད།།
བྲམ་ཟེ་གདོལ་པ་ཁྱི་དང་ཕག།
རང་བཞིན་གཅིག་ཏུ་རོལ་དུ་གསོལ།། ཅེས་པའི་ལན་དུ།

Dir Ni Chö-Nam Zang-Por To
Dü-Pa La Ni The-Tsom Me
Dram-Ze Dol-Pa Khyi Dang Phag
Rang-Shin Chig-Tu Röl-Du Söl

Again the karmavajra makes three prostrations, a lotus roll, and replies:

Here, look at these excellent things!
Don't have any doubt about this gathering.
Brahmins, caṇḍālas, dogs and pigs,
please enjoy as one nature.

བདེ་གཤེགས་ཆོས་ལ་རིང་ཐང་མེད།།
འདོད་ཆགས་ལ་སོགས་དྲི་མ་བྲལ།།
གཟུང་དང་འཛིན་པ་རྣམ་སྤངས་པ།།
དེ་བཞིན་ཉིད་ལ་གུས་ཕྱག་འཚལ།།
ཨ་ཧོ་མཧཱ་སུ་ཁ་ཧོཿ ཞེས་བརྗོད།

De-Sheg Chö La Ring Thang Me
Dö-Chag La Sog Dri-Ma Drel
Zung Dang Zin-Pa Nam Pang-Pa
De-Shin Nyi La Gü Chag-Tsal
Ah ho mahā sukha hoḥ

Say:

There is no price for the Sugata's Dharma.
We prostrate with devotion to suchness,
free from the taints of desire and so on,
free from grasper and grasped.
Ah ho mahā sukha hoḥ

དེ་ནས་ལས་ཀྱི་རྡོ་རྗེ་ལག་པ་གཉིས་པདྨའི་ཕྱག་རྒྱ་ལས་སྲིན་ལག་གཡས་ཀྱིས་སྙིང་གི་བ་ལ་འཛིན་པས་རྡོ་རྗེ་སློབ་དཔོན་ནས་རིམ་བཞིན་མ་ད་ན་འགྲིམ་ཚར་བ་དང་། ཚོགས་ཀྱི་རྫས་རྣམས་མ་ཚང་བ་མེད་པ་སློབ་དཔོན་ལ་ཉིས་འགྱུར་སོགས་དཔོན་སློབ་ཐམས་ཅད་ལ་ལག་པ་གཉིས་ཀས་འབུལ་ཞིང་ལེན་པ་པོས་ཀྱང་ལག་པ་གཉིས་ཀས་པད་ཀོར་གྱིས་བླང་བར་བྱ།

Next, the karmavajra makes the lotus mudra with both hands, and takes bala on his right Ring finger. Beginning from the Vajramaster, he distributes the madana and offers the complete Ganapūjā substances with both hands to everyone, the master and students, with a double portion to the master. Also, they take it after a lotus roll with both hands.

ཨ་ཧོ་མཧཱ་སུ་ཁ་ཧོཿ ཞེས་བརྗོད་ཅིང་བླང་དགོས་ཏེ་ཏེ་བརྡ་ལས། པདྨའི་ལག་པས་བླང་བ་དང་། །དེ་ཉིད་ཀྱི་ནི་ལག་པས་འབུལ། །ཞེས་གསུངས་པའི་ཕྱིར་དེ་ནས་ཐམས་ཅད་ལ་ཕུལ་ཟིན་པ་དང་། ས་རྗེན་ལ་མི་འཇོག་ཅིང་སློབ་དཔོན་གྱིས།

Recite and take [Tsog]:

Ah ho mahā sukha hoḥ

The purpose of taking is stated in the Hevajra Tantra, "Take with lotus hands, also give with those hands." After completing the [Tsog] distributions, which are not to be placed on the bare ground.

ཐམས་ཅད་ཚོགས་ལ་རོལ་བར་ཞུ། ཞེས་བརྗོད།

Tham-Ché Tsog La Röl-War Shu

The master says:

Enjoy the Tsog everyone!

འདི་དག་གི་སྐབས་སུ་སྣོད་དང་མི་ལྡན་པའི་སྐྱེ་བོས་དབེན་པར་བྱས་ལ། དཔོན་སློབ་ཐམས་ཅད་ཀྱིས་གཙང་རྨེའི་རྣམ་རྟོག་མི་བྱ་བར་སྙིང་གའི་བཾ་ཡིག་སངས་རྒྱས་ཐམས་ཅད་འདུས་པའི་ངོ་བོར་མཆོད་པའི་བསམ་པས་རྫས་ཐམས་ཅད་ཚིམས་པར་ལོངས་སྤྱོད། ཁྱད་པར་དགེ་སློང་རྡོ་རྗེ་འཛིན་པ་ལྟ་བུའི་སྡོམ་པ་འོག་མའི་བཅས་པ་བསྲུང་བའི་བསམ་པས་མ་ད་ན་དང་ཕྱི་དྲོའི་ཁ་ཟས་སྤོངས་སེམས་ཀྱི་ཚོགས་རྫས་ཁྱད་དུ་བསད་ན་རྩ་ལྟུང་དུ་འགྱུར་ཏེ། དམ་ཚིག་རྫས་ནི་ཇི་བཞིན་རྙེད། །མི་བསྟེན་པ་ནི་བཅུ་གསུམ་པ། །ཞེས་གསུངས་པའི་ཕྱིར་རོ། ། ཚོགས་ཀྱི་དུས་ཐམས་ཅད་དུ་རྩོད་པ་དང་ཁ་ཤག་འཕྱེད་པ་སོགས་མི་བྱ་བར་ཆོས་ཀྱི་གླེང་བརྗོད་དང་རྡོ་རྗེའི་གླུ་གར་ལ་སོགས་པས་དུས་འདའ་བར་བྱའོ། །དེ་ཡང་ཚོགས་ཀྱི་སྐབས་སུ་ཤ་ལ་བྷ་ལ་དང་། ཆང་ལ་མ་ད་ན་ལ་སོགས་པའི་བརྡ་སྐད་བྱ་དགོས་ཏེ། ཧེ་བཛྲ་ཀྱི་རྒྱུད་ལས། །གལ་ཏེ་སངས་རྒྱས་གསང་བའི་སྐད། །མི་གསུང་ན་ནི་འགྲོངས་པར་འགྱུར། །ཞེས་དང་། གསང་བའི་སྐད་ཀྱིས་མི་སྨྲ་བ། །དེ་ཡི་དམ་ཚིག་ཉམས་པར་ནི། །འགྱུར་བ་འདི་ལ་ཐེ་ཚོམ་མེད། །ཞེས་གསུངས་པའི་ཕྱིར། དེ་ནས་ཐམས་ཅད་ཀྱི་ཚིམས་པར་ལོངས་སྤྱོད་པའི་རྗེས་སུ། ལས་ཀྱི་རྡོ་རྗེས་སྣོད་གཅིག་ཏུ་མས་རིམ་གྱི་ཚོགས་ལྷག་སྡུས་ལ།མཚན་མོ་ཡིན་ན་གྲིབ་གནོན་གྱི་གདོན་བསྲུང་བའི་ཕྱིར་དཔལ་འབར་དང་བཅས་རྡོ་རྗེ་སློབ་དཔོན་གྱི་མདུན་དུ་སྟེགས་ཀྱི་སྟེང་དུ་བཞག ཆུ་གཙང་དང་སློབ་དཔོན་གྱིས་ཆང་གི་ཁ་སྦྱ་འབར་བའི་ཕྱག་རྒྱའི་བར་ནས་གཏོར་ཞིང་།

In these circumstances, one must avoid people who are not suitable vessels. Without concepts of pure and impure, the master and disciples imagine that they are making an offering to the syllable Vaṁ (བཾ), the essence that combines all the Buddhas, and enjoy with satisfaction. In particular, if bhikṣus are holder of the vajra, who dismiss the Ganapūjā substances thinking that they must avoid madana and eating in the afternoon with the intention of guarding their lower vows, then it becomes a root downfall because it is said that "The thirteenth root downfall is not taking whatever samaya substances are given." During all times of the Ganapūjā there must be no fighting or fooling around. One should pass the time conversing Dharma, singing vajra songs [on page 289], and so on. Furthermore, during the Ganapūjā, it is necessary to use the symbolic language of bala for meat and madana for wine. The Hevajra Tantra states, "If the Buddha's secret language is not spoken, one will die" and "There is no doubt that one's samaya will be impaired by not speaking the secret language."

Next, after everyone is satisfied, the karmavajra collects the remainders of the Ganapūjā in a single container from the lower seats to the higher. If it is night time, it is placed on the table in front of the vajramaster with a torch [burning incense stick] to guard against contaminating spirits. Clean water is sprinkled on it, and the vajramaster spits some alcohol through the blazing mudra.

ཨོཾ་ཨཿ ཧཱུྃ་གིས་བདུད་རྩིའི་རྒྱ་མཚོར་བྱིན་གྱིས་བརླབས་ལ།

It is blessed as an ocean of amrita with:

Oṁ āḥ hūṁ

ཕཻཾ་ཞེས་དང་། ཨོཾ་ཁ་ཁ་ཁཱ་ཧི་ཁཱ་ཧི་ཨུཙྪིཥྚ་བ་ལིཾ་ཏ་བྷཀྵ་སི་སྭཱ་ཧཱ། ཞེས་ལན་གསུམ་བརྗོད།

Phaiṁ

Recite three times:

Oṁ kha kha khāhi khāhi ucchishta baliṁta bhakshasi svāhā

འབྱུང་པོ་ལྷག་མ་ལ་དབང་བ་རྣམས་ལ་སྦྱིན་ནོ། །ངོམས་ཤིང་ཚིམས་པའི་སྐལ་བ་ལྡན་པར་གྱུར་ཅིག ཅེས་ཕྱི་རོལ་དུ་དོར། རྔ་དཔྱལ་དང་རོལ་མོའི་སྒྲ་ཆེར་བྱ་ཞིང་།

Jung-Po Lhag-Ma La Wang-Wa Nam La Jin-No, Ngom Shing Tsim-Pay Kal-Wa Den-Par Gyur Chig

This is given to the bhūtas, who has power to consume the remainders, be endowed with the good fortune of contentment and satisfaction!

Take this outside and make a great sound of damaru, bell and music.

བཀྲ་ཤིས་གང་ཞིག་ཆོས་ཀྱི་དབྱིངས་ལས་ལེགས་བྱུང་བའི། །
ཧེ་རུ་ཀ་དཔལ་འཇིགས་བྱེད་རྒྱལ་པོ་འབར་བའི་སྐུ། །
ཤེས་རབ་ཕག་མོའི་པདྨ་ར་རྡོ་རྗེས་རོལ་མཛད་པའི། །
བདེན་པ་དེས་ཀྱང་བདེ་མཆོག་ལ་གནས་བཀྲ་ཤིས་ཤོག །

Tashi Gang Shig Chö-Kyi Jing Lé leg Jung-Way
He-Ru-Ka Pal Jig-Je Gyal-Po Bar-Way Ku
She-Rab Phag-Moy Pad-Mar Dor-Jé Röl Zé-Pay
Den-Pa Dey Kyang De-Chog La Ne Ta-Shi Shog

Recite the auspicious prayers and aspiration:

May any fortunate ones have the good fortune to dwell in great bliss by the truth of
the vajra of Shrī Heruka — the blazing body of the terrifying king,
who arose perfectly from the dharmadhātu —
sporting in the lotus of the prajñā, Vārāhī.

སེམས་ཅན་ཐམས་ཅད་བདེ་གྱུར་ཅིག །
སེམས་ཅན་ཐམས་ཅད་སྐྱོན་མེད་པར། །
གང་གི་ལམ་གྱིས་གྲོལ་འགྱུར་བ། །
དེས་ནི་སངས་རྒྱས་ཉིད་འཐོབ་ཤོག ། ཅེས་པས་བཀྲ་ཤིས་སྨོན་ལམ་བྱ།

Sem-Chen Tham-Ché De Gyur Chig
Sem-Chen Tham-Ché Kyon Me-Par
Gang Gi Lam Gyi Dröl Gyur-Wa
Dey Ni Sang-Gyé Nyi Thob Shog

May all sentient beings be happy.
May all sentient beings be without faults.
May they attain buddhahood
with some liberating path.

ཚོགས་མཆོད་འདི་ལ་ཕྱག་ལེན་རྒྱས་བསྡུས་སྣ་ཚོགས་ཡོད་ཀྱང་སྨོར་ཆེན་རྡོ་རྗེ་འཆང་གི་མཛད་པ་འདི་དོན་ཚང་ཞིང་འཇུག་བདེ་བར་ཡོད། གོང་གི་ཞུ་འབུལ་རྣམས་མ་བྱས་ཀྱང་ཆད་སྐྱོན་མེད་དོ།

Though there are various Ganapūjās, extensive and abbreviated, this one composed by Morchen Vajradhara is both complete and easy to engage. Even if one does not do the requests above, there is no fault.

Conclusion Ritual

རྗེས་ཀྱི་ཆོ་ག་ནི།

མཆོད་པ་རྣམས་ཁ་གསོས་ཤིང་།

ཨོཾ་སུམྦྷ་ནི་སུམྦྷ་ཧཱུྃ་ཧཱུྃ་ཕཊ།

ཨོཾ་གྲྀཧྞ་གྲྀཧྞ་ཧཱུྃ་ཧཱུྃ་ཕཊ།

ཨོཾ་གྲྀཧྞ་པ་ཡ་གྲྀཧྞ་པ་ཡ་ཧཱུྃ་ཧཱུྃ་ཕཊ།

ཨོཾ་ཨཱ་ན་ཡ་ཧོཿ་བྷ་ག་ཝཱན་བིདྱཱ་རཱ་ཛ་ཧཱུྃ་ཧཱུྃ་ཕཊ། ཀྱིས་བསང་།

Replenish the offerings and cleanse them with:

Oṁ sumbha nisumbha huṁ hūṁ phaṭ

Oṁ grihaṇa grihaṇa huṁ hūṁ phaṭ

Oṁ grihaṇapaya grihaṇapaya huṁ hūṁ phaṭ

Oṁ ānayaho bhagavān vidyārāja huṁ hūṁ phaṭ

ཨོཾ་སྭ་བྷཱ་ཝ་ཤུདྡྷཿ་སརྦ་དྷརྨཱཿ་སྭ་བྷཱ་ཝ་ཤུདྡྷོ྅ཧཾ། གིས་སྦྱངས།

Purify with:

Oṁ svabhāva shuddhaḥ sarva dharmāḥ svabhāva shuddho' haṁ

སྟོང་པའི་ངང་ལས་ཨ་ལས་ཡེ་ཤེས་ཀྱི་ཀ་པཱ་ལ་ཡངས་ཤིང་རྒྱ་ཆེ་བ་རྣམས་ཀྱི་ནང་དུ། ཧཱུྃ་ཞུ་བ་ལས་བྱུང་བའི་ལྷ་རྫས་ལས་གྲུབ་པའི་མཆོད་ཡོན། ཞབས་བསིལ། མེ་ཏོག བདུག་སྤོས། མར་མེ། དྲི་ཆབ། ཞལ་ཟས། རོལ་མོ་ལ་སོགས་པ་དངོས་ཤིང་ཐོགས་པ་མེད་པ་ནམ་མཁའི་མཐའ་དང་མཉམ་པར་གྱུར།

Tong-Pay Ngang Lé Ah Lé Ye-She Kyi Ka-Pa-La Yang Shing Gya-Che-Wa Nam Kyi Nang-Du Hūṁ Shu-Wa Lé Jung-Way Lha Zé Lé Drub-Pay Chö-Yon, Shab-Sil, Me-Tog, Dug-Po, Mar-Me, Dri-Chab, Shel-Ze, Röl-Mo La Sog Pa Dang Shing Thog-Pa Me-Pa Nam-Khay Tha Dang Nyam-Par Gyur

From the state of emptiness arises an *Ah* (ཨ), from which arises wide and vast wisdom skullcups. Inside of each skullcup, from dissolving and melting of *Hūṁ* (ཧཱུྃ) arises all the offerings made from divine substances — pure and unimpeded drinking water, washing water, flowers, incense, lamps, scent, food, music, and so on — which fill all of space.

ཨོཾ་བཛྲ་ཨརྒྷཾ་ཨཱཿ ཧཱུྃ། ཨོཾ་བཛྲ་པཱདྱཾ་ཨཱཿ ཧཱུྃ། ཨོཾ་བཛྲ་པུཥྤེ་ཨཱཿ ཧཱུྃ། ཨོཾ་བཛྲ་དྷཱུཔེ་ཨཱཿ ཧཱུྃ།
ཨོཾ་བཛྲ་ཨཱ་ལོ་ཀེ་ཨཱཿ ཧཱུྃ། ཨོཾ་བཛྲ་གནྡྷེ་ཨཱཿ ཧཱུྃ། ཨོཾ་བཛྲ་ནཻ་ཝི་དྱེ་ཨཱཿ ཧཱུྃ། ཨོཾ་བཛྲ་ཤབྡ་
ཨཱཿ ཧཱུྃ། ཞེས་བྱིན་རླབས་བྱ།

Thus bless.

Oṁ vajra arghaṁ āḥ hūṁ
Oṁ vajra pādyaṁ āḥ hūṁ
Oṁ vajra puṣpe āḥ hūṁ
Oṁ vajra dhūpe āḥ hūṁ
Oṁ vajra āloke āḥ hūṁ
Oṁ vajra ghande āḥ hūṁ
Oṁ vajra naividye āḥ hūṁ
Oṁ vajra shabda āḥ hūṁ

ཨོཾ་སརྦ་ཏ་ཐཱ་ག་ཏ་བཛྲ་ཡོ་གི་ནཱི་ས་པ་རི་ཝཱ་ར་ཨརྒྷཾ་པྲ་ཏཱིཙྪ་པཱུ་ཛ་མེ་གྷ་ས་མུ་དྲ་སྥ་ར་ཎ་
ས་མ་ཡེ་ཨཱཿ ཧཱུྃ།

Oṁ sarvatathāgata vajra yoginī saparivāra argham praticcha pūja megha samudra sapharaṇa samaye āḥ hūṁ

ཨོཾ་སརྦ་ཏ་ཐཱ་ག་ཏ་བཛྲ་ཡོ་གི་ནཱི་ས་པ་རི་ཝཱ་ར་པཱ་དྱཾ་པྲ་ཏཱིཙྪ་པཱུ་ཛ་མེ་གྷ་ས་མུ་དྲ་སྥ་ར་ཎ་
ས་མ་ཡེ་ཨཱཿ ཧཱུྃ།

Oṁ sarvatathāgata vajra yoginī saparivāra pādyaṁ praticcha pūja megha samudra sapharaṇa samaye āḥ hūṁ

ཨོཾ་སརྦ་ཏ་ཐཱ་ག་ཏ་བཛྲ་ཡོ་གི་ནཱི་ས་པ་རི་ཝཱ་ར་པུཥྤེ་པྲ་ཏཱིཙྪ་པཱུ་ཛ་མེ་གྷ་ས་མུ་དྲ་སྥ་ར་ཎ་
ས་མ་ཡེ་ཨཱཿ ཧཱུྃ།

Oṁ sarvatathāgata vajra yoginī saparivāra puṣpe praticcha pūja megha samudra sapharaṇa samaye āḥ hūṁ

ཨོཾ་སརྦ་ཏ་ཐཱ་ག་ཏ་བཛྲ་ཡོ་གི་ནཱི་ས་པ་རི་ཝཱ་ར་དྷཱུ་པེ་པྲ་ཏཱིཙྪ་པཱུ་ཛ་མེ་གྷ་ས་མུ་དྲ་སྥ་ར་ཎ་
ས་མ་ཡེ་ཨཱཿ ཧཱུྃ།

Oṁ sarvatathāgata vajra yoginī saparivāra dhūpe praticcha pūja megha samudra sapharaṇa samaye āḥ hūṁ

ཨོཾ་སརྦ་ཏ་ཐཱ་ག་ཏ་བཛྲ་ཡོ་གི་ནཱི་ས་པ་རི་ཝཱ་ར་ཨཱ་ལོ་ཀེ་པྲ་ཏཱིཙྪ་པཱུ་ཛ་མེ་གྷ་ས་མུ་དྲ་སྥ་
ར་ཎ་ས་མ་ཡེ་ཨཱཿ ཧཱུྃ།

Oṁ sarvatathāgata vajra yoginī saparivāra āloke praticcha pūja megha samudra sapharaṇa samaye āḥ hūṁ

ཨོཾ་སརྦ་ཏ་ཐཱ་ག་ཏ་བཛྲ་ཡོ་གི་ནཱི་ས་པ་རི་ཝཱ་ར་གྷནྡྷེ་པྲ་ཏཱི་ཙྪ་པཱུ་ཛ་མེ་གྷ་ས་མུ་དྲ་སྥ་ར་ཎ་
ས་མ་ཡེ་ཨཱཿ ཧཱུྃ།

Oṁ sarvatathāgata vajra yoginī saparivāra ghande praticcha pūja megha samudra sapharaṇa samaye āḥ hūṁ

ཨོཾ་སརྦ་ཏ་ཐཱ་ག་ཏ་བཛྲ་ཡོ་གི་ནཱི་ས་པ་རི་ཝཱ་ར་ནཻ་ཝི་དྱེ་པྲ་ཏཱི་ཙྪ་པཱུ་ཛ་མེ་གྷ་ས་མུ་དྲ་སྥ་ར་
ཎ་ས་མ་ཡེ་ཨཱཿ ཧཱུྃ།

Oṁ sarvatathāgata vajra yoginī saparivāra naividye praticcha pūja megha samudra sapharaṇa samaye āḥ hūṁ

ཨོཾ་སརྦ་ཏ་ཐཱ་ག་ཏ་བཛྲ་ཡོ་གི་ནཱི་ས་པ་རི་ཝཱ་ར་ཤབྡ་པྲ་ཏཱི་ཙྪ་པཱུ་ཛ་མེ་གྷ་ས་མུ་དྲ་སྥ་ར་ཎ་
ས་མ་ཡེ་ཨཱཿ ཧཱུྃ།

Oṁ sarvatathāgata vajra yoginī saparivāra shabda praticcha pūja megha samudra sapharaṇa samaye āḥ hūṁ

ཨོཾ་བཛྲ་གྷཎྚེ་ར་ཎི་ཏ། པྲ་ར་ཎི་ཏ། སཾ་པྲ་ར་ཎི་ཏ། སརྦ་བུདྡྷ་ཀྵེ་ཏྲ་པྲ་ཙ་ལི་ཏེ། པྲཛྙཱ་པཱ་
ར་མི་ཏ་ནཱ་ད་སཾ་བྷ་ཝེ་ཏ། བཛྲ་དྷརྨ་ཧྲི་ད་ཡ་སནྟོ་ཥ་ཎི་ཧཱུྃ་ཧཱུྃ་ཧཱུྃ་ཧོ་ཧོ་ཧོ་ཨ་ཁཾ་སྭཱ་ཧཱ།
ཞེས་རོལ་མོ་དང་བཅས་པས་མཆོད།

Thus offer with music:

Oṁ vajraghaṇḍe raṇita praraṇita saṁpraraṇita sarvabuddha kṣetra pracalite prajñāpāramitā nāda saṁbhaveta vajradharma hridaya santoṣaṇi hūṁ hūṁ hūṁ ho ho ho akhaṁ svāhā

ཨོཾ་སརྦ་ཏ་ཐཱ་ག་ཏ་བཛྲ་ཡོ་གི་ནཱི་ས་པ་རི་ཝ་ར་ཨོཾ་ཨཱཿ ཧཱུྃ་གིས་ནང་མཆོད་འབུལ།

Make the inner offering:

Oṁ sarvatathāgata vajra yoginī saparivara oṁ āḥ hūṁ

དཔལ་ལྡན་རྡོ་རྗེ་མཁའ་འགྲོ་མ།།
མཁའ་འགྲོ་མ་ཡི་འཁོར་ལོས་སྒྱུར།།
ཡེ་ཤེས་ལྔ་དང་སྐུ་གསུམ་བརྙེས།།
འགྲོ་བ་སྐྱོབ་ལ་ཕྱག་འཚལ་ལོ།།

Pal-Den Dor-Je Khan-Dro-Ma
Khan-Dro-Ma Yi Khor-Lö Gyur
Ye-She Nga Dang Ku Sum Nye
Dro-Wa Kyob La Chag Tsal Lo

The glorious Vajraḍākinī,
the empress of all ḍākinīs,
the one who has attained the five wisdoms and three kāyas,
I pay homage to the protector of migrating beings.

ཇི་སྙེད་རྡོ་རྗེ་མཁའ་འགྲོ་མ།།
ཀུན་ཏུ་རྟོག་པའི་འཆིང་གཅོད་ཅིང་།།
འཇིག་རྟེན་བྱ་བར་རབ་འཇུག་མ།།
དེ་སྙེད་རྣམས་ལ་ཕྱག་འཚལ་ལོ།།

Ji Nye Dor-Je Khan-Dro-Ma
Kün-Tu Tog-Pay Ching Chö Ching
Jig-Ten Ja-War Rab Jug Ma
De Nye Nam La Chag Tsal Lo

I pay homage to Vajraḍākinī,
who eliminates the bondage of all concepts,
those who attain
full engagement in the activities of the world.

རྗེ་བཙུན་རྡོ་རྗེ་རྣལ་འབྱོར་མས་བདག་དང་སེམས་ཅན་ཐམས་ཅད་དག་པ་མཁའ་སྤྱོད་
དུ་འཁྲིད་པར་མཛད་དུ་གསོལ། འཇིག་རྟེན་དང་འཇིག་རྟེན་ལས་འདས་པའི་དངོས་གྲུབ་
མ་ལུས་པ་སྩལ་དུ་གསོལ། ཞེས་གསོལ་བ་བཏབ།

Je-Tsün Dor-Je Nal-Jor-Mé Dag Dang Sem-Chen Tham-Ché Dag-Pa Kha-Chö Du Ti-Par Zé-Du Söl, Jig-Ten Dang Jig-Ten Lé Dé-Pay Ngö-Drub Ma-Lü-Pa Tsal Du Söl

Offer the supplication:
Jetsun Vajrayoginī, please lead myself and all sentient beings to Khecarī and please grant all mundane and transcendent siddhis.

ཨོཾ་ཤྲཱི་བཛྲ་ཧེ་རུ་ཀ་ས་མ་ཡ་མ་ནུ་པཱ་ལ་ཡ། ཧེ་རུ་ཀ་ཏྭེ་ནོ་པ་ཏིཥྛ། དྲྀ་ཌྷོ་མེ་བྷ་ཝ། སུ་ཏོ་
ཥྱོ་མེ་བྷ་ཝ། ཨ་ནུ་རཀྟོ་མེ་བྷ་ཝ། སུ་པོ་ཥྱོ་མེ་བྷ་ཝ། སརྦ་སིདྡྷི་མྨེ་པྲ་ཡཙྪ། སརྦ་ཀརྨ་
སུ་ཙ་མེ་ཙིཏྟཾ་ཤྲཱི་ཡཾ་ཀུ་རུ་ཧཱུྃ། ཧ་ཧ་ཧ་ཧ་ཧོཿ བྷ་ག་ཝན། བཛྲ་ཧེ་རུ་ཀ་མཱ་མེ་མུཉྩ། ཧེ་
རུ་ཀོ་བྷ་ཝ། མ་ཧཱ་ས་མ་ཡ་སཏྭ་ཨཱཿཧཱུྃ་ཕཊ། ཞེས་ལན་གསུམ་བརྗོད།

Recite three times:

Oṃ shṛī vajraheruka samayamanupālaya heruka tvenopatiṣṭha dṛiḍho mebhava sutosyo mebhava anurakto mebhava suposyo mebhava sarva sidhhim meprayaccha sarva karmasucame cittaṃ shriyaṁkuru hūṁha ha ha ha hoḥ bhagavān vajraheruka mā me muñca heruko' bhava mahāsamayasattva āḥ hūṁ phaṭ

མ་འབྱོར་པ་དང་ཉམས་པ་དང་།།
གང་ཡང་བདག་རྨོངས་བློ་ཡིས་ནི།།
བགྱིས་པ་དང་ནི་བགྱིད་སྩལ་བ།།
དེ་ཀུན་མགོན་པོས་བཟོད་པར་གསོལ།།

Ma Jor-Pa Dang Nyam-Pa Dang
Gang-Yang Dag Mong Lo Yi Ni
Gyi-Pa Dang Ni Gyi Tsal-Pa
De Kün Gon-Po Zö-Par Söl

Whatever was not prepared or was damaged,
or that I did with a confused mind,
or asked [others] to do,
protector, please be patient with it all.

བདག་ཅག་ལས་དང་པོ་པའི་རྟེན་གྱི་གང་ཟག་ཏུ་གྱུར་པས་ཏིང་ངེ་འཛིན་མི་གསལ་བ་དང་བྱིང་བ་དང་རྒོད་པའི་དབང་དུ་གྱུར་པ་ཐམས་ཅད་དང་ཚིག་ལྷག་པ་དང་ཆད་པར་གྱུར་པ་དང་མཆོད་པའི་ཡོ་བྱད་མ་འབྱོར་པ་དང་ཉམས་པ་དང་དཀྱིལ་འཁོར་སྒྲུབ་པ་ལ་སྐྱོན་དུ་གྱུར་པ་གང་ཡིན་པ་དེ་དག་ཐམས་ཅད་བཟོད་པར་གསོལ་ལོ་ཞེས་ལྷག་ཆད་ཁ་བསྐང་བར་བྱའོ།

Dag Chag Lé Dang-Po-Pay Ten Gyi Gang-Zag Tu Gyur-Pé Ting Nge-Zin Mi Sal-Wa Dang Jing-Wa Dang Gö-Pay Wang-Du Gyur-Pa Tham-Ché Dang Cho-Ga Lhag-Pa Dang Ché-Par Gyur-Pa Dang Chö-Pay Yo-Je Ma Jor-Pa Dang Nyam-Pa Dang Kyil-Khor Drub-Pa La Kyon Du Gyur-Pa Gang Yin-Pa De-Dag Tham-Ché Zö-Par Söl Lo

Since we are beginners, all unclear samādhi and falling under the power of lethargy and agitation, excesses and omissions to the rite, incomplete or using damaged articles of offering and all faults in accomplishing the maṇḍala, for all of them I request your patience.

Thus supplement the excesses and omissions.

ཕྱོགས་བཅུ་ན་བཞུགས་པའི་སངས་རྒྱས་དང་བྱང་ཆུབ་སེམས་དཔའ་ཐམས་ཅད་བདག་ལ་དགོངས་སུ་གསོལ། ཇི་སྲིད་ནམ་མཁའ་མཐའ་དང་མཉམ་པའི་སེམས་ཅན་ཐམས་ཅད་མི་གནས་པའི་མྱ་ངན་ལས་འདས་པའི་ས་ལ་མ་བཞག་གི་བར་དུ་རྒྱལ་བ་རྣམས་མྱ་ངན་ལས་མི་འདའ་བར་བསྟན་པར་བཞུགས་སུ་གསོལ། བྱེ་བྲག་ཏུ་ཡང་སྐུ་གཟུགས་ཀྱི་རྟེན་འདི་རྣམས་ལ་བསྐྱེད་ཅིང་སྤྱན་དྲངས་པའི་ལྷ་ཚོགས་རྣམས་ཇི་སྲིད་འབྱུང་བ་བཞིའི་གནོད་པས་མ་ཞིག་གི་བར་དུ་བསྟན་པར་བཞུགས་སུ་གསོལ། བསྟན་པར་བཞུགས་ནས་བདག་དང་སེམས་ཅན་ཐམས་ཅད་ཀྱི་མགོན་དང་སྐྱབས་དང་དཔུང་གཉེན་དམ་པ་མཛད་དུ་གསོལ།

Chog Chu Na Shug-Pay Sang-Gyé Dang Jang-Chub Sem-Pa Tham-Ché Dag La Gong Su Söl, Ji-Si Nam-Kha Tha Dang Nyam-Pay Sem-Chen Tham-Ché Mi Ne-Pay Nya Ngen Lé Dé-Pay Sa La Ma Shag Gi Bar-Du Gyal-Wa Nam Nya Ngen Lé Mi Da-War Ten-Par Shug Su Söl, Je-Drag Tu Yang Ku Zug Kyi Ten Di Nam La Kye Shing Chen Drang-Pay Lha Tsog Nam Ji-Si Jung-Wa Shiy Nö-Pé Ma Shig Gi

Bar-Du Ten-Par Shug Su Söl, Ten-Par Shug Ne Dag Dang Sem-Chen Tham-Ché Kyi Gon Dang Kyab Dang Pung Nyen Dam-Pa Zé Du Söl

All Buddhas and Bodhisattvas residing in the ten directions, heed me! Until all sentient beings equal with space are placed on the stage of nonabiding nirvana, please remain firm without passing into the nirvana. In particular, the assemblies of deities that have been generated and invited into the images of your forms, please remain firm for as long as your forms are not damaged by the four elements. Through remaining firm, please be the protector, refuge and defender of myself and all sentient beings.

ཨོཾ་སུ་པྲ་ཏིཥྛ་བཛྲ་ཡེ་སྭཱ་ཧཱ། ཞེས་བརྗོད་ཅིང་རྟེན་ལ་མེ་ཏོག་གཏོར་ཞིང་བརྟན་བཞུགས་བྱ།

Recite the following and scatter flowers on the images so they remain firm:

Oṁ supratishta vajraye svāhā

མཚལ་གྱི་ཡེ་ཤེས་པ་དང་བུམ་ནང་གི་ཡེ་ཤེས་པ་དང་རྟེན་མེད་པའི་གཏོར་མགྲོན་གྱི་ཡེ་ཤེས་པ་རྣམས།

ཨོཾ་ཁྱེད་ཀྱིས་སེམས་ཅན་དོན་ཀུན་མཛོད།།

རྗེས་སུ་མཐུན་པའི་དངོས་གྲུབ་སྩོལ།།

སངས་རྒྱས་ཡུལ་དུ་གཤེགས་ནས་ཀྱང་།།

སླར་ཡང་འབྱོན་པར་མཛད་དུ་གསོལ།།

Oṁ

Khye-Kyi Sem-Chen-Dön Kün Zö

Je Su Thün Pay Ngö-Drup Tsöl

Sang-Gyé Yül Du Shek Ne Kyang

Lar-Yang Jön-Par Zé-Du-Söl

To the jñānasattva of the maṇḍala, the jñānasattva inside the vase and the jñānasattva of the tormas guests without an image:

Oṁ

Will you please perform all benefits for sentient beings.
Grant the corresponding siddhis!
Though depart to Buddhas' pureland,
please return again!

བཛྲ་མུཿ། ཡེ་ཤེས་པ་རང་བཞིན་གྱི་གནས་སུ་གཤེགས། དམ་ཚིག་པ་རྣམས་ཛཿ ཧཱུྃ་བཾ་ཧོཿ བདག་ཉིད་ལ་གཉིས་སུ་མེད་པར་ཐིམ་པར་གྱུར།

Vajra muḥ, Ye-She-Pa Rang-Shin Gyi Ne Su Sheg, Dam-Tsig-Pa Nam Jaḥ hūṁ vaṁ hoḥ Dag-Nyi La Nyi-Su Me-Par Thim-Par Gyur

Vajra muḥ, the jñānasattva return to their natural abodes.
The samayasattvas dissolve into oneself nondually with,
Jaḥ hūṁ vaṁ hoḥ

རང་གི་སྙིང་གའི་བཾ་ཡིག་སྔགས་ཕྲེང་དང་བཅས་པ་ལས་འོད་ཟེར་འཕྲོས་ཁམས་གསུམ་ཐམས་ཅད་ཁྱབ། གཟུགས་མེད་ཁམས་འོད་ཟེར་སྔོན་པོའི་རྣམ་པས་ལུས་ཀྱི་སྟོད་ཀྱི་ཆ་ལ་ཐིམ། གཟུགས་ཁམས་འོད་ཟེར་དམར་པོའི་རྣམ་པས་བར་གྱི་ཆ་ལ་ཐིམ། འདོད་ཁམས་འོད་ཟེར་དཀར་པོའི་རྣམ་པས་སྨད་ཀྱི་ཆ་ལ་ཐིམ། རང་ཡང་སྟོད་སྨད་ནས་རིམ་བཞིན་འོད་དུ་ཞུ་ནས་ཚོས་འབྱུང་ལ་ཐིམ། དེ་ཟླ་བ་ལ། དེ་སྔགས་ཕྲེང་ལ། དེ་བཾ་གྱི་མགོ་བོ་ལ། དེ་ཟླ་ཚེས་ལ། དེ་ཐིག་ལེ་ལ། དེ་ནཱ་ད་ལ། དེ་ཇེ་ཕྲ་ཇེ་ཕྲ་མི་དམིགས་པར་གྱུར།
ཅེས་སེམས་བརྗོད་བྲལ་དུ་ཅི་གནས་བཞག དེའི་ངང་ལས།

Rang Gi Nyin-Gay Vaṁ Yig Ngag Treng Dang Ché-Pa Lé Ö-Zer Trö Kham Sum Tham-Ché Khyab, Zug-Me Kham Ö-Zer Ngon-Poy Nam-Pé Lü Kyi Tö Kyi Cha La Thim, Zug-Kham Ö-Zer Mar-Poy Nam-Pé Bar Gyi Cha La Thim, Dö-Kham Ö-Zer Kar-Poy Nam-Pé Me Kyi Cha La Thim, Rang Yang Tö-Me Ne Rim-Shin Ö-Du Shu Ne Chö-Jung La Thim, De Da-Wa La, De Ngag Treng La, De Vaṁ Gyi Go-Wo La, De Da-Tse La, De Thig-Le La, De Na-Da La, De Je-Tra Je-Tra Mi Mig-Par Gyur

Rays of light shine from the *Vaṁ* (བྃ) and the mantra garland in one's heart spreading to all of the three realms. The formless realm in the form of blue light dissolves into the upper part of one's body. The form realm in the form of red light dissolves into the middle part of one's body. The desire realm in the form of white light dissolves into the lower part of one's body. The upper and lower parts of one's body gradually melt into light and dissolve into the dharmakara, which dissolves into the moon, which dissolves into the mantra garland, which dissolves into the *Vaṁ* (བྃ), which dissolves into the head, which dissolve into the crescent moon, which dissolves into the bindu, which dissolves into the nada, which becomes smaller and smaller, then disappears.

Remain free from thought and expression for as long as possible.

རང་ཉིད་རྡོ་རྗེ་རྣལ་འབྱོར་མའི་སྐུར་ལམ་གྱིས་གསལ་བའི་གནས་རྣམས་སུ་ལྷ་བའི་
དཀྱིལ་འཁོར་གྱི་སྟེང་དུ། ལྟེ་བར་ཨོཾ་བྃ་དམར་མོ་རྡོ་རྗེ་ཕག་མོ། སྙིང་གར་ཧཱུྃ་ཡོཾ་སྔོན་མོ་
ག་ཤིན་རྗེ་མ། ཁར་ཧྲིཾ་སྨོཾ་དཀར་མོ་རྨོངས་བྱེད་མ། དཔྲལ་བར་ཧྲིཾ་ཧྲིཾ་སེར་མོ་སྐྱོད་བྱེད་

མ། སྤྱི་གཙུག་ཏུ་ཧཱུྃ་ཧཱུྃ་ལྗང་ཁུ་སྐྲག་བྱེད་མ། ཡན་ལག་ཐམས་ཅད་ལ་ཕཊ་ཕཊ་དུད་ཁ་ཙཎྜི་ཀའི་ངོ་བོ་གྱུར་ཅེས་བརྗོད།

Rang Nyi Dor-Je Nal-Jor-May Kur Lam Gyi Sal-Way Ne Nam Su Da-Way Kyil-Khor Gyi Teng Du, Te-War Oṁ Vaṁ Mar-Mo Dor-Je Phag-Mo, Nying Gar Haṁ Yoṁ Ngon-Mo Shin-Je-Ma, Khar Hriṁ Moṁ Kar-Mo Mong-Je-Ma, Trel-War Hriṁ Hriṁ Ser-Mo Kyö-Je-Ma, Chi Tsug Tu Hūṁ Hūṁ Jang Khu Tag-Je-Ma, Yen-Lag Tham-Ché La Phaṭ Phaṭ Dü-Kha Chan-Di-Kay Ngo-Wo Gyur

From that state:

Oneself in the clear form of Vajrayoginī, on top of moon discs at these locations on one's body are:

red *Oṁ Vaṁ* (ཨོཾ་བཾ) on the navel,
the essence of Vārāhī;

blue *Haṁ Yoṁ* (ཧཾ་ཡོཾ) on the heart,
the essence of Yāminī;

white *Hriṁ Moṁ* (ཧྲིཾ་མོཾ) on the mouth,
the essence of Mohinī;

yellow *Hriṁ Hriṁ* (ཧྲིཾ་ཧྲིཾ) on the forehead,
the essence of Saṁcālinī;

green *Hūṁ Hūṁ* (ཧཱུྃ་ཧཱུྃ) on the crown,
the essence of Saṁtrāsinī;

smoky *Phaṭ Phaṭ* (ཕཊ་ཕཊ) on all the limbs,
the essence of Caṇḍikā.

ༀ་སུམྦྷ་ནི་སུམྦྷ་ཧུྃ་ཧཱུྃ་ཕཊ།

ༀ་གྲིཧྞ་གྲིཧྞ་ཧུྃ་ཧཱུྃ་ཕཊ།

ༀ་གྲིཧྞ་པ་ཡ་གྲིཧྞ་པ་ཡ་ཧུྃ་ཧཱུྃ་ཕཊ།

ༀ་ཨཱ་ན་ཡ་ཧོཿ བྷ་ག་ཝཱན་བིདྱཱ་རཱ་ཛ་ཧུྃ་ཧཱུྃ་ཕཊ།

སྔགས་ཚར་གཉིས་ཕྱག་རྒྱ་དང་བཅས་པས་ཕྱོགས་གཡོན་བསྐོར། མཚམས་གཡས་བསྐོར་གྱིས་བསྲུང་བ་བྱ།

Repeat the mantra twice along with the mudras, and protect with a cycle to turning left in the main directions, and cycle to the right in the intermediate directions.

Oṁ sumbha nisumbha huṁ hūṁ phaṭ

Oṁ grihaṇa grihaṇa huṁ hūṁ phaṭ

Oṁ grihaṇapaya grihaṇapaya huṁ hūṁ phaṭ

Oṁ ānayaho bhagavān vidyārāja huṁ hūṁ phaṭ

Aspiration and Auspicious Prayers

མཁའ་སྤྱོད་ཞལ་བཟང་བལྟ་བའི་སྨོན་ལམ་དང་བཀྲ་ཤིས་བཅས་བཞུགས་སོ།།

"Aspiration to See the Excellent Face of Khecarī" and "Auspicious Prayers".

ན་མོ་བཛྲ་ཙཎྜ་ལཱི་ཡེ། མཁའ་སྤྱོད་ཞལ་བཟང་ལྟ་བའི་སྨོན་ལམ་བཞུགས་སོ།

Namo vajra chandaliye, "Aspiration to See the Excellent Face of Khecarī".

ན་མོ་བཛྲ་ཝཱ་རཱ་ཧྱེ།
མཐའ་ཡས་རྒྱལ་བའི་བདེ་སྟོང་ཟློས་གར་ནི།།
སྲིད་ཞིའི་མིག་འཕྲུལ་ཅིར་ཡང་སྣང་བ་ལས།།
དེང་འདིར་མཁའ་སྤྱོད་དཔལ་མོ་ཡིད་འོང་མ།།
སྙིང་ནས་དྲན་ནོ་འཁྱུད་པའི་རྩེ་དགས་སྐྱོངས།།

Namo vajravārāhye
Tha-Ye Gyal-Way De-Tong Dö-Gar Ni
Si Shiy Mig Trul Chir-Yang Nang-Wa Le
Deng Dir Kha-Chö Pal-Mo Yi Ong Ma
Nying Ne Dren-No Khyü-Pay Tse Ge Kyong

Namo vajravārāhye
From the dance of bliss and emptiness of limitless Jinas,
appearing as any of the enchantments of samsara and nirvana,
now, here is beautiful Sri Khecarī,
recalled from the heart, protect me with your playful embrace.

འོག་མིན་གནས་ན་ལྷན་སྐྱེས་རྒྱལ་ཡུམ་མ།།
ཉེར་བཞིའི་ཡུལ་ན་ཞིང་སྐྱེས་ཌཱ་ཀི་མ།།
ནོར་འཛིན་ཁྱབ་པར་ཀརྨ་མུ་དྲ་མ།།
རྣལ་འབྱོར་བདག་གི་སྐྱབས་མགོན་རྗེ་བཙུན་མ།།

Og-Min Ne Na Lhen-Kye Gyal Yum-Ma
Nyer Shiy Yül Na Shing Kye Da-Ki-Ma
Nor-Zin Khyab-Par Kar-Ma Mu-Dra-Ma
Nal-Jor Dag Gi Kyab-Gön Je-Tsün-Ma

The connate mother of Jinas in Akanistha,
the place-born dakīnis in the twenty four lands,
karmamudras spreading across the earth,
Jetsunma is the yogi's refuge and protector.

ཁྱོད་ནི་སེམས་ཉིད་སྟོང་པའི་རང་རྩལ་ཏེ།།
རྡོ་རྗེ་གྲོང་ན་ཨེ་དབྱིངས་བཾ་གྱི་ངོས།།
སྒྱུ་མའི་གླིང་ན་འཇིགས་རུང་སྲིན་མོ་དང་།།
འཛུམ་དཀར་གཡོ་བའི་ལང་ཚོ་གསལ་བར་སྟོན།།

Khyo Nï Sem-Nyi Tong-Pay Rang Tsal Te
Dor-Je Drong Na E Ying Vaṁ Gyi Ngö
Gyu-May Ling Na Jig Rung Sin-Mo Dang
Zum Kar Yo-Way Lang-Tso Sal-War Ton

You are the intrinsic potency of emptiness, the nature of the mind,
The nature of *E* that is the actuality of *Vaṁ* in the vajra city,
clearly shown as a fearsome ogress
and a brightly smiling maiden traipsing on the island of illusion.

ད་ནི་བདག་གིས་ཇི་ལྟར་བཙལ་གྱུར་ཀྱང་།།
བདེན་པར་གྲུབ་པའི་ངེས་པ་མ་རྙེད་ནས།།
སྤྲོས་པས་དུབ་པའི་སེམས་ཀྱི་སྐྱེས་བུ་དེ།།
བརྗོད་བྲལ་ནགས་ཀྱི་ཁང་བུར་ངལ་གསོ་བསྟེན།།

Da Nï Dag Gi Ji-Tar Tsal Gyur Kyang
Den-Par Drub-Pay Nge-Pa Ma Nye Ne
Trö-Pé Dub-Pay Sem Kyi Kye-Bu De
Jo-Drel Nak Kyi Khang-Bur Ngal-So Ten

Now, also however I search,
having never acquired a certainty of the truly established,
that person, exhausted with mental proliferations,
relies on relaxing in the forest hermitage free from speech.

ཨེ་མ་ད་ནི་ཌཱ་ཀི་དབྱིངས་ནས་བཞེངས།།
ཧེ་རུ་ཀ་དཔལ་རྒྱུད་ཀྱི་རྒྱལ་པོ་ལས།།
རྡོ་རྗེ་བཙུན་མོའི་ཉེ་བའི་སྙིང་པོ་མཆོག།
བཀླགས་པས་འགྲུབ་ཅེས་གསུང་བའི་བདེན་པས་སྐྱོངས།།

E Ma Da Ni Da-Ki Ying Ne Sheng
He-Ru-Ka Pal Gyü Kyi Gyal-Po Le
Dor-Je Tsun-Moy Nye-Way Nying-Po Chog
Lag-Pé Drub Che Sung-Pay Den-Pé Kyong

Amazing! Dākinī, arise now from the dharmadhatū;
protect me with the truth of the teaching,
"There will be accomplishment by reciting the supreme near essence of the Vajra Queen."
in Sri Heruka, the King of Tantras.

ཨོ་ཌི་ཡ་ནའི་བས་མཐའི་ནགས་ཁྲོད་དུ།།
གྲུབ་པའི་དབང་ཕྱུག་རྡོ་རྗེ་དྲིལ་བུ་པ།།
འཁྱུད་དང་ཙུམྦའི་བདེ་བས་རྗེས་བསྐྱངས་ནས།།
མཁའ་སྤྱོད་གནས་སུ་ཁྲིད་བཞིན་བདག་ཀྱང་སྐྱོངས།།

O-Di-Ya-Nay Be-Thay Nag To Du
Drub-Pay Wang-Chug Dor-Je Dril-Bu-Pa
Khyü Dang Tsum-Bay De-We Je Kyong Ne
Kha-Chö Ne-Su Ti Shin Dag Kyang Kyong

In the secluded jungles of Oḍḍiyāna[11],
having protected Vajraghantapada, lord of Siddhas,
with the bliss of embrace and a kiss,
led him into the abode of Khecarī, likewise protect me.

---

[11] Here Oḍḍiyāna may refer to Odivisha.

གངྒཱའི་གླིང་དུ་རྗེ་བཙུན་ཀུ་སཱ་ལི།།
མངོན་སུམ་ནམ་མཁའི་དབྱིངས་སུ་ཁྲིད་པ་དང་།།
དཔལ་ལྡན་ནཱ་རོ་ཏཱ་པ་རྗེས་བཟུང་ལྟར།།
བདག་ཀྱང་མཁའ་སྤྱོད་དགའ་མའི་གྲོང་དུ་ཁྲིད།།

Gan-Gay Ling Du Je-Tsün Ku-Sa-Li
Ngön-Sum Nam-Khay Ying Su Ti-Pa Dang
Pal-Den Na-Ro-Ta-Pa Je Zung Tar
Dag Kyang Kha-Chö Ga-May Dong Du Ti

Having led Lord Kusali on a Ganges island
into the expanse of space in person,
and as you took Sri Narotapa,
also lead me to Khecarī, the city of maidens.

རྩ་བརྒྱུད་བླ་མ་རྣམས་ཀྱི་ཐུགས་རྗེ་དང་།།
རྒྱུད་ཆེན་གསང་མཐའི་ཟབ་ལམ་མྱུར་ཆེད་དང་།།
རྣལ་འབྱོར་བདག་གི་ལྷག་བསམ་དག་པའི་མཐུས།།
མཁའ་སྤྱོད་དགའ་མའི་འཛུམ་ཞལ་མྱུར་མཐོང་ཤོག།
ཅེས་པའང་ཐལ་བྱུང་དུ་སྨྲས་སོ།། ཞེས་ཚར་ཆེན་རྡོ་རྗེ་འཆང་གིས་མཛད་པའོ།།

Tsa-Gyü La-Ma Nam Kyi Thug-Je Dang
Gyü Chen Sang Thay Zab-Lam Nyur Che Dang
Nal-Jor Dag Gi Lhag-Sam Dag-Pay Thü
Kha-Chö Ga-May Zum Shal Nyur Thong Shog

By the compassion of the root and lineage Gurus,
with the special, swift, and profound path of the ultimate-secret tantra,
and I, the yogin with pure wishes,
may the beautiful countenance of the maiden Khecarī be swiftly seen.

Speaking whatever arose spontaneously, this was composed by Tsharchen Vajradhara.

ལྷ་མོ་ཚད་མ་དམ་ཚིག་ཚད་མ་དང་།།
དེས་གསུངས་ཚིག་ཀྱང་ཚད་མའི་མཆོག་ཡིན་པས།།
བདེན་པ་དེ་དག་གིས་ནི་བདག་ཅག་རྣམས།།
རྟག་ཏུ་རྗེས་སུ་འཛིན་པའི་རྒྱུར་གྱུར་ཅིག།

Lha-Mo Tse-Ma Dam-Tsig Tse-Ma Dang
De Sung Tsig Kyang Tse-May Chog Yin-Pe
Den-Pa De-Dag Gi Ni Dag-Chag Nam
Tag-Tu Je-Su Zin-Pay Gyur Gyur Chig

The goddess is authentic, the samaya is authentic,
and also those words are supremely authentic.
By all these truths,
may we always be continually cared for!

[དེ་ལྟར་ཚེ་འདིར་མཁའ་སྤྱོད་དབང་མོའི་ཞལ།།
མངོན་སུམ་མཐོང་བའི་སྐལ་བ་མེད་ན་ཡང་།།
འཆི་བའི་རྣམ་རྟོག་འཕོ་བས་མཚམས་སྦྱར་ནས།།
བར་དོ་མེད་པར་མཁའ་སྤྱོད་འགྲུབ་པར་ཤོག།

Dé-Tar Tsé-Dir Kha-Chö Wang-Moy Zhal
Ngön-Sum Thong-Way Kal-Wa Mé-Na Yang
Chi-Way Nam-Tok Pho-Wé Tsam-Jar Né
Bar-Do Mé-Par Kha-Chö Drup-Par Shok

As such, even if I do not have the fortune to see
the face of powerful Khecari in person,
may I accomplish the Khechari realm without the bardo
through the connection to transform the concept of death.

གལ་ཏེ་རྣམ་ཤེས་བར་དོར་འཁྱམས་སྲིད་ན།།
འཇིག་པའི་སྒྲ་བཞི་ཉམས་ངའི་གཡང་ས་གསུམ།།
མ་ངེས་རྟགས་དྲུག་ལ་སོགས་ཤར་བའི་ཚེ།།
དེ་ཡི་ཁྱེན་གྱིས་དྲིན་ཆེན་བླ་མ་དང་།།
དགའ་བ་གསུམ་གྱི་རྣལ་འབྱོར་དྲན་པའི་མཐུས།།
དེ་མ་ཐག་ཏུ་མཁའ་སྤྱོད་དབང་མོ་དང་།།
དཔའ་བོ་མཁའ་འགྲོའི་ཚོགས་ཀྱིས་མདུན་བསུས་ནས།།
ཕྱིན་ཆད་ལས་ངན་སྐྱེ་སྒོ་ཆོད་པར་ཤོག།
ཞེས་ཚིགས་སུ་བཅད་པ་གསུམ་པོ་འདི་ཀུན་དགའ་དཔལ་གྱིས་གསུངས།

Gal-Té Nam-Shé Bar-Dor Khyam Si-Na
Jik-Pay Dra Shi Nyam-Ngay Yang-Sa Sum
Ma-Ngé Tak Druk La-Sok Shar-Way Tsé
Dé Yi Kyen-Gyi Drin-Chen La-Ma Dang
Ga-Wa Sum Gyi Nal-Jor Dren-Pé Thü
Dé-Ma-Thak-Tu Kha-Chö Wang-Mo Dang
Pa-Wo Khan-Droy Tsog Kyi Dün-Sü Né
Chin Ché-Lé Ngan Kyé-Go Chö-Par Shok

If it is possible the consciousness wandering in the bardo
while the four terrifying sounds, the three fearful abysses,
and the six signs of uncertainty, and so on arising,
through the condition of recalling the greatly kind guru
and through the power of recalling the yoga of the three joys,
having being immediately greeted by powerful Khechari
and the assembly of heroes and ḍākinīs,
henceforth, may the door to be born resulting from negative
karma be shut off.

These three verses were spoken by Kunga Pal.

ནམ་ཤིག་སྒྱུ་མའི་སྐྱེས་ཆེན་འདེགས་པའི་ཚེ།།
རང་སེམས་སྐྱེ་མེད་རྡོ་རྗེ་རྣལ་འབྱོར་མ།།
དྲིན་ཆེན་བླ་མའི་ཐུགས་ཀར་རྒྱངས་ཀྱིས་འཕོས།།
མཁའ་སྤྱོད་དག་པའི་ཞིང་དུ་ཡུད་ཀྱིས་སྤོར།།

Nam-Shik Gyu-May Kyé-Chen Dek-Pay Tsé
Rang-Sem Kyé-Mé Dor-Je Nal-Jor-Ma
Drin-Chen La-Mé Thuk-Kar Gyang Gyi Phö
Kha-Chö Dak-Pay Shing Du Yü-Kyi Por

When lifted up by the illusory great person,
one's mind is the nonarising Vajrayoginī,
shifted far away into the heart of the greatly kind guru,
instantly transferred into pure realm of Khecari.

བླ་མ་ཡི་དམ་ཆོས་སྲུང་ཐུགས་རྗེ་དང་།།
མཁའ་འགྲོ་ཆོས་སྐྱོང་ནོར་ལྷའི་མཐུ་སྟོབས་དང་།།
ཆོས་ཉིད་འགྱུར་མེད་རྟེན་འབྲེལ་བསླུ་མེད་མཐུས།།
སྨོན་པའི་གནས་འདི་གེགས་མེད་འགྲུབ་གྱུར་ཅིག།
ཅེས་ཚིགས་བཅད་གཉིས་པོ་འདི་འང་ཚར་ཆེན་རིན་པོ་ཆེས་མཛད་དོ།

La-Ma Yi-Dam Chö-Sung Thuk-Jé Dang
Khan-Dro Chö-Kyong Nor-Lhé Thu-Top Dang
Chö-Nyi Gyur-Mé Ten-Drel Lu-Mé Thü
Mön-Pay Né Di Gek-Mé Drup Gyur-Chik

By the compassion of the guru, the yidam, and the
dharmapāla,
the magic power of the ḍākinī, Dharma guardians, and
wealth deities,
and the force of unchanging dharmatā, unerring dependent
origination,
may this place of aspiration be accomplished without
impediment.

These two verses were composed by Tsharchen Rinpoche.]

འཆི་ཆོ་མགོན་དང་དཔའ་བོ་མ་ཚོགས་ཀྱིས།།
མེ་ཏོག་གདུགས་དང་རྒྱལ་མཚན་ཐོགས་ནས་སུ།།
རོལ་མོ་གླུ་དབྱངས་སྒྲ་སྙན་སོགས་མཆོད་ཅིང་།།
མཁའ་ལ་སྤྱོད་པའི་གནས་སུ་འཁྲིད་པར་ཤོག། ཅེས་སྨོན་ལམ་བཏབ།

Chi Tse Gon Dang Pa-Wo Ma Tsog Kyi
Me-Tog Dug Dang Gyal-Tsen Thog Ne Su
Röl-Mo Lu Yang Dra Nyen Sog Chö Ching
Kha La Chö-Pay Ne-Su Ti-Par Shog

At the time of death, may the protector with an assembly of heroes and heroines,
bearing flowers, parasols, and victory banners,
making offerings of music, melodies, and songs pleasing to hear, and so on,
guide us to the Khecarī realm.

Thus, offer aspirations.

དེ་ནས་བཀྲ་ཤིས་ནི།
ཕུན་ཚོགས་དགེ་ལེགས་ཀུན་གྱི་དཔལ་མངའ་བ།།
རྡོ་རྗེ་འཆང་ཆེན་པཎ་ཆེན་ནཱ་རོ་སོགས།།
དཔལ་ལྡན་བླ་མ་དམ་པའི་ཚོགས་རྣམས་ཀྱི།།
བྱིན་རླབས་མྱུར་དུ་འཇུག་པའི་བཀྲ་ཤིས་ཤོག།

Phun-Tsog Ge-Leg Kün Gyi Pal Nga-Wa
Dor-Je Chang Chen Pan-Chen Na-Ro Sog
Pal-Den La-Ma Dam-Pay Tsog Nam Kyi
Jin-Lab Nyur-Du Jug-Pay Ta-Shi Shog

Next, recite the auspicious prayer:

The glorious sovereigns of all prosperous abundance,
such as Vajradhara, Mahapandita Naropa, and so on,
the assembly of sublime glorious gurus,
may there be the auspiciousness of receiving swift blessings!

རྒྱལ་བའི་ཡུམ་མཆོག་ཤེས་རབ་ཕ་རོལ་ཕྱིན།།
རང་བཞིན་འོད་གསལ་གདོད་ནས་སྤྲོས་དང་བྲལ།།
བརྟན་གཡོའི་དངོས་ཀུན་སྤྲོ་དང་སྡུད་མཛད་མ།།
མཁའ་སྤྱོད་ཆོས་ཀྱི་སྐུ་ཡི་བཀྲ་ཤིས་ཤོག།

Gyal-Way Yum Chog She-Rab Pha-Röl Chin
Rang-Shin Ö-Sal Dö Ne Trö Dang Dral
Ten Yoy Ngö Kün Trö Dang Dü-Zé-Ma
Kha-Chö Chö Kyi Ku Yi Ta-Shi Shog

The supreme mother of the victors, Prajñāpāramitā,
natural luminosity from the beginning, free of proliferation,
from whom all things animate and inanimate manifest and dissolve.
May there be the auspiciousness of the dharmakāya of Khecarī.

མཚན་དཔེའི་དཔལ་འབར་རབ་མཛེས་བརྗིད་པའི་སྐུ།།
དྲུག་ཅུའི་དབྱངས་ལྡན་ཐེག་མཆོག་སྒྲོགས་པའི་གསུང་།།
ཡེ་ཤེས་ལྡ་ལྡན་བདེ་གསལ་མི་རྟོག་ཐུགས།།
ལྷན་སྐྱེས་ལོངས་སྤྱོད་རྫོགས་པའི་བཀྲ་ཤིས་ཤོག།

Tsen Pey Pal Bar Rab-Ze Ji-Pay Ku
Drug-Chui Yang Den Theg Chog Dog-Pay Sung
Ye-She Nga Den De Sal Mi-Tog Thug
Lhen-Kye Long-Chö Zog-Pay Ta-Shi Shog

Whose body is magnificent, blazing with the beautiful major and minor marks.
Whose voice endows with sixty tones, proclaiming the supreme vehicle.
Whose mind endows with five wisdoms, which is blissful, clear and nonconceptual.
May there be the auspiciousness of the connate sambhogakāya!

སྣ་ཚོགས་ཞིང་དུ་སྣ་ཚོགས་གཟུགས་སྐུ་ཡི།།
སྣ་ཚོགས་ཐབས་ཀྱིས་སྣ་ཚོགས་གདུལ་བྱའི་དོན།།
སྣ་ཚོགས་བསམ་པ་ཇི་བཞིན་སྒྲུབ་མཛད་མ།།
ཞིང་སྐྱེས་སྤྲུལ་པའི་སྐུ་ཡི་བཀྲ་ཤིས་ཤོག།

Na-Tsog Shing Du Na-Tsog Zug Ku Yi
Na-Tsog Thab Kyi Na-Tsog Dul-Jay Don
Na-Tsog Sam-Pa Ji-Shin Drub Zé-Ma
Shing Kye Trül-Pay Ku Yi Ta-Shi Shog

Her various rupakāyas in various buddhafields,
accomplish the benefits of various disciples
according to their various wishes with various methods.
May there be the auspiciousness of the place-born
nirmāṇakāya!

པདྨ་རཱ་གའི་མདོག་མཚུངས་རྗེ་བཙུན་མ།།
འཛུམ་ཁྲོའི་ཉམས་ལྡན་ཞལ་གཅིག་ཕྱག་གཉིས་ཀྱིས།།
གྲི་ཐོད་ལེགས་འཛིན་ཞབས་ཟུང་བརྐྱང་བསྐུམ་ཚུལ།།
སྔགས་སྐྱེས་མཁའ་སྤྱོད་མཆོག་གི་བཀྲ་ཤིས་ཤོག།

Pad-Ma Ra-Gay Dog Tsung Je-Tsün-Ma
Zum Toy Nyam-Den Shal Chig Chag Nyi Kyi
Dri Thö Leg Zin Shab Zung Kyang Kum Tsul
Ngag Kye Kha-Chö Chog Gi Ta-Shi Shog

Jetsunma, the lotus in the same color as ruby,
with one face possessing a wrathful smiling mood and two
hands,
holding a curved knife and a skull, her pair of legs are
extended and contracted.
May there be the auspiciousness of the supreme mantra-born
Khecarī!

གང་གི་རྣམ་འཕྲུལ་གྲངས་མེད་བྱེ་བ་ཕྲག།
སྟོང་ཕྲག་བདུན་ཅུ་རྩ་གཉིས་ཚོགས་རྣམས་ཀྱིས།།
སྒྲུབ་པ་པོ་ཡི་བར་ཆད་ཀུན་སེལ་ཞིང་།།
འདོད་དོན་དངོས་གྲུབ་སྩོལ་བའི་བཀྲ་ཤིས་ཤོག།

Gang Gi Nam-Trul Dang Me Je-Wa Trag
Tong Trag Dun-Chu Tsa Nyi Tsog Nam Kyi
Drub-Pa-Po Yi Bar-Ché Kün Sel Shing
Dö Don Ngö-Drub Tsöl-Way Ta-Shi Shog

With her countless emanations,
seven hundred twenty billion embodiments,
remove yogins' all obstacles.
May there be the auspiciousness of all desired siddhis granted!

Appendix

The Shrine of Vajrayoginī Self-Initiation

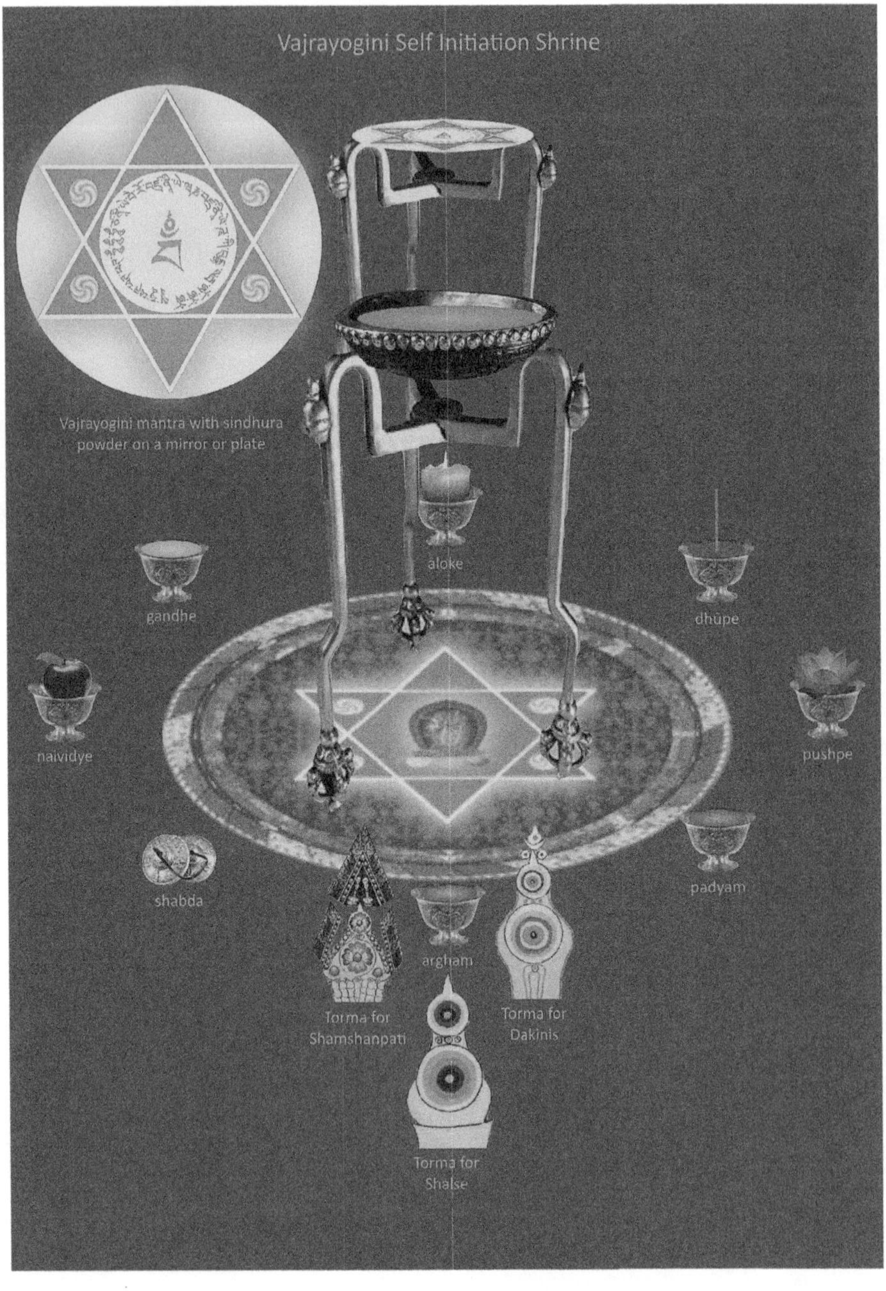

The Vajra Song

The Musical Cloud of Sublime Eternal Great Bliss

རྗེ་བཙུན་རྡོ་རྗེ་རྣལ་འབྱོར་མའི་ཚོགས་ཀྱི་མཆོད་པའི་རྡོ་རྗེའི་གླུ་བདེ་ཆེན་རྟག་པ་དམ་པའི་སྤྲིན་གྱི་རོལ་མོ་ཞེས་བྱ་བ།།

The Musical Cloud of Sublime Eternal Great Bliss, a Vajra Song for the Ganapūjā of Jetsun Vajrayoginī

འོད་གསལ་རྣམ་ཀུན་མཆོག་ལྡན་ཡེ་ཤེས་ཀྱི་རོལ་མོ།།
ཟུང་འཇུག་དྭངས་མའི་གཟུགས་སྐུར་མངོན་སུམ་དུ་ཤར་བ།།
དྲན་པས་སྙིང་གི་གདུང་སེལ་དཔལ་ལྡན་གྱི་བླ་མས།།
བདེ་སྟོང་ཡེ་ཤེས་སྐྱེས་བར་བྱིན་གྱིས་རང་རློབས་ཤིག།

Ö-Sal Nam-Kün Chog-Den Ye-She Kyi Röl-Mo
Zung-Jug Dang-May Zug-Kur Ngön-Sum Du Shar-Wa
Dren-Pé Nying Gi Dung-Sel Pal-Den Gyi La-Mé
De-Tong Ye-She Kye-War Jin Gyi Rang Lob Shig

The play of wisdom, luminosity endowed with the supreme of all aspects,
arising in person as the pure form of union,
may the glorious guru, whose recollection removes the woes of the heart,
bless us so that the wisdom of bliss and emptiness may arise.

ཨེ་དབྱིངས་ཤིན་ཏུ་རྣམ་དག་སྤྲོས་བྲལ་གྱི་གནས་ལུགས།།
ཝཾ་ཡིག་བཅུ་དྲུག་དགའ་བའི་མཚན་དཔེ་རུ་བཞེངས་པའི།།
ལྷན་སྐྱེས་མཁའ་ལ་སྤྱོད་པ་རྣལ་འབྱོར་གྱི་དབང་མོས།།
རླུང་སེམས་དབུ་མར་ཐིམ་པའི་དངོས་གྲུབ་ཞིག་སྩོལ་དང་།།

E Ying Shin-Tu Nam-Dag Trö-Dral Gyi Ne-Lug
Vaṁ Yig Chu-Drug Ga-Way Tsen-Pe Ru Sheng-Pay
Lhen-Kye Kha La Chö-Pa Nal-Jor Gyi Wang-Mö
Lung Sem Wu-Mar Thim-Pay Ngö-Drup Shig Tsöl Dang

E, the very pure dhātu, is the reality free from proliferation,
The syllable Vaṁ arises as the major and minor marks of the sixteen joys.
Yoginī, the queen who flies in the connate space,
grants the siddhi of dissolving the vāyu and mind into the central channel.

ཡུལ་ཆེན་ཉི་ཤུ་རྩ་བཞིར་རང་བཞིན་གྱིས་སྣང་བའི།།
ཐབས་ཤེས་ཕྱག་རྒྱའི་གཟུགས་འཆང་དཔའ་བོ་དང་མཁའ་འགྲོས།།
ཞིང་སྐྱེས་ཕོ་ཉའི་ཚོགས་ཀྱི་འདུ་བ་ལ་བརྟེན་ནས།།
བདེ་ཆེན་ཉམས་བརྒྱུས་སྒེག་པའི་སྐལ་བཟང་ལ་སྦྱོར་ཞིག།

Yül-Chen Nyi-Shu Tsa Shir Rang-Shin Gyi Nang-Way
Thab-She Chag Gye Zug Chang Pa-Wo Dang Khan-Dro
Shing-Kye Pho Nyay Tsog Kyi Du-Wa La Ten-Ne
De-Chen Nyam Gye Geg-Pay Kel-Zang La Jor Shig

Naturally appearing in the twenty-four great lands,
the heroes and ḍākinīs embracing the form of the method and wisdom,
in dependence on gathering the assembly of the place-born messengers,
May there be union with a charming fortunate one with one hundred experiences of great bliss.

སྟོང་ཉིད་མཁའ་ལ་བྲིས་པའི་ཏིང་འཛིན་གྱི་ཉམས་འགྱུར།།
ངོ་མཚར་དབང་པོའི་གཞུ་བཞིན་སྣ་ཚོགས་སུ་འཆར་བའི།།
སྔགས་སྐྱེས་རྡོ་རྗེ་བཙུན་མོའི་བསམ་གཏན་གྱི་དགའ་མ།།
ཅིར་སྣང་བདེ་ཆེན་འདྲེན་པའི་སྐྱོ་གྲོགས་ལ་ཕེབས་དང་།།

Tong-Nyi Kha La Tri-Pay Ting-Zin Gyi Nyam Gyur
Ngo-Tsar Wang-Pö Shu Shin Na-Tsog Su Char-Way
Ngag Kye Dor-Je Tsun-Moy Sam-Ten Gyi Ga-Ma
Chir Nang De-Chen Dren-Pay Kyo-Drog La Pheb Dang

The dance of samādhi drawn in the sky of emptiness
arises in many colors like the amazing bow of Indra.
The mantra-born vajra queen, the beautiful maiden of the concentration,
welcome to be friend, lead to the great bliss of whatever appears.

རྨད་བྱུང་རྡོ་རྗེ་ཐེག་པའི་ལམ་བཟང་གི་མཐར་ཐུག།
རྣལ་འབྱོར་གསང་མཐའི་བདུད་རྩིའི་དགའ་སྟོན་ལ་སྤྱོད་པས།།
བརྟན་གཡོའི་ཚུལ་དུ་ཤར་བའི་ཐ་མལ་གྱི་དངོས་ཀུན།།
ཧེ་རུ་ཀ་དཔལ་འགྲུབ་པའི་སྨོན་ལམ་ཞིག་ཞུའོ།།

Me-Jang Dor-Je Theg-Pay Lam-Zang Gi Thar-Thug
Nal-Jor Sang Thay Dü-Tsiy Ga-Ton La Chö-Pay
Ten-Yoy Tsul Du Shar-Way Tha-Mal Gyi Ngö-Kün
He-Ru-Ka Pal Drup-Pay Mon-Lam Shig Shu'o

The excellent path of the marvelous Vajrayāna is ultimate;
enjoy the feast of the amrita of the ultimate secret yoga.
All ordinary things arise in the form of the animate and inanimate.
I request through an aspiration to accomplish glorious Sri Heruka.

ཞེས་པའང་འཇམ་མགོན་བླ་མ་རིན་པོ་ཆེ་ངག་གི་དབང་ཕྱུག་བྱམས་པ་ཕུན་ཚོགས་དཔལ་བཟང་པོས་འདི་ལྟར་བྲིས་ཞེས་རྡོ་རྗེའི་བཀའ་སྐུལ་གྱི་ངོར་མཆོད་དེ། བྱ་བྲལ་བ་ཀུན་ཏུ་རྒྱུ་མཉྫུ་གྷོ་ཥས་གསོལ་བ་བཏབ་པ་སིདྡྷི་རསྟུ།།

This is composed by wandering Chadralwa Manjughosa to fullfil the vajra command by Jamgon Lama Rinpoche Ngagi Wangchuk Jam-Pa Phuntsok Palzangpo.

༄༅། །ན་རོ་མཁའ་སྤྱོད་མའི་སྒྲུབ་ཐབས་ཐུན་མིན་བསྡུས་པ།།

Concise Uncommon Vajrayoginī Sādhana

༄༅། །ན་མོ་གུ་རུ་བཛྲ་ཡོ་གི་ནཱི་ཡེ།

Namo Guru Vajrayoginīye

དེ་ལ་འདིར་དབང་ཐོབ་ཅིང་། བྱིན་བརླབ་ཟབ་མོས་རྒྱུད་སྨིན་པའི་གང་ཟག་གིས། བསྡུས་པའི་ཚུལ་གྱིས་རྡོ་རྗེ་རྣལ་འབྱོར་མ་སྒོམ་པར་འདོད་པས། སྐྱབས་ཡུལ་གསལ་བཏབ་ནས།

Now then, here, a person who has obtained the empowerment, whose continuum has been ripened by the profound blessing and who wishes to practice the meditation of Vajrayoginī in a concise fashion, having visualized the objects of refuge, should recite the following three times:

བདག་སོགས་འགྲོ་ཀུན་དེང་ནས་བྱང་ཆུབ་བར།།
བླ་མ་དཀོན་མཆོག་གསུམ་ལ་སྐྱབས་སུ་མཆི།།
རྫོགས་བྱང་གོ་འཕང་ལ་བཀྟེན་སེམས་ཅན་ཀུན།།
བསྒྲལ་ཕྱིར་ཟབ་མོའི་རྣལ་འབྱོར་བསྒོམ་པར་བགྱི། །ལན་གསུམ།

Dak-Sok Dro-Kün Deng-Né Jang-Chup Bar, La-Ma Kön-Chok Sum-La Kyap-Su Chi, Dzok Jang Go-Phang La-Ten Sem-Chen Kün, Dral-Chir Sab-Mö Nal-Jor Gom-Par Gyi

I and all migrating beings from now until awakening go for refuge to the Guru and the Three Jewels. I will meditate this profound yoga in order to place all sentient beings on the stage of perfect awakening.

རང་གི་སྤྱི་བོར་པདྨ་ཟླ་བའི་སྟེང་། །བླ་མ་རྡོར་སེམས་ཡབ་ཡུམ་གསལ་བ་ཡི། །སྐུ་ལས་
བདུད་རྩིའི་རྒྱུན་བབས་སྡིག་ལྟུང་བཀྲུས། །དབང་བཞི་ཐོབ་ཅིང་གསང་གསུམ་བྱིན་
བརླབས་གྱུར།

Rang Gi Chi-Wor Pad-Ma Da-Way Teng, La-Ma Dor-Sem Yap-Yum Sal-Wa Yi, Ku-Lé Dü-Tsiy Gyün Bap Dik-Tung Trü, Wang Shi Thop Ching Sang Sum Jin-Lap Gyur

On top of a lotus and moon on one's crown appears Guru Vajrasattva father and mother. A stream of amrita falls from their bodies washing away misdeeds and downfalls; one attains the four empowerments and one's three secrets are blessed.

ॐ श्री वज्रहेरुक समयमनुपालय । हेरुक त्वेनोपतिष्ठ । दृढो मे भव । सुतोष्यो मे भव । अनुरक्तो मे भव । सुपोष्यो मे भव । सर्वसिद्धिं मे प्रयच्छ । सर्वकर्मसु च मे चित्तं श्रियं कुरु हूं । ह ह ह ह होः भगवान् । वज्रहेरुक मा मे मुञ्च । हेरुको भव । महासमयसत्त्व आः हूं फट्।

ཨོཾ་ཤྲཱི་བཛྲ་ཧེ་རུ་ཀ་ས་མ་ཡ་མ་ནུ་པཱ་ལ་ཡ། ཧེ་རུ་ཀ་ཏྭེ་ནོ་པ་ཏིཥྛ། དྲྀ་ཌྷོ་མེ་བྷ་ཝ། སུ་ཏོ་
ཥྱོ་མེ་བྷ་ཝ། ཨ་ནུ་རཀྟོ་མེ་བྷ་ཝ། སུ་པོ་ཥྱོ་མེ་བྷ་ཝ། སརྦ་སི་དྡྷིཾ་མྨེ་པྲ་ཡཙྪ། སརྦ་ཀརྨ་
སུ་ཙ་མེ་ཙིཏྟཾ་ཤྲི་ཡཾ་ཀུ་རུ་ཧཱུྃ། ཧ་ཧ་ཧ་ཧ་ཧོཿ བྷ་ག་ཝཱན། བཛྲ་ཧེ་རུ་ཀ་མཱ་མེ་མུཉྩ། ཧེ་
རུ་ཀོ་བྷ་ཝ། མ་ཧཱ་ས་མ་ཡ་སཏྭ་ཨཱཿ ཧཱུྃ་ཕཊ། ཡིག་བརྒྱ་ཅི་ནུས་བཟླས་མཐར།

Oṃ shrī vajraheruka samayamanupālaya heruka twenopatiṣṭha dṛiḍho me bhava sutosyo me bhava anurakto me bhava suposyo me bhava sarva sidhhim me prayaccha sarva karmasu ca me cittaṃ shriyaṁ kuru hūṁ ha ha ha ha hoḥ bhagavān vajraheruka mā me muñca heruko' bhava mahāsamayasattva āḥ hūṁ phaṭ

(recite the one hundred syllables as much as one can)

བླ་མ་ཐོག་མཐའ་མེད་པའི་སེམས་དཔའ་ཡིས། །བདག་གིས་སྔོན་བསགས་སྡིག་སྒྲིབ་
ཉེས་ལྟུང་ཀུན། །བྱང་ཞིང་དག་པར་བྱིན་གྱིས་བརླབ་ཏུ་གསོལ། །སྤྱི་བོའི་རྡོར་སེམས་
འོད་ཞུ་རང་ལ་ཐིམ།།

La-Ma Thok Tha Me-Pay Sem-Pa Yi, Dak-Gi Ngon Sak Dik Drip Nye-Tung Kün, Jang Shing Dak-Par Jin-Gyi Lap-Tu Söl, Chi-Wö Dor-Sem Ö-Shu Rang La Thim

Guru Vajrasattva without beginning or end, please bless me so that all of my misdeeds, obscurations, faults and downfalls gathered in the past are cleansed and purified. Vajrasattva on the crown melts into light and dissolves into oneself.

Uncommon Guru Yoga:

བླ་མའི་རྣལ་འབྱོར་ཐུན་མིན་ནི། རང་མདུན་ནམ་མཁར་སེང་ཁྲི་པད་ཟླའི་སྟེང་། །རྩ་བའི་བླ་
མ་སངས་རྒྱས་རྡོ་རྗེ་ཆོས། །མཐར་སྐོར་པད་ཟླར་བརྒྱུད་པའི་བླ་མ་རྣམས། །དཔའ་བོ་
རྡོ་རྗེ་ཆོས་ཀྱི་རྣམ་པར་བཞུགས། །མཐའ་སྐོར་སྐྱབས་གནས་རྒྱ་མཚོ་གསལ་བ་ཡི། །
གནས་གསུམ་འོད་ཀྱིས་སྐྱབས་གནས་མ་ལུས་པ། སྤྱན་དྲངས་བསྟིམས་པས་སྐྱབས་
གནས་ཀུན་འདུས་གྱུར།།

Rang-Dün Nam-Khar Seng-Ti Pe-Day Teng, Tsa-Way La-Ma Sang-Gyé Dor-Jé Chö, Thar-Kor Pe-Dar Gyü-Pay La-Ma-Nam, Pa-Wo Dor-Jé Chö-Kyi Nam-Par Shuk, Tha-Kor Kyap-Né Gya-Tso Sal-Wa Yi, Ne-Sum Ö-Kyi Kyap-Né Ma-Lü-Pa, Chen-Drang Tim-Pé Kyap-Né Kün-Dü Gyur

In the space in front of oneself on top of a lion throne, lotus and moon is one's root guru, Buddha Vajradharma, surrounded by the lineage gurus on lotus and moon seats, seated in the form of Vira Vajradharma. An ocean of refuge objects surround them. Light rays from their three places invite all the refuge objects which dissolve into them, and they each become the combination of all refuge objects.

གང་གི་དྲིན་གྱིས་བདེ་ཆེན་ཉིད། །སྐད་ཅིག་ཉིད་ལ་འཆར་བ་གང་། །བླ་མ་རིན་ཆེན་ལྟ་བུའི་སྐུ། །རྡོ་རྗེ་ཅན་ཞབས་པད་ལ་འདུད། །སྐྱབས་གནས་ཀུན་འདུས་བླ་མ་རིན་པོ་ཆེ། །དྲིན་ཅན་ཆོས་ཀྱི་རྗེ་ལ་གསོལ་བ་འདེབས། །མཉམ་མེད་བཀའ་དྲིན་ཅན་གྱི་ཐུགས་རྗེ་གཟིགས། །འདི་ཕྱི་བར་དོ་ཀུན་ཏུ་བྱིན་གྱིས་རློབས།།

Gang-Gi Drin-Gyi De-Chen Nyi, Ke-Chik Nyi-La Char-Wa Gang, La-Ma Rin-Chen Ta-Bü Ku, Dor-Je Chen Shap Pe-La Dü, Kyap-Né Kün-Dü La-Ma Rin-Po-Che, Dri-Chen Chö-Kyi Je-La Söl-Wa Dep, Nya-Mé Ka-Drin Chen-Gyi Thuk-Je Sik, Di-Chi Bar-Do Kün-Tu Jin-Gyi Lop

"I bow to the lotus feet of the guru, whose body is like a jewel, endowed with the three vajras,[12] by whose kindness great bliss arises in an instant. I supplicate the Precious Guru, the combination of all objects of refuge, the kind lord of Dharma, look after me with unequalled kind compassion, bless me always, in this life, the next and the bardo."

---

[12] Following Chogyal Phagpa's explanation of this verse in Sa skya bka' 'bum, vol pa, pg. 110

Giving up attachment:

ཞེན་པ་སྤང་བ་ནི། བདག་གི་ཉོན་མོངས་རང་གཟུགས་ལུས་ལོངས་སྤྱོད།།
དགྲ་གཉེན་བར་མའི་སྣང་བ་ཇི་སྙེད་པ། །རྗེ་བཙུན་བླ་མ་འཁོར་དང་བཅས་ལ་འབུལ།།
གཟུང་འཛིན་རྣམ་རྟོག་ཞི་བར་བྱིན་གྱིས་རློབས།།

Dak-Gi Nyön-Mong Rang-Suk Lü Long-Chö, Dra-Nyen Bar-May Nang-Wa Ji-Nye-Pa, Je-Tsün La-Ma Khor Dang Ché-La Bül, Zung Zin Nam-Tok Shi-War Jin-Gyi Lop

All of my afflicted appearances of my body, wealth, enemies, relatives and those neutral are offered to the Venerable Guru and the assembly; bless me so that my dualistic concepts are pacified.

Giving offerings:

མཆོད་པ་འབུལ་བ་ནི། ཕྱི་མཆོད་ཉེར་སྤྱོད་ནང་མཆོད་བདུད་རྩིའི་སྤྲིན། །གསང་བ་སྙོམས་
འཇུག་བདེ་སྟོང་དེ་ཁོ་ན། །འཁོར་གསུམ་དམིགས་མེད་ཕྱག་རྒྱ་ཆེན་པོ་ཡིས། །རྩ་
བརྒྱུད་དཀོན་མཆོག་རྒྱ་མཚོའི་ཚོགས་རྣམས་མཆོད།།

Chi-Chö Nyer-Chö Nang-Chö Dü-Tsiy Trin, Sang-Wa Nyom-Juk De-Tong De-Kho-Na, Khor-Sum Mik-Mé Chak-Gya Chen-Po Yï, Tsa-Gyü Kön-Chok Gya-Tsö Tsog-Nam Chö

The outer offerings, the sense objects; the inner offerings, a cloud of amrita; the secret offering, the empty bliss of union; and the tathatā offering, mahāmudra beyond the perception of the three circles, are offered to the oceanic assembly of root and lineage Gurus and the Three Jewels.

Gathering the Kusali Accumulations:

ཀུ་སཱ་ལིའི་ཚོགས་བསགས་ནི། རང་སེམས་རྣལ་འབྱོར་མ་དཔལ་མཁའ་ལ་ཐོན། །ཕྱག་
གཡས་གྲི་གུག་ཕུང་པོའི་སྨིན་མཚམས་སུ། །རེག་པ་ཙམ་གྱིས་ཐོད་པ་ལིང་གིས་
བཀོག །མདུན་དུ་ཐོད་པའི་སྒྱིད་བུ་གསུམ་གྱི་སྟེང་། །ལེགས་བཀལ་སྟོང་གསུམ་ཁྱོན་
དང་མཉམ་པར་གྱུར། །རང་ལུས་དུམ་བུར་གཏུབས་ཏེ་དེའི་ནང་བསྐྱུར། །ཡེ་ཤེས་མེ་
འབར་ཐོད་པའི་ནང་རྫས་རྣམས། །ཞུ་ཞིང་ཁོལ་བའི་བདུད་རྩིའི་རྒྱ་མཚོར་གྱུར། །ཨོཾ་
ཨཱཿ ཧཱུྃ་ཧ་ཧོཿ ཧྲཱིཿ། ཞེས་པའི་བྱིན་བརླབ།

Rang-Sem Nal-Jor-Ma Pal Kha-La Thön, Chak-Yé Tri-Guk Phung-Pö Min Tsam-Su, Rek-Pa Tsam-Gyi Thö-Pa Lin-Gi Kok, Dün-Du Thö-Pay Gyi-Bu Sum-Gyi Teng, Lek kal Tong-Sum Khyön Dang Nyam-Par Gyur, Rang-Lü Dum-Bur Tub-Té Dey Nang Kyur, Ye-She Me-Bar Thö-Pay Nang Zé-Nam, Shu-Shing Khöl-Way Dü-Tsiy Gya-Tsor Gyur, Oṁ āḥ hūṁ ha hoḥ hrīḥ

One's own mind as Yoginī is ejected into the sky; through merely touching the body's forehead with the curved knife in her right hand, the skull is completely severed. The skull is well-placed on top of a tripod of skulls in front and becomes equal in size to the three realms. One's body is cut into sections and thrown inside it. The fire of wisdom melts and boils the substances in the skull which become an ocean of amrita.

Bless by saying:

Oṁ āḥ hūṁ ha hoḥ hrīḥ

དྲིན་ཅན་རྩ་བའི་བླ་མའི་ཞལ་དུ་ཨོཾ་ཨཱཿ ཧཱུྃ། ཞེས་ཚར་བདུན།
བརྒྱུད་པའི་བླ་མ་རྣམས་ཀྱི་ཞལ་དུ་ཨོཾ་ཨཱཿ ཧཱུྃ།
སྐྱབས་གནས་དཀོན་མཆོག་རྒྱ་མཚོའི་ཞལ་དུ་ཨོཾ་ཨཱཿ ཧཱུྃ།
རིགས་དྲུག་ལྷར་གསལ་ཞལ་དུ་ཨོཾ་ཨཱཿ ཧཱུྃ།
བདུད་རྩི་མཐོང་རེག་མྱོང་བས་སྒྲིབ་གཉིས་བྱང་།།
ཕུང་པོ་འཇའ་ལུས་སེམས་ཉིད་ཆོས་སྐུར་གྲོལ།།

Drin-Chen Tsa-Way La-May Shal-Du Oṁ āḥ hūṁ
Gyü-Pay La-Ma-Nam Kyi Shal-Du Oṁ āḥ hūṁ
Kyap-Né Kön-Chok Gya-Tsoy Shal-Du Oṁ āḥ hūṁ
Rik-Druk Lhar-Sal Shal-Du Oṁ āḥ hūṁ
Dü-Tsi Thong Rek Nyong-Wé Drip Nyi Jang, Phung-Po Ja-Lü Sem-Nyi Chö-Kur Dröl

Into the mouth of the kind root Guru *Oṁ āḥ hūṁ (repeat 7 times).*

Into the mouths of the lineage Gurus *Oṁ āḥ hūṁ.*

Into the mouths of the refuge objects,
the ocean of Three Jewels *Oṁ āḥ hūṁ.*

Into the mouths of the six classes appearing as deities *Oṁ āḥ hūṁ;* their two obscurations are purified by seeing, touching and tasting the nectar, their bodies become rainbow bodies and their minds are liberated into the dharmakāya.

ས་གཞི་སྤོས་ཆུས་བྱུགས་ཤིང་མེ་ཏོག་བཀྲམ། །རི་རབ་གླིང་བཞི་ཉི་ཟླས་བརྒྱན་པ་འདི། །སངས་རྒྱས་ཞིང་དུ་དམིགས་ཏེ་ཕུལ་བ་ཡིས། །འགྲོ་ཀུན་རྣམ་དག་ཞིང་དུ་སྤྱོད་པར་ཤོག།

Sa-Shi Pö-Chü Jug-Shing Me-Tok Tram, Ri-Rap Ling-Shi Nyi-Dé Gyen-Pa Di, Sang-Gyé Shing-Du Mik-Té Phul-Wa Yi, Dro-Kün Nam-Dak Shing-Du Chö-Par Shok

The ground is smeared with scented water, strewn with flowers, and adorned with Mt. Meru, a sun, a moon and four continents. This is perceived as a Buddhafield. By offering this may all migrating beings enjoy a pure land.

Receiving empowerments:

དབང་བླང་བ་ནི། བླ་མ་སྐྱབས་གནས་རྒྱ་མཚོའི་ཚོགས་རྣམས་ལ། །དབང་བཞི་རྫོགས་པར་གནང་ཞེས་གསོལ་བཏབ་པས། །རྩ་བརྒྱུད་བླ་མས་གནང་བ་ཞུས་ཐོབ་སྟེ། །གཡས་བསྐོར་མས་རིམ་རྩ་བའི་བླ་མར་ཐིམ༔།

La-Ma Kyap-Né Gya-Tsoy Tsog-Nam La, Wang-Shi Dzok-Par Nang-Shé Söl Ta-Pé, Tsa-Gyü La-Mé Nang-Wa Shu Thop-Té, Yé-Kor Mé-Rim Tsa-Way La-Mar Thim

Offer a supplication to the root Guru and the ocean of refuge objects: "Please bestow the four empowerments in full." The root guru requests and obtains permission from the lineage gurus who one by one dissolve clockwise into the root guru.

བླ་མའི་གནས་གསུམ་འབྲུ་གསུམ་འོད་ཟེར་ཚོགས། །རིམ་དང་ཅིག་ཅར་བྱུང་ནས་རང་ལ་ཐིམ།།

La-May Ne-Sum Dru-Sum Ö-Zer Tsog, Rim Dang Chik-Char Jung-Né Rang-La Thim

A mass of light rays from the three syllables at the three places of the guru emerge and dissolve, one by one and then simultaneously,[13] into oneself.

Dissolution of the Guru:

བླམ་བསྒོམ་པ་ནི། རྩ་བའི་བླ་མར་རྩེ་གཅིག་གསོལ་བཏབ་པས། །དགྱེས་བཞིན་འོད་ཞུ་
རང་ལ་ཐིམ་པ་ཡིས། །རང་སེམས་བཾ་ཡིག་སྤྲོས་བྲལ་དབྱིངས་སུ་ཐིམ།།

Tsa-Way La-Mar Tse-Chik Söl-Ta-Pé, Gye-Shin Ö-Shu Rang-La Thim-Pa Yi, Rang-Sem Vaṁ Yik Trö-Dral Ying-Su Thim

Through a one-pointed supplication to the root guru, he is pleased, melts into light and dissolves into oneself; one's mind, the syllable *Vaṁ*, dissolves into the expanse free of proliferation.

དེ་ཡི་ངང་ལས་སྙིང་གར་ཨེ་ཨེ་ལས། །ཆོས་འབྱུང་ཟླ་དཀྱིལ་དབུས་སུ་བཾ་ཡིག་མཐར།
སྔགས་འཕྲེང་འཁོར་བའི་ཟེར་གྱིས་གཞི་ལུས་སྦྱངས།།

De-Yi Ngang-Lé Nyin-Gar E E Lé, Chö-Jung Da-Kyil Wü-Su Vaṁ Yik Thar, Ngak Treng Khor-Way Ser-Gyi Shi-Lü Jang

[13] This refers to how the four empowerments are received: first the lights shine one at a time from each syllable and dissolve into oneself; and for the fourth empowerment, light shines simultaneously from all three syllables and dissolves into oneself.

From that state, in the heart is *E E*, from which

ए ए

ཨེ ཨེ

E E

arises a dharmakāra and moon disk in the middle of which is a *Vaṁ* syllable

वं

བྃ

Vaṁ

surrounded by the mantra rosary, by whose light rays the basis, one's body, is purified and changed into a mass of light.

འོད་ཀྱི་ཕུང་པོར་གྱུར་ལས་སྐད་ཅིག་གིས། །རང་ཉིད་པད་ཉི་དུས་མཚན་འཛིགས་བྱེད་སྟེང་། །རྣམ་སྣང་རིགས་བདག་བཅས་པའི་རྣལ་འབྱོར་མ། །དམར་གསལ་སྤྱན་གསུམ་ནམ་མཁའི་དབྱིངས་སུ་གཟིགས། །ཕྱག་གཡས་གྲི་གུག་ཐུར་དུ་བརྒྱངས་ནས་འཛིན། །གཡོན་པས་ཐོད་ཁྲག་སྟེང་ཕྱོགས་བཟུང་བས་གསོལ། །ཕྲག་པ་གཡོན་པར་

རྡོ་རྗེའི་ཁ་ཊྭཱཾ་བརྟེན། །ཐོད་སྐམ་དབུ་རྒྱན་དོ་ཤལ་ཕྱག་རྒྱས་སྤྲས། །ཞབས་ཟུང་གཡས་བརྐྱངས་གཡོན་བསྐུམ་དོར་སྟབས་བཞེངས། །བདེ་ཆེན་ཉམས་འབར་ཡེ་ཤེས་མེ་དབུས་རོལ།།

Ö-Kyi Phung-Por Gyur-Lé Ke-Chik Gi, Rang Nyi Pe-Nyi Dü-Tsen Jik-Jé Teng, Nam-Nang Rik-Dak Ché-Pay Nal-Jor-Ma, Mar-Sal Chen-Sum Nam-Khay Ying-Su Sik, Chak-Yé Dri-Guk Thur-Du Kyang-Né Dzin, Yön-Pé Thö-Trag Teng-Chok Zung-Wé Söl, Trak-Pa Yön-Par Dor-Jey Kha-Tam-Ga Ten, Thö-Kam Wür-Gyen Do-Shal Chak-Gye Tré, Shap-Zung Yé-Kyang Yön-Kum Dor-Thap Sheng, De-Chen Nyam-Bar Ye-She Mé Wü-Rol

In an instant, oneself is Yoginī standing upon a lotus, sun, Kālarātri and Bhairava, with Vairocana as the master of one's family; vivid red, three eyes, gazing into the depths of space. The right hand holds a curved knife extended downward, with the left hand, one drinks from a skull full of blood held high, supporting a vajra khaṭvāṅga staff on one's left shoulder. One is adorned with a tiara, a necklace of dry skulls and mudras. One's two feet are in a wide stance; the right leg extended, the left leg contracted. One dances in the middle of a wisdom-fire of the experience of great bliss.

ཐུགས་སྲོག་འོད་ཀྱི་སྣོད་བཅུད་དངོས་འཛིན་སྦྱངས། །རྡོ་རྗེ་བཙུན་མོའི་ཞིང་སྐུར་ལམ་གྱིས་གསལ།།

Thuk-Sög Ö-Kyi Nö-Chü Ngö-Zin Jang, Dor-Jé Tsun-Moy Shing-Kur Lam-Gyi Sal

The light rays from the seed syllable in the heart purifies apprehending the universe and living beings as real; these are completely transformed into the realm and forms of the Vajra Queen.

འབར་བའི་ཕྱག་རྒྱ་དང་བཅས། ཕཻཾ།

With the Blazing Mudra:

Phaiṁ

སླར་ཡང་ཐུགས་ཀའི་བཾ་ལས་འོད་འཕྲོས་པས། །ལྷན་སྐྱེས་ཞིང་སྔགས་རྣལ་འབྱོར་མ་དཔལ་ཀུན༏

Lar-Yang Thu-Kay Vaṁ Lé Ö-Trö-Pé, Lhan-Kyé Shing Ngak Nal-Jor-Ma Pal-Kün

Once again from the *Vaṁ* syllable in the heart lights shine and gather all the glorious innate, place-born and mantra-born Yoginīs,

ཚུར་འདུས་ཛཿ ཧཱུྃ་བཾ་ཧོཿ ས་རང་ལ་ཐིམ།།

Tsur-Dü Jaḥ hūṁ vaṁ hos Rang La Thim

Jaḥ hūṁ vaṁ hoḥ, who dissolve into oneself.

དམ་ཚིག་ཡེ་ཤེས་གཉིས་སུ་མེད་པར་གྱུར། །ཡེ་ཤེས་ཞུགས་པའི་རྐྱེན་གྱིས་སྙིང་ཁའི་བཾ། །
འོད་ཞུ་དབུས་སུ་མཁའ་སྤྱོད་དམར་པོ་དང་། །བྱང་ནས་གཡོན་བསྐོར་ལྗང་དམར་སེར་དང་
དཀར། །མཐའ་བསྐོར་སྔགས་ཕྲེང་སུམ་ཅུ་སོ་གཉིས་རྣམས། །རྣལ་འབྱོར་མ་དཔལ་སུམ་ཅུ་
སོ་གཉིས་གྱུར།།

Dam-Tsik Ye-She Nyi-Su Me-Par Gyur, Ye-She Shuk-Pay Kyen-Gyi Nying-Khay Vaṁ, Ö-Shu Wü-Su Kha-Chö Mar-Po Dang, Jang-Né Yön-Kor Jang Mar Ser Dang Kar, Tha-Kor Ngak-Treng Sum-Chu So-Nyi Nam, Nal-Jor-Ma Pal Sum-Chu So-Nyi Gyur

The jñānasattva and the samayasattva become inseparable. Through the condition of the entry of the jñānasattva, the *Vaṁ* at the heart melts into light and becomes red Khecarī, and counter-clockwise from the north, green, red, yellow and white [Khecarī]. The surrounding mantra garland of thirty-two syllables turns into thirty-two Shrī Yoginīs.

ཨོཾ་ཡོག་-ཤུདྡྷཿ སརྦ་དྷརྨཿ ཡོག་-ཤུདྡྷོ྅ ཧཾ།

Oṁ yogaśuddhaḥ sarva dharmāḥ yogaśuddho' haṁ

ལུས་གནས་སོ་སོར་ཟླ་བའི་དཀྱིལ་འཁོར་སྟེང་། །ངོ་བོ་ལྷ་ལ་རྣམ་པ་ཡི་གེའི་གཟུགས།།

Lü-Né So-Sor Da-Way Kyil-Khor Teng, Ngo-Wo Lha-La Nam-Pa Yi-Gay Zuk

In each location of the body on a moon maṇḍala is the essence of the deities in the form of syllables, symbolized by

ཨོཾ་བཾ་ཧཾ་ཡོཾ་ཧྲིཾ་མོཾ་ཧྲིཾ་ཧྲིཾ་དང་། །ཧཱུྃ་ཧཱུྃ་ཕཊ་ཕཊ་རྣམས་ཀྱིས་མཚན་པ་ཡི།།

Oṁ Vaṁ Haṁ Yoṁ Hriṁ Moṁ Hriṁ Hriṁ Dang Hūṁ Hūṁ Phaṭ Phaṭ Nam Kyi Tsen-Pa Yi

Oṁ vaṁ, haṁ yoṁ, hriṁ moṁ, hriṁ hriṁ, hūṁ hūṁ and *phaṭ phaṭ.*

Armor of the Deity

ॐ वं	ཨོཾ་བཾ	Navel	*Oṁ vaṁ*
हं यों	ཧཾ་ཡོཾ	Heart	*haṁ yoṁ*
ह्रीं मों	ཧྲིཾ་མོཾ	Mouth	*hriṁ moṁ*
ह्रीं ह्रीं	ཧྲིཾ་ཧྲིཾ	Brow	*hriṁ hriṁ*
हूं हूं	ཧཱུྃ་ཧཱུྃ	Crown	*hūṁ hūṁ*
फट् फट्	ཕཊ་ཕཊ	Limbs	*phaṭ phaṭ*

ཐུགས་ཀའི་ལུས་དཀྱིལ་གཙོ་མོའི་སྔགས་ཕྲེང་ལས། །འཕྲོས་པའི་འོད་ཀྱིས་འཕགས་མཆོད་འགྲོ་སྒྲིབ་སྦྱངས། །ཕོ་ཉ་གསུམ་གྱི་བྱིན་རླབས་ནུས་མཐུ་ཀུན། །བསྡུས་ཐིམ་མཁའ་སྤྱོད་དངོས་གྲུབ་ཐོབ་པར་གྱུར།།

Thu-Kay Lü-Kyil Tso-Moy Ngak-Treng Lé, Trö-Pay Ö-Kyi Phak-Chö Dro-Drip Jang, Pho-Nya Sum-Gyi Jin-Lap Nü-Thu Kün, Dü-Thim Kha-Chö Ngö-Drup Thop-Par Gyur

Light shines from the mantra rosary of the main deity of the body maṇḍala of the heart, making offerings to the nobles, purifying the obscurations of migrating beings and gathering all the blessings and power of the three messengers which dissolve [into oneself]. One obtains the siddhi of Khecarī.

ॐ ॐ ॐ सर्वबुद्धडाकिनीये । वज्र वर्णनीये । वज्र वैरोचनीये । हूं हूं हूं । फट् फट् फट् स्वाहा ।

ཨོཾ་ཨོཾ་ཨོཾ་སརྦ་བུདྡྷ་ཌཱ་ཀི་ནཱི་ཡེ། བཛྲ་ཝརྞ་ནཱི་ཡེ། བཛྲ་བཻ་རོ་ཙ་ནཱི་ཡེ། ཧཱུྃ་ཧཱུྃ་ཧཱུྃ། ཕཊ་ཕཊ་ཕཊ་སྭཱ་ཧཱ། དམ་བཅའི་གྲངས་ལས་མི་ཉུང་བ་བཟླ། སྒྲོན་ཡིད་བཟླས་སོགས་ཀྱི་མཐར།

Oṁ oṁ oṁ sarvabuddhaḍākinīye vajra varnanīye vajra vairocanīye hūṁ hūṁ hūṁ phaṭ phaṭ phaṭ svāhā

(Do not recite less than one has promised. If one wishes, recite the mental recitation.)

[To continue Vajrayoginī self-initiation, go to page 57, "Front Generation".]

བླ་མ་རྗེ་བཙུན་རྡོ་རྗེ་རྣལ་འབྱོར་མས། །འགྲོ་ཀུན་མཁའ་སྤྱོད་འཁྲིད་པར་མཛད་དུ་གསོལ།།

La-Ma Je-Tsün Dor-Je Nal-Jor-Mé, Dro-Kün Kha-Chö Ti-Par Zé-Du Söl

"May the Guru, Lady Vajrayoginī, place all migrating beings in Khecarī."

ཁམས་གསུམ་འོད་ཞུ་རང་དང་རང་ཉིད་ཀྱང་། །ནཱ་དའི་བར་ཐིམ་འོད་གསལ་དབྱིངས་སུ་ཡལ།།

Kham-Sum Ö-Shu Rang Dang Rang Nyi Kyang, Nā-Day Bar Thim Ö-Sal Ying-Su Yal

The three realms dissolve into light and then into oneself; oneself also dissolves up to the nāda, which disappears into the expanse of luminosity.

སླར་ཡང་རྒྱན་དང་ཕྱག་མཚན་སྤངས་པ་ཡི། །ལྷ་སྐུ་གོ་ཆས་མཚན་པར་གསལ་བའི་ངང་། །སྣང་གྲགས་རྟོག་ཚོགས་ལྷ་སྔགས་ཆོས་ཀྱི་སྐུ། །དགའ་བ་གསུམ་དང་དབྱེར་མེད་འདྲེས་པར་གྱུར།།

Lar-Yang Gyan Dang Chak-Tsan Pang-Pa Yi, Lha-Ku Go-Ché Tsen-Par Sal-Way Ngang, Nang-Drak Tok-Tsog Lha-Ngak Chö-Kyi Ku, Ga-Wa Sum Dang Yer-Mé Dre-Par Gyur

Once again one appears in the state without adornments or hand implements, but clearly adorned with the armor of the deities' forms.

All appearances, sounds and concepts are inseparably integrated with the three blisses: deity, mantra and dharmakāya.

དགེ་བའི་རྩ་བ་འདི་ཡིས་བདག་གཞན་ཀུན། །མཁའ་སྤྱོད་ཆེན་པོའི་གོ་འཕང་འགྲུབ་གྱུར་ནས།། སྲིད་དང་ཞི་བའི་རྒུད་པ་ཀུན་སེལ་ཞིང་། །དོན་གཉིས་ལྷུན་གྱིས་གྲུབ་པའི་བཀྲ་ཤིས་ཤོག།

Ge-Way Tsa-Wa Di-Yi Dak-Shen Kün, Kha-Chö Chen-Poy Go-Phang Drup-Gyur Né, Si-Dang Shi-Way Gü-Pa Kün-Sel Shing, Dön Nyi Lhün-Gyi Drup-Pay Ta-Shi Shok

With this virtue, having established myself and all others in the state of the great Khecarī, and having removed all the disadvantages of saṃsāra and nirvana, may there be the good fortune of the effortless accomplishment of the two benefits.

འཇམ་མགོན་མཁྱེན་བརྩེའི་གསུང་སྒྲུབ་ཐབས་ཐུན་མོང་བ་ལ་ཐུན་མིན་གྱི་འདོན་ཆ་ཅུང་ཟད་སྐད་གཉིས་སྨྲ་བ་དག་དབང་བསམ་གཏན་རྣམ་གཉིས་ཀྱི་ཐུགས་འདོད་ལྟར་སུ་ཀྲ་ཕི་ཏས་བྲིས་པའོ།།

This sadhana was arranged by His Eminence Chogye Trichen Rinpoche.

༄༅། །རྗེ་བཙུན་རྡོ་རྗེ་རྣལ་འབྱོར་མ་ལ་བརྟེན་པའི་རྒྱུན་གྱི་ཚོགས་མཆོད་མདོར་བསྡུས་པ་བསོད་ནམས་རྟག་པ་དམ་པའི་སྤྲིན་ཆེན་ཞེས་བྱ་བ་བཞུགས་སོ།།

The Great Sublime Cloud of Eternal Merit:

Concise Daily Ganapūjā

based on Jetsün Vajrayoginī

ན་མོ་གུ་རུ་བཛྲ་ཡོ་གི་ནཱི་ཡེ།

Namo Guru Vajrayoginīye

གང་ཞིག་སྙིང་རྗེ་ཆེན་པོས་ཡིད་ལྷག་པར་དྲངས་ཏེ། དུས་མྱུར་བ་ཉིད་དུ་གཞན་དོན་རྫོགས་བྱང་གི་གོ་འཕང་ཐོབ་པར་འདོད་པའི་དོན་གཉེར་གྱི་རྡོ་རྗེ་ཐེག་པ་བླ་ན་མེད་པའི་ཐབས་ལ་བརྟེན་ནས་བདེ་སྟོང་དབྱེར་མེད་ཀྱི་རྩིས་ཟིན་པས་ཚོགས་ཟུང་རྒྱ་མཚོ་སྐད་ཅིག་གིས་རྫོགས་པའི་ཐབས་ལྷུར་ལེན་པ་དག་གིས། བཟའ་བཏུང་གི་དངོས་པོ་ལ་བརྟེན་རྒྱུན་གྱི་ཚོགས་མཆོད་མདོར་བསྡུས་ཏེ་བྱ་བའི་ཚུལ་ལ་གསུམ། སྦྱོར་བ། དངོས་གཞི། རྗེས་སོ། །དང་པོ་ནི། རྗེ་བཙུན་རྡོ་རྗེ་རྣལ་འབྱོར་མའི་སྐུ་བྱིན་འབུར་གང་རུང་བའི་སྤྱན་སྔར་རང་ཉིད་ཀྱི་བཟའ་བ་དང་བཏུང་བའི་ཕུད་གཙང་ཞིང་བཀོད་པས་མཛེས་པ་དང་། འབྱོར་ན་མཆོད་པའི་བྱེ་བྲག་གཞན་ཡང་ཇི་ལྟར་རིགས་པ་བཤམ། ནང་མཆོད་ཀུ་ཆང་གིས་བྲན་པའམ། ཆབ་གཙང་མས་བྲན། དངོས་གཞི་ནི། བདག་གི་རྣལ་འབྱོར་སྔོན་དུ་འགྲོ་བའམ། ཐུན་མཚམས་ཀྱི་ལྷ་སྐུ་སྒྱུ་མ་ལྟ་བུའི་ཏིང་ངེ་འཛིན་གྱི་གསལ་སྣང་བརྟན་པོས་བཟའ་བཏུང་གི་དངོས་པོ་རྣམས། སུ་སླུས་བསང་།

For the purpose of someone guided with the best motivation by compassion who wishes to quickly obtain the state of perfect awakening for others' benefit, connected with the elixir of inseparable bliss and emptiness based on the method of unsurpassed Vajrayāna, who has taken on the methods of perfecting an ocean of the pair of accumulations in an instant, there are three topics in the methods of doing the concise regular ganapūjā based on the food and drink articles: the preparations, the main subject and the conclusion:

First, beautifully arrange the clean first portion of one's food and drink in front of any statue, painting or a relief of Jetsun Vajrayoginī, and if one can gather them, arrange any other different offerings. Sprinkle them with the liquid alcohol of the inner offering or sprinkle them with pure water.

Main topic: having done the yoga of self-creation or with the stable clear appearance of the illusory form of the deity in between sessions, cleanse one's food or drink articles with:

ༀ་སུམྦྷ་ནི་སུམྦྷ་ཧུྃ་ཧཱུྃ་ཕཊ།
ༀ་གྲྀཧྞ་གྲྀཧྞ་ཧུྃ་ཧཱུྃ་ཕཊ།
ༀ་གྲྀཧྞ་པ་ཡ་གྲྀཧྞ་པ་ཡ་ཧུྃ་ཧཱུྃ་ཕཊ།
ༀ་ཨཱ་ན་ཡ་ཧོ་བྷ་ག་ཝཱན་བིདྱཱ་རཱ་ཛ་ཧུྃ་ཧཱུྃ་ཕཊ།

Oṁ sumbha nisumbha huṁ hūṁ phaṭ
Oṁ grihaṇa grihaṇa huṁ hūṁ phaṭ
Oṁ grihaṇapaya grihaṇapaya huṁ hūṁ phaṭ
Oṁ ānayaho bhagavān vidyārāja huṁ hūṁ phaṭ

ༀ་སྭ་བྷཱ་ཝ་ཤུདྡྷཿ སརྦ་དྷརྨཱཿ སྭ་བྷཱ་ཝ་ཤུདྡྷོ྅ ཧཾ། གིས་སྦྱངས།

Purify with:

Oṁ svabhāva shuddhaḥ sarva dharmāḥ svabhāva shuddho' haṁ

སྟོང་པའི་ངང་ལས་ཡཾ་ལས་རླུང་། རཾ་ལས་མེའི་དཀྱིལ་འཁོར་གྱི་སྟེང་དུ། ཨ་ལས་ཡེ་ཤེས་ཀྱི་ཀ་པཱ་ལ་ཡངས་ཤིང་རྒྱ་ཆེ་བར་ཚོགས་རྫས་ཤ་ལྔ་བདུད་རྩི་ལྔ་བསྐོལ་ཞིང་འོད་དུ་ཞུ་བ་ལས་བྱུང་བའི་ཡེ་ཤེས་ཀྱི་བདུད་རྩི་འདོད་ཡོན་རྒྱ་མཚོའི་སྤྲིན་ཕུང་འཕྲོ་བར་གྱུར།

Tong-Pay Ngang Lé Yaṁ Lé Lung, Raṁ Lé Mei Kyil-Khor Gyi Teng-Du, Ah Lé Ye-She Kyi Ka-Pa-La Yang Shing Gya-Che-War Tsog-Zé Sha Nga Dü-Tsi Nga Köl Shing Ö-Du Shu-Wa Lé Jung-Way Ye-She Kyi Dü-Tsi Dö-Yön Gya-Tsoy Trin Phung Tro-War Gyur

From the state of emptiness arises *Yaṁ* (ཡཾ) from which arises an air maṇḍala; from *Raṁ* (རཾ) arises a fire maṇḍala, upon which from *Ah* (ཨ) arises a wisdom kapala that is wide and vast, in which the feast substances, the five meats and five amritas boil and transform into an oceanic cloud of the desirable objects of wisdom amrita which comes from [the five meats and five amritas] melting into light.

It is blessed by many recitations of:

ༀ་ཨཱཿ ཧཱུྃ་ཧ་ཧོ་ཧྲཱིཿ། ལན་མང་དུ་བརྗོད་པས་བྱིན་གྱིས་བརླབ།

oṁ āḥ hūṁ ha hoḥ hrīḥ

འབར་བའི་ཕྱག་རྒྱ་དཔྲལ་བའི་དབྱིངས་སུ་གཡོན་དུ་བསྐོར་ཞིང་། ཕཻཾ། ཞེས་བརྗོད་པ་དང་།

Rotate the Blazing mudra counterclockwise at the space of the forehead and recite:

Phaiṁ

རང་གི་སྙིང་ག་ནས་འོད་ཟེར་འཕྲོས་པས་རང་བཞིན་གྱི་གནས་ནས་བླ་མ་རྗེ་བཙུན་རྡོ་རྗེ་རྣལ་འབྱོར་མ་ལ་སངས་རྒྱས་བྱང་སེམས་དཔའ་བོ་མཁའ་འགྲོ་ཆོས་སྐྱོང་སྲུང་མའི་ཚོགས་ཀྱིས་བསྐོར་བ་མདུན་གྱི་ནམ་མཁར་ཨོཾ་བཛྲ་ས་མ་ཛཿ ཞེས་པས།

Rangi Nying-Ga Né Ö-Zer Trö-Pé Rang-Shin Gyi Ne-Né La-Ma Je-Tsün Dor-Jé Nal-Jor-Ma La Sang-Gyé Jang-Sem-Pa-Wo Khan-Dro

Chö-Kyong Sung-May Tso-Gyi Kor-Wa Dün-Gyi Nam-Khar Oṁ vajra samājaḥ

From one's heart light rays radiate and summon the Guru Jetsun Vajrayoginī from her natural abode surrounded by an assembly of buddhas, bodhisattvas, ḍākas, ḍākinīs and dharmapāla guardians into the sky in front by saying, *Oṁ vajra samājaḥ.*

ཚོགས་ཞིང་མཁའ་ཁྱབ་ཏུ་སད་པའི་སྤྱན་སྔར། རང་ལས་སྤྲུལ་པའི་མཆོད་པའི་ལྷ་མོ་རྣམས་ཀྱིས་བདེ་སྟོང་གི་ཉམས་འགྱུར་ཕུན་སུམ་ཚོགས་པས་མཆོད་པའི་སྤྲིན་རྒྱ་མཚོས་མཆོད་པ་ལ་བརྟེན་སྐྱབས་ཡུལ་རྣམས་ཟག་མེད་ཀྱི་བདེ་བས་མཆོག་ཏུ་དགྱེས་པས་བདག་གཞན་ཡིད་ཅན་ཐམས་ཅད་ཀྱི་ཚོགས་ཟུང་མཐའ་དག་སྐད་ཅིག་གིས་རྫོགས་པར་མོས་ལ།

Tsog-Shing Kha Khyap-Tu Sé-Pay Chen-Ngar, Rang-Lé Trül-Pay Chö-Pay Lha-Mo Nam-Kyi De-Tong Gi Nyam-Gyur Phün-Sum Tsog-Pé Chö-Pay Trin Gya-Tsö Chö-Pa La-Ten Kyap Yül-Nam Sak-Me Kyi De-Wé Chok-Tu Gye-Pé Dak-Shen Yi-Chen Tham-Ché Kyi Tsog Zung Tha-Dak Ke-Chik Gi Dzok-Par Mö-La

In the presence of the merit field (which has spread-out in the sky), offering goddesses emanate from oneself offering an oceanic cloud of offerings with the perfected experience of empty bliss. Based upon this, [the merit field] is supremely pleased with the bliss of stainless objects, and the twin accumulations of oneself and all other sentient beings are perfected in a single instant.

Offering to the Gurus and Three Jewels:

ཨོཾ་ཨཱཿ་ཧཱུྃ།།
གང་ཤར་བདེ་སྟོང་རོལ་པ་ལས་བྱུང་བའི།།
ཚོགས་མཆོད་འདོད་ཡོན་བདུད་རྩིའི་སྤྲིན་ཆེན་པོ།།
རྩ་བརྒྱུད་བླ་མ་མཆོག་གསུམ་མཉེས་ཕྱིར་འབུལ།།
བཞེས་ནས་ཐུགས་རྗེས་བྱིན་གྱིས་བརླབ་ཏུ་གསོལ།།

Oṁ āḥ hūṁ
Gang-Shar De-Tong Röl-Pa Lé Jung-Way
Tsog Chö Dö-Yön Dü-Tsiy Trin Chen-Po
Tsa-Gyü La-Ma Chok-Sum Nye-Chir Bül
She-Né Thuk-Jé Jin-Gyi Lap-Tu Söl

Oṁ āḥ hūṁ
Whatever arises is a great cloud of amrita, desirable objects of the ganapūjā arising from the play of bliss and emptiness, offered in order to please the root guru, the lineage gurus, and Three Jewels; having accepted this, please bless me with your compassion.

ॐ गुरु त्रिरत्न सपरिवार ॐ अकारोमुखं सर्वधर्माणां आद्यनुत्पन्नत्वत ॐ आः हूं फट् स्वाहा ।

ཨོཾ་གུ་རུ་ཏྲི་རཏྣ་ས་པ་རི་ཝཱ་ར་ཨོཾ་ཨ་ཀཱ་རོ་མུ་ཁཾ་སརྦ་དྷརྨཱ་ཎཾ་ཨཱ་དྱ་ནུཏྤནྣ་ཏྭ་ཏ་ཨོཾ་ཨཱཿ
ཧཱུྃ་ཕཊ་སྭཱ་ཧཱ། གྱིས་བླ་མ་དང་དཀོན་མཆོག

Oṁ guru triratna saparivāra oṁ akāromukhaṁ sarvadharmāṇāṁ ādyanutpannatvata oṁ āḥ hūṁ phaṭ svāhā (3x)

Offering to the Assembly of Deities:

ཨོཾ་ཨཱཿ ཧཱུྃ།།
གང་ཤར་བདེ་སྟོང་རོལ་པ་ལས་བྱུང་བའི།།
ཚོགས་མཆོད་འདོད་ཡོན་བདུད་རྩིའི་སྤྲིན་ཆེན་པོ།།
ཡི་དམ་དཀྱིལ་འཁོར་ལྷ་ཚོགས་མཉེས་ཕྱིར་འབུལ།།
བཞེས་ནས་མཆོག་ཐུན་དངོས་གྲུབ་རྩལ་དུ་གསོལ།།

Oṁ āḥ hūṁ
Gang-Shar De-Tong Röl-Pa Lé Jung-Way
Tsog-Chö Dö-Yön Dü-Tsiy Trin Chen-Po
Yi-Dam Kyil-Khor Lha-Tsog Nye-Chir Bül
She-Né Chok-Thün Ngö-Drup Tsal-Du Söl

Oṁ āḥ hūṁ
Whatever arises is a great cloud of amrita, desirable objects of the ganapūjā arising from the play of bliss and emptiness, offered in order to please assembled deities of the deity maṇḍala; having accepted this, please grant common and uncommon siddhis.

ॐ मण्डल देव गण सपरिवार ॐ अकारोमुखं सर्वधर्माणां आद्यनुत्पन्नत्वत ॐ आः हूं फट् स्वाहा ।

ཨོཾ་མཎྜ་ལ་དེ་བ་ག་ཎ་ས་པ་རི་ཝཱ་ར་ཨོཾ་ཨ་ཀཱ་རོ་མུ་ཁཾ་སརྦ་དྷརྨཱ་ཎཱཾ་ཨཱ་དྱ་ནུཏྤནྣ་ཏྭ་ཏ་ཨོཾ་ཨཱཿ ཧཱུྃ་ཕཊ་སྭཱ་ཧཱ། ལན་གསུམ་གྱིས་བླམ་ཡི་དམ་གྱི་ལྷ་སྐྱི་དང་།

Oṁ maṇḍala devagaṇa saparivāra oṁ akāromukhaṁ sarvadharmāṇāṁ ādyanutpannatvata oṁ āḥ hūṁ phaṭ svāhā (3x)

Offering to the Vajrayoginī:

ཨོཾ་ཨཱཿ ཧཱུྃ།།

གང་ཤར་བདེ་སྟོང་རོལ་པ་ལས་བྱུང་བའི།།

ཚོགས་མཆོད་འདོད་ཡོན་བདུད་རྩིའི་སྤྲིན་ཆེན་པོ།།

རྣལ་འབྱོར་མ་དཔལ་འཁོར་བཅས་མཉེས་ཕྱིར་འབུལ།།

བཞེས་ནས་བདེ་སྟོང་ཡེ་ཤེས་སྐྱེད་དུ་གསོལ།།

Oṁ āḥ hūṁ
Gang-Shar De-Tong Röl-Pa Lé Jung-Way
Tsog-Chö Dö-Yön Dü-Tsiy Trin Chen-Po
Nal-Jor-Ma Pal Khor-Ché Nye-Chir Bül
She-Né De-Tong Ye-She Kye-Du Söl

Oṁ āḥ hūṁ

Whatever arises is a great cloud of amrita, desirable objects of the ganapūjā arising from the play of bliss and emptiness, offered in order to please Shrī Vajrayoginī with her retinue; having accepted this, please create the wisdom of empty bliss.

ॐ ॐ ॐ सर्वबुद्धडाकिनीये वज्रवर्णनीये वज्रवैरोचनीये हूं हूं हूं फट् फट् फट् स्वाहा । ॐ अकारो मुखं सर्वधर्माणां आद्यनुत्पन्नत्वत ॐ आः हूं फट् स्वाहा ।

ཨོཾ་ཨོཾ་ཨོཾ་སརྦ་བུདྡྷ་ཌཱ་ཀི་ནཱི་ཡེ་བཛྲ་ཝརྞ་ནཱི་ཡེ། བཛྲ་བཻ་རོ་ཙ་ནཱི་ཡེ། ཧཱུྃ་ཧཱུྃ་ཧཱུྃ། ཕཊ་ཕཊ་ཕཊ་སྭཱ་ཧཱ། ཨོཾ་ཨ་ཀཱ་རོ་མུ་ཁཾ་སརྦ་དྷརྨཱ་ཎཱཾ་ཨཱ་དྱ་ནུཏྤནྣ་ཏྭ་ཏ་ཏ་ཨོཾ་ཨཱཿ ཧཱུྃ་ཕཊ་སྭཱ་ཧཱ།

Oṁ oṁ oṁ sarvabuddhaḍākinīye vajravarṇanīye vajravairocanīye hūṁ hūṁ hūṁ phaṭ phaṭ phaṭ svāhā oṁ akāromukhaṁ sarvadharmāṇāṁ ādyanutpannatvata oṁ āḥ hūṁ phaṭ svāhā (3x)

Offering to the Dharmapāla Guardians:

ༀ་ཨཱཿ་ཧཱུྃ།།
གང་ཤར་བདེ་སྟོང་རོལ་པ་ལས་བྱུང་བའི།།
ཚོགས་མཆོད་འདོད་ཡོན་བདུད་རྩིའི་སྤྲིན་ཆེན་པོ།།
རྡོ་རྗེའི་ཆོས་སྲུང་རྒྱ་མཚོ་མཉེས་ཕྱིར་འབུལ།།
བཞེས་ནས་བར་ཆད་ཀུན་སོལ་མཐུན་རྐྱེན་སྒྲུབས།།

Oṁ āḥ hūṁ
Gang-Shar De-Tong Röl-Pa Lé Jung-Way
Tsog-Chö Dö-Yön Dü-Tsiy Trin Chen-Po
Dor-Jey Chö-Sung Gya-Tso Nye-Chir Bül
She-Né Bar-Ché Kün-Söl Thün-Kyen Drup

Oṁ āḥ hūṁ
Whatever arises is a great cloud of amrita, desirable objects of the ganapūjā arising from the play of bliss and emptiness, offered in order to please the ocean of vajradharmapālas; having accepted this, please remove all obstacles and create favorable conditions.

ॐ श्री वज्रधर्मपाल सपरिवार ॐ अकारोमुखं सर्वधर्माणां आद्यनुत्पन्नत्वत ॐ आः हूं फट् स्वाहा ।

ༀ་ཤྲཱི་བཛྲ་དྷརྨ་པཱ་ལ་ས་པ་རི་ཝཱ་ར་ༀ་ཨ་ཀཱ་རོ་མུ་ཁཾ་སརྦ་དྷརྨཱ་ཎཱཾ་ཨཱ་དྱ་ནུཏྤནྣ་ཏྭ་ཏ་ༀ་
ཨཱཿ་ཧཱུྃ་ཕཊ་སྭཱ་ཧཱ། ཞེས་གསུམ་གྱིས་ཆོས་སྐྱོང་སྲུང་མ།

Oṃ shrī vajradharmapāla saparivāra oṁ akāromukhaṁ sarvadharmāṇāṁ ādyanutpannatvata oṁ āḥ hūṁ phaṭ svāhā (3x)

Offering to the ḍākas and ḍākinīs of the three places:

ཨོཾ་ཨཱཿ ཧཱུྃ།།
གང་ཤར་བདེ་སྟོང་རོལ་པ་ལས་བྱུང་བའི།།
ཚོགས་མཆོད་འདོད་ཡོན་བདུད་རྩིའི་སྤྲིན་ཆེན་པོ།།
གནས་གསུམ་དཔའ་བོ་མཁའ་འགྲོ་མཉེས་ཕྱིར་འབུལ།།
བཞེས་ནས་ཟབ་མོའི་ལམ་གྱི་གྲོགས་མཛོད་ཅིག།

Oṁ āḥ hūṁ
Gang-Shar De-Tong Röl-Pa Lé Jung-Way
Tsog-Chö Dö-Yön Dü-Tsiy Trin Chen-Po
Ne-Sum Pa-Wo Khan-Dro Nye-Chir Bül
She-Né Sap-Moy Lam-Gyi Drok Zö Chik

Oṁ āḥ hūṁ
Whatever arises is a great cloud of amrita, desirable objects of the ganapūjā arising from the play of bliss and emptiness, offered in order to please the ḍākas and ḍākinīs of the three places; having accepted this, please be my companions on the profound path.

མཁའ་འགྲོ་སྤྱི་གཏོར་གྱི་སྔགས་སམ།

Recite the general torma mantra of the ḍākinīs:

ॐ ख ख खाहि खाहि सर्व यक्श राक्शस भुत प्रेत पिशाचि । उन्माद । अपस्मार । डाक डाकिन्या दय इमं बलिं गृह्णन्त्य । समय रक्शन्तु । मम सर्व सिद्धिम् मे प्रयच्छन्तु । यथैवं । यथैश्टं । भुज्ञथ । जिघथ । पिपथ । मातिक्रमथ । मम सर्व कर्य । सत्सुखं विशुद्धय । सहायिका भवन्तु हुं हूं फट् फट् स्वाहा ।

ཨོཾ་ཁ་ཁ་ཁཱ་ཧི་ཁཱ་ཧི་སརྦ་ཡཀྵ་རཱཀྵ་ས་བྷུ་ཏ་པྲེ་ཏ་པི་ཤཱ་ཙི། ཨུནྨཱ་ད། ཨ་པསྨཱ་ར། ཌཱ་ཀ་ཌཱ་ཀི་ནྱཱ་ད་ཡ། ཨི་མཾ་བ་ལིཾ་གྲི་ཧྞནྟུ། ས་མ་ཡ་རཀྵནྟུ་མ་མ་སརྦ་སིདྡྷི་མྨེ་པྲ་ཡ་ཙྪནྟུ། ཡ་ཐཻ་བཾ། ཡ་ཐཻཥྚཾ། བྷུཉྫ་ཐ། ཛི་གྷ་ཐ། པི་བ་ཐ། མཱ་ཏི་ཀྲ་མ་ཐ། མ་མ་སརྦ་ཀཱརྻ། སཏྶུ་ཁཾ་བི་ཤུདྡྷ་ཡ། ས་ཧ་ཡི་ཀ་བྷ་བནྟུ་ཧཱུཾ་ཧཱུཾ་ཕཊ་ཕཊ་སྭཱ་ཧཱ། ཞེས་ལན་གསུམ་གྱིས་སྦུལ།

Oṁ kha kha khāhi khāhi, sarva yaksha rākshasa bhuta preta pishāci, unmāda, apasmāra, ḍāka ḍākinyā daya imaṁ baliṁ ghrihaṇantu, samaya rakshantu mama sarva siddhim me prayacchantu, yathaivaṁ, yathaishtaṁ, bhujñatha, jighatha, pipatha, mātikramatha, mama sarva karya, satsukhaṁ vishuddhaya, sahayika bhavantu huṁ hūṁ phaṭ phaṭ svāhā (3x)

Alternately:

ॐ त्रिस्थान डाक डाकिनी सपरिवार ॐ अकारोमुखं सर्वधर्माणां आद्यनुत्पन्नत्वत ॐ आः हूं फट् स्वा हा ।

ཨོཾ་ཏྲི་སྠཱ་ན་ཌཱ་ཀ་ཌཱ་ཀི་ནཱི་ས་པ་རི་ཝཱ་ར་ཨོཾ་ཨ་ཀཱ་རོ་མུ་ཁཾ་སརྦ་དྷརྨཱ་ཎཱཾ་ཨཱདྱ་ནུཏྤནྣ་ཏྭ་ཏ་ཨོཾ་ཨཱཿ ཧཱུཾ་ཕཊ་སྭཱ་ཧཱ། གྱིས་གནས་གསུམ་གྱི་དཔའ་བོ་མཁའ་འགྲོ་འཁོར་དང་བཅས་པར་སྦུལ།

Oṁ tristhāna ḍāka ḍākinī saparivāra oṁ akāromukhaṁ sarvadharmāṇāṁ ādyanutpannatvata oṁ āḥ hūṃ phaṭ svāhā (3x)

དེ་ནས་ཚོགས་ཀྱི་མཆོད་པ་རང་ཉིད་ཀྱིས་རོལ་པའི་སླད་དུ།།

Next, For the purpose of one's enjoyment of the feast recite and imagine the following:

བདག་ཉིད་རྡོ་རྗེ་རྣལ་འབྱོར་མའི། །སྙིང་གར་ཡི་དམ་ལྷ་ཚོགས་དང་།།
ལྟེ་བར་གཏུམ་མོའི་མེ་ལྕེའི་ཕྲོད། །ཆོས་སྲུང་ནོར་ལྷའི་ཚོགས་བཅས་གསལ།།
ཚོགས་མཆོད་ཡེ་ཤེས་བདུད་རྩིའི་རྒྱུན། །ལག་གཉིས་རྡོ་རྗེའི་དགང་བླུགས་ཀྱིས།།
ཕུལ་བས་ཟག་མེད་བདེ་བས་མཉེས། །མཆོག་ཐུན་དངོས་གྲུབ་སྩོལ་བར་གྱུར།།
ཅེས་བརྗོད་ཅིང་བསམ་ལ།

Dak-Nyi Dor-Jé Nal-Jor-May, Nyin-Gar Yi-Dam Lha-Tsog Dang,
Te-War Tu-Moy Me-Chey Trö, Chö-Sung Nor-Lhay Tsog-Ché Sal,
Tsog-Chö Ye-She Dü-Tsiy Gyün, Lak-Nyi Dor-Jey Gang Lug-kyi,
Phül-Wé Zak-Mé De-Wé Nyé, Chok-Thün Ngö-Drup Tsöl-War Gyur

The assembly of deities in the heart of myself, Vajrayoginī, and the mass of flames of Caṇḍalī in the navel appearing as dharmapālas along with wealth deities are pleased with immaculate bliss by the ganapūjā, a stream of wisdom amrita, offered with one's two hands, the vajra ladle and pourer, and bestow the supreme and common siddhis.

ཨོཾ་ཨཱཿ ཧཱུྃ། གིས་ཆོས་ཉིད་གསལ་ཁྱབ་ཀྱི་ངང་དུ་རོལ།

With Oṁ āḥ hūṁ enjoy in a state of dharmatā pervaded with clarity.

ལྷག་མ། ཨོཾ་ཨཱཿ ཧཱུྃ་ཧ་ཧོཿ ཧྲཱིཿ ས་བརླབས།

The remainders are blessed with:

Oṁ āḥ hūṁ ha hoḥ hrīḥ

पैं उश्चित बलिंत भक्शसी ।

ཕཻཾ། ཨུ་ཙྪི་ཏ་བ་ལིཾ་ཏ་བྷཀྵ་སཱི།།

Phaiṁ. Uṣciṭa baliṅgta bhakṣasī

གང་ཤར་བདེ་སྟོང་རོལ་པ་ལས་བྱུང་བའི།
ལྷག་མའི་འདོད་ཡོན་བདུད་རྩིའི་སྤྲིན་ཆེན་པོ།།
འབྱུང་པོ་ལྷག་མར་དབང་བའི་ཚོགས་ལ་སྦྱིན།།
ངོམས་ཤིང་ཚིམས་པའི་སྐལ་བ་ལྡན་གྱུར་ཅིག ཅེས་བརྗོད་ཅིང་ཕྱིར་རོལ་གཙང་སར་བསྐྱལ།

Gang-Shar De-Tong Röl-Pa Lé Jung-Way
Lhak-May Dö-Yön Dü-Tsiy Trin Chen-Po
Jung-Po Lhak-Mar Wang-Way Tsog-La Jin
Ngom-Shing Tsim-Pay Kal-Wa-Den Gyur Chik

Whatever arises is a great cloud of amrita, desirable objects of the ganapūjā arising from the play of bliss and emptiness, given to the assembly of bhūtas[14] who rule the remainders may you be fortunate to be content and satisfied.

Having recited the above, carry the remainders outdoors to a clean place.

---

[14] local elemental spirits

སྤྲོ་ན་རྡོ་རྗེའི་གླུ་འམ་དཔྱིད་ཀྱི་རྒྱལ་མོའི་གླུ་བླངས།

If one wishes, sing the Vajra Song or the Queen of Spring:

གནས···ཀོལླ···གི་རི། ཨི་རེ་ཊྛི···གནས་པ། ཨ་བོ་ལཱ། ···རྡོ་རྗེ། །ཞིང་···མུམྨུ་ཎི···འཐོབ་པ། རེ་ཀཀྐོ་ལཱ།
···པདྨ། ཚོགས་སུ···གྷ་ཎེ་ཀྲྀ་པཱི་ཏཱ···ཅང་ཏེའུ། ཧོ་བཱཛྫ་ཨི། ···དཀྲོལ་བར་བྱེད།། ཀཱ་རུ་ཎེ···སྙིང་རྗེའི།
ཀི···དབང་གིས། ཨ་ཨི་ཎ་རོ་ལཱ། ···ཀུ་ཅོ་མི་བྱ། ཏ་ཧིཾ···དུས་དེར། བ་ལ···ཤ། ཁཱ···བཟའ། ཛྫ་ཨཱི།
འབད་པས···གྷ་ཌེཾ་མ···ཆང་། ཨ་ཎཱ་པཱི་ཛྫ···བཏུང་བར་བྱེད། ཨ་ཨི། ཧ···ཀྱེ། ལེ་ཀཱ་ལིཉྫ་ར་པ་ཎི···
སྐལ་བ་དང་ལྡན་པ་འོང་དུ་གཞུག་གོ ཨ་ཨི། དུདྷུ་ར་བཱཛྫ···སྐལ་མེད་མི་གཞུག་གོ ཨ་ཨི། ཙ་ཨུ་ས་མ···
བཞི་མཉམ། ཀཙྪུ···གླ་རྩི། རཱི་སི་ཧླ། ···དུ་རུ་ཀ ཀཱ་པྤུ་ར···གསུར། ལཱ···བླུག་གོ ཨི་ཨ་ཨི། མཱ་ལ···
ཚོད་མ། ཨིནྡྷ་ཎ···ཤ་ཆེན་ལས་བྱས་པ། སཱ་ལིཉྫ། ཏ···དུས་དེར། ཧིཾ་བྷ་རུ་ཁཱ···མང་དུ་བཟའོ།། ཨི་ཨ
ཨི། ཕྲེཾ་ཁ་ཎ་ཁ···འོང་བ་དང་། ཊ་ཀ···འགྲོ་བ་ལ། ར་ནྟེ། ཤུདྡྷ···དག་པ་དང་། ཨ་ཤུདྡྷ···མ་དག་པར།
ན་མུ་ཎི···མི་བལྟའོ།། ཨ་ཨི། ནི་རཱཾ་སུ···རུས་པའི་རྒྱན། ཨཾ་གེ···ལུས་ལ། ཙ་ཌཱ་ཝི།···གདགས་སོ།། དུས
དེར···ཏ་ཧིཾ་ཛ་ས་རཱ་ཝ་པ་ཎི···སྐྱེས་པའི་རོ་དབྱལ་ལོ། ཨ་ཨི། མ་ལ···འདུ་བའི་དུས་སུ། ཨ་ཛེ་ཀུནྡྷུ་རུ་བཱ
ཊྚ···སྙོམས་འཇུག་བྱའོ།། ཨི། ཌིཎྜི···རེག་མིན། མ་ཏ་ཧིནྣ···དུས་དེར་བསྟེན་ནོ།། བཛྫི་ཨ་ཨི།།

Kolla i re ṭṭhi a bolā, mummuṇi re kakkolā,
ghane kṛipīṭā ho vājja i, kāruṇe ki a i ṇa rolā,
ta hiṁ bala khājja ī, ghadheṁ ma aṇā pījja a i,
ha le kāliñjara paṇi a i, dudhura vājja a i,
cau sama kacchurī sihla, kāppura lā i a i,
māla indhaṇa sāliñja, tahiṁ bharukhā i a i,
phremkhaṇakhaṭa karante, śuddha aśuddha namuṇi a i,
nirāṁsu aṁge caḍāvi, tahiṁ jasarāvapaṇi a i,
mala a je kundhuru bāṭṭa i, ḍindi matahinna vajji a i,

Abiding in Kollagiri and Mummuni, when vajras and padmas gather, continually sound the damaru, with compassion and without conflict.

At that time, eat meat earnestly, one should drink much wine. Ho! The fortunate should stay, avoid the unfortunate. Apply shit, musk, sila, and camphor vegetable stew made from great meat, should be eaten in quantity.

Coming and going without concepts, not thinking of pure or impure, wearing bone ornaments on the body, seat here on the corpse; do not refuse the untouchable; enter into union when gathered.

བཀྲ་ཤིས་གང་ཞིག་ཆོས་ཀྱི་དབྱིངས་ནས་ལེགས་བྱུང་བའི། །ཧེ་རུ་ཀ་དཔལ་འཇིགས་བྱེད་རྒྱལ་པོ་འབར་བའི་སྐུ། །ཤེས་རབ་ཕག་མོའི་པདྨ་ར་རྡོ་རྗེས་རོལ་མཛད་པའི། །བདེན་པ་དེས་ཀྱང་བདེ་མཆོག་ལ་གནས་བཀྲ་ཤིས་ཤོག །འཆི་ཚེ་མགོན་དང་དཔའ་བོ་མ་ཚོགས་ཀྱིས། །མེ་ཏོག་གདུགས་དང་རྒྱལ་མཚན་ཐོགས་ནས་སུ། །རོལ་མོ་གླུ་དབྱངས་སྒྲ་སྙན་སོགས་མཆོད་ཅིང་། །མཁའ་ལ་སྤྱོད་པའི་གནས་སུ་ཁྲིད་པར་ཤོག །ལྷ་མོ་ཚོད་མ་དམ་ཚིག་ཚད་མ་དང་། །དེས་གསུངས་ཚིག་ཀྱང་ཚད་མའི་མཆོག་ཡིན་པས། །བདེན་པ་དེ་དག་གིས་ནི་བདག་ཅག་རྣམས། །རྟག་ཏུ་རྗེས་སུ་འཛིན་པའི་རྒྱུར་གྱུར་ཅིག

Ta-Shi Gang-Shik Chö-Kyi Ying-Né Lek Jung-Way, He-Ru-Ka Pal Jik-Jé Gyal-Po Bar-Way Ku, She-Rap Phak-Mö Pe-Mar Dor-Jé Röl Zé-Pay, Den-Pa Dek-Yang De-Chok La-Né Ta-Shi Shok, Chi-Tsé Gön-Dang Pa-Wo-Ma Tsog Kyi, Me-Tok Duk-Dang Gyal-Tsen Thok-Né

Su, Röl-Mo Lu-Yang Dra-Nyen Sok Chö Ching, Kha-La Chö-Pay Ne-Su Ti-Par Shok, Lha-Mo Tse-Ma Dam-Tsik Tse-Ma Dang, De Sung Tsik Kyang Tse-May Chok Yin-Pé, Den-Pa De-Dak Gi Nï Dak-Chak Nam, Tak-Tu Je-Su Zin-Pay Gyün Gyur Chik

May any fortunate ones have the good fortune to dwell in great bliss by the truth of the vajra of Shrī Heruka — the blazing body of the terrifying king, who arose perfectly from the dharmadhātu — sporting in the lotus of the prajñā, Vārāhī. At the time of death, may protectors and an assembly of ḍākas and ḍākinīs, holding flowers, umbrellas, and victory banners, making offerings of cymbals, songs, vinas, and so on, lead me to abode of Khecarī. Since the goddess is authentic, the samaya is authentic and also those words are supremely authentic, by their truth may we always be continually cared for!

[To continue Vajrayoginī self-initiation, go to page 260, "Conclusion Ritual".]

Outer offerings:

ཨོཾ་གུ་རུ་བཛྲ་ཡོ་གི་ནཱི་ས་པ་རི་ཝཱ་ར་ཨརྒྷཾ་པྲ་ཏཱི་ཙྪ་སྭཱ་ཧཱ།
ཨོཾ་གུ་རུ་བཛྲ་ཡོ་གི་ནཱི་ས་པ་རི་ཝཱ་ར་པཱདྱཾ་པྲ་ཏཱི་ཙྪ་སྭཱ་ཧཱ།
ཨོཾ་གུ་རུ་བཛྲ་ཡོ་གི་ནཱི་ས་པ་རི་ཝཱ་ར་པུཥྤེ་པྲ་ཏཱི་ཙྪ་སྭཱ་ཧཱ།
ཨོཾ་གུ་རུ་བཛྲ་ཡོ་གི་ནཱི་ས་པ་རི་ཝཱ་ར་དྷཱུ་པེ་པྲ་ཏཱི་ཙྪ་སྭཱ་ཧཱ།
ཨོཾ་གུ་རུ་བཛྲ་ཡོ་གི་ནཱི་ས་པ་རི་ཝཱ་ར་ཨཱ་ལོ་ཀེ་པྲ་ཏཱི་ཙྪ་སྭཱ་ཧཱ།
ཨོཾ་གུ་རུ་བཛྲ་ཡོ་གི་ནཱི་ས་པ་རི་ཝཱ་ར་གནྡྷེ་པྲ་ཏཱི་ཙྪ་སྭཱ་ཧཱ།

ཨོཾ་གུ་རུ་བཛྲ་ཡོ་གི་ནཱི་ས་པ་རི་ཝཱ་ར་ནཻ་ཝི་དྱེ་པྲ་ཏཱི་ཙྪ་སྭཱ་ཧཱ།
ཨོཾ་གུ་རུ་བཛྲ་ཡོ་གི་ནཱི་ས་པ་རི་ཝཱ་ར་ཤབྡ་པྲ་ཏཱི་ཙྪ་སྭཱ་ཧཱ། ཞེས་ཕྱི་མཆོད་དང་།

Oṃ guru Vajrayoginī saparivara arghaṁ pratīccha svāhā
Oṃ guru Vajrayoginī saparivara pādyaṁ pratīccha svāhā
Oṃ guru Vajrayoginī saparivara puṣpe pratīccha svāhā
Oṃ guru Vajrayoginī saparivara dhūpe pratīccha svāhā
Oṃ guru Vajrayoginī saparivara āloke pratīccha svāhā
Oṃ guru Vajrayoginī saparivara gandhe pratīccha svāhā
Oṃ guru Vajrayoginī saparivara naividye pratīccha svāhā
Oṃ guru Vajrayoginī saparivara shabda pratīccha svāhā

Inner offerings:

ཨོཾ་ཨཱཿ ཧཱུྃ་གིས་ནང་མཆོད་ཕུལ།།

Oṁ āḥ hūṁ

Praise:

དཔལ་ལྡན་རྡོ་རྗེ་མཁའ་འགྲོ་མ། །མཁའ་འགྲོ་མ་ཡི་འཁོར་ལོས་སྒྱུར།།
ཡེ་ཤེས་ལྔ་དང་སྐུ་གསུམ་བརྙེས། །འགྲོ་བ་སྐྱོབ་ལ་ཕྱག་འཚལ་ལོ།།

Pal-Den Dor-Je Khan-Dro-Ma, Khan-Dro-Ma Yi Khor Lö Gyur
Ye-She Nga Dang Ku-Sum Nyé, Dro-Wa Kyop-La Chak-Tsal Lo

The glorious Vajraḍākinī,
the empress of all ḍākinīs,
the one who has attained the five wisdoms and three kāyas,
I pay homage to the protector of migrating beings.

ཇི་སྙེད་རྡོ་རྗེ་མཁའ་འགྲོ་མ། །ཀུན་ཏུ་རྟོག་པའི་འཆིང་གཅོད་ཅིང་།།
འཇིག་རྟེན་བྱ་བར་རབ་འཇུག་མ། །དེ་སྙེད་རྣམས་ལ་ཕྱག་འཚལ་ལོ།

Jin-Yé Dor-Je Khan-Dro-Ma, Kün-Tu Tok-Payi Ching Chö Ching
Jik-Ten Ja-War Rap-Juk-Ma, De-Nyé Nam-La Chak-Tsal Lo

I pay homage to the Vajraḍākinī
who eliminates the bondage of all concepts,
those who attain full engagement
in the activities of the world.

One hundred syllables:

ॐ श्री वज्रहेरुक समयमनुपालय । हेरुक त्वेनोपतिष्ठ । दृढो मे भव । सुतोष्यो मे भव । अनुरक्तो मे भव । सुपोष्यो मे भव । सर्वसिद्धिं मे प्रयच्छ । सर्वकर्मसु च मे चित्तं श्रियं कुरु हूं । ह ह ह ह होः भगवान् । वज्रहेरुक मा मे मुञ्च । हेरुको भव । महासमयसत्त्व आः हूं फट्।

ཨོཾ་ཤྲཱི་བཛྲ་ཧེ་རུ་ཀ་ས་མ་ཡ་མ་ནུ་པཱ་ལ་ཡ། ཧེ་རུ་ཀ་ཏྭེ་ནོ་པ་ཏིཥྛ། དྲྀ་ཌྷོ་མེ་བྷ་ཝ། སུ་ཏོ་ཥྱོ་མེ་བྷ་ཝ། ཨ་ནུ་རཀྟོ་མེ་བྷ་ཝ། སུ་པོ་ཥྱོ་མེ་བྷ་ཝ། སརྦ་སིདྡྷིཾ་མྨེ་པྲ་ཡཙྪ། སརྦ་ཀརྨ་སུ་ཙ་མེ་ཙིཏྟཾ་ཤྲི་ཡཾ་ཀུ་རུ་ཧཱུྂ། ཧ་ཧ་ཧ་ཧ་ཧོཿ བྷ་ག་ཝཱན། བཛྲ་ཧེ་རུ་ཀ་མཱ་མེ་མུཉྩ། ཧེ་རུ་ཀོ་བྷ་ཝ། མ་ཧཱ་ས་མ་ཡ་སཏྭ་ཨཱཿ ཧཱུྂ་ཕཊ།

Oṁ shrī vajraheruka samayamanupālaya heruka twenopatiṣṭha dṛiḍho me bhava sutosyo me bhava anurakto me bhava suposyo me bhava sarva sidhhim me prayaccha sarva karmasu ca me cittaṃ shriyaṁ kuru hūṁ ha ha ha ha hoḥ bhagavān vajraheruka mā me muñca heruko' bhava mahāsamayasattva āḥ hūṁ phaṭ (3x)

Confess mistakes:

མ་འབྱོར་པ་དང་ཉམས་པ་དང་། །གང་ཡང་བདག་རྨོངས་བློ་ཡིས་ནི།།
བགྱིས་པ་དང་ནི་བགྱིད་རྩལ་བ། །དེ་ཀུན་མགོན་པོས་བཟོད་པར་གསོལ།
གྱིས་ནོངས་པ་བཤགས།

Ma-Jor-Pa Dang Nyam-Pa Dang, Gang-Yang Dak Mong Lo-Yi Ni
Gyi-Pa Dang Ni Gyi Tsal-Wa, De-Kün Gön-Pö Zö-Par Söl

Whatever was not prepared or was damaged,
or that I did with a confused mind,
or asked [others] to do,
protector, please be patient with it all.

རྟེན་ཡོད་པ་རྣམས། ཨོཾ་སུ་པྲ་ཏིཥྛ་བཛྲ་ཡ་སྭཱ་ཧཱས་མེ་ཏོག་འཐོར་ཞིང་བརྟན་བཞུགས་བྱ།

If a support exists, scatter flowers and stabilize with:

Oṁ supratiṣtha vajraya svāhā

རྟེན་མེད་པའི་གཏོར་མགྲོན། བཛྲ་མུཿ ས་ག་གཤེགས།

If there is no support, the oblation guests are dismissed with:

Vajra muḥ

Dedication and aspiration:

དགེ་བ་འདི་ཡིས་མྱུར་དུ་བདག།
རྣལ་འབྱོར་མ་དཔལ་འགྲུབ་གྱུར་ནས།།
འགྲོ་བ་གཅིག་ཀྱང་མ་ལུས་པ།།
དེ་ཡི་ས་ལ་འགོད་པར་ཤོག །ཅེས་བསྔོ་སྨོན་དང་།

Ge-Wa Di-Yi Nyur-Du Dak
Nal-Jor-Ma Pal Drup Gyur Né
Dro-Wa Chi-Kyang Ma-Lü-Pa
De-Yi Sa-La Gö-Par Shok

With this virtue, having quickly
accomplished Shrī Vajrayoginī,
may all migrating beings simultaneously
be placed upon her stage.

གནས་འདིར་ཉིན་མོ་བདེ་ལེགས་སོགས་ཞེས་བརྗོད་ཇི་ལྟར་རིགས་པས་མཚམས་སྦྱར་ཏེ་དེ་ལྟར་ཕུལ་བའི་ཚོགས་རྫས་རྒྱ་ཆེ་བ་ཡོད་ན་ཡོན་ཏན་གྱི་ཞིང་བླ་མ་དང་དགེ་འདུན་ལ་ཚོས་སྟོན་དུ་གསོལ་བའམ། ཕན་འདོགས་པའི་ཞིང་ནད་པ་དང་དབུལ་ཕོངས་སོགས་ལ་སྦྱིན་པས་མཚོན་སྔར་ཡང་ཚོགས་ཟུང་སྤེལ་བའི་ཐབས་ལ་བརྩོན་པར་བྱའོ། །ཞེས་པའང་ཡོངས་ཀྱི་དགེ་བའི་བཤེས་གཉེན་ཆེན་པོ་དཔལ་ལྡན་བླ་མ་དམ་པ་དག་གི་དབང་ཕྱུག་བྱམས་པ་ཕུན་ཚོགས་ཀྱིས་འདི་ལྟར་བྲིས་ཞེས་ལྷ་རྫས་ཀྱི་མེ་ཏོག་དང་བཅས་བཀའ་སྩལ་ཕེབས་པ་གུས་པས་མཆོད་དེ་བྱ་བྲལ་བ་འཇམ་དབྱངས་མཁྱེན་བརྩེའི་དབང་པོས་བྲིས་པའི་དགེ་བས་འགྲོ་ཀུན་ཚོགས་ཟུང་རྒྱ་མཚོ་མྱུར་དུ་རྫོགས་ནས་མཁའ་སྤྱོད་རྡོ་རྗེ་བཙུན་མོའི་གོ་འཕང་ཚེ་གཅིག་ཁོ་ནས་རེག་པའི་རྒྱུར་གྱུར་ཅིག

Join with benedictions such as "May there be excellent happiness in this place during the day..." and so on. As such, it is said "If one is doing very a extensive offering presentation, endeavor in methods to increase the two accumulations i.e. supplicate the field of qualities, the Guru and the Sangha or express generosity to the field of providing benefits, the ill and the poor," and also the completely great kalayanamitra Shrī Gurottama Ngag gi Wangchug Jampa Phuntsog stated "Write something like this", and having received his command along with divine flowers, this is offered with devotion. May the virtue of this writing by the carefree Jamyang Khyentse Wangpo become a cause for all migrating beings to quickly reach in only a single life the stage of the Vajra Queen, Khecari after that quickly perfecting the ocean of the two accumulations.

Made in the USA
Las Vegas, NV
10 August 2024

93548357R00194